# Improving Academic Achievement

This is a volume in the Academic Press
**EDUCATIONAL PSYCHOLOGY SERIES**

*Critical, comprehensive reviews of research knowledge, theories, principles, and practices*

Under the editorship of Gary D. Phye

# Improving Academic Achievement

## Impact of Psychological Factors on Education

EDITED BY

## Joshua Aronson

*Department of Applied Psychology*
*New York University*
*New York, New York*

## ACADEMIC PRESS

An imprint of Elsevier Science

*Amsterdam    Boston    London    New York    Oxford    Paris*
*San Diego    San Francisco    Singapore    Sydney    Tokyo*

Cover images © 2002 PhotoDisc, Inc.

The sponsoring editor for this book was Nikki Levy, the editorial coordinator was Barbara Makinster, and the book production manager was Kristi Anderson. The cover was designed by Suzanne Rogers. Composition was done by Kolam Information Services, India and the book was printed and bound by Maple Press in York, PA.

This book is printed on acid-free paper. ∞

Academic Press
*An imprint of Elsevier Science.*
525 B Street, Suite 1900, San Diego, California 92101-4495, USA
http://www.academicpress.com

Academic Press
Harcourt Place, 32 Jamestown Road, London NW1 7BY, UK
http://www.academicpress.com

Library of Congress Catalog Card Number: 2001096798

International Standard Book Number: 0–12–064455–X

PRINTED IN THE UNITED STATES OF AMERICA
02  03  04  05  06  07  MM  9  8  7  6  5  4  3  2  1

# Contents

# Introductory Chapter

## 1. SELF AND SELF-BELIEF IN PSYCHOLOGY AND EDUCATION: A HISTORICAL PERSPECTIVE

*Frank Pajares and Dale H. Schunk*

# Revisiting and Extending Classic Lessons

## 2. THE PYGMALION EFFECT AND ITS MEDIATING MECHANISMS

*Robert Rosenthal*

## 3. MESSAGES THAT MOTIVATE: HOW PRAISE MOLDS STUDENTS' BELIEFS, MOTIVATION, AND PERFORMANCE (IN SURPRISING WAYS)

*Carol S. Dweck*

## 4. THE PARADOX OF ACHIEVEMENT: THE HARDER YOU PUSH, THE WORSE IT GETS

*Edward L. Deci and Richard M. Ryan*

## 5. IMPROVING THE ACADEMIC PERFORMANCE OF COLLEGE STUDENTS WITH BRIEF ATTRIBUTIONAL INTERVENTIONS

*Timothy D. Wilson, Michelle Damiani, and Nicole Shelton*

## 6. SELF-HANDICAPPING AND SCHOOL: ACADEMIC SELF-CONCEPT AND SELF-PROTECTIVE BEHAVIOR

*Frederick Rhodewalt and Michael W. Tragakis*

## 7. THE WISDOM OF PRACTICE: LESSONS LEARNED FROM THE STUDY OF HIGHLY EFFECTIVE TUTORS

*Mark R. Lepper and Maria Woolverton*

## 11. INTELLIGENCE IS NOT JUST INSIDE THE HEAD: THE THEORY OF SUCCESSFUL INTELLIGENCE

*Robert J. Sternberg*

# Current Lessons

## 12. BEING AND BECOMING A GOOD PERSON: THE ROLE OF EMOTIONAL INTELLIGENCE IN MORAL DEVELOPMENT AND BEHAVIOR

*David A. Pizarro and Peter Salovey*

## 13. MOZART AND THE MIND: FACTUAL AND FICTIONAL EFFECTS OF MUSICAL ENRICHMENT

*Frances H. Rauscher*

## 14. STEREOTYPE THREAT: CONTENDING AND COPING WITH UNNERVING EXPECTATIONS

*Joshua Aronson*

## 15. A BARRIER OF MISTRUST: HOW NEGATIVE STEREOTYPES AFFECT CROSS-RACE MENTORING

*Geoffrey L. Cohen and Claude M. Steele*

## 16. TOWARD A RESOLUTION OF AN AMERICAN TENSION: SOME APPLICATIONS OF THE HELPING MODEL OF AFFIRMATIVE ACTION TO SCHOOLING

*Anthony R. Pratkanis, Marlene E. Turner, and Stanley B. Malos*

## 17. SOCIAL EXCLUSION IN THE CLASSROOM: TEACHERS AND STUDENTS AS AGENTS OF CHANGE

*Amanda W. Harrist and K. Denise Bradley*

# Contributors

*Numbers in parentheses indicate the pages on which the authors' contributions begin.*

**Elliot Aronson** (209), Distinguished Visiting Professor, Stanford University, Stanford, California 94305

**Joshua Aronson** (279), Department of Applied Psychology, New York University, New York, New York 10003

**K. Denise Bradley** (363), Department of Educational Psychology, University of Texas at Austin, Austin, Texas 78712

**Geoffrey L. Cohen** (303), Department of Psychology, Yale University, New Haven, Connecticut 06520–8205

**Michelle Damiani** (89), University of Virginia, Charlottesville, Virginia 22904

**Edward L. Deci** (61), Department of Psychology, University of Rochester, Rochester, New York 14627

**Carol S. Dweck** (37), Department of Psychology, Columbia University, New York, New York 10027

**Jacquelynne Eccles** (159), University of Michigan, Ann Arbor, Michigan 48109

**Andrew J. Elliot** (xix), Department of Clinical Social Sciences in Psychology, University of Rochester, Rochester, New York 14727

**Pamela J. Gaskill** (185), The Ohio State University, Columbus, Ohio 43210

**Amanda W. Harrist** (363), Oklahoma State University, Stillwater, Oklahoma 74078

**Mark R. Lepper** (135), Department of Psychology, Stanford University, Stanford, California 94305–2130

**Stanley B. Malos** (329), Department of Organization and Management, San Jose State University, San Jose, California 95192

**Frank Pajares** (3), Division of Educational Studies, Emory University, Atlanta, Georgia 30322

**David A. Pizarro** (247), Department of Psychology, Yale University, New Haven, Connecticut 06511

**Anthony R. Pratkanis** (329), Department of Psychology, University of California, Santa Cruz, Santa Cruz, California 95064

**Frances H. Rauscher** (267), Department of Psychology, University of Wisconsin Oshkosh, Oshkosh, Wisconsin 54901

**Frederick Rhodewalt** (109), Department of Psychology, University of Utah, Salt Lake City, Utah 84112

**Robert Rosenthal** (25), Department of Psychology, University of California, Riverside, Riverside, California 92521

**Richard M. Ryan** (61), Department of Psychology, University of Rochester, Rochester, New York 14627

**Peter Salovey** (247), Department of Psychology, Yale University, New Haven, Connecticut 06511

**Dale H. Schunk** (3), School of Education, The University of North Carolina at Greensboro, Greensboro, North Carolina 27402–6171

**Nicole Shelton** (89), Princeton University, Princeton, New Jersey 08544

**Claude M. Steele** (303), Department of Psychology, Stanford University, Stanford, California 94305

**Robert J. Sternberg** (227), Yale University, New Haven, Connecticut 06520–8205

**Michael Tragakis** (109), Department of Psychology, University of Utah, Salt Lake City, Utah 84112

**Marlene E. Turner** (329), Department of Organization and Management, San Jose State University, San Jose, California 95192

**Allan Wigfield** (159), University of Maryland, College Park, Maryland 20742

**Timothy D. Wilson** (89), University of Virginia, Charlottesville, Virginia 22904

**Anita Woolfolk Hoy** (185), The Ohio State University, Columbus, Ohio 43210

**Maria Woolverton** (135), Department of Pediatrics, Child Development Center, Georgetown University Medical Center, Washington, D.C. 20007

# Foreword

Providing children with a quality education is a value near and dear to the hearts and minds of parents, teachers, administrators, politicians, and the community at large. The experiences children have at school are formative. School is not only a place where children accumulate facts and learn academic skills, but it is also a place in which their basic motivation toward competence and achievement is established, their affiliative tendencies and relational patterns take root, their view of themselves as persons of worth and value develops, and their sense of the world as a safe or dangerous place is formulated. What transpires at school can have a foundational impact on a child's life, serving as an impetus for or impediment to future growth and functioning.

This quality education that we hold in such high regard would appear to be jeopardized by many recent developments in school settings. A concern over "slipping standards" and global rankings in subjects such as math and science has evoked numerous supposed remedies, many of which are likely to exacerbate rather than eradicate the perceived problem. An unusually large number of children appear to be divesting from intellectual pursuits and the standard educational process altogether, for reasons that are grounded in the school experience and beyond (i.e., social stratification, family structure). School violence of unimaginable proportions is becoming increasingly common, to the point that physical safety is no longer a given, but is a concern that prevents students, teachers, and administrators from allocating full energy and attention to the learning process.

These problems that plague our educational system are clearly in need of immediate and extensive attention. However, we must not allow the negative to overshadow the positive. The majority of children today, as in the past, undoubtedly receive a good education in a safe school environment delivered by teachers and administrators firmly and energetically dedicated to the training and well-being of the students under their care.

Psychologists, and perhaps social psychologists in particular, would seem unusually well-positioned to provide guidance regarding how to address what ills our educational system, and how to build on the strengths and resources currently present. Many of the issues that are part and parcel of social-psychological study are of direct applicability to the educational process, and the contents of this edited volume nicely bear testimony to this fact. Among the foci of this volume are such central social-psychological topics as intrinsic motivation, achievement motivation, the self-concept, attribution theory, social-cognitive strategies, self-efficacy, stereotyping and prejudice, and interpersonal relations. Given the natural interface between social psychology and education, it is surprising that there are few works presently available that address this connection. In fact, to the best of my knowledge one could count the number of such works on a single hand. As such, this volume represents a valuable addition to a dramatically underdeveloped literature.

In this volume, we not only have discussions of some of the core topics of psychology (particularly social psychology) as they relate to education, but we are also guided in these discussions by some of the most influential scholars in the field today. Indeed a number of the chapters are written by individuals who have made *a* or even *the* seminal contribution to their topic of inquiry. Thus, this book not only fills a lacuna in the literature, but it does so with the help of an unusually qualified and adept set of scholars.

Kurt Lewin, a pioneer in the field of social psychology, offered the oft quoted dictum, "There is nothing as practical as a good theory." The chapters in this volume nicely illustrate the veracity of this statement, as the authors clearly articulate the direct educational implications of basic, empirically established, theoretical principles from social psychology and beyond. Many have made passing reference to the applicability of such principles to the classroom or have sounded the call for work in this area; the present volume answers this call in explicit, elaborate, and expert fashion.

Another noteworthy and unusual aspect of this volume is that it includes coverage of both cutting-edge, contemporary research, and the more established work that deservedly bears the label "classic." These chapters on classic research programs such as the jigsaw classroom and the impact of teacher expectations on student achievement are perhaps particularly noteworthy, because they not only reiterate the basic premises fundamental to the classic contributions, but they also overview the research that has been conducted in these areas over the years, and suggest directions for subsequent empirical and/or conceptual development. In a field in which researchers and theorists too often exhibit a tendency to bypass the old and established in search of the new and innovative, a reiteration of the enduring value of these classic contributions, and indeed a demonstration of their continued relevance, is quite welcome.

In short, this edited volume is a rich compilation that represents an important contribution to the literature. It should be of equal value to psychologists interested in exploring the way in which research and theory can be directly applied "in the field," and to educators seeking to ground their classroom and school wide practices in solid empirical and conceptual work. As we enter the 21st century, surely rectifying what ills our educational system and building on the strengths and resources already in place must be among our top priorities. It is books such as this that will help us achieve this important task.

*Andrew J. Elliot*
University of Rochester

# Preface

I decided to create this book when I became aware that some wonderful educational research was unfamiliar to its most likely beneficiaries. A few years ago I was asked to talk about my research to a large audience of education students, most of whom were about to graduate and begin their teaching careers. A funny thing happened. Early on in my talk, I made reference to a classic line of social psychological research that demonstrated the powerful effects of subtle social dynamics on student motivation and achievement. I thought it was research so classic and so relevant to educational practice that I could simply refer to it by name. A puzzled look came over the faces of several students in the audience. So I very briefly described the research. Still, no light of recognition came into the eyes in front of me. I paused and asked for a show of hands: "How many of you have heard of professor X and her research on motivation?" Out of about four hundred students, maybe five raised their hands. I was surprised; I thought this was research that everyone knew. Several times during the remainder of my talk I repeated my little poll, each time asking about a different "landmark" study on the social psychology of education, and each time finding, at best, only sparse recognition. This was especially surprising given the location—one of the top ranked schools of education in the country. Thus, I couldn't easily shrug this off as a local problem; if they weren't familiar with research here, chances are that across the country many freshly minted teachers were starting their careers missing out on some very useful and inspiring knowledge.

The question, of course, is why? One answer is that we psychologists do a rather poor job of communicating our research to nonscientists. Because of the institutional rewards for doing so, we publish mainly in psychology or education journals, we write in jargon, and we generally shy away from talking about applications of our theories in all but the remotest terms. Thus we tend to communicate mainly with one another and often neglect the concerns of the educators who are interested in theory, but who mainly want to know how to use it to be better educators. As a result, some of the psychology research that psychologists are particularly proud of—research that made me want to become an educational psychologist—is not presented in educational psychology textbooks and remains unexposed to education students. This book is intended to fill this gap. It is research and theory that I think will be of interest to students of both education and psychology, but that reflects the practical concerns of educators as much as the theoretical interests of scientists.

A second reason for the book and the specific form it takes is to address a broader problem of a gulf between scientists and educators, one I am frequently confronted with when working with educators in the field. The problem is that educational practice is often highly politicized, both in localities and nationally. Although people care deeply about the welfare of their students, they are often rightfully confused about research purporting to improve educational practice—a general wariness among nonscientists that virtually any claim can be validated by research. This you-can-prove-anything-with-statistics notion is not true, but it is certainly understandable given the frequency with which each side in a political debate about education cites "research" in support of their favored position. This skepticism is intensified by the common use, particularly during political campaigns, of the word "crisis" to describe the state of American education. To be sure, there are plenty of particulars to lend weight to the impression that our schools are in unprecedented trouble. Discussions of *school choice, vouchers, standards and accountability, the Columbine massacre, race gaps in performance*, and so on—all suggest an image of schools in chaos and abandon.

While the importance of these issues is undeniable, the word "crisis" to describe the state of our schools has an unfortunate consequence for discussions of how to improve academic achievement. It implies that schools have fallen from some higher plane of excellence and that improving education requires a return to a "golden age" when schools worked because they employed traditional principles of imparting knowledge. Thus, in response to the crisis, we often hear the plea that our students would be better educated—and more civil, respectful, fulfilled, and so on—if only we would just get "back to basics," and start educating students according to the commonsense principles that guided the education of our parents and grandparents. An unfortunate consequence of this perception is that it tends to narrow our thinking about the process of education; it creates a false dichotomy between commonsense or traditional notions of how to teach, how to motivate, how to praise people, and so on—and everything else. And this can foster a general suspicion of innovation—even well established innovation with a long-standing tradition of improving education.

In the following chapters the authors present what I think is a powerful counterpoint to the distrust of social science research on education. In my experience working with education students, careful study of social psychological principles is an eye-opening experience, one that can help students distinguish between genuinely useful approaches from those that are less useful—whether the approach is traditional or not. The reader of this volume will learn that many commonsense assumptions about education—whether we got them from our own experiences in school, from behaviorist psychology, political rhetoric, or *The Little Engine That Could*—simply do not hold up when looked at scientifically. They will learn, for example, that doling out rewards to motivate students or praising them for a "job well done" often is counterproductive, that boosting self-esteem has little or no effect on school performance, that test scores can rise dramatically depending on how a test is described, that "healthy" competition is sometimes anything but healthy in classrooms, and so on. Familiarity with the lessons offered in this book, in addition to offering specific research-based strategies for boosting performance, can help potential teachers make wiser decisions about how to teach—often by directly refuting conventional wisdom about the way students think and learn.

Presenting both classic and contemporary contributions, the authors describe their work in a style accessible to anyone interested in what psychologists have learned about improving educational practice and boosting achievement. We wrote primarily with two audiences in mind—students in education and in psychology. For the education students, I sought material likely to be of greatest interest and use to them as future teachers or educators, with a balance between theory and recommendations for practice. Both sides of this coin—theory *and* practice—are critical to educators interested in improving achievement. It is critical that both are sufficiently understood. I have seen a number of theoretically derived interventions for boosting achievement (a few of which of are described in this book) fail because some critical aspect of the theory was left out. Such failures are seldom benign. Often, the intervention is cast aside, rejected as just another useless "fad" handed down from ivory tower scientists who don't understand how things work in the "real world." Therefore, for the most part, we stress theory and application in equal measure, reflecting the equal emphasis on each that is required for improving achievement. These qualities make the book of equal value to students of psychology as well. The work is presented in a way that highlights core psychological principles relevant to education, such as intelligence, attribution theory, emotions, motivation, self-concept and self-esteem, group dynamics, and prejudice to educational applications, demonstrating the utility of the theories that are presented in social, cognitive, and educational psychology courses.

The reader will notice a few departures from the standard way of organizing edited books. First, the book is not explicitly organized around topics; instead I have divided the book into two sections—*classic* and *contemporary lessons from psychology*. In this way, the interested reader will be aware of which research has entered the pantheon of studies considered classic. Yet the classics are not out of date; all share the timeless objective of improving achievement or school behavior and all are presented here updated with new research and fresh commentary. I also decided not to organize by topic because doing so would have required using arbitrary and, in some cases, misleading labels. For example, Carol Dweck's chapter on using praise to motivate children could just as easily be placed under the heading "intelligence" as under the heading "motivation" or "the self" or "social influence," or "attribution." To locate it in any single area of psychology risks obscuring its relevance to others. This is true of a number of the chapters. My hope is that readers will read all the chapters and decide for themselves into which sub-areas of psychology or education they best fit.

In a second departure from standard practice, this selection of readings by no means covers the full terrain of how to use psychology to enhance educational practice. That would require a book many times this size. Rather, it covers the areas at the intersection of what I find most important, most exciting, and, in my own experience working with educators and teachers-in-training, most under-appreciated and misunderstood. For example, Robert Rosenthal's classic work on how teacher expectations can shape student learning is probably the most familiar to teachers. But its details—which are critical to current discussions of how to improve education—are widely misunderstood. Similarly, most people have probably heard about the "Mozart effect," which refers to Frances Rauscher and her colleagues' exciting discovery that studying classical music has the potential to increase certain cognitive abilities. But misunderstandings of the effects (partially fueled by popular books trying to capitalize on the research) have led politicians to waste time and money piping Mozart into schools and skeptics to reject the notion of the Mozart effect altogether. Thus, a special effort was made to include work that is widely misunderstood—and to address these misunderstandings.

Additionally, the authors were chosen in large part, not only because they have made seminal contributions to the psychology of education, but also because they write well. The result is a selection of chapters that is both important and readable. Although this is far from everything one needs to know about the subject, it is research everyone who wants to improve education should know about.

Finally, bearing in mind the desire to narrow the divide between scientists and educators, we had veteran teachers read the chapters in the book, posing questions that forced the authors to address their real world concerns as teachers. I learned a lot from these question-and-answer sessions and I hope readers will too.

*Joshua Aronson*

# Acknowledgments

I have many people to thank for helping with this book. First and foremost, I thank the authors for their chapters, their inspiring research, and for their patience with this project, which was slowed considerably by my changing universities midway through the project. I also thank Diana Cordova, whose early efforts as co-editor made the book stronger. I am very grateful to the educators, Sarah Feldman, Nancy McCullough, and Jennifer Barr, who read drafts of chapters and provided the questions to pose to authors in the Q & A that appear at the end of most chapters. I thank also my students and research assistants, Catherine Good, Michael Inzlicht, and Linda McKay, and my wife, Stacey, who provided editorial feedback on my own writing in this volume. I am also grateful to the National Science Foundation, the William T. Grant Foundation, and the Russell Sage Foundation for generous support of my research and time working on this book. Finally, I thank my wife, Stacey, and my daughter, Eliana, for putting up with me during the less enjoyable phases of this process. This book is dedicated, with love, to you.

# PART
# I

# Introductory Chapter

# CHAPTER 1

# Self and Self-Belief in Psychology and Education: A Historical Perspective

FRANK PAJARES

*Division of Educational Studies, Emory University*

DALE H. SCHUNK

*School of Education, The University of North Carolina at Greensboro*

We begin this chapter with a critical assumption that we hope all readers will find sound. The assumption is that the beliefs that children create and develop and hold to be true about themselves are vital forces in their success or failure in all endeavors and, of particular relevance to educators, to their success or failure in school. Rather obvious is it not? After all, any parent or teacher knows well that the beliefs that young people get into their heads become the rules that govern their actions, for good or, regretfully, sometimes for ill.

The assumption that children's self-beliefs are inextricably tied to their thinking and functioning seems so sound, so obvious, and so commonsensical one might well think that research on academic motivation and achievement (research on why students do the things they do in school and why they achieve or fail to achieve) should naturally focus, at least in great part, on the things that children come to believe about themselves. In other words, one would think that, if psychologists are interested in understanding the reasons why students select some activities and avoid others, why they succeed in some academic pursuits and fail at others, or why they are filled with either anticipation or panic at the thought of doing this or that task, then researchers should quite carefully investigate the things and ways that students believe about themselves. As Jerome Bruner (1997) has argued, "if agency and esteem are central to the construction of a concept of Self, then the ordinary practices of school need to be examined with a view to what contribution they make to these two crucial ingredients of personhood."

And as we begin a new millennium this is indeed the case. So much so, in fact, that reviewing the current state of knowledge related to theories and principles of motivation for the 1996 *Handbook of Educational Psychology*, Sandra Graham and Bernard Weiner observed that current research in educational psychology "reflects what is probably the main new direction in the field of motivation—the study of the self." Current interest in self-constructs is so pervasive that Graham and Weiner concluded that "it is evident that the self is on the verge of dominating the field of motivation."

This focus on a child's sense of "self" seems so reasonable that one would think it has always been instrumental in framing the discussion around educational concerns. Consequently, one would think that psychologists and educators have always made the self a focus of educational research. Alas, either this has not been the case, or, when it has, results have been, to say the least, problematic. During the past century, interest in the self and in self-beliefs in psychological and educational research has waxed and waned. For long periods attention to these concepts was scrupulously avoided. At other times rigor in empirical research left much to be desired. Still at other times the application of research findings and scholarly thinking produced mixed results.

So what happened? How did psychology and education lose their interest in the self and in the self-beliefs of individuals? Before we proceed further, this seems an appropriate juncture at which to remind ourselves of two aphorisms appropriate to these questions. The first is Voltaire's dictum that "common sense is not so common." The second is Wittgenstein's lament, "may God grant philosophers the wisdom to see what is before their very eyes." If Wittgenstein believed that philosophers tend to ignore the obvious, we dread to imagine what he would have thought of psychologists.

In this chapter, our primary aim is to provide a historical overview of research on the self and on self-beliefs over the past century that we hope will help explain how it is that psychology has often skirted common sense and declined the wise invitation to see what has always been before its very eyes (and, may we add, what poets, playwrights, novelists, and children's storytellers have always known): that understanding critical issues related to our children's sense of self is crucial to understanding the manner in which they deal with all of life's tasks and challenges. We end the chapter by reviewing two psychological concepts that are responsible for the current resurgence of interest in self-beliefs in recent years and by providing a brief discussion of some of the major educational implications that result from this renewed focus on students' self-beliefs in school.

## HISTORICAL DEVELOPMENT OF RESEARCH
## ON THE SELF

Drawings on caves suggest that some time during the dawn of history, human beings began to give serious thought to their nonphysical, psychological selves. With the advent of written history, writers would describe this awareness of self in terms of spirit, psyche, or soul. Greek philosophers such as Socrates, Plato, and Aristotle defined self in terms of the soul, as immaterial and spiritual. Their conception of an individual's sense of self as a spiritual entity separate from the physical formed the foundation for subsequent conceptions of mind and body duality. During the Middle Ages the concept was further developed by theologians such as Thomas Aquinas, who stressed the immortality and superiority of the soul to the body in which it dwelled.

A turning point in the thinking about this nonphysical being came in 1659, when Rene Descartes wrote his *Principles of Philosophy*. Descartes proposed that doubt was a principal tool of disciplined inquiry, yet he could not doubt that he doubted. He reasoned that if he doubted, he was thinking, and therefore he must exist. Although the emphasis on mind and body duality that Cartesian rationalism came to represent has largely been discarded in recent times, its emphasis on inner processes of self-awareness—on "metacognitive" process—remains a powerful force in philosophical and psychological thought. Other philosophers of this period, among them Spinoza and Leibnitz, added their ideas about the mystery of the nonphysical aspect of individuals. Terms such as mind, soul, psyche, and self were often used interchangeably, with scant regard for invariant vocabulary or scientific experimentation. For the most part, a general state of metaphysical disorganization regarding the concept of self existed well into the present century (and, to some extent, continues). As for belief, it was typically relegated to the realm of religion.

### Early Interest in the Self in American Psychology

At the turn of the last century, when American psychology began to take its place among the other academic disciplines, there was a great deal of interest both in the self and in the role that self-beliefs play in human conduct. For example, when William James (1891a, 1891b) wrote the *Principles of Psychology*, his chapter on "The Consciousness of Self" was the longest in the two volumes. James suggested that "the total self of me, being as it were duplex," is composed of "partly object and partly subject." As a consequence, he differentiated between the self as knower, or the *I*, and the self as known, or *me*. He referred to the *I* as pure ego and suggested that this component of self is consciousness itself. The *me*, on the other hand, is one of the many things that the *I* may be conscious of, and it consists of three components, one physical or material, one social, and one spiritual.

It is not difficult to become captivated by James' seductive conception of self as knower and self as known. After all, the distinction of self in terms of *I* and *me* is almost intuitive ("*I* talk to *myself*"; "*I* want people to like *me*"). On other levels it is also charming and amusing. However, psychologists critical of this intramind type of dualism point out that self-reflection entails shifting the perspective of the same self rather than reifying different selves regulating each other. Bandura (1997), for example, argued that people think, act, and reflect on their actions:

> but it is the one and the same person who is doing the thinking and later evaluating the adequacy of one's knowledge, thinking skills, and action strategies. The shift in perspective does not transform one from an agent to an object as the dualist view of the self would lead one to believe. One is just as much an agent reflecting on one's experiences as in executing courses of action. Rather than splitting the self into object and agent, in self-reflection individuals are simultaneously agent and object. (p. 7)

James had been careful to hedge his conception, however, pointing out that the *I* and the *me* are discriminated aspects of self rather than "separate things," but the truth is that they come off rather separate in his description of them.

James (1896/1958) was also one of the first writers to use the term *self-esteem*, which he described as a self-feeling that "in this world depends entirely on what we back ourselves to be and do" (p. 54). James even provided a mathematical formula for self-esteem that suggests that, in essence, how we feel about ourselves depends on the success with which we accomplish those things we wish to accomplish.

$$\text{Self-esteem} = \frac{\text{Success}}{\text{Pretensions}}$$

Self-esteem may be raised, James argued, either by succeeding in our endeavors or, in the face of incessant disappointments, by lowering our sights and giving up certain pretensions or aims.

In 1902, Charles Horton Cooley introduced the metaphor of the *looking-glass self* to illustrate the idea that individuals' sense of self is formed primarily as they develop self-beliefs that have been created by their perceptions of how others perceive them. That is, the appraisals of others act as mirror reflections that provide the information we use to define our own sense of self. Hence, we are in very great part what we think other people think we are. This conception of self brought to the forefront of psychological thought an emphasis on the importance of early child rearing and schooling as well as the critical role of social comparisons with peers in the development of self. The idea of the looking-glass self underscored the great power that parents, siblings, family members, teachers, and significant others have in shaping children's identity, especially early in a child's life. After all, these are the people who provide us with the first reflections through which we can contemplate our "selves."

James (1896/1958) had viewed the process of self-formation differently. He argued that, because children are conscious of what other people are before they become conscious of what they are themselves, the self is developed primarily through the process of imitation. That is, children create a sense of who they are by imitating the mental and behavioral habits of parents and other influential people in their lives. Both for James and for Cooley, however, the growth of a child's sense of self is deeply influenced—they would argue that it is in fact nearly determined—by the beliefs and actions of others. This, then, is the great blessing or tragedy of self and self-belief construction and development, that we become the kind of person we see reflected in the eyes of others.

## Self, Ego, and the Psychoanalysts

A milestone in the quest for understanding internal processes came in the writings of psychoanalysts such as Sigmund Freud (1923), who framed the self as the regulating center of an individual's personality and shed light on self-processes under the guise of id, ego, and superego functioning. Freud's work was so influential that it would be reasonable to say that few concepts in psychology are as closely associated with the concept of self in modern parlance as that of *ego*. When we say that individuals have a "big ego," we generally mean that they have an exaggerated sense of self-importance. The words that have evolved from ego, such as egotist and egomaniac, describe one who is self-absorbed and self-aggrandizing. These are not the conceptualizations of ego that Freud had in mind.

When Freud introduced the hypothetical construct of ego, he did so to help explain what he considered to be a psychic struggle all individuals must undergo: that between instinctual drives, sociocultural norms, and the world of reality. Freud offered a structural theory of mind, complete with a tripartite model, to explain this psychic conflict and account for human agency. In this model, it is the function of the ego (in German the *ich*, or "I") to mediate and resolve the conflict between the *id* (or "it"), the *superego* (in German *uberich*, or "greater than I"), and the external world. The id consists of the pleasure-seeking, instinctual drives with which all individuals are born; the superego consists of the conscience and ego ideal developed as a result of sociocultural and familial influences. It is the task of the ego to delay, rechannel, or if necessary circumvent id gratification and adapt the individual to the reality of the world at large.

Freud also argued that the ego is part unconscious, and so its executive function is not always thought to reflect intentionality and conscious purpose. This feature of the ego does not distinguish it from traditional conceptions of the self, but it clearly distinguishes it from self-beliefs such as self-esteem, which are generally considered to exist at a conscious level of awareness. Yet, Freudians and neo-Freudians hesitated to make the self a primary psychological unit or to give it central prominence in their theoretical formulations. In part, this was due to the psychodynamic emphasis of the biological processes in human development, hence the oft-repeated Freudian maxim that "biology is destiny." Erik Erikson, a prominent psychoanalyst who would bring this psychological view to the forefront of American psychology, later focused on critical aspects of self and self-belief to trace adolescents' development of their ego identity.

## Other Early Proponents of the Self

Other prominent theorists also wrote prominently about the self early in the century. For example, George Herbert Mead (1913, 1934) made the concept of self a major part of his theoretical writings on the philosophy of transactions with the environment. He argued that personality, rather than being anchored on biological variables, is determined by social-psychological factors. In a manner similar to that of Lev Vygotsky, a young psychologist in Russia whose writings had not yet been translated into English, Mead argued that the self results from an interaction between the social process and what Vygotsky (1935/1978) had called the psychological tools individuals use to make sense of and share social symbols. The primary tool, language, aids individuals in making sense of their inner processes and coming to define their sense of what they are. Mead also made use of James' *I* and *me* dichotomy to help explain that "if the I speaks, the me hears." By listening and making sense of this linguistic exchange, self is realized.

Other psychologists were also instrumental in keeping alive the idea of the importance of studying individuals' conceptions of the self. Kurt Lewin (1935) viewed the self as a central and relatively permanent organization that gave consistency to the entire personality. Goldstein (1939) analyzed the processes of self-actualization, as contrasted with those of the sick organism that must constantly worry about preservation. This was a forerunner of the comprehensive work of Abraham Maslow, who would later write so powerfully about self-actualization. Lecky (1945) contributed the notion of self-consistency as a primary motivating force in human behavior.

Theorists such as Bertocci (1945), clearly influenced by James, reemphasized the two aspects of self, again distinguishing between the self as object, the "me," and the self as subject, the "I." Murphy (1947) discussed the origins and modes of self-enhancement and how the self is related to the social group. Ramey (1948) introduced measures of self-concept in counseling interviews and argued that psychotherapy is primarily a process of changing the self-concept.

We have spent some time covering the major figures involved in self-research and outlining some of the key ideas involved in that research primarily to illustrate that, during the first half of the 20th century, discussions of what components and characteristics might constitute an individual's sense of self were prominent in the mainstream of psychological thinking. These discussions were so prominent, in fact, in the 1949 presidential address before the American Psychological Association, Ernest Hilgard defended the thesis that the self could be a unifying concept in problems of motivation.

## THE INSURGENCE OF BEHAVIORIST THEORIES

Notwithstanding the efforts of James, Mead, the psychoanalysts, and other powerful proponents of the self, during the first half of the 20th century psychologists rallied around various schools of thought characterized by ardent advocacy of their own theoretical viewpoints and unrestrained hostility to those of others. Most prominent among these was the school of thought espousing a *behaviorist* orientation. Even as James promulgated his ideas emphasizing the critical role played by the self in human functioning, the Russian school of reflexology, known today to psychology students primarily through the work of Ivan Pavlov and his discovery of the principle of conditioned reflexes, was having a profound influence on European psychologists. Theirs was a view of human functioning in which only observable experience was deemed worthy of scientific scrutiny.

This behaviorist perspective, which traveled to the United States by way of Edward Titchener, Edward L. Thorndike, and others, soon began to capture the discipline of psychology. It was a movement that wanted a discipline in which self-perceptions and other internal mental states played no meaningful role in a scientific psychology. Adherents swelled their ranks by pointing out that all theories except their own placed self and consciousness at the center of human functioning despite the fact that only a person's tangible, observable, and measurable behavior was fit for scientific inquiry. They solidified their position by conducting empirical investigations that produced convincing research results grounded on what they maintained was sound scientific inquiry.

When the smoke cleared, the behaviorism of Pavlov, Thorndike, John Watson (1925), and later B. F. Skinner (1938) carried the day. Psychology was redirected, attention was turned to observable stimuli and responses, and the inner life of the individual was labeled as beyond the scope of scientific psychology. Self, self-belief, and self-perception as psychological constructs were largely abandoned, along with such internal constructs as mind, consciousness, awareness, and will. With the advent of behaviorist thinking, the self received diminishing attention from the behavior-oriented psychologists who quickly tightened their grip on American psychology.

A critical sidelight to all this is that psychological theories have always had a strong influence on education. Through the years, teachers have followed the prescriptions of psychologists, from William James with his emphasis on the self to J. B. Watson with his stress on observable and measurable behavior. For example, James' educational ideas, particularly his call for attention to self-processes and to the needs and dispositions of the child as outlined in his *Talks* to *Teachers*, were embraced by the educational community of his day and served as the prevailing influence on most educators during the first two decades of the century. In 1903 John Dewey referred to James' *Principles* as the "spiritual progenitor" of the progressive education movement that Dewey was launching at the University of Chicago, and James' ideas even served as foundational for the scientific pedagogy that educational psychologists such as G. Stanley Hall and Edward L. Thorndike would later promulgate. It was unavoidable, then, that when psychology abandoned the self in favor of behaviorist principles of pedagogy, so did education.

Although the decline of interest in the self was encouraged by behaviorist psychologists, all the fault for its neglect cannot be laid at their door. Very little of the literature on the self from early to midcentury was based on what psychologists commonly refer to as disciplined inquiry. Rather, it continued to be philosophic or conceptual in nature, with few studies attempting or reporting empirical findings. Those few who advocated the importance of the self weakened their position with a profound neglect of rigorous experimentation and scientific inquiry.

## THE HUMANISTIC REVOLT

Very nearly coinciding with the zenith of behavioristic influence at midcentury came what is now often referred to as the humanistic revolt in psychology. Dissatisfied with the direction that psychology was taking and apprehensive about what they considered the narrow and passive view of human functioning that behaviorism represented, a group of psychologists called for renewed attention to inner experience, internal processes, and self constructs. In concert with existential and phenomenological movements of the day, the writings of these new theorists caught the attention of scholars and researchers and, during the 1950s, the humanistic movement was born.

The most powerful voice in the new movement was that of Abraham Maslow (1954), now generally recognized as the father of modern humanistic psychology. Maslow began his academic career as a behaviorist (he worked under the noted behaviorist Edward L. Thorndike) but came to find the theory disturbingly deterministic and limited in scope and depth. Maslow believed that all individuals have inner lives and potential for growth, creativity, and free choice. In 1943, with the publication of "A Dynamic Theory of Human Motivation," he outlined a motivational process based on the view that human beings are motivated by basic needs that must be satisfied and that are hierarchically ordered. He argued that the goal of each individual is to achieve self-actualization, defined broadly as the motivation to develop one's full potential as a human being and to reach self-fulfillment, inner peace, and contentment. As Diggory (1966) noted, "the fact that the new self psychologists were able to argue substantive matters of learning theory and motivation with the heirs of the behaviorists made the latter pay attention and finally agree that there might be something to the idea of self after all" (p. 57).

Another eloquent and significant voice of this new humanistic movement was that of Carl Rogers. In an influential series of articles, books, and lectures, Rogers presented a system of psychotherapy called "client-centered," which was built around the importance of the self in human adjustment. In Rogers' client-centered approach, the self is the central aspect of personality and is a phenomenological concept (a pattern of conscious perceptions experienced by the individual) that is of primary importance to that individual's behavior and adjustment. Rogers described the self as a social product, developing out of interpersonal relationships and striving for consistency. He believed that there is a need for positive regard both from others and from oneself and that in every human being there is a tendency toward self-actualization and growth so long as this is permitted and nurtured by environmental forces. Rogers' approach went far toward linking earlier notions about the self. In fact, his impact was powerful and influential enough that his general approach soon became known as "self theory."

Another notable influence in reintroducing the concept of the self into psychology and education were the writings of Arthur Combs and Donald Snygg. In their 1959 book *Individual Behavior*, they proposed that the basic drive of the individual is the maintenance and enhancement of the self. They also proposed that all behavior, without exception, is dependent on the individual's personal frame of reference. In other words, behavior is determined by the totality of experience of which an individual is aware at an instant of action, the phenomenal field. Combs and Snygg's insistence on giving major importance to the ways in which people see themselves and their world was a significant contribution to both psychology and education.

Fueled by the eloquent arguments of humanist theorists, during the 1960s and 1970s there was an enthusiastic renaissance of interest in internal and intrinsic motivating forces and affective processes, particularly with reference to the dynamic importance of the self. One especially prominent voice was that of Gordon Allport, who throughout his career emphasized the importance of self in contemporary psychology and argued for purposeful, rational individuals aware of themselves and controlling their future through their aspirations. The research and writing of Wilbur Brookover and of Stanley Coopersmith, among others, provided deeper understandings of the dynamics of the self in influencing behavior.

This resurgence of interest in the self resulted in increased efforts by many educators and psychologists to promote an emphasis on the importance of a healthy self-concept and positive self-regard. Also born in schools at about this time was the *self-enhancement* view of academic functioning. That is, the view that, because a child's self-esteem is the critical ingredient and primary cause of academic achievement, teacher practices and academic strategies should be aimed at fostering students' self-esteem.

And yet, the surge of interest in self-processes that the humanistic movement brought to education from the 1950s to the late 1970s had profoundly uneven results. In great part, this was because research on the relationship between self-esteem and adaptive functioning either was inconclusive or provided inconsistent results. Highly respected researchers reviewed decades of self-esteem studies and reported that correlations between self-esteem and academic achievement ran the gamut from strongly positive to dismally negative (Handford & Hattie, 1982), which is to say that in some studies low self-esteem was actually associated with higher achievement. The researchers also reported that when they actually evaluated the validity of a study, the better studies tended to show the less significant connections between self-esteem and academic achievement.

More recently, after a thorough review of self-esteem studies in various areas of psychology, and keep in mind that there have been more than 10,000 such studies to date, scholars at the University of California concluded that the association between self-esteem and its expected consequences were mixed, insignificant, or absent. The nonrelationship holds between self-esteem and teenage pregnancy, and self-esteem and child abuse, and self-esteem and most cases of alcohol and drug abuse. As regards self-esteem and social outcomes, self-esteem has been positively and negatively correlated with aggression. And some researchers have provided qualified support for the contention that delinquent behavior might actually serve to enhance self-esteem. Some studies have even shown that high self-esteem correlates positively with increased sexual activity by teens (see Beane, 1991; Kohn, 1994; McMillan, Singh, & Simonetta, 1994).

What followed, of course, was not only a reduced interest in self research in education but a backlash against humanistic psychology and against the self-esteem movement itself. Some critics of the humanist's influence on education viewed humanistic psychology as a form of secular humanism and, therefore, an effort to undermine religion. Reduced interest in the self was also brought about by the many gimmicks introduced into the educational milieu. The gap from theory to practice proved difficult to breach, and many laudable but misguided efforts to nurture the self-esteem of children fell prey to excesses and, ultimately, ridicule. The goal of fostering positive self-perceptions became mired in controversies over the value of self-esteem education, controversies that continue unabated to this day.

## THE COGNITIVE REVOLUTION

The humanistic movement waned during the 1980s as psychologists shifted their interest to cognitive processes and information-processing views of human functioning. This *cognitive revolution*, as it came to be called, was influenced by technological advances and by the advent of the computer, which became the movement's signature metaphor. Much like their humanistic predecessors, the new wave of theorists emphasized internal, mental events, but this emphasis was primarily on cognitive tasks such as encoding and decoding human thinking, information processing strategies, higher-order thinking, memory processes, and problem solving rather than on issues related to the self.

And schools followed suit. Alarmed by what they perceived to be plummeting academic standards and fueled by international studies that erroneously made it appear as if American children graduated from high school practically illiterate (see Berliner & Biddle, 1995), parents and educators demanded a back-to-basics approach to curriculum and practice. In this back-to-basics national mood, students' emotional concerns were regarded as irrelevant to their academic achievement. Reforms were accompanied by an effort to dictate curricular practices according to their success in raising achievement test results. What was called for, critics cried, was a return to the old values of hard work and hard knocks. As a consequence, research on the self and self-beliefs did not merely wane, it was viewed as antithetical to sound educational understandings, as a type of "psychology-lite" undertaking.

## RETURN OF INTEREST IN THE SELF

During the last two decades, prominent voices in psychology and in education have signaled a shift in direction with respect to the issues critical to human functioning, and the self has again become the focus for educational psychology research and practice on academic motivation. In important ways, the shift represents a marked departure from previous conceptions of self-referent thought. If, as Graham and Weiner (1996) contended, the construct of self is on the verge of dominating research and theory on academic motivation, this is due primarily to interest in and research on two self-beliefs: self-efficacy and self-concept. To better understand the resurgence of interest in these ideas, let us take a moment to provide a brief overview of these two constructs.

### Self-Efficacy Beliefs

One of the most prominent among recent voices calling for renewed attention to the self has been that of Albert Bandura, professor of psychology at Stanford University. Like Maslow, Bandura was initially trained as a behaviorist. Early on, however, Bandura was deeply discomforted by the "thought-less" nature of behaviorist notions. He was also aware that a key element was missing from the prevalent learning theories of the day. In 1977, with the publication of "Self-Efficacy: Toward a Unifying Theory of Behavioral Change," he identified an important piece of that missing element—that individuals create and develop self-perceptions of capability that become instrumental to the goals they pursue and to the control they are able to exercise over their environments.

In 1986, Bandura proposed a social cognitive theory of human functioning that emphasized the critical role of self-beliefs in human cognition, motivation, and behavior. Rejecting the behaviorists' indifference to self-processes, Bandura argued that individuals possess a self system that enables them to exercise a measure of control over their thoughts, feelings, and actions. In doing so, he reinvigorated the nearly abandoned focus on the self in the study of human processes that William James had initiated nearly a century earlier. In Bandura's theory, individuals are viewed as proactive and self-regulating rather than as reactive and controlled either by environmental or by biological forces.

According to Bandura, how people behave can often be better predicted by the beliefs they hold about their capabilities, which he called *self-efficacy beliefs*, than by what they are actually capable of accomplishing, for these self-perceptions help determine what individuals do with the knowledge and skills they have. Indeed, Bandura contended that self-efficacy is the most influential arbiter in human functioning. Recently, Bandura (1997) further situated self-efficacy within a theory of personal and collective agency that operates in concert with other sociocognitive factors in regulating human well-being and attainment.

Self-efficacy beliefs influence students' behavior in a number of ways. First, they influence the choices that students make: students engage in tasks about which they feel confident and avoid those tasks about which they are not confident. At lower levels of schooling, this can be a moot issue, for students often have very little choice over the activities in which they must engage. As they get older, however, they have greater control over course and activity selection, and their confidence influences these decisions. Self-efficacy beliefs also help determine how much effort students will expend on an activity and how long they will persevere: the higher the sense of efficacy, the greater the effort expenditure and persistence. This function of self-efficacy beliefs helps create a type of self-fulfilling prophecy, for the perseverance associated with high self-efficacy leads to increased performance, which, in turn, raises sense of efficacy, whereas the giving-in associated with low self-efficacy limits the potential for raising confidence. Self-efficacy beliefs also affect behavior by influencing students' emotional reactions. Students with low self-efficacy can come to believe that things are tougher than they really are, a belief that fosters anxiety, stress, and a narrow vision of how best to solve a problem. High self-efficacy, on the other hand, creates feelings of serenity in approaching difficult tasks, increases optimism, lowers anxiety, raises self-esteem, and fosters resilience.

A strong sense of efficacy enhances human accomplishment and personal well-being. Confident students approach difficult tasks as challenges to be mastered rather than as threats to be avoided. They have greater intrinsic interest and deep engrossment in activities, set themselves challenging goals and maintain strong commitment to them, and heighten and sustain their efforts in the face of failure. Moreover, they more quickly recover their confidence after failures or setbacks, and they attribute failure to insufficient effort or deficient knowledge and skills that are acquirable. For confident students, failure is a healthy reminder that they need to work harder. Conversely, students with low self-efficacy may believe that things are tougher than they really are, a belief that fosters stress, depression, and a narrow vision of how best to solve a problem. When students lack confidence in their capabilities, they are likely to attribute their failure to low ability, which they perceive as inborn, permanent, and not acquirable. For them, failure is just another reminder that they are incapable. Students who doubt their academic ability envision low grades often before they even begin an examination.

As Alexander Dumas wrote, "A man who doubts himself is like a man who would enlist in the ranks of his enemies and bear arms against himself. He makes his failure certain by himself being the first person to be convinced of it." Linus, of Peanuts fame, once quipped that "there is no burden quite as heavy as a great potential." Teachers know that academic potential seldom can be realized in the absence of the child's belief in that potential. Clearly, the Roman poet Virgil was correct: "They are able who think they are able."

In all, Bandura's social cognitive theory paints a portrait of human behavior and motivation in which the beliefs that people have about their capabilities are critical elements. The tenets of this theory are consistent with the basic assumption with which we began this chapter: that individuals' self-beliefs are critical forces in their academic motivation and achievement.

## Self-Concept Beliefs

Current interest in the self and in self-beliefs has also been characterized by renewed research into *self-concept*, a construct with a long ancestry (recall that William James wrote extensively on self-concept more than 100 years ago). Recent definitions of self-concept have been informed by James's conception that the self-concept is an individual's representation of all of his or her self-knowledge. Combs (1962) argued that an individual's self-concept is, in essence, "what an individual believes he is" (p. 52). Consequently, the accuracy of the self-appraisals that one makes rests in part on how well one knows oneself. This suggests that one's self-concept is made up of the beliefs that one holds to be true about one's experience.

Researchers generally agree that children develop a self-concept primarily through their interpretations of the reflected appraisals of others. Recall that early in the century Cooley (1902) used the metaphor of the self as mirror, as a reflection of how others see us. Coopersmith (1967) later wrote that "each person's self-concept, to a considerable extent, is a mirror reflection of how he has been (and is) seen by others who are important to him" (p. 201).

Early theorists defined and used self-concept in general terms as global perceptions of self-worth, or self-esteem. But individuals perceive themselves primarily in terms of the various facets of their self-system, each facet carrying a different description and evaluation. How we may feel about ourselves in one area of our life may be unrelated to how we feel in another. For example, how we perceive our self as a teacher or student may differ markedly from how we perceive our self as a parent, spouse, son or daughter, sibling, athlete, or spouse. Even as a student, we may perceive our self quite differently in differing academic areas. We may have a positive self-concept in mathematics but a negative one in writing. This is not to argue that self-concept beliefs do not generalize and influence each other, nor does it mean that one does not possess a general view of oneself. Rather, it is to emphasize that self-concept can differ across differing domains of functioning, and it is our self-concept in specific areas of our lives that is most likely to guide us in those areas (see Shavelson & Marsh, 1986).

It bears emphasizing that self-efficacy and self-concept beliefs represent quite different views of oneself. Recall that self-efficacy is a judgment of capability to perform a task or engage in an activity. Self-concept, on the other hand, is a self-descriptive judgment that includes an evaluation of competence and the feelings of self-worth associated with the judgment in question. In other words, self-efficacy is a judgment of one's own *confidence*; self-concept is a description of one's own perceived self accompanied by a judgment of *self-worth*.

Clearly, when individuals tap into their self-efficacy or their self-concept beliefs, they must ask themselves quite different types of questions. Self-efficacy beliefs revolve around questions of "can" (Can I write well? Can I drive a car? Can I solve this problem?), whereas self-concept beliefs reflect questions of "being" and "feeling" (Who am I? Do I like myself? How do I feel about myself as a writer?). The answers to the self-efficacy questions that individuals pose to themselves reveal whether they possess high or low confidence to accomplish the task or succeed at the activity in question; the answers to the self-concept questions that individuals pose to themselves reveal how positively or negatively they view themselves, as well as how they feel, in those areas. It is for these reasons that self-efficacy beliefs are often referred to as "confidence" and self-concept beliefs as "self-esteem." What is clear is that students' self-concept and self-efficacy beliefs each influence motivation and academic achievement. As Bandura (1986) observed, both "contribute in their own way to the quality of human life" (p. 410).

## WHY THE RESURGENT INTEREST IN SELF-BELIEFS IS WARRANTED

As we have illustrated, the historical road leading to research on the self and self-beliefs has been a rocky but ultimately productive one, resulting in focusing our attention on ideas that are of some consequence to human functioning. Moreover, there is now ample research evidence to the effect that students' academic behaviors and achievement are directly influenced by the beliefs they hold about themselves and about their academic potentialities. The import of these scholarly findings is that students' difficulties in basic academic skills are often directly related to their beliefs that they cannot read, write, handle numbers, or think well—that they cannot learn—even when such things are not objectively true. That is to say, many students have difficulty in school not because they are incapable of performing successfully but because they are incapable of believing that they can perform successfully; they have learned to see themselves as incapable of handling academic work or to see the work as irrelevant to their life.

Consequently, parents and teachers do well to take seriously their share of responsibility in nurturing the self-beliefs of their children and students, for it is clear that these self-beliefs can have beneficial or destructive influences. Bandura has argued that beliefs of personal competence constitute the key factor of *human agency*, the ability to act intentionally and exercise a measure of control over one's environment and social structures. As children strive to exercise control over their surroundings, their first transactions are mediated by adults who can empower them with self-assurance or diminish their fledgling self-beliefs. Because young children are not proficient at making accurate self-appraisals, they rely on the judgments of others to create their own judgments of confidence and of self-worth. As we have pointed out, it is during early childhood that the metaphor of the "looking-glass self" is at its most powerful. Parents and teachers who provide children with challenging tasks and meaningful activities that can be mastered, and who chaperone these efforts with support and encouragement, help ensure the development of a robust sense of self-worth and of self-confidence. Early mastery experiences are predictive of children's cognitive development, and there is evidence to suggest they work independently of critical variables such as socioeconomic status.

Social comparisons with peers are critical to the development of self-beliefs. Self-concept researchers have described the Big-Fish-Little-Pond effect, which describes how students form their self-concept in part by comparing their academic ability with the perceived abilities of other students in their reference group (Marsh, 1993). Self-concept is increased when one views oneself as more capable than one's peers but, conversely, lowered when others are viewed as more capable. Social-comparative school practices that emphasize standardized, normative assessments involve ability grouping and lock-step instruction, use competitive grading practices, and encourage students to compare their achievement with that of their peers work to destroy the fragile self-beliefs of those who are less academically talented or prepared. These are practices that convert "instructional experiences into education in inefficacy" (Bandura, 1997, p. 175).

Educators have long known that when classroom structures are individualized and instruction is tailored to students' academic capabilities, social comparisons are minimized and students are more likely to gauge their academic progress according to their own standards rather than compare it to the progress of their classmates. To some degree, students will inevitably evaluate themselves in relation to their classmates regardless of what a school or teacher does to minimize or counter these comparisons. In cooperative and individualized learning settings, students can more easily select the peers with whom to compare themselves. Individualized structures that lower the competitive orientation of a classroom and school are more likely than traditional, competitive structures to increase confidence and improve students' self-concept.

It may even be reasonably argued that teachers should pay as much attention to students' self-beliefs as to actual competence, for it is the belief that may more accurately predict students' motivation and future academic choices. Assessing students' self-beliefs can provide schools with important insights about their pupils' academic motivation, behavior, and future choices. For example, unrealistically low self-efficacy, not lack of capability or skill, can be responsible for maladaptive academic behaviors, avoidance of courses and careers, and diminishing school interest and achievement. Students who lack confidence in skills they possess are less likely to engage in tasks in which those skills are required, and they will more quickly give up in the face of difficulty. Given the generally lower confidence of most girls related to boys in areas such as mathematics and computer technology, it seems that young women may be especially vulnerable in these areas (Zeldin & Pajares, 2000). In such cases, in addition to continued skill improvement, schools must work to identify their students' inaccurate judgments and design and implement interventions to challenge them.

There are also ways of maintaining a joint focus on the development of competence and of the self-beliefs that accompany that competence. In the area of writing, instructional programs such as the Writers' Workshop approach to writing instruction have as a key priority the building of a child's sense of confidence in writing (Atwell, 1987; Calkins, 1994). Writers' workshop advocates stress the idea that children must gain confidence in themselves as writers if they are to improve and grow in this skill. Attention to children's self-beliefs is made an explicit feature of teacher education in such programs, and teachers are encouraged to assess both competence and the accompanying confidence as part of regular writing evaluations. Students' self-evaluations typically include self-reflection geared to understanding their own self-beliefs.

It seems clear that many of the difficulties that people experience throughout their lives are closely connected with the beliefs they hold about themselves and their place in the world in which they live. Similarly, students' academic failures in basic subjects, as well as the misdirected motivation and lack of commitment often characteristic of the underachiever, the dropout, the student labeled "at risk," and the socially disabled, are in good measure the consequence of, or certainly exacerbated by, the beliefs that students develop about themselves and about their ability to exercise a measure of control over their environments.

Some cautions are in order. The first deals with the care that should be taken as regards the nature of interventions designed to increase academic self-beliefs. Because mastery experience is the most influential source of self-efficacy information, social-cognitive theorists focus on the important task of raising competence *and* confidence through authentic mastery experiences. Decades earlier, Erik Erikson (1959/1980) put it this way:

> Children cannot be fooled by empty praise and condescending encouragement. They may have to accept artificial bolstering of their self-esteem in lieu of something better, but what I call their accruing ego identity gains real strength only from wholehearted and consistent recognition of real accomplishment, that is, achievement that has meaning in their culture. (p. 95)

The second caution deals with the warnings that have quite rightly been made regarding the tyranny that can result from an unbridled self-oriented emphasis in education (see McMillan et al., 1994). It can be a short voyage from self-reflection and self-fulfillment to self-obsession, self-absorption, self-centeredness, self-importance, and selfishness. Children taught that the nurturance, maintenance, and gratification of their sense of self are the prime directive of their own personal and social development do not easily learn to nurture others, to maintain lasting and mutually satisfying relationships, or to defer or postpone their own perceived needs (Beane, 1991; Kohn, 1994). Artificial self-esteem is naked against adversity; unwarranted confidence is cocky conceit. When what is communicated to a child from an early age is that nothing matters quite as much as how he or she feels or how confident he or she should be, one can rest assured that the world will sooner or later teach that child a lesson in humility that may not be easily learned. Some researchers have observed that an obsession with one's sense of self is responsible for an alarming increase in depression and other mental difficulties.

As is evident from the proliferation of self-esteem kits, programs, and gimmicks, complex issues related to self-esteem have been oversimplified and caricatured. We concur with the judgment of researchers who question whether self-esteem programs of the sort that have been in fashion are effective in raising either self-esteem or achievement. As we have argued, concern for the affective needs of students should not be divorced from concerns about their cognitive (and social and physical) needs. And we believe that in most cases efforts are better aimed at transforming schools, classrooms, and teaching practices than at altering students' psyches (Kohn, 1994). But institutional transformation and a focus on students' intellectual development are not incompatible with concern for students' self-beliefs.

The aim of education must transcend the development of academic competence. Schools have the added responsibility of preparing self-assured, fully functioning individuals capable of pursuing their hopes and their ambitions. Nel Noddings (1992) observed that the ultimate aim of schools should be to nurture the "ethical self," that is "to produce competent, caring, loving, and lovable people" (p. 174). Schools can aid their students in these pursuits by helping them to develop the habit of excellence in scholarship while at the same time nurturing the self-beliefs necessary to maintain that excellence throughout their adult lives. As Bandura (1986) argued,

> educational practices should be gauged not only by the skills and knowledge they impart for present use but also by what they do to children's beliefs about their capabilities, which affects how they approach the future. Students who develop a strong sense of self-efficacy are well equipped to educate themselves when they have to rely on their own initiative. (p. 417)

One need only cast a casual glance at the American landscape to see that attending to the affective concerns of students is both a noble and a necessary enterprise. It is our hope that psychological and educational research during the next century will provide an uninterrupted series of insights to that end.

More than 100 years ago, William James ended his lectures to the nation's teachers with the gentle admonition that if they could but see their pupils as young creatures composed of good intentions, and love them as well, they would be "in the best possible position for becoming perfect teachers." As this is our aim, we do well to take heed.

# References

Atwell, N. (1987). *In the middle*. Portsmouth, NH: Boynton/Cook–Heinemann.

Bandura. A. (1977). Self-efficacy: Toward a unifying theory of behavioral change. *Psychological Review, 84*, 191–215.

Bandura, A. (1986). *Social foundations of thought and action: A social cognitive theory*. Englewood Cliffs, NJ: Prentice–Hall.

Bandura, A. (1997). *Self-efficacy: The exercise of control*. New York: Freeman.

Beane, J. A. (1991). Sorting out the self-esteem controversy. *Educational Leadership, 49*, 25–30.

Berliner, D. C., & Biddle, B. J. (1995). *The manufactured crisis: Myths, fraud, and the attack on America's public schools*. Reading, MA: Addison–Wesley.

Bertocci, P. A. (1945). The psychological self, ego and personality. *Psychological Review, 52*, 91–99.

Bruner, J. (1997). *The culture of education*. Cambridge, MA: Harvard University Press.

Calkins, L. (1994). *The art of teaching writing*. Portsmouth, NH: Heinemann.

Combs, A. W. (1962). Perceiving, behaving, becoming. In *Yearbook of the Association for Supervision and Curriculum Development*. Washington, DC: Education Association.

Combs, A. W., & Snygg, D. (1959). *Individual behavior* (2nd ed.). New York: Harper & Row.

Cooley, C. H. (1902). *Human nature and the social order*. New York: Scribner.

Coopersmith, S. (1967). *The antecedents of self-esteem*. San Francisco: Freeman.

Diggory, J. C. (1966). *Self-evaluation: Concepts and studies*. New York: Wiley.

Erikson, E. (1959/1980). *Identity and the life cycle*. New York: Norton.

Freud, S. (1923). *The ego and the id*. New York: Norton.

Goldstein, K. (1939). *The organism*. New York: American Book.

Graham, S., & Weiner, B. (1996). Theories and principles of motivation. In D. C. Berliner & R. C. Calfee (Eds.), *Handbook of educational psychology* (pp. 63–84). New York: Simon & Schuster Macmillan.

Hansford, B. C., & Hattie, J. A. (1982). The relationship between self and achievement/performance measures. *Review of Educational Research, 52*, 123–142.

Hilgard, E. R. (1949). Human motives and the concept of the self. *American Psychologist, 4*, 135–142.

James, W. (1891a). *The principles of psychology* (Vol. 1). Cambridge, MA: Harvard University Press.

James, W. (1891b). *The principles of psychology* (Vol. 2). Cambridge, MA: Harvard University Press.

James., W. (1896/1958). *Talks to teachers*. New York: Norton.

Kohn, A. (1994). The truth about self-esteem. *Phi Delta Kappan, 76*, 272–283.

Lecky, P. (1945). *Self-consistency: A theory of personality*. New York: Island Press.

Lewin, K. (1935). *A dynamic theory of personality*. New York: McGraw–Hill.

Marsh, H. W. (1993). Academic self-concept: Theory, measurement, and research. In J. Suls (Ed.), *Psychological perspectives on the self* (Vol. 4, pp. 59–98). Hillsdale, NJ: Lawrence Erlbaum.

Maslow, A. H. (1943). A dynamic theory of human motivation. *Psychological Review, 50*, 370–396.

Maslow, A. H. (1954). *Motivation and personality*. New York: Harper & Row.

McMillan, J. H., Singh, J., & Simonetta, L. G. (1994). The tyranny of self-oriented self-esteem. *Educational Horizons, Spring*, 141–145.

Mead, G. H. (1913). The social self. *Journal of Philosophy, Psychology and Scientific Methods, 10*, 374– 380.

Mead, G. H. (1934). *Mind, self and society*. Chicago: University of Chicago Press.

Murphy, G. (1947). *Personality: A biosocial approach to origins and structure*. New York: Harper & Row.

Noddings, N. (1992). *The challenge to care in schools: An alternative approach to education*. New York: Teachers College Press.

Ramey, V. C. (1948). Self-reference in counseling interviews. *Journal of Consulting Psychology, 12*, 153–163.

Shavelson, R. J., & Marsh, H. W. (1986). On the structure of self-concept. In R. Schwarzer (Ed.), *Self-related cognition in anxiety and motivation* (pp. 79–95). Hillsdale, NJ: Erlbaum.

Skinner, B. F. (1938). *The behavior of organisms*. Englewood Cliffs, NJ: Prentice Hall.

Vygotsky, L. S. (1935/1978). *Mind in society: The development of higher psychological processes*. Cambridge, MA: Harvard University Press.

Watson, J. B. (1925). *Behaviorism*. New York: Norton.

Zeldin, A. L., & Pajares, F. (2000). Against the odds: Self-efficacy beliefs of women with math-related careers. *American Educational Research Journal, 37*, 215–246.

## Suggested Reading

Bandura, A. (1997). *Self-efficacy: The exercise of control*. New York: Freeman.

Hattie, J. (1992). *Self-concept*. Hillsdale, NJ: Lawrence Erlbaum.

Kohn, A. (1994). The truth about self-esteem. *Phi Delta Kappan, 76*, 272–283.

Pajares, F. (1997). Current directions in self-efficacy research. In M. Maehr & P. R. Pintrich (Eds.), *Advances in motivation and achievement* (Vol. 10, pp. 1–49). Greenwich, CT: JAI Press.

Schunk, D. H. (1991). Self-efficacy and academic motivation. *Educational Psychologist, 26*, 207–231.

# PART

## II

# Revisiting and Extending Classic Lessons

# The Pygmalion Effect and Its Mediating Mechanisms

ROBERT ROSENTHAL

*Department of Psychology, University of California, Riverside*

In the mid-1950s I nearly ruined the results of my doctoral dissertation at UCLA. The sordid details are available elsewhere (Rosenthal, 1985) but briefly, it appeared that I might have treated my research participants in such a way as to lead them to respond in accordance with my experimental hypothesis or expectancy. All of this was quite unwitting, of course, but it did raise a sobering question about the possibility of interpersonal expectancy effects in the psychological laboratory. If it were my unintentional interpersonal expectancy effect or my "unconscious experimenter bias" that had led to the puzzling and disconcerting results of my dissertation then presumably we could produce the phenomenon in our own laboratory and with several experimenters rather that just one. Producing the phenomenon in this way not only would yield the scientific benefit of demonstrating an interesting and important concept; it would also yield the very considerable personal benefit of showing that I was not alone in having unintentionally affected the results of my research by virtue of my bias or expectancy.

This Chapter is based in part on an invited address given to the Teachers of Psychology in the Secondary Schools (TOPSS) and subsequently published in *Psychology Teacher Network (PTN)*, 1998, Vol. 8, pp. 2–4, 9. It is an updated version of papers cited in the references of the *PTN* paper.

Correspondence concerning this chapter should be addressed to Robert Rosenthal, Department of Psychology, University of California, Riverside, CA 92521-0426.

## SOME EARLY RESULTS

### Human Subjects

In the first of our studies employing human subjects, 10 students of psychology, both undergraduate and graduate, served as the experimenters (Rosenthal & Fode, 1963b). All were enrolled in an advanced course in experimental psychology and were already involved in conducting research. Each student–experimenter was assigned as his or her research participants about 20 students of introductory psychology. The procedure was for the experimenters to show a series of 10 photographs of people's faces to each of their participants individually. Participants were to rate the degree of success or failure shown in the face of each person pictured in the photos. Each face could be rated at any value from −10 to +10, with −10 meaning extreme failure and +10 meaning extreme success. The 10 photos had been selected so that, on the average, they would be seen as neither successful nor unsuccessful, but quite neutral, with an average numerical score of zero.

All 10 experimenters were given identical instructions on how to administer the task to their participants and were given identical instructions to read to them. They were cautioned not to deviate from these instructions. The purpose of their participation, it was explained to all experimenters, was to see how well they could duplicate experimental results that were already well-established. Half the experimenters were told that the "well-established" finding was such that their participants should rate the photos as of successful people (ratings of +5) and half the experimenters were told that their participants should rate the photos as being of unsuccessful people (ratings of −5). Results showed that experimenters expecting higher photo ratings obtained higher photo ratings than did experimenters expecting lower photo ratings. Subsequent studies tended to obtain generally similar results (Rosenthal, 1969; Rosenthal & Rubin, 1978).

### Animal Subjects

Pfungst's work with Clever Hans and Pavlov's work on the inheritance of acquired characteristics had both suggested the possibility of experimenter expectancy effects with animal subjects (Gruenberg, 1929; Pfungst, 1965). In addition, Bertrand Russell (1927) had noted this possibility, adding that animal subjects take on the national character of the experimenter. As he put it: "Animals studied by Americans rush about frantically, with an incredible display of hustle and pep, and at last achieve the desired result by chance. Animals observed by Germans sit still and think, and at last evolve the solution out of their inner consciousness" (pp. 29–30).

But it was not only the work of Pavlov, Pfungst, and Russell that made us test the generality of experimenter expectancy effects by working with animal subjects. It was also the reaction of my friends and colleagues who themselves worked with animal subjects. That reaction was: "Well of course you'd find expectancy effects and other artifacts when you work with humans; that's why we work with rats."

A good beginning might have been to replicate with a larger sample size Pfungst's research with Clever Hans; but with horses hard to come by, rats were made to do (Rosenthal & Fode, 1963a).

A class in experimental psychology had been performing experiments with human participants for most of a semester. Now they were asked to perform one more experiment, the last in the course and the first employing animal subjects. The experimenters were told of studies that had shown that maze-brightness and maze-dullness could be developed in strains of rats by successive inbreeding of the well and the poorly performing maze runners. Sixty laboratory rats were equitably divided among the 12 experimenters. Half the experimenters were told that their rats were maze-bright and the other half were told their rats were maze-dull. The animal's task was to learn to run to the darker of two arms of an elevated T-maze. The two arms of the maze, one white and one gray, were interchangeable; and the "correct" or rewarded arm was equally often on the right as on the left. Whenever animals ran to the correct side they obtained a food reward. Each rat was given 10 trials each day for 5 days to learn that the darker side of the maze was the one that led to the food.

Beginning with the first day and continuing on through the experiment, animals believed to be better performers became better performers. Animals believed to be bright showed a daily improvement in their performance, while those believed to be dull improved only to the third day and then showed a worsening of performance. Sometimes an animal refused to budge from the starting position. This happened 11% of the time among the allegedly bright rats; but among the allegedly dull rats it happened 29% of the time. When animals did respond and correctly so, those believed to be brighter ran faster to the rewarded side of the maze than did even the correctly responding rats believed to be dull.

When the experiment was complete, all experimenters rated their rats and their own attitudes and behavior vis-à-vis their animals. Those experimenters who had been led to expect better performance viewed their animals as brighter, more pleasant, and more likable. These same experimenters felt more relaxed in their contacts with the animals and described their behavior toward them as more pleasant, friendly, enthusiastic, and less talkative. They also stated that they handled their rats more and also more gently than did the experimenters expecting poor performance.

The next experiment with animal subjects also employed rats, this time using not mazes but Skinner boxes (Rosenthal & Lawson, 1964). Because the experimenters (39) outnumbered the subjects (14), experimenters worked in teams of two or three. Once again about half the experimenters were led to believe that their subjects had been specially bred for excellence of performance. The experimenters who had been assigned the remaining rats were led to believe that their animals were genetically inferior.

The learning required of the animals in this experiment was more complex than that required in the maze learning study. This time the rats had to learn in sequence and over a period of a full academic quarter the following behaviors: to run to the food dispenser whenever a clicking sound occurred; to press a bar for a food reward; to learn that the feeder could be turned off and that sometimes it did not pay to press the bar; to learn new responses with only the clicking sound as a reinforcer (rather than the food); to bar-press only in the presence of a light and not in the absence of the light; and, finally, to pull on a loop that was followed by a light that informed the animal that a bar-press would be followed by a bit of food.

At the end of the experiment the performance of the animals believed to be superior *was* superior to that of the animals believed to be inferior, and the difference in learning favored the allegedly brighter rats in all five of the laboratory sections in which the experiment was conducted.

## TEACHER EXPECTATION EFFECTS

If rats became brighter when expected to, then it would not be farfetched to think that children could become brighter when expected to by their teachers. Indeed, Kenneth Clark (1963) had for years been saying that teachers' expectations could be very important determinants of intellectual performance. Clark's ideas and our research should have sent us right into the schools to study teacher expectations; but that is not what happened.

What did happen was that after our laboratory had completed about a dozen studies of experimenter expectancy effects (we no longer used the term *unconscious experimenter bias*), I summarized our results in an article for the *American Scientist* (Rosenthal, 1963). I concluded this article by wondering whether the same interpersonal expectancy effects found in psychological experimenters might not also be found in physicians, psychotherapists, employers, and teachers: "When the master teacher tells his apprentice that a pupil appears to be a slow learner, is this prophecy then self-fulfilled?" (p. 280).

Among the reprint requests for this paper there was one from Lenore F. Jacobson, the principal of an elementary school in South San Francisco, California. I also sent her a stack of unpublished papers and thought no more about it. Soon after, Lenore Jacobson wrote me a letter telling of her interest in the problem of teacher expectations. She ended her letter with the following line: "If you ever 'graduate' to classroom children, please let me know whether I can be of assistance." I gratefully accepted Lenore's offer of assistance and asked whether she would consider collaborating on a project to investigate teacher expectancy effects. A tentative experimental design was suggested in this letter as well.

Lenore replied, mainly to discuss concerns over the ethical and organizational implications of creating false expectations for superior performance in teachers. If this problem could be solved, her school would be ideal, she felt, with children from primarily lower-class backgrounds. Lenore also suggested gently that I was "a bit naive" to think one could just *tell* teachers to expect some of their pupils to be "diamonds in the rough." We would have to administer some new test to the children, a test the teachers would not know.

Phone calls and letters followed, and in January of 1964, a trip to South San Francisco to settle on a final design and to meet with the school district's administrators to obtain their approval. This approval was forthcoming because of the leadership of the school superintendent, Dr. Paul Nielsen. Approval for this research had already been obtained from Robert L. Hall, Program Director for Sociology and Social Psychology for the National Science Foundation, which had been supporting much of the early work on experimenter expectancy effects.

## The Pygmalion Experiment

All of the children in the study were administered a nonverbal test of intelligence, which was disguised as a test that would predict intellectual "blooming." The test was labeled the Harvard Test of Inflected Acquisition. There were 18 classrooms in the school, 3 at each of the six grade levels. Within each grade level the 3 classrooms were composed of children with above-average ability, average ability, and below-average ability, respectively. Within each of the 18 classrooms approximately 20% of the children were chosen at random to form the experimental group. Each teacher was given the names of the children from his or her class who were in the experimental condition. The teacher was told that these children had scored on the Harvard Test of Inflected Acquisition such that they would show surprising gains in intellectual competence during the next 8 months of school. The only difference between the experimental group children and the control group children, then, was in the mind of the teacher.

At the end of the school year, 8 months later, all the children were retested with the same test of intelligence. Considering the school as a whole, the children from whom the teachers had been led to expect greater intellectual gain showed a greater intellectual gain than did the children of the control group (Rosenthal & Jacobson, 1966, 1968, 1992).

## An Unexpected Finding

At the time the Pygmalion experiment was conducted there was already considerable evidence that interpersonal self-fulfilling prophecies could occur, at least in laboratory settings. It should not then have come as such a great surprise that teachers' expectations might affect pupils' intellectual development. For those well-acquainted with the prior research, the surprise value was, in fact, not all so great. There was, however, a surprise in the Pygmalion research. For this surprise there was no great prior probability, at least not in terms of many formal research studies.

At the end of the school year of the Pygmalion study, all teachers were asked to describe the classroom behavior of their pupils. Those children in whom intellectual growth was expected were described as having a better chance of becoming successful in the future, as more interesting, curious, and happy. There was a tendency, too, for these children to be seen as more appealing, adjusted, and affectionate, as less in need of social approval. In short, the children in whom intellectual growth was expected became more intellectually alive and autonomous, or at least were so perceived by their teachers.

But we already know that the children of the experimental group gained more intellectually, so that perhaps it was the fact of such gaining that accounted for the more favorable ratings of these children's behavior and aptitude. But a great many of the control group children also gained in IQ during the course of the year. We might expect that those who gained more intellectually among these undesignated children would also be rated more favorably by their teachers. Such was not the case. The more the control group children gained in IQ the more they were regarded as *less* well-adjusted, as *less* interesting, and as *less* affectionate.

From these results it would seem that when children who are expected to grow intellectually do so, they are benefited in other ways as well. When children who are not specifically expected to develop intellectually do so, they seem either to show accompanying undesirable behavior or at least are perceived by their teachers as showing such undesirable behavior. If children are to show intellectual gain, it seems to be better for their real or perceived intellectual vitality, and for their real or perceived mental health, if their teacher has been expecting them to grow intellectually. It appears worthwhile to investigate further the proposition that there may be hazards to unpredicted intellectual growth (Rosenthal, 1974).

## Reactions to Pygmalion

Reactions to Pygmalion were extreme. Many were very favorable, many were very unfavorable. Elsewhere we have noted in considerable detail the best known of these negative criticisms and given reasons in considerable detail why they were not compelling (Rosenthal, 1985, 1987, 1995; Rosenthal & Rubin, 1971, 1978). For our present purposes, it will be enough to give a very brief overview of these criticisms and why they were not compelling.

1. The analyses of the data were criticized on the grounds that the analyses should have focused on classrooms as a whole rather than on individual children. In fact, we had analyzed the data both ways, that is, by

classrooms and by children, a fact made clear in our report, and both ways gave essentially the same results.

2. A second criticism claimed that because the same IQ test had been employed for both the pretest and the posttest, the study might suffer from practice effects. It puzzles us how practice effects could bias the results of a randomized experiment. If practice effects were so great as to drive everyone's performance up to the limit, or ceiling, of the test, then practice effects could operate to *diminish* the effects of the experimental manipulation but they could not operate to increase those effects.

3. A third criticism was that teachers themselves administered the group tests of IQ. As it turned out, however, when children were retested by testers who were blind to the experimental conditions, indeed to the existence of experimental conditions, the effects of teacher expectations actually increased rather than decreased.

4. A fourth criticism was that we had employed group tests of IQ, tests that were less reliable than individually administered tests of IQ. This criticism suggested that the teacher expectancy effect might be due to this greater unreliability of the test instrument. As it turns out, however, lower reliability of a test instrument makes it harder, not easier, to obtain statistically significant results.

5. A fifth criticism was that the IQ of the youngest children had been measured with low validity. Actually, the validity of the measures of even these youngest children ($r = 0.65$) was substantially higher than the validity of many IQ tests, and much higher than the validity of psychological tests in general (Cohen, 1988). Incidentally, even if we set aside the results from these youngest children, ample evidence remains for the operation of teacher expectancy effects.

6. A sixth criticism suggested that the data should have been transformed mathematically before being analyzed. Critics then transformed the original data of Pygmalion in eight different ways. Some of these transformations were seriously biased (e.g., discarding data showing greater teacher expectancy effects). Despite this, however, none of the transformations gave results noticeably different from those reported in the Pygmalion experiment. For total IQ, every transformation gave a significant result when one had been reported in the Pygmalion experiment. When verbal IQ and reasoning IQ were considered separately, the various transformations yielded *more* significant teacher expectancy effects than had been reported in Pygmalion.

## A Heuristic Note

Before leaving the topic of negative criticisms of Pygmalion, one casual observation should be offered for any possible heuristic value it may hold. The bulk of the criticism of Pygmalion came neither from mathematical statisticians, nor from experimental social psychologists, nor from educators (though the president of a large teachers' union attacked Pygmalion bitterly as an affront to the good name of the teacher or the teachers' union). The bulk of the negative reactions came from workers in the field of educational psychology. Perhaps it was only they who would have been interested enough to respond. That seems unlikely, however, as many other kinds of psychologists regarded the Pygmalion effect as of great interest. We leave the observation as just a curiosity, one that might be clarified by future workers in the fields of the history, the sociology, and the psychology of science.

## REPLICABILITY OF PYGMALION EFFECTS

Psychological researchers are, and should be, a skeptical lot. They demand that claims to knowledge be based on credible empirical evidence. But that is not enough. We demand also that phenomena claimed as knowledge be replicable. A finding is not believed for long if it cannot be replicated by other workers in the field.

For the research area of interpersonal expectations in general, there have been nearly 500 replication studies, the vast majority of which have found that what one person expects of another tends to elicit that behavior from that other person. The average magnitude of the effect can be expressed as a correlation of about 0.30 (a very substantial magnitude) between what has been expected from research participants and what has been obtained from research participants (Rosenthal, 1984, 1991a, 1991b, 1998).

Summaries of replications are also available for just the effects of interpersonal expectations on pupils' IQ performance (Raudenbush, 1984, 1994; Smith, 1980). Both Raudenbush and Smith found significant overall effects of interpersonal expectations on students' IQ. Raudenbush's analysis (1994) was designed to investigate the relationship between the credibility of the expectancy induction and the magnitude of the teacher expectancy effect on pupil IQ. He reasoned that inductions of expectations in teachers would be credible only to the extent that teachers did not already know the children and, thus, had not already established expectations on the basis of their direct experience. Although the effects of teacher expectations were significant for his full set of 19 studies, he found dramatic differences in effect sizes as a function of how long teachers had known pupils before the induction of the expectation. Of the studies in which teachers knew pupils only 2 weeks or less, 91% showed results in the predicted direction, compared with only 12% of the studies in which teachers knew pupils longer than 2 weeks. This was very strong evidence that simply telling teachers that pupils will do well is not very effective if there are strong prior bases for teachers having formed their own expectations.

It may be of interest to note the typical magnitude of the effect on IQ of experimentally induced favorable teacher expectations. For the studies summarized by Raudenbush in which the teacher knew the children 2 weeks or less, the typical (median) size of the IQ increase due to induced favorable teacher expectations was about a quarter of a standard deviation. For the best known of the individually administered tests of IQ, that represents about 4 IQ points; in terms of SAT scores, that would represent a gain of about 25 points.

In sum, it seems clear, then, based on the accumulated evidence, as well as on the evidence provided by the original Pygmalion experiment, that the educational self-fulfilling prophecy (Merton, 1948) has now been well established, and that is the first step in the scientific study of any phenomenon (Merton, 1987).

For many years the central question in the study of interpersonal expectancy effects was whether there was any such thing. The replication evidence has answered that question sufficiently, based on the current full number of 479 studies, so that simple additional replications will add little new knowledge. The central questions in the study of interpersonal expectancy effects have changed so that now the more interesting questions include the specification of the variables that (a) *moderate* expectancy effects and (b) *mediate* expectancy effects. Moderator variables are preexisting variables such as sex, age, and personality that are associated with the magnitude of interpersonal expectancy effects; mediating variables refer to the behaviors by which expectations are communicated.

## THE FOUR-FACTOR "THEORY"

On the basis of the first 30 or so published studies relevant to mediation, a four-factor "theory" of the mediation of teacher expectancy effects was proposed (Rosenthal, 1973, 1974). The "theory" describes four major groupings of teacher behaviors hypothesized to be involved in mediation. The first factor, *climate*, refers to the warmer socioemotional climate that teachers tend to create for high-expectancy students, a warmth that can be communicated both verbally and nonverbally. The *input* factor refers to the tendency for teachers to teach more material to their "special" students. The *output* factor refers to the tendency for teachers to give their "special" students greater opportunities for responding. Finally, the *feedback* factor refers to the tendency for teachers to give more differentiated feedback to their "special," high-expectancy students. By differentiated, we mean that the feedback will be contingent on the correctness or incorrectness of the student's response and that the content of the feedback will tend to be directly related to what the student has said.

A series of analyses conducted by Harris and Rosenthal (1985, 1986) were designed to summarize the many studies examining these four factors. While all four factors received ample support in terms of significance testing, the magnitudes of the effects for the *climate* and *input* factors were especially impressive. Teachers appear to teach more and to teach it more warmly to students for whom they have more favorable expectations.

From these results we cannot infer that if we select warmer and more material-presenting teachers our nation's children will learn more. We also cannot infer from these results that training teachers to be warmer and more material-presenting will lead to improved learning on the part of our nation's children. Our results, however, do suggest that conducting the research required to determine the benefits of selection and training for *climate* (or affect) and *input* (or effort) may well yield substantial benefits both for science and for society.

## Teachers' Questions and Answers

**Q:**   Faculty lounges are a place where often most of the conversation among teachers revolves around specific students: their accomplishments, needs, who is a good student, who is not. By listening to these conversations, teachers often form well-defined expectations of them. What happens if for no fault of his or her own (i.e., different subject matter, teaching style) that student fails to live up to those expectations in future classes? Are there any adverse effects for the student? Was this phenomenon observed in any of your studies?

**A:**   The faculty lounge as a place for the dissemination of expectations about students was a topic frequently raised by teachers and principals. However, the specific questions raised here about the effects on students of their not living up to the expectations held for them, I cannot answer. We just do not know. In our own studies, and in the studies of others, this question has never been properly addressed. It would be my hope that some of the readers of this book might be the ones to investigate this topic in a creative and rigorous manner!

**Q:**   How do you measure teacher expectations? By the challenge level of the work they give to students? By the positive and negative statements they make to students?

**A:**   There are many ways to measure teacher expectations including those suggested by this question. Some of these methods are more direct, some less direct. More direct procedures include asking teachers to make global overall assessments of the expectations they hold for each of the children in their class (e.g., on a 1 to 9 rating scale indicate the intellectual potential of Jessica, Steve, Emily, Darius, etc.) Somewhat less global, more specific, estimates can be obtained from teachers by asking, for each of their students, the grade level at which they will be reading at the end of the year, or the percentile level they will achieve on any one of a number of standardized achievement tests.

A less direct, less obtrusive, estimate of teachers' expectations can be obtained by examining the feedback teachers give their students, for example, on written work in English and social studies. Detailed feedback may be an indication that the teacher feels the child is worth the effort. Accepting shoddy work and giving grades higher than merited by the child's performance can be an indication of a teacher's belief that the child cannot improve over her or his current level. (Such beliefs about students are rarely warranted whether one is working in special education at the elementary school level or with doctoral students at major research universities.)

**Q:**  When greater intellectual gains are expected of children by adults, why does this work to result in higher student achievement? What is taking place there?

**A:**  There is considerable evidence now that the two most important factors mediating the effects of teachers' favorable expectations are *affect* and *effort*. *Affect* refers to the tendency of teachers to provide warmer, more pleasant socioemotional climates for students for whom they hold more favorable expectations. *Effort* refers to the tendency to teach more material to students for whom they hold more favorable expectations. Emotional warmth combined with high standards (tough warmth) may well communicate to students "I'm with you and I know you can do it."

# References

Clark, K. B. (1963) Educational stimulation of racially disadvantaged children. In A. H. Passow (Ed.), *Education in depressed areas.* New York: Bureau of Publications, Teachers College, Columbia University.

Cohen, J. (1988) *Statistical power analysis for the behavioral sciences* (2nd ed.). Hillsdale, NJ: Lawrence Erlbaum.

Gruenberg, B. C. (1929). *The story of evolution.* Princeton, NJ: Van Nostrand.

Harris, M. J., & Rosenthal, R. (1985). The mediation of interpersonal expectancy effects: 31 meta-analyses. *Psychological Bulletin, 97,* 363–386.

Harris, M. J., & Rosenthal, R. (1986). Four factors in the mediation of teacher expectancy effects. In R. S. Feldman (Ed.), *The social psychology of education* (pp. 91–114). New York: Cambridge University Press.

Merton, R. K. (1948). The self-fulfilling prophecy. *Antioch Review, 8,* 193–210.

Merton, R. K. (1987). Three fragments from a sociologist's notebooks: Establishing the phenomenon, specified ignorance, and strategic research materials. *Annual Review of Sociology, 13,* 1–28.

Pfungst, O. (1965). *Clever Hans* (C. L. Rahn, Trans.). New York: Holt, Rinehart & Winston. (Original work published 1911)

Raudenbush, S. W. (1984). Magnitude of teacher expectancy effects on pupil IQ as a function of the credibility of expectancy induction: A synthesis of findings from 18 experiments. *Journal of Educational Psychology, 76,* 85–97.

Raudenbush, S. W. (1994). Random effects models. In H. Cooper & L. V. Hedges (Eds.), *The handbook of research synthesis.* New York: Russell Sage Foundation.

Rosenthal, R. (1963). On the social psychology of the psychological experiment: The experimenter's hypothesis as unintended determinant of experimental results. *American Scientist, 51,* 268–283.

Rosenthal, R. (1969). Interpersonal expectations. In R. Rosenthal & R. L. Rosnow (Eds.), *Artifact in behavioral research* (pp. 181–277). New York: Academic Press.

Rosenthal, R. (1973). The mediation of Pygmalion effects: A four factor "theory." *Papua New Guinea Journal of Education, 9,* 1–12.

Rosenthal, R. (1974). *On the social psychology of the self-fulfilling prophecy: Further evidence for Pygmalion effects and their mediating mechanisms* (Module 53, pp. 1–28). New York: MSS Modular Pub.

Rosenthal, R. (1984). *Meta-analytic procedures for social research.* Newbury Park, CA: Sage.

Rosenthal, R. (1985). From unconscious experimenter bias to teacher expectancy effects. In J. G. Dusek, V. C. Hall, & W. J. Meyer (Eds.), *Teacher expectancies* (pp. 37–65). Hillsdale, NJ: Lawrence Erlbaum.

Rosenthal, R. (1987). Pygmalion effects: Existence, magnitude, and social importance. *Educational Researcher, 16,* 37–41.

Rosenthal, R. (1991a). *Meta-analytic procedures for social research* (rev. ed.). Newbury Park, CA: Sage.

Rosenthal, R. (1991b). Teacher expectancy effects: A brief update 25 years after the Pygmalion experiment. *Journal of Research in Education, 1,* 3–12.

Rosenthal, R. (1995). Critiquing Pygmalion: A 25-year perspective. *Current Directions in Psychological Science, 4,* 171–172.

Rosenthal, R. (1998). Interpersonal expectancy effects: A forty year perspective. *Psychology Teacher Network, 8,* 2–4, 9.

Rosenthal, R., & Fode, K. L. (1963a). The effect of experimenter bias on the performance of the albino rat. *Behavioral Science, 8,* 183–189.

Rosenthal, R., & Fode, K. L. (1963b). Three experiments in experimenter bias. *Psychological Reports, 12,* 491–511.

Rosenthal, R., & Jacobson, L. (1966). Teachers' expectancies: Determinants of pupils' IQ gains. *Psychological Reports, 19,* 115–118.

Rosenthal, R., & Jacobson, L. (1968). *Pygmalion in the classroom.* New York: Holt, Rinehart & Winston.

Rosenthal, R., & Jacobson, L. (1992). *Pygmalion in the classroom* (expanded ed.). New York: Irvington.

Rosenthal, R., & Lawson, R. (1964). A longitudinal study of the effects of experimenter bias on the operant learning of laboratory rats. *Journal of Psychiatric Research, 2,* 61–72.

Rosenthal, R., & Rubin, D. B. (1971). Pygmalion reaffirmed. In J. D. Elashoff & R. E. Snow (Eds.), *Pygmalion reconsidered* (pp. 139–155). Worthington, OH: C. A. Jones.

Rosenthal, R., & Rubin, D. B. (1978). Interpersonal expectancy effects: The first 345 studies. *The Behavioral and Brain Sciences, 3,* 377–386.

Russell, B. (1927). *Philosophy.* New York: Norton.

Smith, M. L. (1980). Teacher expectations. *Evaluation in Education, 4,* 53–55.

# Messages That Motivate: How Praise Molds Students' Beliefs, Motivation, and Performance (in Surprising Ways)

CAROL S. DWECK

*Department of Psychology, Columbia University, New York*

Why do some very bright students do poorly in school and end up achieving little in life? Why do other, seemingly less bright students rise to the challenges and accomplish far more than anyone ever expected? Much of my career has been devoted to answering these questions, and that's where social psychology comes in.

One of the most important things social psychology has done is to show us how profoundly people's beliefs affect their behavior. This has been shown very clearly in the realm of students' motivation and achievement. Do students believe their intelligence is a fixed trait or an expandable quality? Do they believe their failures are due to a lack of effort or to a lack of ability? Do they believe they are doing a task to learn something new or to show how smart they are? These beliefs are key components of students' eagerness to learn, their love of challenge, and their ability to persist and thrive in the face of difficulty. This is why they are key factors in what students achieve—quite apart from their intellectual ability.

The most exciting thing about this is that beliefs can be changed. So, even more important than showing that beliefs matter for students' motivation and achievement is showing that when you change their beliefs, you change their motivation and achievement.

It is sometimes amazing to those who are not social psychologists that what look like minor belief-changing interventions—teaching students a different view of intelligence, teaching them a different interpretation for failure, or orienting them toward different reasons for achieving—end up up having real effects on students' school engagement and achievement. I have seen researchers from other fields be completely baffled by these results because they are used to seeing hugely expensive, large-scale, long-term, multifaceted interventions that yield only small effects. Yet, social psychologists understand the power of a carefully targeted intervention that changes a key belief and refocuses students' motivation in highly productive ways.

In this chapter, I show how the feedback we give to students can mold their beliefs about their intelligence and, in turn, their motivation and achievement, sometimes in very surprising ways.


## THE ROLE OF MOTIVATION IN ACHIEVEMENT

What role does motivation play in achievement? There are many researchers who argue that motivation is the key ingredient not only in outstanding achievement, but also in extraordinary achievement. Their work suggests that creative genius itself grows out of the ability to sustain intense commitment for very long periods in the face of obstacles (Runco, Nemiro, & Walberg, 1998; see also Hayes, 1989; Nickerson, 1999; Perkins, 1994; Weisberg, 1986, 1999). They tell us, much to our surprise, that many well-known geniuses were pretty much ordinary children who then became obsessed with something and, because of that obsession, ended up making enormous contributions (Howe, 1999; Simonton, 1999). This is true in science: Darwin's father was deeply disappointed in how ordinary his son seemed as a child (Simonton, 1999). It is true in philosophy: John Stuart Mill's father in fact was tickled to show that a child with mediocre intelligence could be trained to be a world-famous philosopher (Howe, 1999). Tolstoy and William James were also seen as unexceptional children (Howe, 1999).

Even Mozart, whom we think of as composing in infancy, did not produce really original and noteworthy works until after more than 10 years of nonstop composing (Bloom, 1985; Hayes, 1989; Weisberg, 1999). His early compositions were amateurish hodgepodges of other people's compositions. The same principle applies in athletics as well. We all know the story of how Michael Jordan was cut from his high school basketball team—which only increased his commitment and relentless practice until he became one of the greatest athletes of all time.

Yet, much of society is stubbornly wedded to the idea that accomplishment, especially outstanding accomplishment, is about endowment. We ignore the fact that Mozart, Darwin, Michael Jordan, and Tiger Woods practiced feverishly and singlemindedly for years, and instead believe that they were simply born with one-in-a-million ability. As for Thomas Edison's claim that genius is 99% perspiration and only 1% inspiration, we think he was just being modest. And when we read that the ringlike structure of benzene came to Kekule, the great chemist, in a dream and that the brilliant poem *Kubla Khan* came to Samuel Taylor Coleridge in an opium-induced delirium, we think "Ah yes, that's genius," forgetting the years of commitment and training that led to these achievements.

I have to confess that in my teaching, even I am often amazed at what students can achieve with the right beliefs and the right commitment. Every year, I come across students who just don't seem to have it or don't seem to get it. That is, they just don't think the right way to do well in my courses. Each year I think maybe this is the one who cannot profit from instruction and motivational training. Each year I am wrong. As my teaching assistants and I work with them, things happen and these students raise their exam scores 20, 30, and 40 points, sometimes joining the ranks of the top students in the course.

Let's take a look at the beliefs that can do this.

## THE ROLE OF BELIEFS IN MOTIVATION: OVERVIEW OF THE CHAPTER

In discussing beliefs that play a key role in motivation, I focus on one particular kind of belief, namely, students' "theories" about their intelligence. I begin by describing the two theories of intelligence that students hold: the belief that intelligence is a *fixed trait* that cannot be developed versus the idea that intelligence is a *malleable quality*, a potential that can be cultivated. I then show how these beliefs affect the tasks students take on, the effort they are willing to exert, their ability to cope with setbacks, and ultimately their academic performance.

As you will see, the belief in fixed intelligence leads even the most able students to worry about how smart they are, to think they're dumb when they fail, to dislike and avoid effort, and to show impaired performance when they face academic difficulty (which even top students can experience when they enter a new school). The belief that intelligence can be developed, in contrast, makes students want to do just that: It leads them to value learning over looking smart, to enjoy effort and challenges, and to thrive in the face of difficulty.

How are these beliefs learned and how can they be changed? I go on to show how messages from adults can mold the two beliefs. Some messages are quite direct, such as when a view of intelligence is directly taught. But some are indirect, and very surprising. We have found, for example, that praising students' intelligence after a job well done—which sounds like a great thing to do—plunges them into the fixed view with all of its vulnerabilities. On the other hand, praising their effort, which may sound like a consolation prize, instead fosters the malleable view with all its hardiness and resilience.

But before looking at the two views of intelligence and their impact let us ask: What is the correct view of intelligence? Is it fixed or is it something that can be developed? Psychologists have always taken and still take both views. Alfred Binet (1909/1973), the inventor of the IQ test, however, was a radical proponent of the idea that intelligence can be developed. He believed that children's most basic capcacity to learn could be transformed through education, and he devoted much of his career to designing educational programs that might do that. He invented the IQ test simply to identify candidates for his educational intervention, that is, children who were not profiting from the schooling they were currently receiving. Today, more and more psychologists are taking the view that intelligence or important components of it can be developed through motivation and learning (Brown & Campione, 1996; Perkins, 1995; Resnick, 1983; Sternberg, 1985), and as I noted earlier a goodly number even argue that genius itself is a product of high levels of motivation over long periods.

My work does not directly address the question of the true nature of intelligence, but it does show the critical importance of what students believe about intelligence.

## STUDENTS' "THEORIES OF INTELLIGENCE"

How do we measure students' beliefs about their intelligence? Generally, we asked them to agree or disagree with statements like the following: "You have a certain amount of intelligence and you really can't do much to change it"; "Your intelligence is something very basic about you that you can't really change." Students who agree with these statements hold the fixed view, whereas students who disagree with them hold the malleable view. In studies with older students, we also include direct statments of the malleable view for students to agree or disagree with, for example: "Anyone, no matter who they are, can increase their intelligence substantially." (Having both versions tends to confuse the younger students; see Dweck, 1999.)

Let us now look at the motivational worlds these beliefs create for students. These two different worlds are depicted in Table 1.

**TABLE I**
**Theories of Intelligence**

| | Intelligence is fixed | Intelligence is malleable |
|---|---|---|
| Students' goal | To look smart even if sacrificing learning | To learn new things even if hard or risky |
| What does failure mean? | Failure means low intelligence | Failure means low effort, poor strategy |
| What does effort mean? | Effort means low intelligence | Effort activates and uses intelligence |
| Strategy after difficulty | Less effort | More effort |
| Self-defeating defensiveness | High | Low |
| Performance after difficulty | Impaired | Equal or improved |

# The Belief in Fixed Intelligence

## What Is Students' Goal in School?

When students believe that their intelligence is fixed what is it they want most to accomplish through their academic work? The answer is they want to look smart. Because intelligence is such a deeply valued commodity and they only have a fixed amount of it, students want to feel as though they have the right amount. In many studies with grade school, junior high school, and college students, we give students a choice between a challenging task, from which they can learn important new things, and a "safer" task at which they can look smart. Most students with the fixed view take the task that will make them look smart (Dweck & Leggett, 1988; Stone & Dweck, 1998). This means that rather than risk making errors, they sacrifice valuable learning opportunities. On our questionnaires, they agree with such statements as "I have to admit that I would rather do well in a class than learn a lot" and "If I knew I wasn't going to do well at a task, I probably wouldn't do it even if I might learn a lot from it" (Dweck & Sorich, 1999; Mueller & Dweck, 1998).

A recent study shows exactly how self-defeating this can be. At the University of Hong Kong (the premier institution of higher learning in Hong Kong), all classes, class assignments, and examinations are in English. But not all students come to the university knowing much English. In this study (Hong, Chiu, Dweck, Lin, & Wan, 1999), we assessed new students' theories about their intelligence and we obtained their scores on their English proficiency exams. We then asked them if they would be willing to take a remedial English course if the faculty offered it. Students who had low English proficiency and believed in malleable intelligence said yes, but students with low English proficiency and a fixed view of intelligence did not. They were not willing to expose their ignorance or risk errors, even though, by not doing so, they were placing their academic career in jeopardy.

## What Does Failure or Difficulty Mean?

You might think that students who believe in fixed intelligence would form an opinion of their intelligence and stick to it, but this is not the case. Why not? Because, although they believe intelligence is fixed, intelligence is an invisible, internal thing that cannot be observed directly, so they just have to guess its level from their performance. This means that one day students with the fixed view can think their fixed ability is high because they've done well, but the next day they can think it is low because they haven't.

A study by Stone and Dweck (1998) illustrates this clearly. In this study, fifth grade students were questioned about what their performance on our task would mean to them. They had earlier been told simply that the task measured an important ability. Now they were asked to rate the truth of the following statements: "This task will tell me how good I am at this type of problem"; "It will tell me how smart I am"; "It will tell me how smart I'll be when I grow up." Students with the malleable view of intelligence agreed only with the first statement (since this was essentially what we had told them), but students with the fixed view agreed—and agreed nearly equally—with all three statements. They were investing one little task with the power to tell them about their permanent intelligence!

In my work, I have been very interested in how students understand and cope with the academic difficulties they might encounter. Not surprisingly, we have found over and over that students who believe in fixed intelligence see academic setbacks as meaning something very negative about their intellectual abilities (Grant, & Dweck, 2001; Dweck & Sorich, 1999; Henderson & Dweck, 1990; Mueller & Dweck, 1998). This is even true of bright students at top schools.

In one study (Dweck & Sorich, 1999) we asked junior high school students to imagine that they really liked a new class they were taking in school. They studied for the first test, but did really poorly. What would they feel and what would they think? They told us they would feel stupid and would think "I'm just not good at this subject" and "I wasn't smart enough." Again, one test has the power to define them.

What would they do? Work harder? Guess again.

## What Do These Students Believe about Effort?

Other students believe that effort can compensate for lower ability, that you can get to the same place by working that much harder, but not these students. They tell us that if you don't have ability, forget it: You're not going anywhere. Your effort just won't work. Specifically, they agree that "If you're not good at a subject, working hard won't make you good at it" and "It doesn't matter how hard you work—if you're smart you'll do well, if you're not smart you won't."

So what *would* they do after doing poorly on that test? Compared with students with the malleable view, students with a fixed view of intelligence: "would spend *less* time on the subject from now on" and "would try to cheat on the next test." If effort does not work, these are, sadly, the options they see for themselves.

Even when they have not done poorly, effort is threatening. Students with the fixed view believe that if you have to work hard at something it automatically means you are no good at it, and that "If you're really smart at something, you shouldn't have to work hard at it" (Dweck & Sorich, 1999). So, it should not be surprising when these students tell us that one of their main goals in school is to work as little as possible (Dweck & Sorich, 1999).

What a bind these students put themselves in. They very much want to feel and look smart. But they can't feel or look smart by working hard, because working hard is direct evidence of being dumb. They want to do well, but not by working at it. Moreover, if they happen not to do well, there is no remedy. Effort can't compensate.

I believe there is no more damaging view for students than the belief that effort is unnecessary (if you're smart) and ineffective (if you're not). And it goes right along with a belief in fixed intelligence.

## Choosing Defenses over Achievement

Students who believe their effort measures them are prone to a variety of self-defeating behavior. In fact, these students are likely to choose failure over effort. Trying hard is simply too much of a risk. This is why, for example, many students leave things to the last minute: if they hardly study and still do well, then they're really smart; if they don't do well, then, after all, they didn't really try (Rhodewalt, 1994; Rhodewalt and Tragakis, Chapter 6 in this volume; see Berglas, 1990). This is also why we see many students withdraw their efforts from their studies when school becomes difficult. They are preserving their sense of their ability. They are sacrificing their actual achievement so they can hold onto the belief that they *could* have done well.

They also suddenly "lose interest" in the difficult subject (Dweck & Sorich, 1999). This way it's not that they couldn't do it, but that they weren't really into it.

In short, a belief in fixed intelligence can lead students to place their futures in jeopardy so they won't feel bad about themselves in the present.

## What Happens to Performance?

No surprises here either. If failure means they are dumb and that their effort is useless, it is no wonder that many students' achievement eventually suffers when they hold the fixed view.

Actually, the need to prove your intelligence can be highly motivating when things are going well, but it does not serve students well when the going gets tougher. To examine this, we have done several large studies of students making the transition to junior high school (Dweck & Sorich, 1999; Henderson & Dweck, 1990). This is when students leave the cocoon of grade school in which teachers have time to be more nurturant, the work is more individualized, and the grading tends to be more generous. Suddenly, students find themselves in a new, more impersonal world with harder work and more stringent grading. This is a particular threat to students with the fixed view, whose intelligence is now on line.

In each of our studies, we have found that this is a time when their grades and achievement test scores suffer compared with their classmates who hold the more malleable view. Regardless of their past achievement, students with the fixed view are more likely to show lower academic performance. Some students who were among the highest achievers before are now in trouble.

Now let's look now at the alternative.

## The Belief in Malleable Intelligence

### What Is Their Goal in School?

When students believe their intelligence is a potential they can develop, they focus not so much on looking smart, but on challenges and learning. When we offer *them* a choice of tasks, they reject the task that would simply make them look smart in favor of the task that allows them to learn something new, even with the risk of making errors.

These students agree with the following statements: "It is much more important for me to learn things in my classes than it is to get the best grades"; "I like school work I can learn from even if I make a lot of mistakes."

For these students, the name of the game is not the quick fix of outdoing others, but rather personal mastery over time: "I feel successful when I improve in school even if other students get a higher score than me."

### What Does Failure or Difficulty Mean?

It sends a message about your effort or strategy, not your fixed ability. Mistakes are simply a natural part of learning, and give you information about what to do next. Failure, although never welcome, is also a signal to do something. When these students receive a disappointing grade, they tell us they would find out what went wrong, engage in remedial work, and study more the next time (Dweck & Sorich, 1999; Grant, 2001; Hong et al., 1999). In other words, they take the bull by the horns and work toward improvement in the future.

We saw how students with the fixed view become trapped in a failure, worrying about their ability. Interestingly, students with the malleable view, even students who do not have much confidence in their intelligence, are motivated to step up their efforts instead of worrying about whether they have or don't have enough fixed ability.

## What Does Effort Mean?

Everything. For these students, effort is what powers their ability and allows them to use it to the fullest. Even geniuses, they believe, have to work hard for their accomplishments. In this, they are in sync with Thomas Edison and his 99% perspiration. They also believe that even if you're not that good at something, effort will certainly help you achieve, for effort is the way to overcome setbacks.

In short, they agree that "The harder you work at something, the better you will be at it" (Dweck & Sorich, 1999).

## Choosing Achievement over Defenses

Because difficulty and effort are part of learning, students with the malleable view have less need for all those face-saving, self-defeating strategies. Rather than feel that when something is hard they have to pull back or lose interest, they see it as a plus: "If an assignment is hard, it means I'll probably learn a lot from it"; "When something is difficult it just makes me want to work more on it, not less."

## What Happens to Performance?

In line with their emphasis on challenge, effort, and learning, these students are able to do well as they make difficult educational transitions. As I've reported, they outshine their classmates with the fixed view in grades and achievement test scores as they confront the challenges of a new school (Dweck & Sorich, 1999; Henderson & Dweck, 1990). Even many students who had not done that well in grade school were seen to blossom (Henderson & Dweck, 1990).

## CAN THEORIES OF INTELLIGENCE BE CHANGED?

Yes, they can. Even though when left alone students' theories tend to be pretty stable, students can be temporarily oriented toward a different view or can be taught a different view in a more permanent way.

In a number of experiments, psychologists have tested the effects of orienting students toward a fixed view of ability (by telling them that the ability required by the task is inborn, or is one that you either have or don't have) verus a malleable view of ability (by telling them that the ability could be learned over time with practice or effort) (Aronson, 1998; Jourden, Bandura, & Banfield, 1991; Tabernero & Wood, 1999; Wood & Bandura, 1989). These studies have found that when students are oriented toward the malleable view they choose more challenging goals for themselves, they maintain confidence and high, effective persistence in the face of setbacks, and they end up outperforming the students oriented toward the fixed view. What is also interesting is that the students given the malleable view maintain their interest in the activity even when they are experiencing difficulty.

In a fascinating study, Joshua Aronson, Carrie Fried, and Catherine Good (in press) taught college students a malleable view of their intelligence and looked at the impact on their actual engagement and achievement in school. As Aronson reports in Chapter 14 of this book, students who were taught this theory, especially minority students, showed greater engagement in their studies and higher grade point averages than groups of comparable students who were not. This study shows what a profound effect a short belief-changing experience can have on a student's academic life.

Recently, we have been examining some common practices that can, inadvertently, alter students' theories about their intelligence.

## The Effects of Praise

A few years ago, Melissa Kamins, Claudia Mueller, and I began to wonder if some very common and very well-meant practices might be having unwanted effects on students. We started thinking about how students with the fixed view of intelligence were so fixated on their intelligence, so worried about how smart they were, and so concerned with how their performance measures them. Well, we thought, when you praise a student's intelligence after a job well done, aren't you telling the student that intelligence is what it is all about and that intelligence can be measured directly from performance?

Now, of course, this is not what people mean to do when they praise intelligence. They mean to boost students' confidence and motivate them to do well in the future. In fact, in a survey of parents we conducted, more than 80% of parents agreed that it was *necessary* to praise children's ability to make them feel good about themselves. However, to see what intelligence praise *really* does, we conducted a series of studies with late grade school children and kindergartners. To foreshadow our findings, I will tell you that the power of intelligence praise was astounding to us. Let us look first at the older children.

In six studies (Mueller and Dweck, 1998), we gave children interesting puzzlelike problems to solve. These problems were part of a popular nonverbal IQ test. The first set of problems they worked on was challenging but well within their range, and virtually all children did really well. After this success, children received one of three forms of praise. One-third of the children were given intelligence praise: "Wow, you did really well on these problems. You got (eight) right. That's a really high score. You must be smart at these problems." One-third were given effort praise: "Wow, you did really well....That's a really high score. Your must have worked hard at these problems." And one-third of the children were simply told "Wow, you did really well on these problems....That's

**TABLE 2**
**Impact of Praise**

|  | Intelligence praise | Effort praise |
|---|---|---|
| Theory of intelligence | Promotes a fixed theory | Promotes a malleable theory |
| Students' goal | To look smart even if sacrificing learning | To learn new things even if hard or risky |
| What does failure mean? | Failure means low intelligence | Failure means low effort |
| Enjoyment after difficulty | Low | High |
| Persistence after difficulty | Low | High |
| Defensiveness after difficulty (lying) | High | Low |
| Performance after difficulty | Impaired | Improved |

a really high score," but were not praised for their ability or their effort. Remember, all three groups of students were similar when they entered the study. The only thing that differed was the feedback they received.

After achieving the success and receiving the praise, students went on to a second set of problems, but these were much harder and they did not do nearly as well.[1] Did they still enjoy the problems and did they still want to take them home to practice? How did they explain their difficulty—was it a matter of ability or a matter of effort?

Finally, children worked on a third set of problems that were equal to the first set in difficulty. How did the different groups of students do on these, after their experience with difficulty on the second set?

We asked these and other questions, and the answers we received are summarized in Table 2.

## Impact of the Praise on Students' Theories of Intelligence

In two of the studies we looked at the whether the different forms of praise actually taught students different views of intelligence. In one study, after the first (successful) set of problems, we found that students who were given intelligence praise now bought into the fixed view of intelligence far more than the students who were given the effort praise. (The third group tended to fall pretty much in the middle on this and other measures, so for the sake of simplicity I focus mainly on the intelligence-praised and effort-praised groups.)

Well, maybe the intelligence-praised students bought into the fixed view because it was in their self-interest to adopt this view. After all, they had just

---

[1]In all of our research, we make very sure that all children later have a mastery experience on the harder problems and leave feeling very proud of their performance.

been told they were smart at something, so why not feel even better by thinking this intelligence is a permanent part of themselves? So in another study, we asked students about their theories of intelligence after the difficult problems. And again we found a strong difference. Intelligence-praised students agreed with the fixed theory, and effort-praised students endorsed the malleable theory. The different forms of praise really did orient students toward different views of intelligence, with intelligence praise implying that the adult was judging some deep-seated ability that dwelt within them and the effort praise implying that skills are more acquirable and can be expanded through effort.

In this second study, in addition to asking students how much they agreed or disagreed with the fixed theory of intelligence, we asked them to explain intelligence in their own words by completing the following sentence: "I think intelligence is...." More students who had received the effort praise included malleable or motivational terms ("how much you know" or "trying your best") in their definitions.

Thus, the different forms of praise had a clear impact on students' theories of intelligence. Did they have an impact on the other things we know theories of intelligence affect?

## Did They Want to Look Smart or Learn?

In the first three studies, we tried to find out out what students' goals were after the different forms of praise. Were they more interested in continuing to look smart, or did they prefer to take on a challenging opportunity to learn? To answer this question, we offered them a choice of tasks. Some tasks were described as tasks that were perfect for avoiding mistakes and showing how smart you are, while others were described as not good for looking smart but excellent for learning something new and important. In every one of these studies, the majority of the intelligence-praised students chose a task that would allow them to look smart and rejected a challenging task that would allow them to learn a lot but would not necessarily make them look good. The effort-praised students did completely the opposite: 80–90% of them preferred the task that would allow them to learn a lot and rejected the task that would just make them look smart. So, intelligence praise, rather than making students eager for challenge and learning, did just the opposite. It was effort praise that made students eager to jump right in and learn.

Another of our measures brings home this point. In two studies (in one study right after the praised success, and in the other, after the difficulty) we asked students to tell us which of two folders they would prefer to read: one that contained "interesting new strategies" for solving the problems or one that contained scores that other (unfamiliar) children had earned on the same problems. In both studies, more than three-quarters of the effort-praised children chose the folder from which they could learn new strategies, whereas more than three-quarters of the intelligence-praised children chose the other folder, the one that would tell them how their scores compared with those of other children. Once again, intelligence-praised children passed up an opportunity to learn in order to shore up their egos; effort-praised students wanted to immerse themselves in information that could teach them more.

## What Does Failure Mean?

If praising students' intelligence did in fact teach them to measure themselves from their performance, then they should have measured themselves from their poorer performance on the second set of problems, and that is exactly what they did. When asked to rate different explanations for why they had trouble with those problems, intelligence-praised students agreed strongly that "I'm not good enough at the problems" and "I'm not smart enough." What the intelligence praise gave them, one experience with difficulty took away. The effort-praised students hardly blamed their ability at all. Instead they agreed strongly that "I didn't work hard enough," something they could easily remedy.

Another of our measures spoke pointedly to the meaning of failure for intelligence-praised children's egos. In one study, we told students that we would be doing our study in another school and it would be nice if they could write a short description of the problems for the kids in that school. On the same sheet they were asked to report the number of problems they had gotten right in the hard set. Almost 40% of the intelligence-praised children lied about their score, all of them artificially raising it. Only 13% of the effort-praised children did so. This means that intelligence-praised children were so invested in their performance—saw it as such a reflection of themselves—that many could not tell the truth even to someone they would never meet.

## What Did Difficulty Do to Enjoyment?

How did the difficulty affect children's enjoyment of the task? We assessed this by asking students how much fun they thought the problems were and how much they liked working on them. When students answered these questions right after the praised success, students from all groups thought the task was great fun. And when students were asked these questions after the hard problems, impressively, the difficulty did not change the enjoyment one bit for the effort-praised students. They really seemed engaged and challenged by the difficulty. But the enjoyment of the intelligence-praised students declined significantly after the difficulty. If they did not do well they could not enjoy it as much.

Another common way to measure students' feelings about an activity is to see how much they would want to do it in their spare time. So we asked: "How much would you like to take these problems home to work on?" Once again, right after the praised success, all groups of children registered a strong desire to take the problems home. And again, the effort-praised group showed no decline after the difficulty, but the intelligence-praised students showed a sharp decline. If they did not do well on the problems, they did not want to deal with them in the future. This is certainly not a productive way to overcome a deficiency.

In short, effort praise, but not intelligence praise, allowed students to maintain their interest and commitment.

## What Happened to Performance?

In four studies, we tracked students' performance over the three sets of problems, and looked at what happened from the first set (on which all three groups did equally well) to the third set (which was equivalent to the first set in difficulty, but came after the difficult second set). The effort-praised students did the best of the three groups on the final set and they improved significantly from the first set to the third. This means that their continued involvement and effort paid off. They actually became better ("smarter") at the problems.

In contrast, the intelligence-praised students did the worst of the three groups on the last set of problems, and *declined* significantly from the first to the third set. So, not only does this mind-set lead to self-denigration and loss of enjoyment in the face of difficulty, but it also leads to impaired performance.

In short, intelligence praise had powerful, but not good, effects on students' motivation and performance. This is not to say that the students did not enjoy the intelligence praise. To the contrary. When students received the intelligence praise, they often displayed a proud, satisfied smile that they did not display in the other conditions. That smile was, however, short-lived, as the students were soon overwhelmed by a host of concerns. In contrast, the effort praise, although perhaps not as thrilling initially, had a host of beneficial effects. By the way, we meant the effort praise to stand for a category of praise—process praise—where the emphasis is on what students put into their work to achieve an admirable result. As we will see, the praise could as easily refer to their strategies and the like, not simply sheer effort.

Why did the two forms of praise lead to such dramatically different results? As I suggested earlier, intelligence praise orients students toward a fixed intelligence mind-set in which maintaining the aura of intelligence becomes all important, and setbacks have dire implications for intelligence. Effort praise, on the other hand, puts students in the malleable intelligence mind-set in which learning, effort, and process are all important, leading students to become fully engaged with the task and giving them a recipe for overcoming obstacles.

Do these findings apply to a small segment of the student population? I don't think so. We conducted these studies with students of varying ethnicity (Caucasian, Hispanic, African-American) and varying socioeconomic level. Some of the studies were in more rural Midwestern communities, while others were in large urban centers. The results were the same.

Could it be that some students, for example, those with poor academic histories, simply didn't buy into the intelligence praise and didn't show the effects? Could it be that the "truly" intelligent students remained confident in their abilities and didn't show the negative effects? We looked at this by examining students' performance on the first set of problems, and then observing whether this had an impact on their acceptance of the high-ability message or their responses on the different measures. It did not make any difference. The effect cut across all levels of actual proficiency at the task.

## Other Types of Trait Praise

In a study with younger (kindergarten) children (Kamins & Dweck, 1999), we wondered whether other kinds of "trait" or "person" praise could also be problematic. What about praising traits other than intelligence, such as the child's goodness, after a fine job? What about expressing approval of the child as a whole when he or she does something laudable?[2] So we tried three different kinds of trait/person praise and measured their effects. Specifically, after a job well done, some children were given ability praise: "you're really good at this"; some were given goodness praise: "you're a good girl/boy"; and some were given general approval of themselves as a whole: "I'm very proud of you."

We also tried two different kinds of "process" praise with other children. Specifically, after a good job, some children were given effort praise: "You must have really tried hard." Others were given strategy praise: "You found a good way to do it. Can you think of other ways that may also work?"

After three praised tasks, children in all the groups rated themselves as extremely happy. They also said they felt they were good at what they had done, and that they felt like a good boy or girl, a nice boy or girl, and a smart boy or girl. Children then encountered two setbacks. Did the praise they had received affect how they reacted to these setbacks?

Just as with the older students, children who had received trait/person praise coped poorly with the setbacks. Telling children, on the basis of their performance, that they were good or smart or that you were proud of them made them highly vulnerable. They now told us that they did not feel they were good, smart, and worthy of pride—and they thought that badness was a more fixed quality. They were also less persistent in trying to solve the problem. In fact, when asked to tell us what would happen next, these children, instead of coming up with ways to fix their mistakes, often reiterated their failure or expressed regret or fear. That is, in line with their feelings of incompetence, badness, or blameworthiness, they said "I didn't do it right," "I'd feel sad," or "I'd be punished."

---

[2]This does *not* mean that children should not feel that you are proud of them in general or feel that they are good kids. It simply means they should not think that this judgment depends on a particular behavior.

In sharp contrast, the children who had received the process praise still felt they were smart and good, and they were highly persistent, coming up with many constructive solutions to fix their mistakes. Once again, it must be remembered that all the groups were the same at the beginning. All that differed was the praise they received. This praise, however made a big difference in how they felt about themselves and their abilities after difficulty, as well as whether they were able to cope effectively with the difficulty. Thinking you are a bad or dumb child is paralyzing, whereas thinking that you need to exert more effort or use a different strategy is energizing.

## Feedback in the Real World

What are the different ways these trait versus process messages might be communicated to kids in the real world? Chauncy Lennon and I ( Dweck & Lennon, 2001) began thinking seriously about this issue when he called to my attention a very strange finding from a large-scale study of thousands of students across the country: The more time parents spent with their children on homework, the less well the students did! Now of course it might be the case that parents felt they had to spend more time with poorer students. But it also could be that spending a lot of time with students on their homework sends them the message that they are not capable. So, we started thinking about all the good things parents do that can send their kids a trait message—or that can send their kids a process message—and we developed a questionnaire to ask students about this. (These students were in their first year of junior high school.)

What we did was develop a series of 11 scenarios in which we asked students to imagine that their parents did something: "Imagine that your parents offer to help you with your schoolwork. Why would they do this?" We then offered them a series of four reasons to rate. Each reason represented a trait message ("They are worried that I'm not smart emough to figure it out on my own") or a process message ("They want to make sure I learn as much as I can from my schoolwork"). The trait messages focused on judgments of smartness–dumbness or goodness–badness, whereas the process messages focused on learning, challenge, effort, strategies, and understanding. Here are some more examples.

"Imagine your parents spend time talking with you about your schoolwork. Why would they do this?" Trait message: "They want to see whether I am smart or not." Process message: "They want to encourage me to do challenging work."

"Suppose that your parents are very excited when you bring home some good grades. Why would they be this way?" Trait message: "They think it means I'm smart in school." Process message: They think I worked hard to get good grades. We included positive trait messages like this so that the trait-focused messages would not always be the more negative messages.

We then looked at what these trait versus process messages predicted. First, the trait message predicted a more fixed theory of intelligence, whereas the process message predicted a more malleable theory.[3]

The messages also predicted students' effort beliefs. Students who said their parents sent a trait message believed that high effort means you have low ability.

Next, the trait versus process messages predicted students' explanations for a failure. Here we asked them to imagine that they were enjoying a new course in school, studied for the first exam, but did poorly. What does that mean? Students who told us that their parents' feedback sent a trait message said that the failure would mean they were no good at the subject and would make them feel that they weren't smart enough. They also said that after an experience like that they would not like the subject any more.

Finally, students who told us that their parents sent a process message ended up earning high grades across their transition to junior high school.

## (More) Implications for Education

Our findings on trait versus process feedback tell a consistent story. They show that practices that focus students on judgments of their intelligence lead to a belief in fixed intelligence with all of its vulnerabilities. On the other hand, practices that focus students on effort, challenge, or strategies lead to a belief in malleable intelligence with all of its benefits. Let's look at some of the implications of these findings.

### Anyone Can Give Process Feedback

One thing that excites me about these findings is that the process message is pretty easy to incorporate into a parent's or teacher's existing practices. A parent or teacher may be very structured or unstructured, very autocratic or democratic, very warm or formal—it doesn't matter. A process message can fit into any of these styles.

The same thing is true for parents. In some cultures, the parents rule the roost and children must simply comply. In other cultures, there is a higher premium on understanding the child's point of view and in having a more equal give-and-take between parent and child. Still, a process message can be integrated into either style without asking parents to develop a whole new philosophy of child rearing that may or may not fit with their culture.

---

[3]Of course, we do not know from these findings whether there are real differences in parents' messages that are causing the different theories or the other effects that I will report in a moment, or whether students who already have a fixed theory interpret their parents' practices differently from students who have a malleable theory. Both would be interesting and we are looking at this question in our current studies.

## What Are Some Ways to Give Process Feedback?

The first thing to do is to stop giving trait-focused feedback. Do not praise children for low-challenge, low-effort, no-mistake success. This tells them they are smart and praiseworthy only when they do things quickly, easily, and perfectly. This will not make them love learning and challenge. When I encounter such a situation, I tell a child: "O-oops, I'm sorry I wasted your time. Let's go onto something harder that you can learn from."

Teachers can also model the excitement of confronting a challenge and using mistakes as clues for the next strategy: "Wow, this is hard, this is fun. Well, that strategy didn't work; it tells us that's not the right way. What should we try next?"

Process praise should be given both when a student succeeds and when a student fails, for a process focus is the way to repeat the success in the future and the way to overcome failures. But process praise after failure is not simply telling the student to try harder, for without showing them how, effort feedback can sometimes be unhelpful. This means that process praise places a bigger responsibility on the educator both to give students the right mind-set *and* to help them gain the skills they may need to implement it successfully.

Some people think that our findings mean we should not praise children as much as we do. But they do not mean that at all. We can praise as often and as enthusiastically as we like, but the focus of the praise should be the process in which the student is engaged, not the student's smartness. In fact, I would argue that the process praise is more appreciative of the student than the intelligence praise. With intelligence praise, you simply survey the work and declare the child smart. But with process praise, you really have to appreciate what went into producing what the students produced: what went into the ideas, the strategies, the choices, the development, the execution of the project. It becomes an interchange with the student rather than simply an evaluation.

## Aren't Performance Goals Also Important?

I have discussed how students with the malleble theory of intelligence value learning something new (a learning goal) over validating their intelligence through their performance (a performance goal). But given our society, are performance goals also important? Yes, they are.

To my mind, it is the balance that counts—a balance between valuing learning and valuing performance. Grades matter, and many students who want to go on to top schools need good grades. Problems arise when students come to care so much about their performance that they sacrifice important learning opportunities and limit their intellectual growth, as they do with a fixed theory of intelligence.

Problems also arise when students equate their grades with their intelligence or their worth. This can be very damaging, for when they hit difficulty they may quickly feel inadequate, become discouraged, and lose their ability or their desire to perform well in that area.

For me the best mix is a combination of (a) valuing learning and challenge and (b) valuing grades but seeing them as merely an index of current performance, not a sign of intelligence or worth.

## How Can Classrooms Balance Both Kinds of Goals?

First, here's what *not* to do.

When I was in sixth grade, my teacher seemed to equate our worth with our IQ scores. We were seated around the room in IQ order. If you did not have a high IQ, she would not let you clean the blackboard erasers, carry the flag in the assembly, or carry a note to the principal. She let us know that in her mind, a high IQ reflected not only basic intelligence but also character. The lower-IQ students felt terrible, and the higher-IQ students lived in fear that they would take another IQ test and lose their status. It was not an atmostphere that fostered love of learning and challenge.

This doesn't mean that a classroom that stresses performance can't also stress the importance of facing learning challenges. First and foremost, it must be made clear to students that their performance reflects their current skills and efforts, not their intelligence or worth. In this case, if students are disappointed in their performance, there is a clear and constructive implication: Work harder, avail yourself of more learning opportunities, learn how to study better, ask the teacher for more help, and so on.

Students who are taught that their performance simply measures their current skills can still relish learning and challenges, for mistakes and setbacks should not be undermining.

By the way, this stance characterizes many top athletes. They are *very* performance-oriented during a game or match, but they do not see a negative outcome as reflecting their underlying ability or potential to learn. Moreover, between games they are very learning-oriented. They review tapes of past games, try to learn from their mistakes, talk to their coaches about how to improve, and work ceaselessly on new skills.

## Are Higher Standards the Way to Go?

The current zeal for higher standards and more testing follows a period in which many educators believed that giving students lots of successes would boost their self-esteem and love of learning. This did not work. Instead students became used to low effort and became uninterested in challenges. Nor did self-esteem rise. That's why so many educators are eager to forget about self-esteem and return to the good old days of high standards, with the risk of widespread failure. What's the answer?

As I have shown, there is another approach, one that addresses students' achievement *and* their self-esteem: teaching students about malleable intelligence; teaching them to value hard work, learning, and challenges; teaching them how to cope with disappointing performance by planning new strategies and exerting more effort; and helping to provide them with the skills that will put them more in charge of their own learning. In this way, educators can be highly demanding of students but not run the risk that large numbers of students will be labeled as failures.

## What about "Gifted" Labels and Programs?

Calling a student gifted can be just like intelligence praise. This means that labeling kids as gifted can sometimes do more harm than good by feeding into a fixed theory of intelligence. The label "gifted" implies that students have received some magical quality (the gift) that makes them special and more worthy than others. Some students are in danger of getting hung up on this label. They may become so concerned with deserving the label and so worried about losing it—that is, they may become so concerned with bolstering their fixed, superior intelligence—that they may lose their love of challenge and learning. Such students may begin to prefer only things they can do easily and perfectly, thus limiting their intellectual growth.

In line with what I discussed earlier, psychologists who study creative geniuses point out that the single most important factor in creative achievement is willingness to exert tremendous effort and to sustain this effort in the face of obstacles. It would be a tragedy if by labeling students as gifted, we limited their creative contributions.

We can, however prevent this by making clear to students that "gifted" simply means that if they work hard and keep on learning and stretching themselves, they will be capable of noteworthy accomplishments. Of course, that is true of many kids, not just those considered gifted.

## What about Girls?

Girls, especially bright girls, have traditionally underestimated themselves and shied away from challenges. Don't they *need* a message that they are smart?

As I have shown, the way to motivate students and to give them more lasting motivation and confidence is not by telling them they're smart, but by focusing them on the processes that create achievement. In fact, my great fear is that in our zeal to bolster the confidence of girls (and minority students as well), we have lavished intelligence praise on them, thereby making them perhaps even more vulnerable than they were before.

## PYGMALION AND THE MALLEABLE THEORY

The idea of beliefs affecting behavior was dramatically demonstrated in the original "Pygmalion in the Classroom" studies by Rosenthal and Jacobson

(1968; see Rosenthal, Chapter 2 in this volume). It was *teachers'* beliefs and *teachers'* behavior that were influenced, but the impact was on students' achievement.

At the beginning of a school year, teachers were told that some students in their classes had the potential to blossom intellectually. These students had in fact been randomly selected, but by the end of the year, especially in the younger grades, many of these students actually showed marked gains in achievement.

This study is often interpreted to mean that when teachers think students are smart, they treat them differently. But teachers were not told that the students were simply smart. They were given a malleable theory of those students' intelligence, and it may well be the malleable theory of intelligence that produced the results. This would mean that it is not only students' theories of intelligence that matter, but those of teachers too (see Dweck, 2001).

## CONCLUSION

I have shown how students' theories about their intelligence can play a central role in their achievement and I have shown how our practices can affect these theories. In particular, I have shown how some of our most well-meaning practices, such as praising students' intelligence, can actually put their motivation and achievement in jeopardy—and how other practices, such as praising students' efforts and strategies, can create the motivated achievers we hope for.

### Teachers' Questions and Answers

**Q:** Like many parents, I suppose, my young child strikes me as the most brilliant child I've ever met. I'm constantly amazed at her use of language and finding myself telling her how smart she is, not, as with your research subjects, in response to completing a task, but rather at her automatic understanding of language and the world around her. Should I hold my tongue? Won't intelligence praise given early in life and in a general, noncontingent way help her create an enduring sense that she is smart?

**A:** By praising your child's automatic understanding, you are telling her that she is smart when things come to her quickly and easily (and not when she has to work hard for them). By praising her intelligence in a general, noncontingent way, you would be telling her that you admire her for some mysterious trait she happens to have (not for the effort and concentration she applies to master new things). What will happen when she encounters something that is difficult for her? Will she doubt her smartness? Will she worry about losing your admiration? How will she learn that all worthwhile pursuits involve periods of confusion, of trying new strategies, of prolonged effort in the face of uncertainty. The important thing for childern to learn is that they can master most challenging tasks through effort over time, not that they are smart and praiseworthy when they do things that are easy for them.

**Q:** How can heterogeneous groupings in cooperative learning exercises help promote motivational strategies?

**A:** Too often we hope that when we do good things (like praising intelligence), helpful motivational strategies will automatically follow. Heterogeneous grouping and cooperative learning are seen as good things, but helpful motivational strategies will not automatically follow from them. Both have potential pitfalls. In heterogeneous grouping, students who need more time and effort may come to think of themselves as dumb. In cooperative learning exercises, those students may feel as though they are less capable, less valuable members of the team. This means that ANY educational practice needs to build in explicit messages about intelligence, learning, and effort.

**Q:** How can teachers start to change students' cognitive messages to themselves so that they will be open to work that requires significant effort?

**A:** Students do indeed talk to themselves in helpful or in harmful ways. In the harmful messages to themselves they express fear of challenge, reveal anxiety over being found lacking, explain setbacks in terms of low ability, and tell themselves to give up when they have performed poorly. Therefore, teachers must teach these students a new language. The teachers should speak warmly and excitedly about challenges as wonderful opportunities, they should talk to mistakes as though they are fascinating and helpful friends, they should exhort themselves and the students to concentrate and apply effort to a knotty problem, and they should always point with wonder to the fruits of the effort—learning important new things that they didn't know before. In this way, students can learn a whole new repertoire of helpful messages to guide their future learning.

# References

Aronson, J. (1998). *The effects of conceiving ability as fixed or improvable on responses to stereotype threat.* Unpublished manuscript, University of Texas.

Aronson, J., Fried, C., & Good, C. (in press). Reducing the effects of stereotype threat on African American college students by shaping theories of intelligence *Journal of Experimental Social Psychology.*

Berglas, S. (1990). Self-handicapping: Etiological and diagnostic considerations. In R. L. Higgins (Ed.), *Self-handicapping: The paradox that isn't* (pp. 151–186). New York: Plenum.

Binet, A. (1909/1973). *Les idees modernes sur les enfants* [Modern ideas on children]. Paris: Flamarion.

Bloom, B. S. (1985). *Developing talent in young people.* New York: Ballantine.

Brown, A. L., & Campione, J. C. (1996). Psychological theory and the design of innovative learning environments: On procedures, principles, and systems. In L. Schauble & R. Glaser (Eds.), *Innovations in learning: New environments for education* (pp. 289–325). Mahwah, NJ: Erlbaum.

Dweck, C. S. (1999). *Self-theories and goals: Their role in motivation, personality, and development*. Philadalphia: Taylor & Francis/Psychology Press.

Dweck, C. S. (2001). The development of ability conceptions. In A. Wigfield and J. Eccles (Eds. ). *The development of achievement motivation*. Academic Press.

Dweck, C. S., & Leggett, E. L. (1988). A social-cognitive approach to motivation and personality, *Psychological Review, 95*, 256–273.

Dweck, C. S., & Lennon, C. (2001, April). *Person versus process-focused parenting styles*. Symposium paper presented at the Biennial Meeting of the Society for Research in Child Development, Minneapolis, MN.

Dweck, C. S., & Sorich, L. (1999). Mastery-oriented thinking. In C. R. Snyder (Ed. ). *Coping*. New York: Oxford University Press.

Grant, H. (2001). *Dimensions of achievement goals and their impact on achievement*. Doctoral dissertation, Columbia University.

Grant, H., & Dweck, C. S. (2001). Clarifying achievement goals and their impact. Manuscript submitted for publication.

Gutman, R. W. (2000). *Mozart: A cultural biography*. New York: Harcourt Brace.

Hayes, J. R. (1989). Cognitive processes in creativity. In J. Glover, R. Ronning, & C. Reynolds (Eds.), *Handbook of creativity*. New York: Plenum.

Henderson, V., & Dweck, C. S. (1990). Achievement and motivation in adolescence: A new model and data. In S. Feldman & G. Elliott (Eds.), *At the threshold: The developing adolescent*. Cambridge, MA: Harvard University Press.

Hong, Y., Chiu, C., Dweck, C. S., Lin, D., & Wan, W. (1999). A test of implicit theories and self-confidence as predictors of responses to achievement challenges. *Journal of Personality and Social Psychology, 77*, 588–599.

Howe, M. J. (1999). Prodigies and creativity. In R. J. Sternberg (Ed.) *Handbook of creativity*. New York: Cambridge University Press.

Jourden, F. J., Bandura, A., & Banfield, J. T. (1991). The impact of conceptions of ability on self-regulatory factors and motor skill acquisition. *Journal of Sport and Exercise Psychology, 13*, 213–226.

Kamins, M., & Dweck, C. S. (1999). Person versus process praise: Implications for contingent self-worth and coping. *Developmental Psychology, 35*, 835–847.

Mueller, C. M., & Dweck, C. S. (1998). Intelligence praise can undermine motivation and performance. *Journal of Personality and Social Psychology, 75*, 33–52.

Nickerson, R. S. (1999). Enhancing creativity. In R. J. Sternberg (Ed.) *Handbook of creativity*. New York: Cambridge University Press.

Perkins, D. N. (1994). Creativity: Beyond the Darwinian paradigm. In M. A. Boden (Ed.), *Dimensions of creativity*. Cambridge, MA: MIT Press.

Perkins, D. N. (1995). *Outsmarting IQ: The emerging science of learnable intelligence*. New York: Free Press.

Resnick, L. B. (1983). Mathematics and science learning: A new conception. *Science*, 477–478.

Rhodewalt, F. (1994). Conceptions of ability, achievement goals, and individual differences in self-handicapping behavior: On the application of implicit theories. *Journal of Personality, 62*, 67–85.

Rosenthal, R., & Jacobson, L. (1968) *Pygmalion in the classroom: Teacher expectation and pupils' intellectual development*. New York: Holt, Rinehart & Winston, 1968.

Runco, M. A., Nemiro, J., & Walberg, H. J. (1998). Personal explicit theories of creativity. *Journal of Creative Behavior, 32*, 1–17.

Simonton, D. (1999). *Origins of genius: Darwinian perspectives on creativity*. New York: Oxford.

Sosniak, L. A. (1985). Learning to be a concert pianist. In B. S. Bloom (Ed.), *Developing talent in young people*. New York: Ballantine.

Sternberg, R. J. (1985). *Beyond IQ*. New York: Cambridge University Press.

Stone, J., & Dweck, C. S. (1998). *Theories of intelligence and the meaning of achievement goals*. Unpublished manuscript, Columbia University.

Tabernero, C., & Wood, R. E. (1999). Implicit theories versus the social construal of ability in self-regulation and performance on a complex task. *Organizational Behavior and Human Decision Processes, 78*, 104–127.

Weisberg, R. W. (1986). *Creativity: Genius and other myths*. New York: Freeman.
Weisberg, R. W. (1999). Creativity and knowledge: A challenge to theories. In R. J. Sternberg (Ed.) *Handbook of creativity*. New York: Cambridge University Press.
Wood, R., & Bandura, A. (1989). Impact of conceptions of ability on self-regulatory mechanisms and complex decision-making. *Journal of Personality and Social Psychology, 56*, 407–415.

# The Paradox of Achievement: The Harder You Push, the Worse It Gets

EDWARD L. DECI AND RICHARD M. RYAN

*Department of Psychology, University of Rochester, New York*

Politicians, educators, and parents all seem deeply concerned about the achievement of students within the American educational system. In the wake of stiff global competition, politicians have called for tougher standards that, they say, will put American education at the top of the heap. States such as New York have implemented stringent new testing programs that are intended to motivate students to live up to higher standards. Educational administrators and teachers feel increasingly compelled to assign unprecedented amounts of homework and to "teach to the tests" because in many cases they and their schools are being evaluated on the basis of the students' test scores. Parents, wanting their children to get ahead, try to help them cope with the pressures and demonstrate their competence.

In this chapter we discuss motivation for learning and achievement, considering the impact of various policies and practices on motivation and performance. We base our discussion on self-determination theory (SDT) (Deci & Ryan, 1985) and the research it has stimulated, arguing that some ways to motivate achievement are more effective than others. During this pressured time, with achievement being so ardently endorsed, some politicians, educators, and parents are advocating and adopting approaches that not only fail to yield their intended outcomes but in fact are counterproductive. At the same time, others have recommended and implemented approaches to motivation that enhance both the achievement and well-being of students.

## EXCELLENCE IN EDUCATION

Nearly everyone wants our educational system to be excellent, and most people agree that excellence in education involves students' displaying the highest level of achievement of which they are capable. However, although some politicians and pundits maintain that achievement, as indexed by standardized tests, is the only important criterion for judging the excellence of education, most teachers and parents believe that truly excellent education involves a much fuller and more complex set of goals.

These teachers and parents, of course, want students to achieve their full potentials, learning material that is deep, meaningful, and of lasting value and developing a greater capacity to think critically and creatively about problems. But most teachers and parents would like even more than that. They would also like the students to be curious and interested in learning, rather than grade-focused or work-avoidant, and to gain a sense of confidence and competence as they learn. And they want the students, whatever their level of performance, to display initiative, to carry through on commitments, to be respectful and feel respected, and to be contributing, well-rounded members of the community.

In short, when addressing the issue of how to promote students' motivation, it is important to consider a differentiated set of educational criteria, recognizing that high scores on standardized achievement tests do not ensure excellent education. Having students attain high achievement test scores is but one criterion for excellent education, and, despite the pervasive rhetoric, it may not even be the most important. The goals outlined above, which are relevant for all students, from those with the highest to the lowest achievement scores, must also be achieved for educational systems to be excellent. Unfortunately, some approaches to promoting higher achievement test scores may even interfere with excellent education in the broader sense implied above. For example, the test-driven reforms essentially deform school climates with their narrow focus and pressuring methods, resulting in less than excellent experiences for the preponderance of students who encounter them.

Like most people, our goal is to see excellent education for our children, and of course we expect excellent educational systems to facilitate learning and achievement. But we hasten to add that our evaluation of an educational endeavor focuses on the students' affective outcomes as well as on their cognitive ones. Our work, based in SDT, accordingly stresses a variety of outcomes, including the quality of experience, the depth of learning, the creativity of performance, and the well-being of students. These outcomes have as much to do with how students feel about themselves as with what material they learn.

In this chapter, we argue that, when students are provided an educational climate that nurtures their fundamental psychological needs, they likely attain not only high levels of achievement but also growth, development, and well-being. However, when the climate pressures students to achieve high test scores, not only will the motivational and emotional costs be substantial, but high-quality achievement will also typically suffer for the vast majority of students. Thus, the paradox of achievement: the harder you push the less you get.

## A MOTIVATIONAL ANALYSIS

Self-determination theory is concerned with the social conditions that promote versus forestall motivation; however, the theory recognizes that there are different types or qualities of motivation and that different social factors give rise to them. Thus, for example, SDT examines the conditions that promote versus forestall rigid or superficial types of motivation as well as those that affect motivation involving a deep commitment to and interest in learning.

Like all current theories of motivation and behavior change, SDT distinguishes between being *amotivated* (i.e., being unmotivated) and being *motivated*. Amotivation means not having an intention to act (i.e., not trying to attain an outcome), and it may manifest as lethargy and lack of behavior or as behavior that is not intended, in other words, just going through the motions. Motivation, in contrast, involves intentionality; it involves acting with the desire to accomplish some outcome such as the long-term accumulation of a straight-A record. The more strongly a person values an outcome and believes he or she is capable of achieving it, the stronger will be that person's motivation.

Unlike most other theories, SDT is less concerned with the strength of a person's motivation and more concerned with the type. In other words, SDT has focused on differentiating the concept of motivation by specifying different types of motivation and exploring the antecedents and consequences of the different types. A central concept in the theory is the degree to which behaviors are autonomous versus controlled, so types of motivation are organized with respect to their relation to the dimension of autonomy versus control. *Autonomous behaviors* are fully volitional; they are freely pursued and wholly endorsed by the self. *Controlled behaviors*, on the other hand, are pressured and directed, whether by external or internal forces, leaving people feeling like they have to do the behaviors, like they have no choice. To examine the motivational basis of autonomy versus control in human behavior, we began by distinguishing between intrinsic motivation and extrinsic motivation.

## Intrinsic and Extrinsic Motivation

*Intrinsic motivation* is a manifestation of people's proactive nature. People have a general propensity to explore, to learn, to exercise capacities, to take on optimal challenges. These are not behaviors that must be entrained or programmed but instead represent inherent tendencies. They are an innate part of who we are, and people are inclined to do them unless something interferes.

Intrinsic motivation is a type of self-motivation in which people do activities that *interest* them, provide spontaneous pleasure or enjoyment, and do not require any "reward" beyond this inherent satisfaction. Children love to play, and through playing, they learn. It is not necessary to offer them candy or gold stars to get them to play and explore; that is what they do naturally. And in that natural, self-directed activity, they imitate older children, they express and work through their feelings, they try to do what their parents do. Quite simply, children are intrinsically motivated for the types of behaviors that foster learning and development. Although intrinsic motivation is pervasively evident in young children, it is also a powerful source of learning throughout the life span. Indeed, much of what people learn stems from spontaneous interests, curiosity, and their natural desire to master problems and affect the surroundings. One of the things about intrinsic motivation that makes it so important for our investigations is that it is the prototype of human autonomy. Intrinsic motivation is the epitome of volition and is accompanied by feelings of interest, enjoyment, and freedom. When intrinsically motivated, people are engrossed in the activity, and they are not easily distracted. The initiative is theirs, and often they persist for long periods.

White (1959) suggested that effectance (i.e., having an effect on one's surroundings) is an inherent motivational propensity. Stated differently, people are inherently motivated to be competent and to feel competent. deCharms (1968) added that people also have an innate desire to be causal agents, to feel a sense of self-initiation and control. That is, people prefer to feel like an "origin" rather than a "pawn" with respect to the regulation of their behavior. Building on these ideas, Deci (1975) proposed that intrinsically motivated behaviors involve people's innate needs to be *competent* and *self-determining*.

In contrast to intrinsic motivation where the behavior itself is interesting and satisfying, *extrinsic motivation* concerns doing a behavior to obtain some separate consequence that has been made contingent on the behavior. Seeking rewards and avoiding punishments represent prototypic extrinsic motivations. When extrinsically motivated, people engage in activities because the activities are instrumental; that is, they are means to desired ends (Ryan & Deci, 2000). Achievement-related behaviors can be motivated by either intrinsic or extrinsic motivation and are often motivated by a combination of the two. In the discussion that follows, we examine these motivations in more detail, considering their relation to each other and the conditions that promote each.

Subsequently, we address the educational outcomes that typically result from the different types of motivation.

## Research on Intrinsic Motivation

The intrinsic–extrinsic distinction has now been widely investigated. When people do an activity because they find it interesting and are receiving no apparent external consequence for doing it, they are considered intrinsically motivated; whereas, if they do it to attain an external consequence, such as earning money, receiving a good grade on an exam, or getting into a highly ranked college, they are extrinsically motivated. Researchers have reliably assessed whether people are intrinsically or extrinsically motivated both by examining the reasons they endorse for why they are doing a behavior and by making inferences based on observations of behavior and the conditions within which it occurs.

Research on intrinsic motivation began with an examination of how factors in the social environment affect people's intrinsic motivation. SDT makes predictions about how various environmental events will affect intrinsic motivation based on their anticipated impact on people's feelings of competence and autonomy. Social conditions that allow satisfaction of the needs for competence and autonomy while doing an activity are predicted to maintain or enhance intrinsic motivation for the activity, whereas conditions that thwart satisfaction of these needs are predicted to decrease intrinsic motivation.

### Perceived Competence

Several studies have examined how factors hypothesized to be related to perceived competence affect intrinsic motivation. For example, Danner and Lonky (1981) and Harter (1978) found that people select and express more positive affect when working on tasks that are optimally challenging. If tasks are too easy, people tend to be bored; if too hard, they tend to be anxious. Optimally challenging tasks are possible to master, but they are difficult enough to stretch people's capacities, so succeeding at them leaves the people feeling competent. The Danner and Lonky study further showed that although children tend spontaneously to select optimal challenges, they are less intrinsically motivated and choose easier tasks when they are extrinsically rewarded.

Numerous studies have found that positive performance feedback enhances intrinsic motivation because it supports their perceived competence (Deci, 1971), while negative performance feedback undermines intrinsic motivation because it diminishes their perceived competence (Deci & Cascio, 1972). Thus, telling people they did well at an activity tends to increase their interest in the activity, but telling them they did badly tends to diminish their interest (Vallerand & Reid, 1984). However, subsequent studies by Fisher (1978) and

Ryan (1982) indicated that perceived competence enhances intrinsic motivation only if it is accompanied by supports for autonomy. For example, a teacher's saying to a boy, "That's good, you did just as you should," is likely to leave the student feeling like a pawn, like he just did what the teacher thinks he should. It takes the emphasis away from his initiation, leaving no room for him to feel like an originator of his own action. This might result in his being extrinsically motivated to get the teacher's praise, but it will not support his intrinsic motivation for the activity itself. In contrast, saying to the student "That's nice work, I like the way you took the initiative to do it" conveys that he did the task both competently and autonomously. This positive feedback is more likely to enhance intrinsic motivation. The important point here is that feeling competent is necessary for people to be motivated—to be either intrinsically motivated or extrinsically motivated. However, only when people perceive themselves to be autonomous will the competence affirmation enhance their *intrinsic* motivation.

## Perceived Autonomy

deCharms (1968) used the concept of perceived locus of causality (PLOC) to emphasize that, when people feel autonomous, they experience the initiation of their behavior to be within themselves and they become more intrinsically motivated. On the other hand, when the PLOC is external to themselves, they tend to lose intrinsic motivation because their need for autonomy is not satisfied. Thus, any factor that conduces toward an external perceived locus of causality (E-PLOC) is predicted to diminish intrinsic motivation, and any factor that fosters an internal perceived locus of causality (I-PLOC) is predicted to enhance intrinsic motivation. The example above, of the teacher who told the student he did just as he should, was intended to illustrate how even the language the teacher uses can lead the student's perceived locus of causality to be more external.

Hundreds of studies have tested the general hypothesis that factors prompting an external PLOC tend to undermine intrinsic motivation whereas factors prompting an internal PLOC tend to enhance it. The best known of these concern the undermining of intrinsic motivation by extrinsic rewards, a phenomenon that first appeared in early experiments by Deci (1971). He found that college students who were given monetary rewards for completing interesting puzzles were less likely to persist at the puzzles during a later free-play period than were participants who solved the same puzzles without being rewarded. Puzzle solving for the rewarded participants seemed to become dependent on rewards, so the individuals were less likely to persist at the puzzles if rewards were not forthcoming. Studies of high school students in the United States (Harackiewicz, 1979) and in Israel (Kruglanski, Friedman, & Zeevi, 1971) showed that rewards led the students to report less interest in the target task than their counterparts who did not get rewards, and undermining of intrinsic motivation by expected rewards has been found even in nursery school children (Lepper, Greene, & Nisbett, 1973).

According to SDT, the use of contingent rewards tends to foster an E-PLOC and the perception that one's behavior is being controlled, thus diminishing the experience of autonomy that is necessary for maintaining intrinsic motivation. This undermining of intrinsic motivation by tangible extrinsic rewards has been demonstrated not only across age groups, but also across a variety of reward types and reward contingencies (Ryan, Mims, & Koestner, 1983).

SDT recognizes that rewards can be quite effective in controlling behavior, a point that has been made by behaviorists for decades. However, SDT emphasizes that when extrinsic rewards control behavior, they interfere with people's self-regulation. In other words, if your aim is to encourage students to motivate and regulate themselves, controlling their behavior with rewards will work against that aim. As such, we begin to see how important it is to think about different types of motivation. It is possible to motivate people with rewards, that is, to motivate them extrinsically, but this is not self-motivation and thus is not the type of motivation that thoughtful educators hope to engender in their students.

The finding that tangible rewards tend to undermine intrinsic motivation has been extremely controversial, with behaviorists adamantly denying that there are any notable negative consequences to the use of tangible rewards for motivating effective performance (e.g., Eisenberger & Cameron, 1996). However, a recent meta-analysis of nearly 100 experiments examining the effects of tangible rewards on intrinsic motivation revealed that if people were rewarded contingent on doing, completing, or performing well on an interesting activity, the rewards undermined their intrinsic motivation for the activity (Deci, Koestner, & Ryan, 1999). On the other hand, if people did not expect the rewards while doing the activity or did not even have to do the activity to get the rewards, they were unlikely to experience the rewards as controllers of their behavior so the rewards did not have a detrimental effect on intrinsic motivation. Another important result from the meta-analysis was that the undermining of intrinsic motivation by contingent tangible rewards was found to be worse for children than for college students, thus indicating that the use of extrinsic rewards such as gold stars, tokens, and awards as a motivational strategy in primary schools is particularly problematic.

Additional studies have examined the effects on intrinsic motivation of other external events relevant to classroom practices. Experiments indicate that threats of punishment (Deci & Cascio, 1972), external evaluations (Harackiewicz, Manderlink, & Sansone, 1984; Smith, 1975), deadlines (Amabile, DeJong, & Lepper, 1976), and imposed goals (Mossholder, 1980), all of which foster an E-PLOC, also undermine intrinsic motivation. On the other hand, providing choice (Zuckerman, Porac, Lathin, Smith, & Deci, 1978) and acknowledging task-related feelings (Koestner, Ryan, Bernieri, & Holt, 1984), which conduce toward an I-PLOC, can enhance intrinsic motivation. These findings support the idea that factors experienced as controlling (i.e., as pressure to think, feel, or behave in specific ways) diminish intrinsic motivation, whereas those experienced as autonomy supportive (i.e., as encouragement for self-initiation and choice) facilitate intrinsic motivation.

Other research has revealed that the style and language people use in administering external events such as offering rewards or setting limits also significantly affect intrinsic motivation and, in some cases, can counteract the effects of the events themselves. For example, Ryan et al. (1983) found that when performance-contingent rewards (those based on the quality of one's performance) were administered with a controlling style using language such as "you should" or "you have to," they undermined intrinsic motivation. That, of course, was to be expected in light of the studies showing that rewards undermined intrinsic motivation even when the style was not explicitly controlling. However, Ryan et al. also found that when performance-contingent rewards were administered with a more autonomy-supportive style (i.e., in a way that acknowledged the recipients' good performance with an interested tone that did not involve controlling language), the rewards were less likely to be undermining. Thus, although there is a strong tendency for tangible rewards to undermine intrinsic motivation, they will be less detrimental if the rewarder has established an autonomy-supportive relationship with the person being rewarded. If parents or teachers have a secure, autonomy-supportive relationship with a child, the occasional use of rewards for good performance is unlikely to be detrimental to the child, but if those adults rely on the use of rewards as a motivational strategy, the rewards are indeed likely to take a significant toll on the child's intrinsic motivation.

Kast and Connor (1988) did a comparable experiment in which they provided positive feedback with either a controlling or noncontrolling style and found that controlling positive feedback undermined intrinsic motivation, whereas positive feedback that was clearly noncontrolling enhanced it. This experiment, therefore, supported the example provided earlier in the chapter about the importance of giving positive feedback in a way that also supports autonomy. In another study, Koestner et al. (1984) found that, whereas directive limit setting was detrimental to children's intrinsic motivation, setting limits in a way that provided choice and acknowledged the children's feelings did not undermine intrinsic motivation.

To summarize, events such as rewards, deadlines, and limits tend to undermine intrinsic motivation, whereas events such as providing positive feedback tend to support intrinsic motivation. However, the interpersonal style people use in administering the events interacts with the events to determine their effects. Specifically, when people's style is controlling and pressuring it diminishes intrinsic motivation, even for positive feedback, whereas when the interpersonal relationship is supportive it tends to enhance intrinsic motivation and events such as rewards and limits administered with such a style are less detrimental. In short, the interpersonal style people use to provide feedback, convey expectations, or administer rewards can significantly affect the impact of those events on intrinsic motivation. Insofar as your goal is to promote intrinsic motivation for schoolwork, then it is important to be sensitive to the students' needs for autonomy support both at home and in the classroom.

Taken together, the experiments underscore the importance of the inter-personal relationship that an authority figure—a teacher or parent, for example—has with students. Being controlling starts from the adult's perspective, conveying what the adult wants the student to do while failing to take account of the student's desires or feelings. Being autonomy supportive, in contrast, recognizes and acknowledges the student's desires and feelings and moves on from there. Using an autonomy-supportive style, adults accept that a student might find the material boring or that it is not optimal for his or her skill level, and then the adults might explain why the material is important or they might adjust the difficulty level, as seems appropriate at the time. The idea, quite simply, concerns being responsive to the student rather than simply being demanding of him or her.

## Intrinsic Motivation in the Classroom

Some studies of the conditions that promote versus diminish intrinsic motivation have been done in classrooms. For example, Deci, Schwartz, Shein-man, and Ryan (1981) assessed whether teachers were oriented toward sup-porting students' autonomy versus controlling students' behavior. Reasoning that a teacher's orientation is a critical factor in creating the climate within a classroom, the researchers examined how these teacher orientations toward autonomy support versus control related to students' intrinsic motivation.

Deci et al. provided teachers a set of vignettes, each describing a typical problem in schools, such as a student having been listless and uninvolved recently or a student having not completed homework assignments. Following each problem were four ways of responding, and teachers were asked to rate each response in terms of how appropriate they believed it to be. One way, which involved the teacher prescribing the solution and using external contin-gencies (e.g., stay in from recess) as a motivational device, was highly control-ling. Another, considered moderately controlling, involved emphasizing what the student *should* do about the problem. A third, viewed as moderately autonomy supportive, encouraged the student to observe other students to see how they dealt with such situations. And the fourth, which was highly autonomy supportive, involved encouraging the student to talk about the problem from his or her own perspective and to think about ways of handling it. In these examples, one can observe a clear progression from external control toward encouragement of children's self-regulation.

In this study, Deci et al. (1981) found that teacher who more strongly endorsed the autonomy-supportive, relative to the controlling, strategies had students who were more intrinsically motivated and had higher self-esteem. In a follow-up study, teachers were preselected in terms of whether they tended to be more autonomy supportive or more controlling. Then, the intrinsic motivation and self-esteem of their students was assessed on the second day of the school year and again 2 months later. Results showed that over the first 2 months of the school year, students in the classrooms with the more autonomy-supportive teachers tended to show increases in intrinsic motivation and self-esteem, relative to students in the classrooms with more controlling teachers.

A study by Ryan and Grolnick (1986) showed that students' *perceptions* of their teachers' being more autonomy supportive, relative to controlling, were also associated with the students' having higher levels of intrinsic motivation. Specifically, children who perceived classroom teachers to be controlling or pressuring were less interested and curious in school, less desirous of challenge, and overall less confident in their feelings about schoolwork than were children who experienced support for their autonomy.

These and numerous other studies of classroom climates (see Ryan & LaGuardia, 1999) represent real-world parallels to the laboratory experiments that showed that more controlling techniques and orientations tend to be detrimental to intrinsic motivation whereas techniques and orientations that are more supportive of people's autonomy tend to enhance their intrinsic motivation.

## Extrinsic Motivation: Controlled or Self-Determined?

Extrinsic motivation is more complex than intrinsic motivation in terms of its relation to autonomy and psychological need satisfaction. Extrinsically motivated behaviors are those that a person does because they are instrumental to some separable consequence rather than because they are a source of spontaneous enjoyment and satisfaction. For example, when people act specifically to get rewards, they are extrinsically motivated, and, as we saw, numerous studies have indicated that this tends to decrease perceived autonomy and intrinsic motivation. In other words, behavior that is intended to obtain tangible rewards is controlled. However, there are many different "extrinsic reasons" why a person might do an activity, and these reasons can be quite different in terms of the degree to which they are controlled versus autonomous.

Consider extrinsically motivated behaviors that are approval-driven, done specifically to feel appreciated. In such cases, people behave not because they enjoy the activity, or even because they value the activity itself, but instead because they believe it will bring them approval that they would not otherwise get. Within SDT, the third innate psychological need, in addition to competence and autonomy, is the need for interpersonal relatedness or connectedness. Behavior that is motivated by the desire for approval could bring the person satisfaction of the need for relatedness; however, when people behave for this extrinsic reason, which is undoubtedly quite common among students, they are in the unfortunate position of needing to trade off satisfaction of one need for that of another. In other words, they are being controlled by the approval that they would not otherwise get, so, by doing what they have to do to get the approval, the students are sacrificing satisfaction of the need for autonomy to gain satisfaction of the need for relatedness. As such, this type of extrinsic motivation, like extrinsic motivation that is explicitly aimed at attainment of a tangible reward or avoidance of a punishment, is also quite controlled, and teachers who make their approval contingent on particular behaviors are being controlling.

There are still other forms of extrinsic, or instrumental, motivation, however, and some are not controlled. People can be extrinsically motivated because they personally value an activity, that is, because they consider it important for their long-term, self-selected goals. For example, students who do not find organic chemistry interesting may study it with a full sense of volition because they understand and accept its importance for becoming a good doctor. They would have achieved a state of valuing the learning itself even though it is instrumental rather than interesting. In other words, although some premed students feel pressured and controlled because they have to study the subject, others, on whom we are here focusing, have assimilated the importance of the material for their chosen future, so they engage it because it is valuable to them. They study quite willingly (Black & Deci, 2000).

Recognizing various reasons for doing extrinsically motivated behaviors, SDT proposes that extrinsic motivation can be differentiated into meaningful subtypes that result from the degree to which people have internalized and integrated the regulation of an uninteresting behavior (i.e., a behavior that is not intrinsically motivated). In other words, socially sanctioned values can be more or less fully assimilated by the self, resulting in different types of regulation that range from mere compliance to volitional execution of behaviors that have been fully self-endorsed.

The theory specifies four types of extrinsic motivation, referred to as external regulation, introjected regulation, identified regulation, and integrated regulation, which we now address in turn.

## External Regulation

The most superficial level of embracing a behavior is in evidence when people perform a task simply to obtain a reward or avoid a punishment. If students perform tasks only for externally administered consequences, their behavior is externally regulated and has an E-PLOC. External regulation is what was typically contrasted with intrinsic motivation in early studies of the undermining of intrinsic motivation and is the form of motivation focused on by Skinner's (1953) reinforcement theory and the behavior modification programs it spawned. When a person's motivation to behave remains dependent on the continued supply of external consequences the person's behavior is controlled by those consequences, and the person typically experiences low levels of self-determination and task interest.

## Introjected Regulation

A second type of extrinsic motivation results when a regulation has been partially internalized, that is, taken in but not assimilated. Introjected regulation is an internally controlled state (Ryan, 1982) in which behaviors are intended either to avoid anxiety or to experience ego-enhancing pride. When students behave to prove their worth, gain a general sense of approval, or avoid affronts to their self-esteem, they are controlled by introjects. That is, they are motivated by contingent self-esteem (Deci & Ryan, 1995).

A classic form of introjected regulation in school settings is *ego involvement* (Nicholls, 1984; Ryan, 1982), which involves students' proving their worth by comparing their competence with that of others. Ego involvement is a pervasive form of motivation in today's performance-focused, test-oriented schools. A number of experiments (e.g., Ryan, Koestner, & Deci, 1991) have shown that focusing people on ego involvements or introjects induces feelings of pressure and tension and interferes with intrinsic motivation. Introjects are not really experienced as part of the self, but instead as demands on the self, so they have a relatively external PLOC.

## Identified Regulation

A more autonomous or self-determined form of extrinsic motivation occurs when students' actions are regulated by identifications. This involves identifying with, or accepting as one's own, the value of an activity. For example, students may participate in, rather than disrupt, certain classroom activities not because the activities are interesting (intrinsic motivation) or because the students feel they have to behave to gain rewards or feel worthy (external or introjected regulation), but rather because the students believe in the value of an organized lesson for their own learning. In this case, they would be relatively self-determined in their participation. The behavior would still be considered extrinsically motivated, for the students would be doing it not because they find it inherently interesting but instead because of its instrumental value. Through identification, students can come to find personal meaning in learning certain subjects even if they do not find them interesting.

## Integrated Regulation

The most autonomous form of extrinsic motivation occurs when identifications (i.e., consciously endorsed values) have been fully assimilated to the self. This integration requires people to evaluate identifications with respect to other values and needs, bring them into congruence, and thus fully endorse them within the context of their life goals and relationships (Ryan, 1995). Integration represents the deepest form of internalization, results in self-determined behavior, and leads to the experience of being in touch with one's true self (Sheldon & Elliot, 1998). The process of integration, which is a critical developmental process, requires relatively mature cognitive capacities. Thus, school-children may identify with specific values, though fully integrating those values with other aspects of the self is likely to be in evidence only as they move through their teens and into young adulthood.

### The Differentiation of Motivation

Within SDT, the four types of extrinsic motivation (i.e., external, introjected, identified, and integrated) are ordered to reflect increasingly effective internalization and thus more autonomous behavior. Evidence from the United States, Canada, Japan, Russia, and other nations supports the notion that these four types of extrinsic motivation fall along a continuum of autonomy (Ryan & Deci, 2000). Because identified and integrated regulations provide the bases for relatively self-determined extrinsic motivation, they can be understood as approximating intrinsic motivation, which is invariantly autonomous. Nonetheless, it is important to distinguish between intrinsic motivation and autonomous extrinsic motivation because intrinsic motivation in based in finding an activity interesting, whereas well-internalized extrinsic motivation is based in finding an activity personally important for self-selected goals or purposes.

## Promoting Self-Determined Extrinsic Motivation

According to SDT, the type of motivation people manifest within a particular context depends on the satisfaction versus thwarting of the basic psychological needs within that context. To the extent that factors in the social environment support satisfaction of the needs for autonomy, competence, and relatedness, people will not only be more intrinsically motivated but will also be more effective in internalizing and integrating extrinsic motivation so as to be more volitional overall. In contrast, contexts that control, that do not offer optimal challenges, and/or that convey lack of acceptance and caring undermine intrinsic motivation and impair internalization, resulting in more controlled types of regulation or no motivation at all.

A need-supporting classroom allows students to participate in charting their own course of learning and to engage in active types of learning. It provides a context in which students can find optimal challenges and grapple meaningfully with responsibility so they will learn to be more self-governing. In such classrooms, students feel related to their teachers and to other students, for in these noncontrolling contexts students are able to interact in ways that provide a greater sense of competence and autonomy, as well as acceptance.

When teachers create an atmosphere in which all students are respected, the students will be more likely to identify with the goals and values that are manifest by the teachers.

Several studies have examined the relations between contextual factors, such as acknowledging students' perspectives and encouraging their self-initiation, and students' internalization and integration. For example, Grolnick and Ryan (1989) found that when parents were more responsive to their late-elementary-school children, hearing their concerns and offering them choice, the students displayed more fully internalized extrinsic motivation for doing school work. Reeve and Hamm (1999) discovered that when teachers motivated students by listening more, acknowledging quality performance, and being more responsive to the students, the students felt more competent and were more autonomous in their motivation.

Ryan, Stiller, and Lynch (1994) found that seventh through ninth grade students who felt secure and positively related to their teachers were more likely to turn to them for help and were more self-motivated in school than were students who did not feel connected to their teachers. This relatedness to teachers predicted school outcomes above and beyond the children's being securely related to their parents, indicating that both parents and teachers play an important role in children's motivation.

Other studies have experimentally manipulated factors believed to affect internalization and integration. For example, Deci, Eghrari, Patrick, and Leone (1994) did an experiment in which college students were asked to do a highly uninteresting activity. Three variables were manipulated: providing versus not providing a meaningful rationale; acknowledging versus not acknowledging students' feelings that the task is boring; and emphasizing choice versus emphasizing that the students *should* do the behavior. Results of the study showed that these three factors—providing a rationale, acknowledging the students' feelings, and emphasizing choice—all conduced toward greater internalization, as reflected in more task behavior during a subsequent period. Thus, by providing the supports that allow need satisfaction, people will be more likely to internalize the regulation of nonintrinsically motivated activities.

This experiment by Deci et al. revealed another interesting result, namely, in relatively controlling circumstances (i.e., without a rationale and with pressure to perform), not only did students show less internalization of regulations, but the internalization that did occur was only introjected, that is, taken in and used *to pressure themselves*. In contrast, under relatively supportive conditions, there was more internalization and that internalization tended to be integrated. In other words, subsequently, students in the supportive conditions continued to do the activity and felt free rather than controlled in doing so.

To summarize, when students feel support from parents and teachers for basic need satisfaction, the students are more likely to internalize the values and regulations endorsed by their parents and teachers. Feeling related to these significant adults, the children are more likely to turn to and emulate them, and as they feel encouraged to experiment and initiate they will be able to transform those emulations into identifications and become more autonomously motivated with respect to extrinsic, as well as intrinsic, motivation.

# MOTIVATION AND LEARNING OUTCOMES

Various studies have explored the relations between motivation and educational outcomes, examining how different types of motivation, rather than the overall amount of motivation, relate to students' performance and affect. As noted earlier, the outcomes we consider most important are both cognitive and affective, including deep or conceptual learning, creativity, and psychological well-being.

Some of the studies have focused on intrinsic motivation while others have investigated internalized extrinsic motivation. These studies have been of two types. In some, motivation has been assessed with questionnaires and related to outcomes. In the others, experimental conditions have been created that are known to promote different types of motivation and the outcomes of these different conditions have been compared.

## Intrinsic Motivation and Achievement

A few studies have compared student achievement in a condition that supports intrinsic motivation versus a condition that undermines it. For example, Benware and Deci (1984) asked college students to spend about 3 hours learning complex material about neurophysiology. Half the students were told they would be tested on their learning, and the other half were told they would have the opportunity to put their learning to active use by teaching the material to others. The first condition, of course, was expected to represent low intrinsic motivation, and the second, higher intrinsic motivation.

When students returned to the laboratory after studying the material, they were given a questionnaire asking how interesting and enjoyable they had found the material, and then they were all given an examination on the material even though only half of them had been expecting it. The exam was designed to test both rote and conceptual learning. Results showed that students who learned in order to be tested reported finding the material less intrinsically interesting than did the others. Further, those who expected to be tested actually gave worse answers on the conceptual questions than those who learned expecting to put the material to active use, although the two groups did not differ on the rote memorization questions. From this, we conclude, first, that when students are intrinsically motivated they learn better at the conceptual level and, second, that having students learn in order to be tested is detrimental to their being intrinsically motivated.

Grolnick and Ryan (1987) performed an experiment in which fifth graders read material either in a controlling condition, where they were told they would be tested and graded, or in a noncontrolling, autonomy-supportive condition, where they were told they would be asked questions about how interesting and difficult they found the material. Subsequently, all children were asked how interesting they found the material and all were tested on it. The results showed that the more autonomy supportive condition led to more interest in the material and better conceptual understanding than the controlling condition, thus complementing the Benware and Deci (1984) results. It seems that autonomy-support, relative to control, allowed intrinsic motivation to flourish, which resulted in greater depth of processing and better comprehension of the material. Results also indicated that the controlling condition yielded greater rote memorization than the autonomy-supportive condition, but the controlled group also evidenced greater deterioration of memorized material over the subsequent week, leaving the two conditions comparable in terms of rote learning, as had been the case in the Benware and Deci (1984) study.

Other studies have shown that controlling conditions diminish creativity and flexible problem solving, relative to conditions that allow more autonomy. For example, a set of studies summarized by Amabile (1996) showed that when students do artistic projects to get rewards, to win a competition, or to be evaluated—all conditions known to undermine intrinsic motivation—their projects were judged to be less creative than those of students who were not controlled in these ways. Similarly, McGraw and McCullers (1979) found that when students were rewarded for solving problems, they were more rigid in their thinking and problem solving than students who were not rewarded. A recent meta-analysis by Utman (1997) confirms this viewpoint. He examined the impact of more autonomous, compared with more controlled, motivations and found that, whereas both autonomous and controlled motivations can produce performance at simple, algorithmic tasks, more controlled motivations have detrimental effects on creative or complex performance outcomes.

To summarize, convincing evidence indicates that controlling events such as rewards, tests, and deadlines, as well as controlling interpersonal styles, not only decrease intrinsic motivation but also tend to diminish conceptual learning, creativity, and flexible problem solving, all of which are hallmarks of what we consider high-quality achievement.

## Extrinsic Motivation, Achievement, and Adjustment

Controlling conditions have also been found to impair internalization and integration, resulting in a poorer-quality achievement, thus further implying that supporting students' intrinsic need satisfaction rather than controlling their behavior is advantageous for academic performance. For example, Grolnick and Ryan (1987, 1989) found that late-elementary-aged children with more fully internalized extrinsic motivation for school displayed better conceptual learning, received higher grades, and did better on standardized tests than children with less internalized motivation. Miserandino (1996) further showed that, even removing the effects of prior achievement, students who had more autonomous motivation for school not only achieved better grades and test scores but also had more positive classroom experiences. They were more curious, less angry, and less bored.

In fact, numerous studies have found strong ties between autonomous motivation and affective experiences. For example, Ryan and Connell (1989) demonstrated that internalized forms of academic motivation were associated with high levels of interest and confidence and low levels of anxiety. Vallerand, Fortier, and Guay (1997) reported that autonomous, relative to controlled, motivation of high school students was positively related to their remaining in school. Sheldon and Kasser (1998) discovered that when students succeeded at autonomously pursued goals they evidenced enhanced well-being, but success at externally regulated or introjected goals did not enhance well-being. In complementary work, Goodenow (1993) showed that students who felt accepted, connected, and cared for in the classroom (these being conditions that facilitate internalization) not only had more positive attitudes and fewer behavior problems, but also displayed greater achievement than those who felt more detached or disconnected.

In sum, research has now confirmed that autonomous, relative to controlled, motivation is associated with enhanced engagement, learning, and creativity, as well as more positive adjustment and mental health, and further that the need-supporting conditions facilitative of autonomous motivation are also associated with these positive educational outcomes. Such studies make clear why it is so important for educators to think about promoting self-regulation rather than falling back on the more familiar and perhaps easier-to-use techniques that attempt to control students' behavior.

## WHAT LEADS TEACHERS TO CONTROL?

We have been continually pleased, as we have met with groups of teachers, to learn that the great majority of them believe that providing supports for students' psychological needs is an important part of their job. Yet, we have also been distressed during our classroom observations by the degree to which teachers resort to control, evaluation, and pressure as motivational strategies. This seeming discrepancy prompted us to consider the factors that might lead teachers to be controlling.

### Pressure Toward Outcomes

In various meetings with teachers we were struck by how frequently they returned to the issue of feeling pressured and controlled, by how much their own excitement for teaching has been sapped by the increasing demands and controls that have been placed on them. Although one might be inclined to write these comments off as run-of-the-mill gripes, it struck us that there was something very important to be gleaned from the comments. Just as students have needs for competence, autonomy, and relatedness, teachers also have these needs. And it occurred to us that, just as pressures and controls interfere with students' need satisfaction, making them less effective as students, pressures and controls would probably have comparable effects on teachers.

To examine this possibility, Deci, Spiegel, Ryan, Koestner, and Kauffman (1982) did a study in which participants taught a student how to solve puzzles. Half the instructors were told that it was their job to facilitate the student's learning, and the other half were told that it was their responsibility to make sure the student "performed up to high standards." The idea was that the emphasis on high standards would leave the teachers feeling pressured and that this might in turn lead them to be more controlling in their teaching style. Results indicated that, relative to instructors in the nonpressuring condition, instructors in the high-standards condition talked more, were more directive and evaluative, and told the students how to solve the problems rather than allowing them to experiment for themselves.

Thus, the study confirmed what we had expected, namely, by pressuring teachers, which much of the new emphasis on achievement seems to be doing, we may actually be working against what we would ultimately hope to accomplish. The pressure may indeed produce higher standardized test scores because the teachers will likely "teach to the tests." But the result will surely be teachers who are more controlling and less satisfied, and students who are less creative, less well adjusted, and less conceptually sophisticated.

## Pressure from Students

Other studies have suggested that pressure "from above" is not the only troubling force that teachers have to deal with. Students who are listless or rebellious create tension for teachers, which could easily push them to be controlling with these students. In fact, a study by Pelletier and Vallerand (1996) showed that when teachers believe that students were extrinsically motivated for school, they treated them in a more controlling fashion than when they believed the students were intrinsically motivated, even if the two types of students did not actually behave differently. Thus, there seems to be a tendency for teachers to be more controlling when students are less interested, and this tendency may be manifest if teachers *believe* the students are uninterested even if their behavior is no different from that of the other students.

Teachers who have been in the profession for many years report that they are encountering increasing numbers of students who have not been well-socialized, who are disinterested or reactive because they seem not to be getting the attention and support they need at home. This, of course, results in teachers needing to give them more attention, but that can be quite frustrating for the teachers when they have a room full of students to deal with. In fact, Grolnick and Ryan (1989) found that when parents were less involved with their children, teachers spent more time with those children, but the teacher attention was characterized primarily by surveillance, reprimands, constraints, and control. Such attention, rather than facilitating the students' internalization and self-regulation, would of course be likely to perpetuate the cycle of adult control and student alienation.

## What Can We Do?

Many educators are discouraged about the problems that exist in some of our schools, and there certainly is room for improvement. Nonetheless, we have been very encouraged by observing the ways some teachers interact with children—they are models of autonomy-supportive teachers—and we have found such teachers even in very disadvantaged areas. These teachers seem to provide the conditions for all their students to experience satisfaction of the needs for competence, autonomy, and relatedness. We have also encountered educational administrators who support teachers for working to provide autonomy-supportive classrooms. Such dedicated individuals give one hope.

Further, we have seen a few instances of educational reform efforts built around an understanding of what children need in order to learn and feel good about themselves and what teachers need in order to teach well and feel good about themselves. One such effort is the Child Development Project (CDP) which promotes changes intended to allow students to feel competent, related to others, and autonomous. Teachers become facilitators rather than directors, and students play an active role in making classroom decisions. Results from the first few years of CDP show better attendance, fewer behavior problems, and a greater sense of community (Lewis, Schaps, & Watson, 1995).

Another effort is First Things First (FTF), which focuses on reaching higher standards by facilitating changes that allow both teachers and students to satisfy their intrinsic needs (Connell, 1996). Included in FTF is a decrease in the student:teacher ratio during core instructional periods from about 30:1 to about 15:1. This has been done in various ways as decided by the personnel of each school, but among the ways have been to have other college-educated staff such as counselors and assistant principals spend part of each day in a classroom. FTF also involves an increase in the number of years the students spend with a teacher from just 1 to anywhere from 2 or 4 years. The supplemental teachers also stay with the same classes for multiple years. The idea is that teachers and students have to build meaningful relationships for both to be able feel more competent, autonomous, and related. And one of the interesting things that happens through this continuity of care is that teachers tend to develop relationships with family members as well as with the students. Another example is that FTF provides more enriched learning opportunities for students, which is accomplished through more active participation in projects, trips, and problem solving, again as decided by the teachers and school staff. With FTF, most of the changes are ones that must be done at the level of school or district rather than the level of individual teachers, but the use of more autonomy-supportive styles and more interesting learning activities can be implemented by individual teachers.

Furthermore, a study by Hennessey and Zbikowski (1993) indicated that there are ways to help immunize students against being undermined by rewards and controls. They used videotaped training techniques in which late-elementary-aged students talked about how important it is to them to do their school work for its own satisfaction rather than for rewards, and the researchers found that the students who watched the tape did not display the undermining effect when being rewarded for a subsequent activity. This study therefore emphasizes the importance of teachers' not emphasizing rewards and helping students keep focused on the activity itself.

The two reform efforts herein discussed, which are richer and more complex than we have conveyed, as well as the dedicated work of autonomy-supportive educators who emphasize learning rather than rewards, stand in sharp contrast to the so-called reforms that implement stronger controls on school districts, teachers, and students, imagining that these will lead to improved education and, in turn, to students who develop the competencies necessary to assume responsible and productive roles in society. The rhetoric accompanying such efforts is focused on achievement and is full of blame for teachers and administrators. It fails to consider what the teachers and educators, many of whom are very dedicated and hard working, might need to overcome obstacles associated, for example, with working in neighborhoods that are plagued by poverty. The approach instead assumes that high-stakes testing will force the teachers and educators to do better jobs, yet the existing evidence makes clear that this approach, which is prompting increased use of controls at all levels of education, is not only unlikely to produce the desired results, but indeed is actually working against the very goals that thoughtful educators or commentators would hope to attain. What that means, of course, is that, if people are genuinely interested in improved achievement, they will have to think differently about the problem, trying to understand what the real issues are. They will have to be willing to devote the resources necessary to implement the difficult changes that begin with the needs of the students and teachers, so that both will feel empowered and their natural tendencies to learn, develop, and be effective will flourish.

## CONCLUSION

People can be motivated in more controlled ways or more self-determined ways, with intrinsic motivation and well-integrated extrinsic motivation being the bases for self-determination. Evidence suggests that high-quality learning, creativity, and psychological adjustment are enhanced in contexts that provide autonomy support. By encouraging students' experimentation and self-initiation, teachers can foster students' willingness to take on challenges, explore new ideas, persist at difficult activities, and feel good about themselves. Indeed, it appears that the outcomes we all desire are most likely to accrue by focusing on the needs of individuals within the educational system. Yet, the renewed concern with achievement seems to be leading all too many people toward an approach that is based on controlling people's behavior rather than supporting the development of greater self-regulation.

In this chapter we have reviewed an array of evidence suggesting that intrinsic motivation and the internalization of extrinsic motivation flourish in situations of secure relationships that provide opportunities for need satisfaction. By offering optimal challenges, providing feedback that is not evaluative of the person, giving a meaningful rationale for requested behavior, acknowledging feelings, providing greater choice, and setting up cooperative learning opportunities, teachers can foster students' self-determination. Furthermore, by taking account of teachers' needs as well as students' needs, it is possible to begin implementing the types of widespread school reform that, although more difficult than simply emphasizing higher standards and using tougher tests, is nonetheless the most promising prospect we have for bringing about excellent education.

## Teachers' Questions and Answers

**Q:**   You say that tangible extrinsic rewards often undermine intrinsic motivation. Could you give me a list of the specific kind of rewards to avoid and the kind that are more acceptable?

**A:**   The issue is not so much what kind of rewards to avoid and what kind to use but rather is what ways to use them and what ways to avoid. In our theory, the term *informational* use of rewards is contrasted with controlling, and the evidence is clear that informational use of rewards is far more effective. It refers to using rewards to convey real information that can be put to meaningful use by the recipients. Informational rewards are not highly salient, nor intended to make a student do something. Instead, they are used as a personal communication with an individual student, expressing appreciation or conveying competence feedback in a way that is responsive to the student's frame of reference. Some teachers use rewards to make a public spectacle. They announce in front of the class who did best in arithmetic and who did best in history. That is controlling, and students do not feel good about it. Those who were singled out are usually embarrassed and the others feel like losers.

In a sense, the issue begins with you, with your intentions. Ask yourself, "Why am I using this reward? Is my intention to prod the students or change their behavior? Am I feeling pressured to improve the students' performance? In other words, am I trying to control them? Or am I doing what really feels right to me, relating personally to the students?"

Having said that the critical issue is "how" rewards are used rather than "what kind" of rewards are used, there is a bit to be said about what kind. Verbal rewards (i.e., positive performance feedback) are typically more informative and less detrimental than tangible rewards, although even they can be detrimental if used to control. And rewards that are naturally occurring consequences—that follow naturally or logically from behaviors—are more effective than the arbitrary ones most often used, in part because, with naturally occurring consequences, students are learning about real relations that exist in the world, about what is likely to happen when they choose to do certain things.

**Q:**     I agree that the use of very obvious rewards like gold stars and prizes for good performance can backfire. At the same time, as a teacher, I'm forced to set deadlines, give grades, and prepare my students for tests. Is there a way that I can reduce the negative impact of these practices on my students' self-regulation?

**A:**     Deadlines, tests, and grades are "givens" in schools, and they are not necessarily detrimental. Try to treat them simply as givens, taking a positive attitude about them, doing your best not to feel controlled by them and not to pressure your students with them. We realize that is asking a lot, because the most destructive element of deadlines, tests, and grades is the "high stakes" that are increasingly being attached to them. To the extent that they are intended to evaluate rather than inform, to control rather than encourage, they will be detrimental. The high-stakes use of deadlines, tests, and grades functions to make districts compete against each other, schools to compete against each other, and classrooms to compete against each other. The ultimate result, of course, is that they make students compete against each other, and we end up with winners and losers rather than with interested, educated students.

The important thing for you is to keep focused on the educational activities, on enriching learning opportunities, on making the material relevant to students' lives, on being responsive to students' interests, on encouraging students to try things out and initiate for themselves. Begin by asking yourself what might the student want or need in this situation, rather than what am I feeling pressured to do. That way, the tests will simply be one of the givens and will not dominate the day-to-day activities of the classroom. In a sense, your job is, in part, to shelter your students from the storm—to create an autonomy-supportive classroom climate despite the controls that are operating around you. The alternative (or complementary) approach is to become a political activist and work to influence policy.

**Q:**   I couldn't agree more that the pressure we are under to raise standards and test scores makes many of us more controlling of our students. I see this all the time. You seem to be arguing for eliminating or reducing the use of these tests, because, if I read you right, the kind of teaching practices that flow from this testing is pretty shallow and may be producing less able and interested students in the long run. Is this right? If so, how accepted a view is this in psychology and education and why is testing so unquestionably embraced by national decision makers.

**A:**   Yes, we are arguing for the elimination of high-stakes testing. On the other hand, well-formulated, informationally administered tests can serve an important educational function in the classroom. As far as how accepted this view is, there are really two issues that are contained within the question. The first concerns psychological research on the undermining of intrinsic motivation and internalization by extrinsic rewards and other controls. The second concerns the increasing use of high-stakes testing.

The phenomenon of undermining intrinsic motivation by controls has been somewhat controversial within psychology, but it does have fairly widespread acceptance. Some psychologists do not believe in the concepts of intrinsic motivation and a natural developmental tendency to internalize and integrate values and regulations. Naturally, if people do not believe in intrinsic motivation, they will not even consider whether something might undermine it. For such psychologists, what makes sense is controlling people's behavior with techniques such as reward contingencies. But there are far fewer psychologists who believe that than used to be the case.

As for high-stakes testing, it tends to be educational researchers rather than psychological researchers who are addressing this issue. Many educational researchers are very concerned about the increasing use of tests as a motivational strategy. In fact, the American Education Research Association, the most important association of educational researchers, has published a book that takes a stand against the use of these tests for motivating learning (Kellaghan, Madaus, & Raczek, 1996).

As to why national decision makers don't seem to question the tests, it is difficult to speak for other people, but several factors seem to be involved. First, most of the decision makers are not educators and they tend to know relatively little about child development and education. They are business people, lawyers, and politicians who think in different kinds of ways. Second, their focus is on outcomes, so they are trapped in the very paradox that we were attempting to explicate in this chapter. They do not think about processes, about how, for example, such a strong focus on outcomes can affect the processes though which people attempt to achieve the outcomes. Some of the decision makers say, "Go ahead, use whatever are the best methods to achieve these outcomes," without recognizing that their emphasis on the outcomes makes it very difficult for teachers to sustain use of the best methods for achieving those outcomes. The decision makers are inadvertently undermining the processes that stand the best change of yielding the outcomes they claim to be wanting.

Third, discipline, tests, and controls are concrete and easy to understand, so they appeal to a lot of people. It is more difficult to tell people how to be responsive to the psychological needs of students than it is to tell them how to implement reward programs. Good teachers understand intuitively what students need and are able to be responsive to these needs, but many people, including the decision makers, have a much harder time understanding. Interestingly, research shows that orderly classrooms in which teachers are instructing and students are listening are rated more positively by observers than ones in which students are working in groups, experimenting with different ways of doing things, and being active (Boggiano, Barrett, Weiher, McClelland, & Lusk, 1987). The irony, of course, is that the classrooms in which there is control and order are less effective in promoting conceptual understanding and psychological well-being than are those in which students are autonomously motivated and fully engaged.

Fourth, when many people think about classrooms, they are implicitly comparing ones with discipline, tests, and controls to ones in which there is chaos, unruliness, disrespect, and minimal learning. The "be tough" approach versus the "be soft" approach, so to speak. But they are failing to recognize the third approach, in which classrooms have interested students who eagerly experiment, congenial relationships among teachers and students, and engaged learning. So, part of the problem concerns the comparison group that is being used for the controlling methods; if people only see control versus chaos, they will prefer control. But that, of course, misses the point.

# References

Amabile, T. M. (1996). *Creativity in context.* New York: Westview Press.

Amabile, T. M., DeJong, W., & Lepper, M. R. (1976). Effects of externally imposed deadlines on subsequent intrinsic motivation. *Journal of Personality and Social Psychology, 34*, 92–98.

Benware, C., & Deci, E. L. (1984). Quality of learning with an active versus passive motivational set. *American Educational Research Journal, 21*, 755–765.

Black, A. E., & Deci, E. L. (2000). The effects of instructors' autonomy support and students' autonomous motivation on learning organic chemistry: A self-determination theory perspective. *Science Education, 84*, 740–756.

Boggiano, A. K., Barrett, M., Weiher, A. W., McClelland, G. H., & Lusk, C. M. (1987). Use of the maximal-operant principle to motivate children's intrinsic interest. *Journal of Personality and Social Psychology, 53*, 866–879.

Connell, J. P. (1996). *First things first: A framework for successful school-site reform.* Philadelphia: Institute for Research and Reform in Education.

Danner, F. W., & Lonky, E. (1981). A cognitive-developmental approach to the effects of rewards on intrinsic motivation. *Child Development, 52*, 1043–1052.

deCharms, R. (1968). *Personal causation: The internal affective determinants of behavior.* New York: Academic Press.

Deci, E. L. (1971). Effects of externally mediated rewards on intrinsic motivation. *Journal of Personality and Social Psychology, 18,* 105–115.

Deci, E. L. (1975). *Intrinsic motivation.* New York: Plenum.

Deci, E. L., & Cascio, W. F. (1972, April). *Changes in intrinsic motivation as a function of negative feedback and threats.* Paper presented at the meeting of the Eastern Psychological Association, Boston.

Deci, E. L., Eghrari, H., Patrick, B. C., & Leone, D. R. (1994). Facilitating internalization: The self-determination theory perspective. *Journal of Personality, 62,* 119–142.

Deci, E. L., Koestner, R., & Ryan, R. M. (1999). A meta-analytic review of experiments examining the effects of extrinsic rewards on intrinsic motivation. *Psychological Bulletin, 125,* 627–668.

Deci, E. L., & Ryan, R. M. (1985). *Intrinsic motivation and self-determination in human behavior.* New York: Plenum.

Deci, E. L., & Ryan, R. M. (1995). Human autonomy: The basis for true self-esteem. In M. Kernis (Ed.), *Efficacy, agency, and self-esteem* (pp. 31–49). New York: Plenum.

Deci, E. L., Schwartz, A. J., Sheinman, L., & Ryan, R. M. (1981). An instrument to assess adults' orientations toward control versus autonomy with children: Reflections on intrinsic motivation and perceived competence. *Journal of Educational Psychology, 73,* 642–650.

Deci, E. L., Spiegel, N. H., Ryan, R. M., Koestner, R., & Kauffman, M. (1982). The effects of performance standards on teaching styles: The behavior of controlling teachers. *Journal of Educational Psychology, 74,* 852–859.

Eisenberger, R., & Cameron, J. (1996). Detrimental effects of reward: Reality of myth? *American Psychologist, 51,* 1153–1166.

Fisher, C. D. (1978). The effects of personal control, competence, and extrinsic reward systems on intrinsic motivation. *Organizational Behavior and Human Performance, 21,* 273–288.

Goodenow, C. (1993). Classroom belonging among early adolescent students: Relationships to motivation and achievement. *Journal of Early Adolescence, 13,* 21–43.

Grolnick, W. S., & Ryan, R. M. (1987). Autonomy in children's learning: An experimental and individual difference investigation. *Journal of Personality and Social Psychology, 52,* 890–898.

Grolnick, W. S., & Ryan, R. M. (1989). Parent styles associated with children's self-regulation and competence in school. *Journal of Educational Psychology, 81,* 143–154.

Harackiewicz, J. M. (1979). The effects of reward contingency and performance feedback on intrinsic motivation. *Journal of Personality and Social Psychology, 37,* 1352–1363.

Harackiewicz, J., Manderlink, G., & Sansone, C. (1984). Rewarding pinball wizardry: The effects of evaluation on intrinsic interest. *Journal of Personality and Social Psychology, 47,* 287–300.

Harter, S. (1978). Pleasure derived from optimal challenge and the effects of extrinsic rewards on children's difficulty level choices. *Child Development, 49,* 788–799.

Hennessey, B. A., & Zbikowski, A. M. (1993). Immunizing children against the negative effects of reward: A further examination of intrinsic motivation training techniques. *Creativity Research Journal, 6,* 297–307.

Kast, A., & Connor, K. (1988). Sex and age differences in response to informational and controlling feedback. *Personality and Social Psychology Bulletin, 14,* 514–523.

Kellaghan, T., Madaus, G. F., & Raczek, A. (1996). *The use of external examinations to improve student motivation.* Washington, DC: American Educational Research Association.

Koestner, R., Ryan, R. M., Bernieri, F., & Holt, K. (1984). Setting limits on children's behavior: The differential effects of controlling versus informational styles on intrinsic motivation and creativity. *Journal of Personality, 52,* 233–248.

Kruglanski, A. W., Friedman, I., & Zeevi, G. (1971). The effects of extrinsic incentive on some qualitative aspects of task performance. *Journal of Personality, 39,* 606–617.

Lepper, M. R., Greene, D., & Nisbett, R. E. (1973). Undermining children's intrinsic interest with extrinsic rewards: A test of the "overjustification" hypothesis. *Journal of Personality and Social Psychology, 28,* 129–137.

Lewis, C. C., Schaps, E., & Watson, M. (1995). Beyond the pendulum: Creating challenging and caring schools. *Phi Delta Kappan, 76,* 547–554.

McGraw, K. O., & McCullers, J. C. (1979). Evidence of a detrimental effect of extrinsic incentives on breaking a mental set. *Journal of Experimental Social Psychology, 15,* 285–294.

Miserandino, M. (1996). Children who do well in school: Individual differences in perceived competence and autonomy in above-average children. *Journal of Educational Psychology, 88,* 203–214.

Mossholder, K. W. (1980). Effects of externally mediated goal setting on intrinsic motivation: A laboratory experiment. *Journal of Applied Psychology, 65,* 202–210.

Nicholls, J. G. (1984). Achievement motivation: Conceptions of ability, subjective experience, task choice, and performance. *Psychological Review, 91,* 328–346.

Pelletier, L. G., & Vallerand, R. J. (1996). Supervisors' beliefs and subordinates' intrinsic motivation: A behavioral confirmation analysis. *Journal of Personality and Social Psychology, 71,* 331–340.

Reeve, J., & Hamm, D. (1999). *Teachers as resources and obstacles to students' intrinsic motivation.* Unpublished manuscript, University of Iowa.

Ryan, R. M. (1982). Control and information in the intrapersonal sphere: An extension of cognitive evaluation theory. *Journal of Personality and Social Psychology, 43,* 450–461.

Ryan, R. M. (1995). Psychological needs and the facilitation of integrative processes. *Journal of Personality, 63,* 397–427.

Ryan, R. M., & Connell, J. P. (1989). Perceived locus of causality and internalization: Examining reasons for acting in two domains. *Journal of Personality and Social Psychology, 57,* 749–761.

Ryan, R. M., & Deci, E. L. (2000). Self-determination theory and the facilitation of intrinsic motivation, social development and well-being. *American Psychologist, 55,* 68–78.

Ryan, R. M., & Grolnick, W. S. (1986). Origins and pawns in the classroom: Self-report and projective assessments of individual differences in children's perceptions. *Journal of Personality and Social Psychology, 50,* 550–558.

Ryan, R. M., Koestner, R., & Deci, E. L. (1991). Ego-involved persistence: When free-choice behavior is not intrinsically motivated. *Motivation and Emotion, 15,* 185–205.

Ryan, R. M., & La Guardia, J. G. (1999). Achievement motivation within a pressured society: Intrinsic and extrinsic motivations to learn and the politics of school reform. In T. Urdan (Ed.) *Advances in motivation and achievement* (Vol. 11, pp. 45–85). Greenwich, CT: JAI Press.

Ryan, R. M., Mims, V., & Koestner, R. (1983). Relation of reward contingency and interpersonal context to intrinsic motivation: A review and test using cognitive evaluation theory. *Journal of Personality and Social Psychology, 45,* 736–750.

Ryan, R. M., Stiller, J., & Lynch, J. H. (1994). Representations of relationships to teachers, parents, and friends as predictors of academic motivation and self-esteem. *Journal of Early Adolescence, 14,* 226–249.

Sheldon, K. M., & Elliot, A. E. (1998). Not all personal goals are personal: Comparing autonomous and controlled reasons for goals as predictors of effort and attainment. *Personality and Social Psychology Bulletin, 24,* 546–557.

Sheldon, K. M., & Kasser, T. (1998). Pursuing personal goals: Skills enable progress but not all progress is beneficial. *Personality and Social Psychology Bulletin, 24,* 1319–1331.

Skinner, B. F. (1953). *Science and human behavior.* New York: Macmillan.

Smith, W. E. (1975). *The effect of anticipated vs. unanticipated social reward on subsequent intrinsic motivation.* Unpublished dissertation, Cornell University.

Utman, C. H. (1997). Performance effects of motivational state: A meta-analysis. *Personality and Social Psychology Review, 1,* 170–182.

Vallerand, R. J., Fortier, M. S., & Guay, F. (1997). Self-determination and persistence in a real-life setting: Toward a motivational model of high school dropout. *Journal of Personality and Social Psychology, 72,* 1161–1176.

Vallerand, R. J., & Reid, G. (1984). On the causal effects of perceived competence on intrinsic motivation: A test of cognitive evaluation theory. *Journal of Sport Psychology, 6,* 94–102.

White, R. W. (1959). Motivation reconsidered: The concept of competence. *Psychological Review, 66,* 297–333.

Zuckerman, M., Porac, J., Lathin, D., Smith, R., & Deci, E. L. (1978). On the importance of self-determination for intrinsically motivated behavior. *Personality and Social Psychology Bulletin, 4,* 443–446.

CHAPTER

5

# Improving the Academic Performance of College Students with Brief Attributional Interventions

TIMOTHY D. WILSON AND MICHELLE DAMIANI

*University of Virginia, Charlottesville, Virginia*

NICOLE SHELTON

*Princeton University, Princeton, New Jersey*

Two first-year college students, Sam and Sarah, receive Ds on their first calculus test. Sam is very upset and anxious about his performance and finds it difficult to concentrate. Sarah shrugs off her poor performance, buckles down, and studies harder for the next test. Why does one student respond to the poor grade with anxiety and helplessness, whereas the other redoubles her efforts? A key factor is how they explain their poor performance on the first test, namely, their attributions.

Attribution theory originated in the late 1950s and early 1960s with theorists such as Heider (1958), Schachter and Singer (1962), Jones and Davis (1965), Kelley (1967), and Bem (1972). These theorists advocated a phenomenological approach to the study of human behavior. To understand what people will do, they argued, we have to see the world through their eyes, specifically, how people explain the reasons for their own and others' behavior. In the case of

Address all correspondence to Dr. Timothy D. Wilson, Department of Psychology, Gilmer Hall, P. O. Box 400400, University of Virginia, Charlottesville, VA 22904–4400. Fax: (434) 982-4766. E-mail: tdw@virginia.edu.

*Improving Academic Achievement*
Copyright 2002, Elsevier Science (USA). All rights reserved.

the two college students, their reactions to getting a "D" are determined by their attributions about the causes of the poor grade. Note that there is little concern with the *actual* causes of the students' poor performance, such as how intelligent they are or how well prepared they were for the test. Consistent with a phenomenological approach, the focus is on how the students perceive the causes of their poor performance, because these attributions are believed to have important consequences that are independent of the actual causes.

The actual causes of behavior, of course, are not irrelevant. If Sam got a D because he was woefully unprepared for a college calculus class or untalented at math, then how he explains his poor performance will not matter very much. He is unlikely to do very well on the next test. In everyday life, however, people are often in situations in which they have the potential to succeed. Most people taking college courses have the ability to do well; if they did not, they would not have been admitted to college or advanced so far in their academic careers. Attribution theory assumes that within this range of abilities, the explanation people make for their performance is crucial.

As noted by Valins and Nisbett (1972) and Storms and McCaul (1976), many problems become worse the more people worry about them. Further, the degree to which people worry about a problem depends on how they explain its causes. Storms and McCaul (1976) refer to this as an exacerbation cycle, which operates like this: People behave dysfunctionally, such as doing poorly on a test, and make a pejorative attribution about the cause of the behavior, namely, an attribution that implies that they were to blame and that the problem is unlikely to get better. This pejorative attribution causes physiological arousal and anxiety. The arousal and anxiety, in turn, make it more difficult to perform the desired behavior, leading to even more pejorative attributions, further anxiety, and so on, round and round in a viscious cycle.

Sam, for example, might explain his D as due to the fact that he was an admission error who is clearly not intelligent enough to do well in college. The anxiety produced by this self-blame makes it difficult for him to study for the next test. He does poorly again, which serves to increase his self-blame and anxiety, which makes it even more difficult to study, and so on. Sarah, in contrast, explains her D as due to the fact that she did not study hard enough and that the professor purposefully gives a tough first test. She is not very anxious when she thinks about the next test and is able to study hard for it.

How might we help students who make pejorative attributions for their performance? One possibility would be to target the behavior that is causing their problems, namely, their poor academic performance. Perhaps some math tutoring is in order or a program to improve study skills. Another possibility is to target directly the anxiety that is contributing to the academic difficulties. Perhaps we could teach them relaxation strategies or prescribe drugs to alleviate the anxiety.

Although either of these approaches might work, research on attribution theory suggests a third approach. Rather than targeting people's behavior or anxiety, perhaps we could try to change their attributions from pejorative to nonpejorative ones. Doing so might succeed in breaking the exacerbation cycle: People avoid the self-blame that follows from a pejorative attribution, thereby avoiding further increases in anxiety and poor performance (and subsequent self-blame). This is the premise of "attribution therapy" (Ross, Rodin, & Zimbardo, 1969). In this chapter we review attempts to use attribution therapy to help college students improve their academic performance, beginning with a brief review of the history of attribution therapy.

## MISATTRIBUTION RESEARCH

Initial attempts at attribution therapy focused on people's explanations for their physiological arousal. These interventions were based on Schachter and Singer's (1962) two-factor theory of emotion, which argues that emotional experience is a joint function of arousal and an attribution about the cause of the arousal. The same physiological arousal can be attributed to a variety of sources, leading to quite different emotions. Schachter and Singer (1962), for example, demonstrated that people could be led to make quite different attributions about the cause of their arousal, which was actually due to an injection of epinephrine. Some participants attributed the arousal to the fact that they were angry at the experimenters (because another participant acted in an angry manner), whereas others attributed it to the fact that they were quite happy (because another participant acted in a happy-go-lucky manner). This study, and many others like it, demonstrated that the way in which people explain the causes of their internal arousal is influenced by their social environment (e.g., how other people are responding), which can have profound effects on their emotions and behavior.

These studies led to the insight that people experiencing arousal-based problems could be helped by changing their attributions about the cause of the arousal. Storms and Nisbett (1970), for example, reasoned that insomniacs have difficulty sleeping because they are physiologically aroused at bedtime. If people attribute this arousal to pejorative causes, they are caught in the exacerbation cycle described earlier. The dysfunctional behavior—the arousal and sleeplessness people experience when they are trying to sleep—is attributed to pejorative causes (e.g., "I'm a hopeless neurotic"), which produces additional anxiety and further sleep problems, leading to even more pejorative attributions, and so on.

In an attempt to break this cycle of self-blame, the researchers gave insomniacs a placebo to take at bedtime and manipulated the supposed side effects of the pill. Some participants were told that the pill would have arousing side effects such as an increased heart rate. Ironically, these participants reported getting to sleep more quickly than people who were told that the pill had no side effects. Storms and Nisbett (1970) argued that telling people that the pill had arousing effects provided the insomniacs with a nonpejorative explanation for the arousal they typically experienced at bedtime, reducing their self-blame and subsequent anxiety. The exacerbation cycle was broken, allowing participants to get to sleep more quickly.

Although promising, there are some problems with applying misattribution techniques to achievement contexts. First, although the original findings have been replicated by some (e.g., Storms, Denney, McCaul, & Lowery, 1979), other researchers have failed to replicate them (e.g., Kellogg & Baron, 1975; for a review, see Ross & Olson, 1981). Second, this type of intervention is not easy to administer on a large scale. To help college students who are experiencing academic difficulties, for example, it would not be feasible to hand out placebos and tell people that they would have arousing side effects. Finally, misattribution manipulations are limited to dysfunctional behaviors that are accompanied by physiological arousal, such as insomnia. Although students who are getting low grades probably become aroused at times, such as when taking a test, it might be more feasible to target their attributions about their poor academic performance.

## REATTRIBUTION INTERVENTIONS

Reattribution is a technique that attempts to change people's explanations about the dysfunctional behavior itself, regardless of whether that behavior is accompanied by physiological arousal. For example, to help students who get poor grades in their first year of college, we would attempt to change their attributions for their poor academic performance from pejorative (e.g., low intelligence) to nonpejorative (e.g., the difficulty of the transition from high school to college) causes.

Interestingly, the reattribution approach arose from a confluence of different research traditions. As already mentioned, one tradition was research on attribution theory (e.g., Kelley, 1967), which led to early attempts to change people's attributions from pejorative to nonpejorative causes, with mixed success (e.g., Nisbett, Borgida, Crandall, & Reed, 1976). Reattribution interventions can be traced to four other theoretical roots.

### Weiner's Attribution Theory

Bernard Weiner (1986; Weiner, Frieze, Kukla, Reed, Rest, & Rosenbaum, 1972) was among the first to extend attribution theory to the domain of academic achievement. Whereas early attribution theories had focused on the internal–external dimension of causality (whether people attribute an event to themselves or to something external to themselves), Weiner stressed the importance of additional, independent dimensions, notably stability (whether people see the causes as stable and unchangeable or unstable and changeable). Weiner argued that the stability dimension is most related to expectations about future performance and thus is a promising target of interventions. He hypothesized that changing people's attributions for poor performance to an unstable cause, such as low effort (internal, unstable) or bad luck (external, unstable), would raise their expectations about their future performance. Weiner's work spawned attribution retraining studies that focused on the stability dimension, usually with the attempt to convince people that their poor performance was due to low effort. Many of these studies have been successful, by showing that getting people to attribute failures to low effort led to increased effort and improved performance in the future (e.g., Anderson, 1983; Andrews & Debus, 1978).

## Learned Helplessness Theory

Concurrent with initial research on attribution theory, Martin Seligman and his colleagues were developing their theory of learned helplessness in animals (Overmeier & Seligman, 1967; Seligman & Maier, 1967). The emphasis of the theory was on the debilitating effects of a lack of control over negative outcomes. For example, dogs who experienced uncontrollable negative events (e.g., electric shocks) showed more deficits in learning than dogs who received the same shocks but could control their termination. In 1978, Abramson, Seligman, and Teasdale reformulated learned helplessness theory in terms of attributional principles, arguing that the key to understanding humans' reactions to negative events is the way they explain the causes of these events. Reformulated helplessness theory focused on three independent dimensions of causality: internality (whether people see the causes as internal or external to themselves); stability (whether people see the causes as stable and unchangeable or unstable and changeable); and globality (whether people see the causes as applying to one specific situation or as applying to many situations). People who attribute negative events to internal, stable, global causes will experience learned helplessness, which is characterized by depression, lower effort, and difficulty in learning.

Learned helplessness theory has focused mostly on individual differences in patterns of attributions and how these differences are correlated with problems such as depression and health. In a further revision of the theory, for example, Abramson, Metalsky, and Alloy (1989) argued that people who attribute negative life events to stable, global causes are particularly likely to experience a type of depression termed hopelessness. Perhaps due to its emphasis on individual differences in personality, the learned helplessness approach has not generated many interventions that attempt to change people's attributions. The predictions of the theory, however, are quite compatible with the other approaches reviewed here: People experiencing academic difficulties are better off attributing them to external, unstable, specific causes than internal, stable, global ones.

## Dweck's Model of Self-Theories

Drawing on the work of Weiner and learned helplessness theorists, Carol Dweck (1975) was one of the first to show that encouraging people to attribute poor performance to unstable causes (e.g., low effort) improves subsequent effort and performance. She subsequently developed a model that emphasizes people's theories about their own intelligence. People who view their intelligence as a fixed, unchangeable trait (an entity theory) are hypothesized to react to failure very differently than people who view their intelligence as a malleable, changeable skill (an incremental theory). Of most relevance here is how people with these different theories react to failure on a task. Those with an entity theory, Dweck reasoned, are more likely to give up, assuming that they must not have the ability required for the task. Those with an incremental theory are more likely to try harder in the future, assuming they need only increase their efforts to acquire the skills necessary to do well. In a series of fascinating experiments, Dweck and her colleagues have shown that children with incremental theories choose more challenging tasks to perform, persist more in the face of failure, and perform better academically (for a review see Dweck, 1999, and Chapter 3 in this volume).

Dweck's work is firmly rooted in attribution theory. People with an entity theory of intelligence are likely to attribute academic failure to an internal, stable cause (low intelligence that will not change), whereas people with an incremental theory are likely to attribute academic failure to an external, unstable cause (the fact that they have not yet acquired the necessary skills, but can with increased effort). Because these patterns of attribution are rooted in people's self-theories about intelligence, Dweck (1999) argues that the best way to change attributions is to target these theories, rather than specific attributions.

## Self-Efficacy Theory

In contrast, Albert Bandura's (1997) self-efficacy theory points to the importance of people's beliefs about the likelihood that they can perform desired behaviors. The greater people's sense of self-efficacy in a given domain, the more effort they will exert and the more successful they are likely to be. Self-efficacy beliefs are related to attributions, because people who attribute successes to internal, stable factors (e.g., ability) will experience greater self-efficacy than people who attribute their successes to external, unstable factors (e.g., luck). Bandura argues that self-efficacy is a broader, more important concept than attributions, and that in fact the effects of attributional interventions are mediated by changes in self-efficacy. We will return to the issue of what mediates the effects of attributional interventions; for now, we point out that self-efficacy theory, like the other approaches we have reviewed, argues that changing people's attributions for the causes of their behavior can have beneficial effects on future performance.

## IMPROVING THE ACADEMIC PERFORMANCE OF COLLEGE STUDENTS

To summarize, a number of theoretical approaches converge on the same intervention strategy: To help people behaving dysfunctionally, it is helpful to try to change their attributions from pejorative to nonpejorative explanations of their behavior. Although a number of attributional dimensions have been targeted, such as internality, the one that has been addressed the most is the stability dimension, whereby people are encouraged to reattribute their poor performance from stable to unstable causes. By the early 1980s a number of successful interventions had been performed, notably Dweck's work with academic performance in children.

These studies inspired Wilson and Linville (1982, 1985) to try an attributional intervention with college students. They reasoned that students in the first year of college might be especially susceptible to the exacerbation cycle discussed earlier. Academic setbacks are common in the first year of college, as they are in any transition from one level of schooling to the next. Students must deal with more challenging courses, a new social environment, and (for many) life away from home for the first time. The way in which students explain these setbacks is crucial, Wilson and Linville reasoned. Those who make pejorative attributions, blaming their academic difficulties on internal, stable factors, are likely to experience anxiety, lowered effort, and difficulty in learning new material, just as the theories we have reviewed would predict. They might well become caught in a spiral of increasing self-blame, anxiety, and poor performance.

If so, first-year college students might be helped by an intervention that encouraged them to attribute any academic problems they were having to temporary factors. One of way of accomplishing this, Wilson and Linville reasoned, would be to convey the simple message that many beginning college students experience academic difficulties, but that these difficulties tend to improve after the first year. The knowledge that their initial academic problems are not unusual, and are likely to improve over time, might be enough to change people's attributions from pejorative to nonpejorative causes, thereby alleviating anxiety and improving performance.

To find out, Wilson and Linville (1982) targeted first year college students who were especially likely to be caught in the exacerbation cycle. Specifically, they selected students who were worried about their academic performance, felt that they had not done as well as they could have in their first semester courses (and, in fact, did not have extremely high GPAs), and felt that they were intellectually inferior to their classmates. Ostensibly as part of a survey about the college experience, the participants were randomly assigned to a treatment or control condition. In the treatment condition, the students read actual statistics documenting that many students improve their grades after their first year of college. To make this information more concrete, the students also watched videotaped interviews of four upperclass students discussing their college experiences and personal backgrounds. The interviewees reported their grade point average for their first semester of college, second semester of college, and the semester they had just completed. In all four cases, it was clear that the students' grades improved over time. These interviews were intended to convey the following message: "The academic problems you are experiencing are not your fault; they are caused by temporary roadblocks and you will do better in the future." Participants in the control condition did not receive the statistics or view the videotapes.

The effects of this simple intervention were dramatic. Compared with the control condition, students in the treatment condition improved their grades in the following year and were more likely to remain in college. Wilson and Linville (1982) concluded that it may be possible to interrupt the exacerbation cycle, with considerable benefit, with a simple, one-time intervention. These dramatic, counterintuitive results cried out for a replication. Wilson and Linville thus conducted two more studies, with some minor procedural changes (see Wilson & Linville, 1985). When the results of the three experiments were combined, the effects of the attributional manipulation on grade improvement remained significant, though the effects were larger for males than females. The difference in grade improvement for males in the treatment versus control conditions was 0.41 GPA point (on a 4-point scale in which 4 = A, 3 = B, etc.). The difference in grade improvement for females in the treatment versus control conditions was a more modest 0.13 GPA point.

Since the publication of Wilson and Linville's studies a number of other investigators have used similar attributional interventions with college students. Table 1 summarizes the results of all known experimental studies that used attributional interventions to try to improve the academic performance of college students and randomly assigned participants to an intervention or control condition. As can be seen in this table, there have been many successful replications of Wilson and Linville's results. Each of the studies found that a one-time attributional manipulation improved academic performance relative to a randomly assigned control group. Sometimes the dependent measure was a single, multiple-choice test administered in a laboratory setting (e.g., Perry & Penner, 1990); sometimes it was an exam in an actual course (e.g., Noel, Forsyth, & Kelley, 1987; Van Overwalle & De Metsenaere, 1990). Often it was people's overall grade point average in the semester after the intervention (e.g., Aronson, Fried, & Good, in press; Jesse & Gregory, 1986/1987; Nelum-Hart, Schooler, Wilson, & Meyers, 1999; Van Overwalle, Segebarth, & Goldchstein, 1989; Wilson & Linville, 1985).

The consistency of the results summarized in Table 1 is striking. On a variety of dependent measures, one-time attributional interventions have been quite successful in improving college students' academic performance. Table 1 also illustrates, however, that a number of questions remain unanswered.

**TABLE 1**

**Summary of Attributional Retraining Studies Targeting Academic Performance in College Students**

| Study | Participants[a] | Manipulation | Results[b] | Moderators |
|---|---|---|---|---|
| Wilson and Linville (1982, 1985)[c] | Introductory psychology students with below-average grades and high worry about academic performance | Videotaped interview of upperclass students reporting that their grades increased after the first year, statistics indicating that grades increase after the first year | Improved grades the semester after the study; improved test performance (sample GRE[d] items); trend toward increased likelihood of staying in college | Results stronger for males than females |
| Jesse and Gregory (1986/1987) | Introductory psychology students | (a) GPA information: Same as video and statistics of Wilson and Linville (1982), crossed with (b) case histories of two students illustrating benefits of attributing bad performance to unstable, controllable factors | Replicated Wilson and Linville (1982); participants in GPA information condition improved grades next semester more than controls | People who received both the GPA information and the case histories did not improve their grades; people who received only the GPA information did |
| Noel et al. (1987) | Introductory psychology students who had received grade of D or F on first two tests | Videotaped interview of upperclass students reporting that their grades improved; internal, controllable causes of poor performance stressed (e.g., effort) | Better performance on next two tests and final exam | None |
| Van Overwalle et al. (1989) | First-year college students failing an economics course | Videotaped interview of students reporting causes of their poor performance in first year; unstable, controllable causes stressed | Better performance on next exam and higher grade point average at end of year | None |

*continues*

*continued*

| Study | Participants[a] | Manipulation | Results[b] | Moderators |
|---|---|---|---|---|
| Van Overwalle and De Metsenaere (1990, Study 1) | First-year college students in an economics course | Videotaped interview of students reporting causes of their poor performance in first year; unstable, controllable causes stressed | Better performance on final exam | None |
| Van Overwalle and De Metsenaere (1990, Study 2) | First-year law students | Videotaped interview of students reporting causes of their poor performance in first year; unstable, controllable causes of poor performance stressed | Better performance on final exam | Results stronger for students who had moderate grades on midterm (as opposed to low or high grades) |
| Perry and Penner (1990) | Introductory psychology students with a GPA above 2.10 | Videotaped interview of professor describing his first year in college: unstable causes of poor performance and stable, internal causes of good performance stressed | Better performance on multiple-choice tests | Manipulation worked only with students who initially attributed failures to low ability |
| Menec, Perry, Struthers, Schonwetter, Hechter, and Eicholz (1994, Study 1) | Introductory psychology students | Videotaped interview of graduate student emphasizing unstable, internal causes of poor performance (low effort, ineffective strategies) | Better performance on multiple-choice tests | Manipulation worked only with students who had (a) performed poorly on an initial test and (b) received an effective lecture on the test material |

| Study | Participants | Manipulation | Measure | Results |
|---|---|---|---|---|
| Menec et al. (1994, Study 2) | Introductory psychology students who performed poorly on an initial test | Videotaped interview of upperclass students emphasizing unstable, internal causes of poor performance (low effort, ineffective strategies) | Better performance on multiple-choice tests | Manipulation *decreased* performance for students who received an ineffective lecture; manipulation *increased* performance for students who (a) received an effective lecture and (b) had an external locus of control |
| Nelum-Hart et al. (1999) | African-American and white introductory psychology and summer orientation students | Videotaped interviews of African-American and white upperclass students who had improved their GPA; unstable causes of poor performance stressed | Improvement in grades in the following semester | Significant interaction between attributional retraining, race, and level of dispositional worry; the manipulation worked the best for high-worrying African-Americans; there was a nonsignificant tendency for low-worrying African-Americans to do worse in the attributional retraining condition |
| Aronson, Fried and Good (in press) | African-American and white undergraduates | Students wrote letters to middle school students emphasizing the malleability of intelligence (emphasis on internal, unstable causes of poor performance) | Improvement in grades in the following quarter | Effects of treatment slightly larger for African-Americans, but not significantly so |

[a] Unless otherwise noted, no selection criteria were used to select participants.

[b] Unless otherwise noted, all results reported below were significant at $p < 0.05$, when the attributional retraining group was compared with a control condition.

[c] Results are averaged over three studies.

[d] GPA, grade point average; GRE, Graduate Record Exam.

# Who Benefits the Most from
# Attributional Interventions?

In one sense, the studies summarized in Table 1 illustrate that the effects are quite general. Wilson and Linville's (1985) finding that males benefitted more than females appears to have been spurious, as no other study has reported a similar gender difference. Further, there has been some diversity in the samples used, including students of different races, from different countries, in different kinds of courses, and no systematic differences between these groups has been found.

The last column of Table 1, however, highlights some unanswered questions about the type of person who is likely to benefit the most from the attributional intervention. Several studies found that the intervention worked better under some conditions or for certain types of people. For example, one study worked only with participants who initially attributed their poor performance to low ability (Perry & Penner, 1990), whereas another found that initial attributions to low ability did not moderate the results (Van Overwalle et al., 1989). One study found that the intervention worked best with students who had low grades (Menec et al., 1994, Study 1), whereas another found that it worked best with students who had moderate grades (as opposed to low or high) (Van Overwalle & De Metsenaere, 1990, Study 2).

There are two results that are particularly notable, because each suggested that the attributional manipulation *decreased* academic performance in a particular condition or in a particular type of person. After administering an attributional intervention, Menec et al. (1994) showed students a videotaped lecture on a topic relevant to their psychology course. They manipulated the effectiveness of the professor who gave the lecture; in one condition he was highly engaging and expressive, whereas in the other he was inexpressive and humorless. The main dependent measure was people's performance on a multiple-choice test, administered 1 week later, that was based on material in the videotaped lecture. In two studies, the attributional intervention improved test performance only among students who saw the effective lecture. This supported the researchers' hypothesis that the attributional intervention would cause people to try harder to learn the material, but that this would pay off only when they had received effective instruction. In one study, however, the attributional intervention led to a significant *decrease* in test performance among people who saw the ineffective lecture.

Our best guess is that this result was spurious, because in Menec and colleagues' (1994) other study, the attributional manipulation had no significant effect on people who saw the ineffective lecture. Nonetheless, the interaction between attributional interventions and the quality of instruction students receive is worthy of further attention.

Nelum-Hart et al. (1999) examined the extent to which attributional manipulations of the type used by Wilson and Linville (1982) generalized to African

American students. (There were a few African American students in earlier studies, but not enough to examine race differences reliably.) All students saw videotaped interviews of four, upperclass students who reported that their grades had improved since their first year of college and gave specific, unstable reasons for their initial poor performance. Two of the students in the videos were African-American and two were white. Overall, the intervention led to an improvement in GPA in both African-American and white students.

A closer look at the data, however, reveals some interesting differences. Nelum-Hart et al. (1999) included a measure of dispositional worry, in which people rated how much various statements described them, such as "I am a worrier, I worry about everything and anything" and "I wish I didn't worry so much about everything." The sample was divided into four groups: high-worrying African Americans, low-worrying African-Americans, high-worrying whites, and low-worrying whites. As it happened, the attributional manipulation led to improved grades in three of these four groups, all but the low-worrying African-Americans. Unexpectedly, in this latter group, the attributional manipulation led to somewhat lower performance. That is, low-worrying African-Americans who received the attributional manipulation actually had a somewhat lower GPA than low-worrying African-Americans in the control condition.

We should note that the sample sizes were quite low when broken down by the worry variable; for example, there were only six African-Americans in each of the four conditions of the study. Further, the drop in grades among low-worrying African-Americans, when considered by itself, was not statistically reliable. Thus, we cannot say for certain whether the attributional manipulation leads to a reliable drop in performance in this group or simply has no effect. The difference between this group and the other three was striking, however, and further studies should explore why the attributional manipulation did not help low-worrying African-Americans as much as the others.

A hint comes from the fact that the low-worrying African-Americans in the control condition got better grades than other participants in the control condition. The other three control groups—high-worrying African-Americans, low-worrying whites, and high-worrying whites—all showed a drop in grade point average the semester after the study was conducted. In contrast, low-worrying African-Americans' performance in the control condition did not change. Perhaps low-worrying African-Americans had some protective mechanism that allowed them to avoid the exacerbation cycle. Whatever this mechanism was, the attributional retraining manipulation may have short-circuited it, as evidenced by the lower performance of low-worrying African-Americans in the treatment condition.

To summarize, there is a remarkable consistency of results across the studies summarized in Table 1; college students of various backgrounds, selected using different criteria, have benefitted from attributional retraining interventions. Nonetheless, we should not overlook the hint of negative effects in two of the studies. Although the extent to which these negative effects are real or spurious is unclear, they are worthy of further attention.

## Evidence for Mediators of Attributional Retraining Effects

Although the various theoretical approaches reviewed earlier all argue that attributional interventions can benefit college students, they disagree on exactly what mediates the effects. Weiner (1986) has argued that the key is to get people to attribute past failures to unstable causes, so that they expect to do better in the future. Dweck (1999) suggests that the key is to change people's self-theories about intelligence, whereas Bandura (1997) argues that the key is to change people's self-efficacy. The exacerbation cycle we have described suggests that a reduction in anxiety produced by pejorative attributions is crucial. These distinctions are important, because with a clearer picture of exactly what mediates the effects of attributional interventions (e.g., changes in attributions of stability or changes in theories of intelligence), these interventions can be further refined and improved.

Few studies include more than one or two measures of the potential mediators of the effects, making it difficult to assess exactly what is responsible for the improvements in academic performance that have been observed. Further, whereas some studies find the predicted changes in these mediators, others have not. Aronson, Fried, and Good (in press), for example, found that their intervention increased the extent to which students believed intelligence was malleable, supporting Dweck's (1999) theory that changes in these self-theories lead to improvement in performance. Evidence for another possible mediator, that attributional interventions would increase people's expectations that their performance would improve, which would lead to increased effort and actual improvements, has been inconsistent (Wilson & Linville, 1985, found no such evidence for the mediation of expectations, whereas Menec et al., 1994, did.) Further, direct measures of the attributions that the interventions are designed to change have yielded inconsistent results (Perry, Hechter, Menec, & Weinberg, 1993). One complicating factor is that it is not clear that people have access to or can easily report the attributions that mediate their behavior (Nisbett & Wilson, 1977). Thus, our enthusiasm over the success of attributional retraining manipulations should be tempered by the lack of evidence to date about precisely what mediates the effect.

## RECOMMENDATIONS FOR EDUCATORS

As illustrated by our discussion of mediators and potential negative effects, academic psychologists are fond of equivocation. We like to focus on the ''ifs, ands, and buts,'' because exploring the nuances and subtleties of the findings often reveals quite a bit about the conceptual underpinnings of the findings. We recognize, however, that such equivocation can be frustrating for practitioners who need to know what to do now, not in 10 years after some of the theoretical issues have been resolved. The stakes are high, as there are many students at risk of being caught in the exacerbation cycle. In this section we make some specific recommendations for how attributional retraining techniques might be used to help students adjust to college and perform up to their capabilities.

The good news is that a relatively simple, inexpensive, easy-to-implement intervention has been shown to work. Most programs that have been designed to help college students improve their academic performance are expensive, time-consuming, and labor-intensive, such as study skills courses that involve multiple sessions. Whereas such programs might be quite helpful, the research reviewed here suggests that a one-time intervention can have nontrivial effects on students' academic performance, such as the improvement in grade point average of 0.30 to 0.40 points observed by Wilson and Linville (1982) and Nelum-Hart et al. (1999).

The attributional retraining interventions used in these studies could be easily adopted as part of orientation programs for incoming college students or, for that matter, any student experiencing a transition from one level of education to another. Most of the interventions have this in common: students watch videotaped interviews of upperclass students who mention that whereas their grades were low their first year, they improved thereafter. In many of the studies, the students offer specific reasons for their improved performance, emphasizing unstable, controllable reasons for their initial difficulties, such as adjustment to a new environment and learning how to select college courses. It would be relatively easy to make such a videotape (tailoring it to the specific setting, using actual students) and show it at orientation sessions. College advisers, counselors, and professors could convey the same message, or even be supplied with copies of the retraining video to show individual students. In their day-to-day communications with students, teachers could also convey the idea that many students have struggles that can be overcome with perseverance. This would be similar to Lepper and Woolverton's (see Chapter 8 in this volume) approach to expert tutoring; they have found that stressing the difficulty of the material has protective and motivating effects on students. There is good reason to believe that inexpensive, simple approaches such as these will be beneficial.

## Interventions and Experiments

As we write these words, however, the academic researcher part of us is like a little voice in the back of our minds. "What if the hints of negative effects of this intervention are real," this voice says, "such that the videotapes have harmful effects on some subgroups, such as low-worrying African Americans?" And,

"All of the studies have been conducted with students who have begun college and have probably already experienced some academic setbacks. Would the intervention work at an orientation with students who are about to begin college with high hopes and have not yet experienced any setbacks? Maybe the message that the first year will be difficult is too discouraging at that point and is best delivered midway through the first year of college." For example, Jesse and Gregory (1986/1987) intervened in the second week of students' first semester of college. Contrary to Wilson and Linville's (1985) studies, the intervention had negative short-term effects; people who got the intervention did significantly worse on sample items from the Graduate Record Exam. However, these students improved their grades more in the long run than did people in the control condition. Finally, would the intervention work with younger students, such as those beginning middle school or high school? Clearly, we need to know more about such issues as the optimal timing of the intervention.

Though some educators and administrators may want to wait until these questions are answered before implementing the attributional retraining intervention, we have a different suggestion: Be a science-practitioner. Rather than simply making the training video and showing it at a first-year orientation, turn the intervention into an experiment in which some people see the video and a randomly assigned control group does not. Track the performance of both groups to see whether the intervention was successful and whether it was more successful for some types of students than others.

We can think of at least two objections to this suggestion. First, is it ethical to "withhold" the intervention from a control group when there is such good evidence that the intervention is beneficial? We believe it is, given the uncertainty over how the intervention works and which types of students will benefit from it the most. An analogy to drug testing in medical research is apt. Suppose that a new drug was found to alleviate migraine headaches, and yet there was uncertainty about whether it helped all subgroups of people (e.g., males versus females, young versus old). The only way to tell is to continue to test the drug experimentally, in which some people are randomly assigned to get the drug and others are randomly assigned to get a placebo. Once it is clear that the drug is beneficial with few side effects, for most people, the trials are ended and the drug is distributed widely.

We believe that the current status of attributional retraining interventions with college students is analogous to a drug that is in the early stages of testing. The initial results look quite promising, but there are many unanswered questions. Before we can recommend widespread prescriptions, further experimental trials are needed. Rather than waiting for research psychologists to perform these trials, we suggest that college administrators and educators conduct the experiments themselves.

The second objection is whether college administrators and educators have the skills necessary to conduct experimental investigations of attributional retraining interventions. Conducting well-designed, tightly controlled experiments in field settings is not a trivial undertaking; nor would it be easy for nonprofessionals to analyze the results statistically (see Aronson, Wilson, & Brewer, 1998, for an in-depth discussion of methodological issues in experimentation). As experiments go, however, the type we are proposing is not very complicated, essentially involving random assignment to two groups: one that gets the intervention and one that does not. In other words, the intervention would be the same as what would be done otherwise, except for the inclusion of a control group. Further, an advantage of being at a college or university is the proximity of people who are well-versed in methodology and statistics. A professor or graduate student in psychology or education might be interested in helping administrators design and analyze such an experiment.

The payoff of this approach could be quite large. The number of experiments of the type described in Table 1 would quickly multiply, providing answers to the thorny questions of who is most helped by attributional retraining interventions, the optimal timing of the intervention, and so on. The intervention could be fine-tuned to work best in specific locales with specific populations. It might well be, for example, that the intervention best suited for older students at a community college is different from the one best suited for younger students at a large state university or students in high school. The only way to answer these questions is to find out which types of interventions are most effective, and the only way to find that out is to conduct experiments in which the intervention group is compared with a control group.

Science can be an agonizingly slow process, as evidenced by the fact that there have been about 10 experiments on attributional retraining with college students published in the years since Wilson and Linville's (1982) study appeared in the literature. Although our suggestion for educators and administrators to conduct experiments might seem naive or unrealistic, we believe that such a joining of forces would lead to considerable practical and conceptual advances. What is now a simple, promising technique to help college students experiencing academic difficulties might well evolve into a set of seasoned, well-tested interventions tailored for specific populations.

### Teachers' Questions and Answers

**Q:**  What do you suppose happens when a student has an inappropriate or unrealistic view of his or her efficacy? For example, the student who believes she or he can conquer a reading assignment, but actually does not have the skills for that reading level?

**A:**  Good question. As we say in the chapter, convincing a person who does not have the ability to perform a task that his or her difficulties are caused by external, unstable factors is unlikely to help. In fact, we may be doing such people a disservice, by causing them to persist longer at a task they are bound to fail. The assumption many researchers make is that at the college level virtually all the students have the ability to do the work; thus there are unlikely to be many people who truly do not have academic ability and will be harmed by an attributional intervention. This is borne out by the fact that on average, attributional interventions have proved to be beneficial. It would be desirable, of course, to identify in advance those students who are likely to respond well to the interventions and those who will not. Several efforts have been made in this direction, as noted in the chapter, but clearly this is an area in which much more work is needed.

**Q:** From a practical perspective, is there anything to be gained by refreshing the intervention, with either more of the same or perhaps by related teacher prompts that serve as reminders? Do we have any indication of how long these effects last?

**A:** This is another open question. We do know that one-shot interventions can have remarkably long-lasting effects, as in the original Wilson and Linville (1982) study, in which students in the treatment condition achieved better grades and were less likely to drop out of college in the following year. One-time interventions might be enough to break the exacerbation cycle, in which people's worries about themselves and their performance make it difficult to study, leading to more worry, more academic setbacks, and so on. Once this cycle is broken people can in a sense "refresh" the intervention themselves, by reminding themselves that any academic problems might be caused by non-pejorative factors, thereby reducing their anxiety and making it easier to study. Surely, however, some people require a larger "dose" of the intervention than others and are likely to respond to repeated reminders. The danger is that if teachers are constantly reminding students of all the reasons why they could be doing better, the students might feel labeled as underachievers. It would be best to reinforce the intervention at the group level, reminding all students that people often blame themselves inappropriately for academic setbacks.

**Q:** Is part of the power of the intervention the fact that the student sees "people like me" (same general age, at the same university, etc.) or might it be even more powerful to have a high status person, like a professor, talk about her or his obstacles and struggles as a youth and how she or he eventually overcame them?

**A:** In our research, we have assumed that people are most likely to personalize the information if they see people similar to themselves making nonpejorative attributions for academic setbacks. That is why in the Nelum-Hart et al. (1999) study, for example, we had white and African-American students watch videotaped interviews with white and African-American people taking about their academic problems and why they occurred. But we are unaware of any study that has looked at this systematically. It might be that attributional information delivered by a high-status person is as effective or more so.

# References

Abramson, L. Y., Metalsky, G. I., & Alloy, L. B. (1989). Hopelessness depression: A theory-based subtype of depression. *Psychological Review, 96*, 358–372.

Abramson, L. Y., Seligman, M. E. P., & Teasdale, J. D. (1978). Learned helplessness in humans: Critique and reformulation. *Journal of Abnormal Psychology, 87*, 49–74.

Anderson, C. A. (1983). Motivational and performance deficits in interpersonal settings: The effect of attributional style. *Journal of Personality and Social Psychology, 45*, 1136–1147.

Andrews, G. R., & Debus, R. L. (1978). Persistence and the causal perception of failure: Modifying cognitive attributions. *Journal of Educational Psychology, 70*, 154–166.

Aronson, E., Wilson, T. D., & Brewer, M. (1998). Experimentation in social psychology. In D. Gilbert, S. Fiske, & G. Lindzey (Eds.), *The handbook of social psychology* (4th ed., Vol. 1, pp. 99–142). New York: Random House.

Aronson, J., Fried, C. B., & Good (in press). Reducing the effects of stereotype threat on African-American college students by shaping theories of intelligence. *Journal of Experimental Social Psychology.*

Bandura, A. (1997). *Self-efficacy: The exercise of control.* New York: Freeman.

Bem, D. J. (1972). Self-perception theory. In L. Berkowitz (Ed.), *Advances in Experimental Social Psychology* (Vol. 6, pp. 1–62). New York: Academic Press.

Dweck, C. S. (1975). The role of expectations and attributions in the alleviation of learned helplessness. *Journal of Personality and Social Psychology, 31*, 674–685.

Dweck, C. S. (1999). *Self-theories: Their role in motivation, personality, and development.* Philadelphia: Psychology Press.

Försterling, F. (1988). *Attribution theory in clinical psychology.* New York: Wiley.

Heider, F. (1958). *The psychology of interpersonal relations.* New York: Wiley.

Jesse, D. M., & Gregory, W. L. (1986/1987). A comparison of three attribution approaches to maintaining first year college GPA. *Educational Research Quarterly, 11*, 12–25.

Jones, E. E., & Davis, K. E. (1965). From acts to dispositions: The attribution process in social psychology. In L. Berkowitz (Ed.), *Advances in experimental social psychology* (Vol. 2, pp. 219–266). New York: Academic Press.

Kelley, H. H. (1967). Attribution theory in social psychology. In D. Levine (Ed.), *Nebraska symposium on motivation* (Vol. 15, pp. 192–238). Lincoln: University of Nebraska Press.

Kellogg, R., & Baron, S. (1975). Attribution theory, insomnia, and the reverse placebo effect: A reversal of Storms and Nisbett's findings. *Journal of Personality and Social Psychology, 32*, 231–236.

Menec, V. H., Perry, R. P., Struthers, C. W., Schonwetter, D. J., Hechter, F. J., & Eichholz, B. L. (1994). Assisting at-risk college students with attributional retraining and effective teaching. *Journal of Applied Social Psychology, 24*, 675–701.

Nelum-Hart, M. J., Schooler, J. S., Wilson, T. D., & Meyers, J. M. (1999). *Attribution retraining via video role modeling.* Unpublished data, University of Pittsburgh.

Nisbett, R. E., Borgida, E., Crandall, R., & Reed, H. (1976). Popular induction: Information is not necessarily informative. In J. S. Carroll & J. W. Payne (Eds.), *Cognition and social behavior* (pp. 113–134). Hillsdale, NJ: Erlbaum.

Nisbett, R. E., & Wilson, T. D. (1977). Telling more than we can know: Verbal reports on mental processes. *Psychological Review, 84*, 231–259.

Noel, J. G., Forsyth, D. R., & Kelley, K. N. (1987). Improving the performance of failing students by overcoming their self-serving attributional biases. *Basic and Applied Social Psychology, 8*, 151–162.

Nolen-Hoeksema, S., Girgus, J. S., & Seligman, M. E. P. (1986). Learned helplessness in children: A longitudinal study of depression, achievement, and explanatory style. *Journal of Personality and Social Psychology, 51*, 435–442.

Overmeier, J. B., & Seligman, M. E. P. (1967). Effects of inescapable shock upon subsequent escape and avoidance learning. *Journal of Comparative and Physiological Psychology, 63*, 23–33.

Perry, R. P., Hechter, F. J., Menec, V. H., & Weinberg, L. E. (1993). Enhancing achievement motivation and performance in college students: An attributional retraining perspective. *Research in Higher Education, 34,* 687–723.

Perry, R. P., & Penner, K. S. (1990). Enhancing academic achievement in college students through attributional retraining and instruction. *Journal of Educational Psychology, 82,* 262–271.

Ross, L., Rodin, J., & Zimbardo, P. G. (1969). Toward an attribution therapy: The reduction of fear through induced cognitive-emotional misattribution. *Journal of Personality and Social Psychology, 12,* 279–288.

Ross, M., & Olson, J. M. (1981). An expectancy-attribution model of the effect of placebos. *Psychological Review, 88,* 408–437.

Schachter, S., & Singer, J. E. (1962). Cognitive, social, and physiological determinants of emotional states. *Psychological Review, 69,* 379–399.

Schulman, P. (1995). Explanatory style and achievement in school and work. In G. M. Buchanan, M. E. P. Seligman, et al. (Eds.). *Explanatory style* (pp. 159–171). Hillsdale, NJ: Erlbaum.

Seligman, M. E. P., & Maier, S. F. (1967). Failure to escape traumatic shock. *Journal of Experimental Psychology, 74,* 1–9.

Storms, M. D., Denney, D. R., McCaul, K. D., & Lowery, C. R. (1979). Treating insomnia. In I. H. Frieze, D. Bar-Tal, & J. S. Carroll (Eds.), *New approaches to social problems* (pp. 151–167). Hillsdale, NJ: Erlbaum.

Storms, M. D., & McCaul, K. D. (1976). Attribution processes and emotional exacerbation of dysfunctional behavior. In J. H. Harvey, W. J. Ickes, & R. F. Kidd (Eds.), *New directions in attribution research* (Vol. 1, pp. 143–164). Hillsdale, NJ: Erlbaum.

Storms, M. D., & Nisbett, R. E. (1970). Insomnia and the attribution process. *Journal of Personality and Social Psychology, 16,* 319–328.

Valins, S., & Nisbett, R. E. (1972). Attribution processes in the development and treatment of emotional disorders. In E. E. Jones, D. E. Kanouse, H. H. Kelley, R. E. Nisbett, S. Valins, & B. Weiner, (Eds.), *Attribution: Perceiving the causes of behavior* (pp. 137–150). Morristown, NJ: General Learning Press.

Van Overwalle, F., & De Metsenaere, M. (1990). The effects of attribution-based intervention and study strategy training on academic achievement in college freshman. *British Journal of Educational Psychology, 60,* 299–311.

Van Overwalle, F., Segebarth, K., & Goldschstein, M. (1989). Improving performance of freshmen through attributional testimonies from fellow students. *British Journal of Educational Psychology, 59,* 75–85.

Weiner, B. (1986). *An attributional theory of emotion and motivation.* New York: Springer-Verlag.

Weiner, B., Frieze, L., Kukla, A., Reed, L., Rest, S., & Rosenbaum, R. M. (1972). Perceiving the causes of success and failure. In E. E. Jones, D. E. Kanouse, H. H. Kelley, R. E. Nisbett, S. Valins, & B. Weiner (Eds.), *Attribution: Perceiving the causes of behavior* (pp. 95–120). Morristown, NJ: General Learning Press.

Wilson, T. D., & Linville, P. W. (1982). Improving the academic performance of college freshmen: Attribution therapy revisited. *Journal of Personality and Social Psychology, 42,* 367–376.

Wilson, T. D., & Linville, P. W. (1985). Improving the performance of college freshmen using attributional techniques. *Journal of Personality and Social Psychology, 49,* 287–293.

# CHAPTER 6

# Self-Handicapping and School: Academic Self-Concept and Self-Protective Behavior

FREDERICK RHODEWALT AND MICHAEL W. TRAGAKIS

*Department of Psychology, University of Utah, Salt Lake City*

The first author had by all accounts a largely unremarkable childhood and adolescence. He had loving and supportive parents. In fact, at a very young age his mother told him he was destined for great things. He attended high school in a small Pennsylvania town, played sports, had a part time job, and maintained what, at the time, seemed like an active social life. He was also, to put it charitably, a student of modest accomplishment who managed a grade point average that placed him solidly in the bottom quarter of his class. His one notable talent was that he was very good at taking standardized tests. This circumstance led to a number of contradictory interactions that were for him very confusing. On more than one occasion he sat sheepishly in front of his mother as she shook her head in bewilderment at the lone ''C'' on his report card, this ''C'' being the pinnacle of his academic achievement for that school term. She would say, ''Freddie, I just know you could do better if you tried''. Then there were the conferences with the guidance counselor remarking in amazement, ''This SAT score has got to be a fluke, let's face it you are just not college material.'' To make matters worse, Fred had what some would call a self-defeating side to him. Rather than prepare for an exam or write a term paper, he would go to a party or work extra hours at his job. He was never quite prepared and viewed deadlines as mere suggestions. In the end his guidance counselor was right. He was not college material and dropped out of college after 1 year. But his mother was right also; he could do it if he tried.

Save for a few specifics, this story could describe any number of students. The example is commonplace but we believe it illustrates several features of what social psychologists Steven Berglas and Edward E. Jones (1978) termed *self-handicapping behavior*. Self-handicaps are impediments to successful performance created or at least claimed by the person prior to performing. Self-handicaps come before the fact rather than after the threatening outcome has occurred, as in rationalization. According to Berglas and Jones, the person who interviews for a job while slightly drunk or who stays out late the night before taking college entrance exams is manipulating in a self-serving way the conclusions one may draw about the outcome of the interview or exam. Being inebriated or tired decreases the likelihood of getting the job offer or a high score on the SAT, but it also protects the belief that one has the ability to do well. In the terminology of attribution theory, the person is capitalizing on the attributional principles of *discounting* and *augmentation* (Kelley, 1972). That is, conclusions about lack of ability are *discounted*, or downplayed, because the handicap offers an equally plausible explanation for the rejection or failure. In the unlikely event of success, attributions to ability are *augmented*, or accorded greater causal importance, because the good performance occurred despite the handicap. The self-handicapper then is willing to trade the increased likelihood of failure for the opportunity to protect a desired self-image. It is important to point out that the self-handicapper is willing to accept the label of drunkard or lazy to preserve a more central label of competence and worthiness. The label implied by the handicap is almost always to a quality that is believed to be modifiable, while the attribute that is being protected is believed to be fixed and unmodifiable, a point to which we return momentarily.

Just about any device can be used as a self-handicap. Research has documented the self-handicapping function of alcohol and drug consumption, lack of practice, withdrawal of effort, choice of unfavorable performance conditions, and claims of illness, injury, and emotional distress to mention but a few examples. Researchers have suggested several taxonomies of self-handicaps including whether the handicap is internal (i.e., inebriation or illness) or external (i.e., unfavorable performance setting) to the person. We believe that the most meaningful distinction is whether the self-handicap is behavioral or claimed because these two types of handicaps seem to have different relations to actual performance. A behavioral handicap involves actually doing something to sabotage one's performance such as consuming alcohol or procrastinating. A claimed self-handicap involves a verbal declaration that the obstacle to performance is present. Many, but not all, preperformance statements of poor health or lack of motivation and effort are examples of claimed self-handicaps. Most behavioral handicaps directly impede successful performance but their veracity is not in question because they are open to public observation. Claimed handicaps need not have a direct negative link to behavior. The claim of a "pulled muscle" prior to a tennis match may not have any real bearing on the outcome of the match. At the same time, the self-handicapping tennis player must show some evidence that the injury is affecting his or her performance for the handicap to be credible. Thus, claiming a handicap may not be related to performance but supporting the claim may be.

Researchers have only begun to examine the relationship between self-handicapping and performance. For example, in one study in our laboratory, we (Rhodewalt & Fairfield, 1991) asked students to state privately how hard they were going to try at an upcoming test of intelligence (lack of effort being a claimed self-handicap). Unknown to the students, we had manipulated the difficulty of a set of practice items so that half of the students expected to do well and half expected to do poorly. Students who had suspicions that they would not do well on the IQ test *claimed* prior to taking it that they did not intend to put forth as much effort as did students who expected to do well. All students were then administered the same test. What is striking about this experiment is that students who made the claim of low intended effort actually performed significantly worse than did students who did not make the claim. Given that the test was the same for everyone, we assume that stating that they were not going to try led them to try less hard which accounted for their poorer performance. Surely, the relation between the type of self-handicap and performance is complex and warrants additional research.

## SELF-HANDICAPPING MOTIVES

Perhaps the most interesting question in this research area asks why do people self-handicap. We think the question is best answered by thinking of two classes of motives which we have labeled *proximal* and *distal*. Proximal motives are those elements and concerns in the immediate situation that trigger episodes of self-handicapping behavior. For example, the importance of an outcome for the person's self-esteem would be a proximal factor. Distal motives are those characteristics of the person stemming from past personal experiences and learning that would engender a proclivity to self-handicap as opposed to some other performance strategy. Admittedly, the proximal/distal distinction blurs because in many instances proximal influences may more greatly affect some people than others, reflecting the interplay between short-term and long-term motives.

To illustrate the complex etiology of self-handicapping, we have formulated a model that depicts the interplay of these various motives (see Fig. 1). As illustrated in Figure 1, distal motives have two sources. One set of motives stems from a unique history of experiences relevant to the desired competency. For example, two people may wish to believe that they are exceptionally brilliant but differ in the past experiences that would support such a claim.

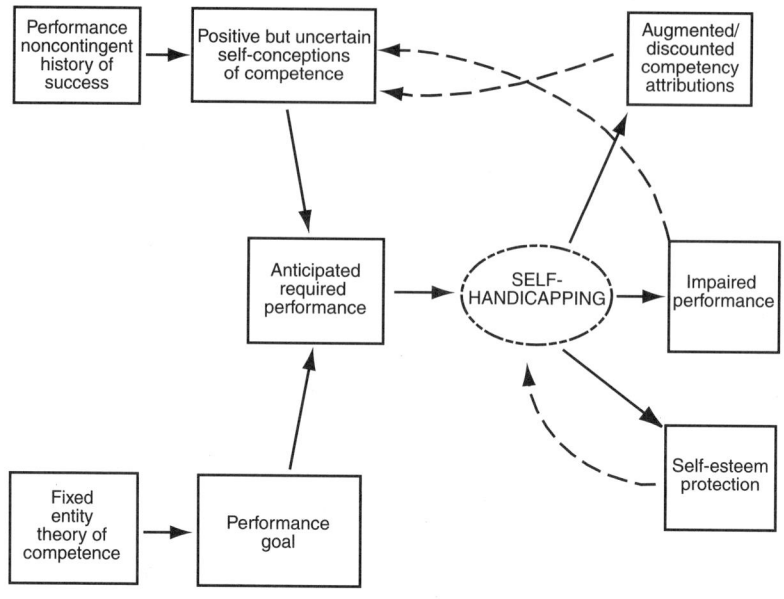

**FIGURE 1**
Model of causes and consequences of self-handicapping behavior.

One person may have had a history of very cunning business decisions and a clear sense of how she arrived at those decisions. The other individual may have also made a number of decisions that worked out well for his or her company. These successful decisions also imply ability but the person is uncertain that other factors such as good fortune were not involved. We would say that the latter person has had a history of response noncontingent success feedback while the former has had a history of response-contingent success feedback. The second set of motives comes from the conclusion that competence is unmodifiable which gives rise to the goal of competency demonstration. We provide a detailed discussion of both motives to understand self-handicapping in academic settings. There is a second noteworthy feature of the model. It is recursive in the sense that the consequences of self-handicapping feed back into the model and either reinforce self-handicapping acts or maintain or, perhaps, exacerbate antecedent motives and concerns. We suggest that all of the pathways outlined in Figure 1 may be important targets for educators concerned with self-handicapping students. Accordingly we use this model to close the chapter with a discussion of various classroom strategies and interventions that might serve to break the cycle of self-defeating, self-handicapping behaviors in students.

Episodes of self-handicapping are precipitated by a fear that one cannot produce evidence of a competence, skill, ability, or attribute. This fear stems from uncertainty that one possesses these desirable qualitites. The story at the beginning of the chapter illustrates this point. Both parent and son wanted to believe that Fred was academically talented but there was a long history of behavioral evidence that was at best ambiguous with respect to this conclusion. He had a mixed history of academic achievement with a set of murky interpretations attached to them; failures were due to lack of effort and successes were questioned because they may have been "flukes." Through it all he could allow himself to believe that he was a reservoir of untapped talent, until he was asked to prove it, that is. The prospect of the SAT looming large on the morrow provided the potential to refute this self-belief. If people are uncertain of their abilities, self-handicapping allows them to preserve their positive self-beliefs in the face of anticipated negative feedback.

Berglas and Jones (1978) stated this idea more formally by proposing that people who have had a positive but capricious reinforcement history with respect to some desired attribute are motivated to self-handicap when called on to provide evidence of that attribute or competency. They demonstrated this hypothesis in a classic experiment that participants believed was a study of the effects of various drugs on intellectual performance. Participants were told that they would be taking two equivalent forms of an IQ test. The first test would be taken under optimal conditions and the second would be taken after the participant had ingested one of a variety of compounds under study. The compounds were allegedly of two kinds: "Actavil," a drug that was thought to improve performance and, "Pandocrin," a drug that was thought to interfere with performance. Participants were told that they could choose the type of drug and its dosage and then were administered the first test. Everyone received feedback that they had done very well, in fact, they were told that they had scored in the upper percentiles of the people who had been tested. For half of the participants, this feedback was response contingent. That is, there was a correct answer for each item on the test so that these participants had a clear idea of what they did to do well. For the other half of the participants, the success feedback was response-noncontingent, meaning that there was no correct answer and thus no connection between their behavior and the feedback they received. These noncontingent feedback, success participants were told that their test results indicated that they were very intelligent but they had no idea what they did to do well on the test. They were then asked to replicate their success on the second test but first they had to select the drug they wanted to be administered before taking the test. The critical question asked who would select the performance-handicapping drug "Pandocrin."[1] The answer was that those participants who were uncertain of why they achieved the initial success (noncontingent success feedback) showed a clear preference for self-handicapping while those who were confident of their ability (contingent success feedback) did not. This finding has been replicated

---

[1]The experiment concluded at this point and no drug was provided.

many times with different handicapping options and for different abilities. Studies like the above clearly illustrate two of the central motives for self-handicapping behaviors. They demonstrate the more distal motive of a history of success experiences that are not clearly related to performance. Such experiences seem to foster uncertain self-conceptions of competence. Then, anticipated threat to that desired, but fragilely held self-conception, in turn, proximally drives self-handicapping.

Two other findings from the Berglas and Jones (1978) study merit discussion. First, there was a difference between males and females in their preference for self-handicapping. More than 80% of the men who experienced noncontingent success feedback chose the self-handicapping drug while less than 40% of the women did so. Although it is not the case that women do not self-handicap at all, as we shall explore in our discussion of individual differences later in the chapter, women do not self-handicap across the wide range of situations nor employ the wide variety of handicaps that men do. The second issue introduced by the Berglas and Jones findings pertains to the notion that in most instances, self-handicapping is a public behavior performed before one or more observers. This fact raises the possibility that people self-handicap to protect their images in the eyes of others rather than to deceive themselves. Berglas and Jones attempted to address this question by varying whether the experimenter would know of the participant's choice to self-handicap. Whether the experimenter was allegedly aware of the self-handicap did not make a difference, leading Berglas and Jones to conclude that self-handicapping was for self-protection. Others (see Kolditz & Arkin, 1982) have produced evidence that self-presentational concerns can increase the likelihood of self-handicapping. Our reading of the literature leads us to conclude that self-handicappers are as concerned about their self-concept in their own eyes as they are concerned about how they appear to others.

Thus far we have considered motivational concerns that arouse specific episodes of self-handicapping. We now consider a set of motives that are more antecedent to self-handicapping behaviors. What experiences lead an individual to consider self-handicapping strategies in general? A logical extension of the Berglas and Jones analysis, one they explicitly endorsed, is that people's self-conceptions of ability are gleaned from a set of ability-relevant learning experiences. People differ in two pertinent respects, in this regard. First, they differ in their self-conceptions of ability or competency. People who do not believe that they possess a certain skill or competence will also not feel the need to self-handicap; there is no positive self-image to protect. As we have already noted, among people with positive competency images, there are differences in the learning histories on which these competency images are grounded. For some, their learning histories are such that there is a clear relation between past performance and its causes. For others, their learning histories have been dotted with positive outcomes but the connection between their underlying ability and these positive outcomes is unclear.

Again, consider the example with which we opened the chapter. There was a very mixed history of academic achievement available to support the claim of intellectual ability. Negative performances were not relevant because they were discounted. Lack of effort was a salient and plausible alternative explanation for the poor grades. But, the protection of a sense of ability through discounting attributions was accomplished by creating causal uncertainty not clarity. One cannot say for sure that lack of ability was operating because lack of effort was also present in the causal mix. Discounting, then, is like being granted a pardon, the judgment is suspended, but underlying competence is still in question. Returning to the opening example, positive outcomes were viewed as diagnostic of ability although there was the suspicion that luck was involved (again with the discounting). The net result was a positive but not confidently held self-image of intellectual competency. One can be comfortable with such fragile self-conceptions until asked to display evidence of the talent.

Berglas and Jones (1978) speculated about a second kind of learning contingency that may also engender the tendency to self-handicap. Berglas and Jones suggested that not only may children experience an ability-relevant history of noncontingent success feedback, but they may also acquire suspicions of conditional love or worth from their parents. Children read from their parents' behavior, either accurately or inaccurately, that they will be loved only if they are competent. For some children this message translates into chronic overachievement in an attempt to avoid their parents' viewing them as incompetent. Other children focus on the communication, "you could do it if you tried." For these children, trying and failing have the added risk of loss of parental love; therefore their only alternative is to withdraw effort. These are interesting hypotheses but ones that, to our knowledge, have not been directly examined in research.

Although Berglas and Jones have pointed to plausible antecedents of the self-handicapping motive, there seems to be a piece missing from the puzzle. Why self-handicap when a number of other responses are available? For example, the person who was unsure of his or her ability could choose to be better prepared or even overprepared for the evaluative performance. Why then is it so imperative to the self-handicapper to avoid failure and preserve a fragile sense of competency? No doubt uncertainty about ability motivates self-handicapping behavior but there must be more to the story.

We (Rhodewalt, 1994) have approached this question by building on the seminal thinking of Carol Dweck and her colleagues (1999, and Chapter 3 in this volume; Dweck & Leggett, 1988; Elliot & Dweck, 1988). Although Dweck's concern is with mastery oriented and helpless achievement behavior, we believe it also extends to an understanding of self-handicapping behavior. Dweck contends that people differ in their beliefs or personal theories about the causes of ability and competency. "Fixed entity" theorists believe that ability is a fixed trait. Whatever one's capacity, it is relatively fixed and unmodifiable. "Incremental" theorists assume that ability can be cultivated through learning, that one's capacities are malleable. It is probably more accurate to say that we all entertain both theories and differ in the extent to which we favor one over the other as the predominant explanation for ability. Surely the most hard-core "fixed-entity" adherent recognizes that one can have a bad day.

According to Dweck, "fixed entity" and "incremental" self-theories are associated with different goals in achievement contexts. The "fixed entity" theorist pursues performance goals, that is, goals of receiving positive feedback and outcomes, such as a high grade or praise from the teacher. In contrast, the "incremental" theorist pursues learning goals, characterized by learning something new or improving on an existing skill. We contend that the linking of self-theories and goals has implications for responses to anticipated threats to the self. Consider two students who are uncertain about their intelligence and who are also facing an important test of that intelligence. For the "incremental theorist/learning goal" student this is clearly an unsettling situation. The evaluation is important and the outcome is uncertain. However, the meaning of that outcome, while potentially disappointing, is not damning. A negative evaluation signals that more training and preparation are required before the student can move on. Now consider the "fixed entity theorist/ performance goal" student facing the same challenge. Failure for this student does not mean that more preparation is required. Rather it signals that ability is lacking and this is a devastating message because, according to the fixed entity view, there is not much one can do to remedy the deficit. Thus, when situations require the demonstration of a certain competence, the performance goals and focus on ability of those who hold fixed theories of competence may also motivate self-protective, self-handicapping tactics.

More formally, our model proposes that the self-handicapping student is the product of two learning histories. First, this student has had a set of socialization experiences that instilled the belief that competency is fixed and can only be demonstrated rather than improved. Second, this student possesses ability self-conceptions that are based on a causally ambiguous and shaky history of success. Thus, these students enter many evaluative situations with the goal of demonstrating an ability of which they are uncertain. It is the confluence of these two learning histories and their more immediate performance demands that set the stage for self-handicapping. Evaluative situations that pose the threat of negative feedback about the self are to be avoided because their implications are so damaging. In these contexts the student will embrace self-handicaps because the trade-off of increased risk of failure for the protection of an ability self-conception is a bargain.

## INDIVIDUAL DIFFERENCES IN SELF-HANDICAPPING TENDENCIES

The foregoing discussion of socialization experiences and distal motives to self-handicap anticipates the proposition that people differ in their propensities to employ self-handicapping strategies. Three classes of individual difference have been investigated (see Rhodewalt, 1990; Hirt, Deppe, & Gordon, 1991, for detailed discussions): (a) a general self-handicapping style, (b) domain/ strategy-specific self-handicapping, and (c) sex differences in self-handicapping.

Most of the research on the chronic self-handicapping style has used the Self-Handicapping Scale (SHS) (Jones & Rhodewalt, 1982; Rhodewalt, 1990). The SHS was designed to be a face valid measure of one's willingness to admit to having engaged in behaviors associated with self-handicapping. The scale includes items such as "I would do a lot better if I tried harder," "I tend to put things off to the last moment," and "I sometimes enjoy being mildly ill for a day or two because it takes off the pressure." The cumulative research evidence indicates that the SHS possesses adequate reliability and validity (see Rhodewalt, 1990, for a review).

Throughout the remainder of this section we highlight research findings that employed the SHS. There are two sets of findings that are pertinent to the discussion of a general self-handicapping style. First, the SHS predicts both behavioral and claimed self-handicapping. In an early study, Rhodewalt, Saltzman, and Witmer (1984) had members of a collegiate men's swimming team complete the SHS and rate each swimming meet in the upcoming season for its importance to the success of the team. Our notion was that more important meets would be more likely than less important meets to pose a challenge or threat to the individual swimmers. Then throughout the season, the coach kept weekly logs on practice attendance and practice effort for each member of the team. SHS-defined high self-handicapping swimmers prepared less than low self-handicapping swimmers before important meets but did not differ prior to less important meets. That is, low self-handicappers increased effort as challenge increased while high self-handicappers did not.

The SHS also predicts claimed self-handicapping as evidenced in a study by Rhodewalt and Fairfield (1991), who provided students with practice problems for an upcoming test of intelligence. Half of the students received relatively easy practice items and half received relatively difficult practice items. The researchers' intention was to give participants the expectation that either they would do poorly or they would do well on the test. Prior to taking the test, the participants reported anonymously how hard they intended to try on the test. High self-handicapping students claimed lower intended effort prior to a test in which they did not expect to do well than did low self-handicapping students. As noted previously, claims of low intended effort were translated into poor test performance for these high self-handicappers.

Further evidence for the validity of the SHS comes from two "classroom studies" (Rhodewalt & Hill, 1994; Feick & Rhodewalt, 1998) in which college undergraduates were administered the SHS and reported their class performance expectations at the beginning of the academic term. Then, prior to the first in-class exam, they completed a checklist of potential obstacles to their performing well on the upcoming test. In both studies, there was a significant positive relation between scores on the SHS at the beginning of the class and number of handicaps claimed prior to taking the examination.

Individual differences in the tendency to self-handicap have also been linked to the motives discussed previously. We probed students in a number of ways about their self-theories of ability (Rhodewalt, 1994). We also asked about their goals in school. In accord with our speculations about motives to self-handicap, participants who scored high on the SHS were more likely to espouse "fixed entity" theories of ability and to pursue performance goals in school than were low scorers on the scale.

A different body of research suggests that there are domain/strategy-specific self-handicappers. By domain/strategy-specific self-handicapping we mean a propensity to use one mode of self-handicapping in one life area rather than a general tendency to self-handicap. For example, a person who has been injured in an accident and experiences chronic pain may come to learn that pain complaints excuse his poor performance at work. In this case, using pain as a self-handicap only in the work setting would be an example of domain/strategy-specific self-handicapping. This type of self-handicapping has been examined most extensively by C. R. Snyder, T. W. Smith, and colleagues, who have shown that "conditions" such as chronic test anxiety and hypochondriasis can serve a self-handicapping function (e.g., Snyder & Smith, 1982). In fact, their research demonstrates that anxiety or symptoms abate when their self-handicapping utility is reduced.

It is important to note that in this class of self-handicapping, the response or behavior was initially performed for other reasons. For example, there can be no doubt that evaluative situations elicit intense anxiety for some people. However, over time and experience these anxious reactions form part of the attributional context in which individuals interpret their ability-related outcomes and, subsequently, take on a self-handicapping function. It follows then that although self-handicapping considerations had nothing to do with establishing certain "dysfunctional" response patterns, they have much to do with maintaining them.

There is no obvious reason that domain/strategy-specific self-handicapping be related to a more general tendency to self-handicap (as indexed by the SHS) save for the possibility that people with a general self-handicapping style may be quicker to see the self-handicapping possibilities of an action or claim. To illustrate this point Rhodewalt, Morf, Hazlett, and Fairfield (1991) manipulated the obvious functionality of a potential handicap. That is, it was suggested that background music played during the test was found to be very distracting by most people (unambiguous handicap) or slightly distracting by some but not other people (ambiguous handicap). Although virtually all participants took advantage of the presence of an obvious self-handicap to excuse a poor performance, only high-SHS participants incorporated an ambiguous handicap into their performance attributions.[2] High-SHS individuals appear to be more facile at perceiving and availing themselves of the self-handicapping potential of obstacles to successful performance. It is likely then that high self-handi-cappers would be quicker to appreciate the self-handicapping opportunities afforded by an illness, injury, or extreme emotional reaction. These facts need to be considered when choosing and implementing interventions.

One of the most consistent findings in the self-handicapping literature is that males and females differ in their self-handicapping behavior. This sex difference has not been studied systematically and consequently is poorly understood. That has not stopped researchers from proposing a number of explanations for the difference, including differences between the sexes in the attributions for competency-relevant outcomes (men attribute success to ability more than women) and the importance of competency to the self (competency plays a more prominent role in the self-conceptions of men than in those of women). Tests of these hypotheses, where they exist, are far from conclusive. Moreover, it is inaccurate to conclude that men self-handicap and women do not. In an earlier review of sex differences in self-handicapping (Rhodewalt, 1990), it was suggested that the sex difference was most consistently observed with behav-ioral self-handicaps. For reasons that are unknown, women do not avail them-selves of behavioral self-handicaps (e.g., drug and alcohol consumption, effort withdrawal) and men do. There is ample evidence that women will use claimed self-handicaps (e.g., test anxiety, illness, stress). We noted in our earlier review that these claimed handicaps often fall into the category of domain/strategy-specific handicaps. One possible implication of these studies is that self-handi-capping is not a generally preferred self-protective strategy for women. Rather, when they do self-handicap it is because they have learned the self-handicap-ping benefits of a behavior that was initially performed for other reasons.

## CONSEQUENCES OF SELF-HANDICAPPING

According to theory, people self-handicap so that they may protect their self-images of competency in the event of failure and enhance these images in the case of success. They are also interested in protecting their public reputations as competent individuals. Does self-handicapping accomplish these self-pro-tective and self-presentational objectives? We have examined these questions in both laboratory (Rhodewalt et al., 1991; Rhodewalt, Sanbonmatsu, Feick, Tschanz, & Waller, 1995) and naturalistic (Rhodewalt & Hill, 1994; Feick & Rhodewalt, 1998) investigations and found that in the short term the answer is ''yes,'' self-handicapping works. But, it is not without costs.

---

[2]This is actually a slight misstatement of the findings. Low-SHS participants who were also low in self-esteem appeared not to self-handicap regardless of how obvious was the opportunity to do so. Of course, these are probably individuals who do not have positive self-images to protect.

With regard to self-protection, there is ample evidence that when faced with failure, self-handicappers discount lack of ability as a cause. In the laboratory Rhodewalt et al. (1991, Study 2) led students to believe that they had performed well on an intelligence test and then were administered a second form of the same test. Half of the students received feedback that they continued to be successful on the second test and half received feedback that they were now failing. Independent of this feedback was the presence or absence of an experimenter-imposed handicap. Those students who failed but had a handicap reported levels of ability and self-esteem equal to those who succeeded on both tests. In contrast, students who failed and did not have a handicap concluded that they had low ability and displayed lowered self-esteem.

This study found no evidence of self-enhancement when participants were successful and handicapping. It appears that people are more likely to handicap for its self-protective benefits than for its self-enhancing function. There are exceptions to this statement. In a separate study, Rhodewalt et al. (1991, Study 1) found that participants who were both high scorers on the SHS and high in self-esteem employed self-handicaps for self-enhancement. This finding raises the possibility that for a subset of students who are confident in their ability, self-handicapping reflects an attempt to self-aggrandize.

We have also conducted naturalistic studies of the consequences of self-handicapping. In these "classroom studies" we examined not only who self-handicaps but the role these handicaps play in reactions to academic feedback. In these studies (Rhodewalt & Hill, 1994; Feick & Rhodewalt, 1998), graded exams were returned to the students and they were asked to make attributions for their performance and to report their state self-esteem at that moment. We categorized by comparing their grades on the exam the exam with their grade expectations reported at the beginning of the term. Students were grouped into those who performed worse than they expected (failure), equal to their expectations (expected success), or better than their expectations (unexpected success). These studies provide clear evidence for both the self-protection and self-enhancement functions of self-handicapping. Compared with students who failed without self-handicapping, self-handicapping failure students inferred that they possessed greater ability and reported significantly higher postfeedback self-esteem. In fact, self-handicapping, failure students displayed self-esteem that was equal to that of non-self-handicapping students who were successful (expected success). Perhaps the most interesting findings were the responses of students whose exam performance far exceeded their expectations. Those students who had self-handicapped and then performed unexpectedly well inferred that they had greater ability and displayed higher levels of postfeedback self-esteem than did students who performed unexpectedly well without having self-handicapped.

There is a small but consistent literature that examines the self-presentational utility of self-handicapping (Luginbuhl & Palmer, 1991; Rhodewalt et al., 1995; Smith & Strube, 1991). This work asks how self-handicappers are perceived by others. These studies uniformly find that observers give self-handicappers the attributional benefit of the doubt by discounting attributions to ability (or lack thereof) following poor performance. It also clear, however, that observers do not like self-handicappers. Along this line, we found that observers will evaluate the same objective performance more negatively when it is produced by a self-handicapping person than when it is produced by a non-self-handicapping person (Rhodewalt et al., 1995). This latter finding suggests that the act of self-handicapping may engender more threatening feedback than one would otherwise normally encounter. It is as if the evaluator recognizes the handicap and does not feel concerned about softening the feedback.

The general conclusion taken from the research reviewed in the preceding paragraphs is that self-handicapping involves trade-offs but appears to serve the short-term goal of self-image protection. However, before the reader concludes that we are advocating self-handicapping as a lifestyle let us consider those few studies that have examined the long-term effects of self-handicapping. To the extent that the student chronically self-handicaps, one would expect that there would be deleterious effects on achievement and accomplishment. We have evidence suggesting that this is true. We created an index of over-/underachievement by using students' SAT/ACT scores as a measure of aptitude and their grade point averages (GPAs) as a measure of achievement (Rhodewalt & Saltzman reported in Rhodewalt, 1990).[3] In samples from two different universities the over-/underachievement index correlated negatively with scores on the SHS. That is, the more a student was a chronic self-handicapper as evidenced by his or her SHS score, the less likely his or her grades were as high as what would be expected from his or her SAT/ACT scores.

Zuckerman, Kieffer, and Knee (1998) provided a follow-up examination of the relation between chronic self-handicapping and academic performance. In two studies these researchers found that individual differences in self-handicapping as measured by the SHS were related to lower academic performance as indexed by GPA. Moreover, the negative relation between SHS and GPA was independent of verbal and quantitative SAT and level of self-esteem. Zuckerman et al. (1998) also measured study habits and found that poor exam preparation seemed to drive the relationship between self-handicapping and poor performance.

It appears then that the self-handicapper gains self-image protection in the short term at the potential long-term cost of lower achievement. From the parent's or educator's perspective, it is often puzzling why certain students persistently engage in such obviously self-defeating acts. The outside observer cannot see that these acts play an important function in the phenomenal well-

[3]The over-/underachievement index was created with the algorithm 1 (+) log(GPA/SAT × 1000 to place the index on an interval scale. Consider three students who all obtained a score of 1200 on their SATs but who had GPAs of 3.0, 2.0, and 1.0 respectively. Their corresponding index scores would be 1.44, 1.22, and 0.92 (see Rhodewalt, 1990).

being of the self-handicapper. Admittedly such self-defeating strategies are detrimental to the long-term success of the individual. We, however, contend that self-handicapping behavior cannot be reduced or eliminated without a recognition of the underlying motives and internal reward structure that drive the development and maintenance of these acts that we have considered here. We turn now to a discussion of the implications of our understanding of self-handicapping for educational settings.

## INDICATIONS FOR THE CLASSROOM

As many educators will attest, students often behave in puzzling and counter-productive ways. Our first goal in this chapter was to remove some of the bafflement around these self-defeating behaviors by placing them within the framework of self-handicapping theory and research. We have shown that self-handicapping in the classroom can serve to protect self-conceptions of competency and to preserve desired images in the eyes of others. Despite the short-term gains that self-handicapping may provide students, there are definite long-term costs to self-handicapping that cannot be ignored. What then can be done to reduce the appeal of self-handicapping in academic settings? The answers to this question are complex but clearly must begin with a consideration of the motives that drive self-handicapping behavior. More specifically, to reduce self-handicapping in the classroom, teachers and parents will need to launch a multifront assault on students' confusion about the causes of academic outcomes and the resulting positive but uncertain self-conceptions. They will have to address the fact that self-handicapping students focus on fixed notions of ability and fear that they are not able to demonstrate evidence of these innate qualities. Breaking these links in the self-handicapping process, as illustrated in our model, can be accomplished by numerous classroom-oriented and individually focused strategies that eliminate or mitigate these contributors to the self-handicapping tendency. It is important to mention that self-handicapping behavior is often multiply determined and interventions that address only one motive or concern will not eradicate self-handicapping. Educators can nonetheless do their best to foster environments and create programs that mollify students' drive to set up obstacles to their own performance.

### Alleviating Outcome Noncontingency

As discussed previously, one of the primary factors contributing to the tendency to self-handicap is a history of noncontingent success (Berglas & Jones, 1978; Berglas, 1990). Such a history fosters a sense that one's successes are not related to one's own instrumental behaviors. Individuals with this type of reinforcement history lack a clear sense of their own role in the successes and rewards they receive, and feel uncertain of their competence and self-worth. Although this pattern of noncontingent success primarily rears its destructive head in the family setting (i.e., parental reinforcement and care taking patterns), it has also been found to be prevalent in many classroom settings. Many academic self-handicappers may be responding to a precarious reinforcement history in the classroom (see Covington & Teel, 1996).

One of the primary contributors to a sense of noncontingent success in scholastic settings is the comparative grading/incentive system which is widely employed in educational settings. Martin Covington, a researcher in the forefront of examining ways to eliminate student failure and lack of motivation, stresses that many classrooms and college courses involve what he and his colleagues call an "ability game," based on comparing students' performance in the classroom (Covington, 1984; Covington & Teel, 1996). Instructors operating within this framework reward and evaluate students based on their accomplishments relative to each other. In a very real sense, students perceive a "zero-sum" distribution of high grades and praise, their own performance necessarily constrained by the other capable students in class.

Unfortunately, many students in this type of incentive system lack a clear sense of their own abilities and skills in their academic pursuits in a nonrelative sense. Grades and evaluations are not assigned with a given student's individual performance and improvement in mind, rather with a consideration of where the student fits in the general class performance scheme. For students who are low achievers and who have experienced consistent uncertainty in their ability to perform well, this evaluative framework can be especially threatening. Such students can never be sure of their true ability, and may withdraw effort, procrastinate, and engage in other self-handicapping strategies to preserve a tenuous sense of competency. A straightforward example of this is a college course where grades are assigned "on the curve." Students who perform well in such a class may receive average grades regardless of their understanding or progress because other students are also progressing at the same rate. Such a lack of clear connection between abilities and grades can trigger self-protective responses.

Educational researchers have offered an alternative incentive system with which to foster student learning and scholastic growth, one that is not founded on comparing students' performance. Based on the notion of mastery learning, this alternative evaluative framework involves evaluating students on the basis of what are called "criterion-referenced standards," rather than on a normative basis (Covington & Omelich, 1984). Standards of excellence are set in advance by the instructor and students strive to meet those standards commensurate with the grade they desire. To clarify, certain criteria are conveyed in which students can earn a given grade. Students can then choose to complete the tasks and achieve the competencies associated with any grade level they choose. There is therefore an equal access to rewards in this framework; any number of students can succeed, provided they accomplish the criteria established.

The contingency of one's efforts and abilities on successful or failing outcomes in this criterion-based evaluative system is much more self-evident to students than it is in an evaluative framework that is more comparative. It becomes very clear exactly what must be accomplished to achieve a given outcome, critical information to students who are uncertain of their ability to perform. In this regard, the responsibility for scholastic achievement is firmly placed on each students' shoulders, rather than on the vagaries of class composition. More important, students come to focus on the learning and tasks at hand, rather than on social comparison processes that prove detrimental to uncertain and low-achieving students. The self-presentational aspects of self-handicapping are also somewhat reduced with the institution of this incentive/grading system, in that students are no longer competing with other students for grades. Protecting one's image of competence in others' eyes will be overshadowed to some extent by the desire to focus on one's own effort and output, achieving criteria that are personally set.

Other traditional systems instituted to evaluate and categorize students also promote a sense of noncontingency between students' efforts and abilities and performance outcomes. Notably, scholastic settings have a tendency to weigh the results of standardized tests heavily when assigning students to different educational "tracks" and in establishing a foundation for performance expectancies (Riggs, 1992). The problem here lies in the fact that students, due to a multitude of factors, such as variable motivation levels, home-life difficulties, and interest in school, may not live up to the success predicted by standardized test results. The fluctuating performance of students on a day-to-day level will not consistently measure up to a given student's scores on standardized tests. Students will then experience a lack of contingency between their own efforts and abilities and their standardized test performance.

Students may find "tracking" on the basis of standardized test scores and the expectations that result particularly daunting and thus withdraw effort in the classroom. This is especially the case for uncertain students who score well on such tests. Self-handicapping strategies may result, providing these students with a comfortable buffer, to protect their sense of an "underlying" capability that may not be corroborated by daily outcomes. The experiences and strategies of the first author, shared in the opening vignette of this chapter, illustrate this dilemma.

To counteract this potent contributor to a sense of noncontingency in student outcomes, less emphasis can be placed on specific grades and outcomes (Covington & Teel, 1996). A more holistic approach can help alleviate the pressures and uncertainties engendered by such tracking systems, which may remain important means to maximize the educational benefit of students with differing ability levels. Moreover, educational theorists maintain that rewarding improvement and emphasizing the acceptable and important role of mistakes in the learning process promote an increased sense of mastery and understanding of one's instrumentality in achieving outcomes (Urdan, Midgely, & Anderman, 1998).

Finally, the support of autonomy in the classroom seems to be yet another influence on the perception that student outcomes are not contingent on their effort and abilities. Research by Ryan and Grolnick (Grolnick & Ryan, 1987; Ryan & Grolnick, 1986) suggests that more directive and autonomy-reducing class environments foster an externalized sense of motivation and self-regulation in accomplishing scholastic goals. This externalized self-regulation translates into a sense that activities in the classroom and resultant outcomes do not derive from the student's own initiative or ability, but from the prodding and direction of the instructor. As with the previous scenarios, without a clear sense of how to create and replicate successful outcomes on one's own, successful but uncertain students will be drawn to self-handicapping. Along this line, externalized self-regulation resulting from low classroom autonomy has been found to be linked to decreased levels of motivation and effort, common reactions for self-handicappers (Riggs, 1992; Berglas & Jones, 1978). Consistent with this thinking, Midgely, Arunkumar, and Urdan (1996) found that self-handicapping was related to a more extrinsic orientation in terms of academic pursuits.

As may be evident, instructors who promote student independence in task choice and class involvement foster greater internalization and autonomous regulation of students' scholastic efforts. Students gain a better sense of the role they play in the outcomes they receive when given such freedom. Moreover, internalized self-regulation promotes increased investment and interest in classroom activities, which should eliminate a concern with performance outcomes (grades, praise, feelings of superiority) characteristic of self-handicappers (Garcia & Pintrich, 1996). Internalization has been shown to foster a wide range of positive outcomes including elevated mood and vitality (Sheldon & Kasser, 1995), scholastic achievement (Grolnick & Ryan, 1989), and a stable sense of self-esteem that is not contingent on performance outcomes (Deci & Ryan, 1995). All of these outcomes should be beneficial in academic settings, especially for those uncertain about their ability to succeed.

## Promoting Positive and Certain Self-Conceptions

Another significant motive for self-handicapping that we have included in our model is the fear that one cannot produce evidence of those competencies that one would like to believe he or she possesses. Conditionality of support, both in the classroom and at home, is a primary basis for this uncertainty that self-handicapping children confront. Students who exhibit self-handicapping and other self-protective behavior often have the sense that their worth and regard from others are conditional on their performance. Self-handicappers then set up personal obstacles to success in an attempt to guide the attributions that others make, protecting a tenuous sense of worthiness in others' eyes. Such conditionality, though, unfortunately leaves students constantly wondering about their own importance and merit. Although parents may be the primary source of this type of conditionality, teachers can also trigger such doubts and suspicions as well.

A central manner in which conditionality of feedback is conveyed to students in academic settings is in the nature of praise received from instructors. Traditional classrooms typically focus on praising successful outcomes and lauding students for their intelligence in achieving those outcomes. Although this method may seem to be beneficial to students and their long-term motivation and achievement, this strategy may prove counterproductive in steering students clear of self-handicapping strategies. Such praise often sends the message that student worth is a function of the outcomes they produce, regardless of the improvement, hard work, and understanding they might demonstrate. In the language of Carol Dweck and her colleagues, students come to focus on performance goals (i.e., demonstrating capability through outcomes) rather than on goals aimed at mastering the material (Dweck, Chapter 3 in this volume; Dweck & Leggett, 1988; Mueller & Dweck, 1998). Moreover, praising students for their intelligence and the outcomes they receive has actually been found to be detrimental to students' motivation and performance in the classroom (Mueller & Dweck, 1998; Baumeister, Hutton, & Cairns, 1990; Graham, 1990). Skilled performance and interest in school have been found to decrease with outcome-focused praise, undermining the educational mission for all students. These research findings on the effects of outcome-focused praise seem to be especially pertinent for students who are uncertain of their ability to perform well consistently.

An intervention for this type of demotivated state would be to shift the basis for praise to a focus on the unique talents of each student as a person, as well as on the achievements of a given student (Covington & Teel, 1996). While outcomes in the classroom may remain important indicators of student understanding and progress, teachers can strive to separate the student from the grades and outcomes they receive. For example, teachers might acknowledge and appreciate each student's participation in class activities regardless of the grades given. Over time, students, especially those who have been operating under the pressures of living up to important others' standards, will become more confident that the support they receive is on the basis of their worth as a person, rather than on evidence of high performance (Riggs, 1992). Again, for low-achieving and uncertain students, decreased conditionality of teacher support will provide a sturdy foundation from which to invest energy and hard work in class. These students are likely to become more confident in their ability to demonstrate their competencies and should rely less on self-protective strategies (see also Covington & Teel, 1996).

## Decreasing the Focus on Ability as a Fixed Factor in Performance

In most educational settings student ability is the focus of teachers and students alike. In Western educational systems, in fact, ability is viewed as the major perceived cause of success in school and drives both students' and teachers' conceptions of student competence and positive evaluations (Covington, 1984). This focus on ability and attributions to ability, though, further contributes to the tendency to self-handicap in uncertain and low-achieving students. Poor scholastic outcomes and otherwise variable performance call students' ability into question, fostering a desire to protect the self from the sting of possible failure. As previously discussed, self-handicappers often are responding to a sense that their academic ability is a fixed entity that can only be demonstrated but not cultivated.

Unfortunately, "nativist" views of ability are promoted by educational practices that use "aptitude" as the basis of attainment and self-worth. For example, research by Covington (1984) related to the Self-Worth Theory of Achievement Motivation revealed that perceived ability is one of the primary contributors to perceptions of worthiness in academic settings. Students are socialized in school to approach success and avoid failure to bolster their sense of self-worth in the classroom. The perceptions of a student's ability and resultant self-worth play critical roles in the investment and dedication of students, as well as in the feedback received from teachers.

Praising students on the basis of their outcomes, as discussed earlier, seems to promote conditional self-worth in academic settings as well as self-uncertainty. Valuing students on the basis of their ability seems to be especially damaging to students with self-handicapping tendencies. Not only is a conditionality of worth triggered by this type of praise, but uncertain students may feel inadequate to preserve ability-related recognition. In addition, students infer subtle, implicit messages from instructors' praise. Research by Sandra Graham (1990) indicated that sometimes praising a child for success can actually convey a message that the student has low ability. Praise for success, if not meted out evenly across students and situations, can create an impression that the given student's success if unexpected. The student would attribute the teacher's praise to his or her low level of ability in need of support and encouragement. Clearly, such an implication would be ardently avoided, especially by those students who are trying to preserve a sense of competency. Self-handicapping strategies may be an attractive response in such contexts.

That causal explanations for academic performance powerfully direct subsequent achievement activity including self-handicapping behavior is clearly shown in developmental studies of attribution and performance. Ability and effort are viewed as two of the most critical factors contributing to student performance (cf. Weiner, 1985). In early childhood, children tend to view ability as fluid and malleable, often reflected by the amount of effort exhibited by a student on a given task (Harari & Covington, 1981; see also Dweck & Leggett, 1988; Dweck & Bempechat, 1983). Because of this more malleable view of ability and an inability to grasp fully the attributional nuances of self-handicapping, strategic self-handicapping behavior tends not to occur in early childhood (Harari & Covington, 1981; Covington, 1984).

In later childhood and early adolescence, though, through years of scholastic socialization and feedback, students begin to see ability as more of a fixed quality. As a result of this static view of ability, young students develop a reciprocal relationship between ability and effort. That is, students begin to see that for a given outcome, effort and ability are interrelated, with increases in effort indicative of lower ability and vice versa (Covington, 1984). As a result, students wishing to protect an uncertain, but fixed sense of ability may tend to withdraw effort or engage in other self-handicapping behaviors. Accordingly, research has indicated that children display self-handicapping as they approach adolescence, sixth grade and beyond (see Kimble, Kimble, & Croy, 1998; Thill, 1993). Shifts in ability to draw causal attributions as well as an increased level of ego involvement seem to drive this emergence of self-handicapping in school-age children.

A number of strategies can be enacted to help alleviate the emphasis on ability that stymies students who are uncertain and low-achieving. Primarily, the bases for praise to students can be altered so as to remove the focus on ability. Notably, unlike praise for ability, praising the effort students invest in classroom activities allows them to focus on the process of learning, rather than on how they measure up to other students. Praise for effort does not promote self-consciousness, which is distracting; rather, praise for effort promotes involvement in the task at hand (see Nicholls, 1984). By emphasizing effort, students focus on their own progress, understanding, and interest in academic activities, all of which obviate the desire to handicap the self.

A variation of the emphasis on effort notion is the idea of attributional training designed to help students reduce the impact that ability attribution has on academic achievement. Research by Wilson and Linville (1985), for example, demonstrated that the short-term performance and long-term performance of college freshmen were improved when it was offered that the causes of their low grades were temporary factors. Conversely, other research indicates that when children feel they have no control over their own outcomes, helplessness and withdrawal of effort result (Dweck & Repucci, 1973). Along this line, a stress on the controllable role of effort, rather than on the seemingly uncontrollable level of ability, frees students to put forth the work and energy necessary to achieve positive outcomes. In a sense, students can be taught to view outcomes as resting primarily on the level of effort exerted. As a result, the role of a fixed and thus limiting conception of ability diminishes, while the empowering role of effort engages students of all ability and confidence levels. Students can thus begin to focus on the goal of learning and improvement, rather than getting bogged down by goals of performance.

## Eliminating the Fear of Unsuccessful Performance

Perhaps the most critical and overarching obstacles for educators to confront in reducing academic self-handicapping are student failure and the weight accorded to performance in students' sense of self-worth. Overcoming these hurdles will quell students' drive to sabotage their own learning or avoid trying their best to grasp new concepts. As previously discussed, the "ability game" currently being "played" in classrooms unfortunately undercuts students' motivation to try, fosters unnecessary comparisons between students, and instills a zero-sum perception of rewards and good grades (Covington & Teel, 1996). This "ability game" promotes student motives to demonstrate their ability through performance outcomes and strive to outperform others. Although grades may continue to be an important means for instructors to assess students learning and progress, a number of innovative strategies can be implemented to eliminate the sting of unsuccessful performance and bring the focus back to learning and growth.

The criterion-referenced standards mentioned earlier can also serve to eliminate the role of performance apprehension. Students working in this framework understand the criteria they must surpass to obtain a given grade; there is no guesswork about how the student might achieve success. Both the teacher and the student can then begin to focus on the tasks and competencies at hand, rather than on how to protect a fragile sense of ability or worth. It has also been offered that in these types of evaluative structures, student planning and the resultant sense of personal control it fosters become an integral part of the process. The encouragement of planning in any evaluative paradigm, but especially with criterion-referenced standards, functions to further reduce students' worries about not being able to display their competence and progress (Covington, & Teel, 1996). Moreover, socializing students to plan their "academic attack" should also promote a more clear sense of the contingency between students' actions and outcomes. Overall, criterion-based evaluation and planning emphases represent important strategies to eliminate the fear of unsuccessful performance and need to self-handicap in students.

The notion of retesting has also been offered as a means to reduce the threat of failure in academic settings. Offering students additional chances to pass examinations or complete assignments not only changes the meaning of failure, but also fosters mastery of the material to be learned (Covington & Omelich, 1984). When students have the opportunity to retake examinations, for example, poor performance is instructive and motivational, rather than defeating. Students are aware that they will have chances to try again to obtain the grade they desire, while they are also informed of the specific topic areas in need of more study. Such a strategy seems to especially aid students who may be less quick to grasp course material, while not hindering those students who succeed with less effort. Retesting clearly removes the drive to self-handicap as one's abilities are put to the test over time, with the role of effort being quite salient and emphasized.

Eliminating student fears of unsuccessful performance can also be accomplished through the use of multiple modes of learning and assessment (Covington & Teel, 1996). In line with Gardiner's (1993) notion of seven types of intelligence, (i.e., linguistic ability, logical-mathematical ability, spatial ability, bodily-kinesthetic ability, musical ability, intrapersonal ability, and intrapersonal ability), different students may have strengths in competence areas that are not traditionally assessed. By offering students the opportunity to demonstrate their knowledge and comprehension via more familiar or more comfortable modes, students who might not otherwise succeed can demonstrate their academic progress. The strategic use of self-protective strategies appears less necessary when students are offered varied and comfortable ways to demonstrate understanding.

Finally, altering the structure of class activities may serve to eliminate the use of self-handicapping in uncertain and low-achieving students. Specifically, instituting collaborative learning in the classroom can eliminate the self-presentational motivations for self-handicapping. As evidenced by research by Sharan (1980), collaborative and cooperative learning promote peer interaction and interdependence and a focus on the exchange of ideas between students. In these learning structures, each student's performance ultimately has an impact on the group to which she or he is assigned. Class methods such as the jigsaw classroom (see Aronson, Chapter 10 in this volume; Aronson & Patnoe, 1997) foster awareness that each student has a responsibility for other students' learning. In this particular scenario, self-handicapping strategies may be socially censured and the responsibility to the greater group should promote classroom engagement.

Armed with increased understanding of academic self-handicapping and the means to confront such tendencies, instructors can begin to address the issue of the variable and perhaps inadequate performance of capable students. Certainly, the underpinnings for procrastination, withdrawal of effort, and other self-handicapping strategies are not without foundation in the past experiences of these students. With an awareness of this foundation teachers can begin to initiate classwide and individually tailored methods to shore up students' sense of confidence and worth. Addressing the sense of outcome noncontingency, positive but uncertain self-conceptions, the focus on fixed notions of ability, and fear of not being able to perform successfully may allow students who may be uncertain of their ability to succeed in school to engage fully in academics. Nonetheless, educators should be aware of the strategic and, at least in the short term, beneficial nature of self-handicapping, which provides students a safety net with which to approach academic endeavors and exploration. Flexibility and innovation will be the watchwords for teachers who attempt to help students make the transition from the use of attributional "crutches" to standing on their own two feet. It is important to add that the indications offered in this chapter by no means confine themselves to ways to reduce self-handicapping in the classroom, but represent positive strategies to motivate students with all levels of ability and interest. With differing student populations and concomitant skill levels, creating a scholastic setting that can appeal to and inspire many different types of students will prove most productive and fruitful for the instructors of today.

## Teachers' Questions and Answers

**Q:** How will I notice if a student is self-handicapping in my class? What should I begin to be looking for?

**A:** Teachers should be looking for any number of behavioral and claimed self-handicaps that will surface most clearly during testing periods or when assignments are due. Behavioral self-handicaps include apathy and withdrawal of effort, alcohol and drug consumption, procrastination, and overinvolvement in extracurricular activities. Self-handicaps that are claimed encompass reports of illness, injury, and anxiety or other emotional distress. Almost any behavior or claim that prevents optimal academic performance might be used as a self-handicap.

**Q:** What can teachers do specifically to promote a classroom environment that will minimize self-handicapping behavior?

**A:** Numerous in-class strategies discussed in this chapter can be used to minimize self-handicapping behavior. Specifically, instructors can institute grading systems, such as criterion-referenced standards, that allow students to establish and attain their own, desired level of achievement. Moreover, less emphasis on specific grades and more emphasis on effort and overall understanding can lessen the drive to self-handicap. Training students to plan out their academic strategies (i.e., concrete planning as to how the student will accomplish his or her assignments over time) is another effective preventative measure that will certainly provide long-term benefit. Finally, the use of multiple modes of learning and assessment will reduce or eliminate the drive to self-handicap in many cases.

**Q:** Given the national trend toward an increase in standardized testing and increased accountability in schools, do you think this will lead to an increase in student self-handicapping behavior as student achievement is increased?

**A:** Depending on which aspect of those current trends in education we refer to, there are actually two answers to this question. On the one hand, with regard to increased teacher accountability to maintain or increase high standards of performance, the keen focus on student outcomes may increase the drive to self-handicap in many students. Instructors may end up focusing too heavily on grades and test scores, spurring uncertain students to protect themselves via self-handicapping. On the other hand, considering the recent institution of mandatory competency examinations across the country, teacher responses to this development may actually reduce self-handicapping. Creative and supportive class techniques and environments, aimed at students' mastery of the material rather than on test scores, should minimize the drive to self-handicap. In general, the more creative and student-centered classes are, the less students will seek out self-handicaps.

# References

Aronson, E., & Patnoe, S. (1997). *The jigsaw classroom: Building cooperation in the classroom*. New York: Longman.

Baumeister, R. F., Hutton, D. G., & Cairns, K. J. (1990). Negative effects of praise on skilled performance. *Basic and Applied Social Psychology, 11*, 131–148.

Berglas, S. (1990). Self-handicapping: Etiological and diagnostic considerations. In R. L. Higgins, C. R. Snyder, & S. Berglas (Eds.), *Self-handicapping: The paradox that isn't* (pp. 152–186). New York: Plenum.

Berglas, S., & Jones, E. E. (1978). Drug choice as a self-handicapping strategy in response to non-contingent success. *Journal of Personality and Social Psychology, 36*, 405–417.

Covington, M. V. (1984). The motive for self-worth. In R. Ames & C. Ames (Eds.), *Research on motivation in education*. Orlando, FL: Academic Press.

Covington, M. V., & Omelich, C. L. (1984). Task oriented versus competitive learning structures: Motivation and performance consequences. *Journal of Educational Psychology, 76*, 1038–1050.

Covington, M. V., & Teel, K. M. (1996). *Overcoming student failure: Changing motives and incentives for learning*. Washington, DC: American Psychological Association.

Deci, E. L., & Ryan, R. M. (1995). Human autonomy: The basis for true self-esteem. In M. H. Kernis, (Ed.), *Efficacy, agency and self-esteem* (pp. 31–49). New York: Plenum.

Dweck, C. S. (1999). *Self-theories: Their role in motivation, personality and development*. Philadelphia: Psychology Press.

Dweck, C. S., & Bempechat, J. (1983). Children's theories of intelligence: Consequences for learning. In S. G. Paris, G. M. Olson, & H. M. Stevenson (Eds.), *Learning and motivation in the classroom*. (pp. 239–256). Hillsdale, NJ: Erlbaum.

Dweck, C. S., & Leggett, E. L. (1988). A social-cognitive approach to motivation and personality. *Psychological Review, 95*, 256–273.

Dweck, C. S., & Repucci, D. N. (1973). Learned helplessness and reinforcement responsibility in children. *Journal of Personality and Social Psychology, 25*, 109–116.

Elliot, E. S., & Dweck, C. S. (1988). Goals: An approach to motivation and achievement. *Journal of Personality and Social Psychology, 54*, 5–12.

Feick, D. L., & Rhodewalt, F. (1998). The double-edged sword of self-handicapping: Discounting, augmentation, and the protection and enhancement of self-esteem. *Motivation and Emotion, 21*, 147–163.

Garcia, T., & Pintrich, P. R. (1996). The effects of autonomy on motivation and performance in the college classroom. *Contemporary Educational Psychology, 21*, 477–486.

Gardiner, H. (1993). *Multiple intelligences: The theory and practive*. New York: Basic Books.

Graham, S. (1990). Communicating low ability in the classroom: Bad things good teachers sometimes do. In S. Graham & V. S. Folkes (Eds.), *Attribution theory: Applications to achievement, mental health and interpersonal conflict* (pp. 17–36). Hillsdale, NJ: Erlbaum.

Grolnick, W. S., & Ryan, R. M. (1987). Autonomy in children's learning: An experimental and individual differences investigation. *Journal of Persoanlity and Social Psychology, 52*, 890–898.

Grolnick, W. S., & Ryan, R. M. (1989). Parent styles associated with children's self-regulation and competence in school. *Journal of Educational Psychology, 81*, 143–154.

Harari, O., & Covington, M. V. (1981). Reaction to achievment behvaior from a teacher and student perspective: A developmental analysis. *American Educational Research Journal, 18*, 15–28.

Hirt, E. R., Deppe, R. K., & Gordon, L. J. (1991). Self-reported versus behavioral self-handicapping: Empirical evidence for a theoretical distinction. *Journal of Personality and Social Psychology, 61*, 981–991.

Jones, E. E., & Rhodewalt, F. (1982). *The self-handicapping scale.* (Available from F. Rhodewalt, Department of Psychology, University of Utah).

Kelley, H. H. (1972). Attribution in social interaction. In E. E. Jones, D. F. Kanouse, H. H. Kelley, R. E. Nisbett, S. Valins, & B. Weiner (Eds.), *Attribution: Perceiving the causes of behavior* (pp. 1–26). Morristown, NJ: General Learning Press.

Kimble, C. E., Kimble, E. A., & Croy, N. A. (1998). Development of self-handicapping tendencies. *Journal of Social Psychology, 138*, 524–534.

Kolditz, T. A., & Arkin, R. M. (1982). An impression management interpretation of the self-handicapping strategy. *Journal of Personality and Social Psychology, 43*, 492–502.

Luginbuhl, J., & Palmer, R. (1991). Impression management aspects of self-handicapping: Positive and negative effects. *Personality and Social Psychology Bulletin, 17*, 655–662.

Midgely, C., Arunkumar, R., & Urdan, T. (1996). "If I don't do well tomorrow, there's reason": Predictors of adolescents' use of academic self-handicapping strategies. *Journal of Educational Psychology, 88*, 423–434.

Mueller, C. M., & Dweck, C. S. (1998). Praise for intelligence can undermine children's motivation and performance. *Journal of Personality and Social Psychology, 75*, 33–52.

Nicholls, J. G. (1984). Achievement motivation: Conceptions of ability, subjective experience, task choice and performance. *Psychological Review, 91*, 328–346.

Rhodewalt, F. (1990). Self-handicappers: Individual differences in the preference for anticipatory self-protective acts. In R. Higgins, C. R. Snyder, & S. Berglas. *Self-handicapping: The paradox that isn't.* New York: Plenum.

Rhodewalt, F. (1994). Conceptions of ability, achievement goals and individual differences in self-handicapping behavior: On the application of implicit theories. *Journal of Personality, 62*, 67–85.

Rhodewalt, F., & Fairfield, M. (1991). Claimed self-handicaps and the self-handicapper: The relation of reduction in intended effort to performance. *Journal of Research in Personality, 25*, 402–417.

Rhodewalt, F., & Hill, S. K. (1994). Self-handicapping in the classroom: The effects of claimed self-handicaps in responses to academic failure. *Journal of Personality and Social Psychology, 16*, 397–416.

Rhodewalt, F., Morf, C., Hazlett, S., & Fairfield, M. (1991). Self-handicapping: The role of discounting and augmentation in the preservation of self-esteem. *Journal of Personality and Social Psychology, 61*, 121–131.

Rhodewalt, F., Saltzman, A. T., & Wittmer, J. (1984). Self-handicapping among competitive athletes: The role of practice in self-esteem protection. *Basic and Applied Social Psychology, 5*, 97–209.

Rhodewalt, F., Sanbonmatsu, D., Feick, D., Tschanz, B., & Waller, A. (1995). Self-handicapping and interpersonal trade-offs: The effects of claimed self-handicaps on observers' performance evaluations and feedback. *Personality and Social Psychology Bulletin, 21*, 1042–1050.

Riggs, J. M. (1992). Self-handicapping and achievement. In A. K. Boggiano & T. S. Pittman (Eds.), *Achievment and motivation: A social-developmental perspective* (pp. 244–267). Cambridge: Cambridge University Press.

Ryan, R. M., & Grolnick, W. S. (1986). Origins and pawns in the classroom: Self-report and projective assessments of individual differences in children's perceptions. *Journal of Personality and Social Psychology, 50*, 550–558.

Sharan, S. (1980). Cooperative learning in small groups: Recent methods and effects on achievement, attitudes and ethnic relations. *Review of Educational Research, 50*, 241–271.

Sheldon, K. M., & Kasser, T. (1995). Coherence and congruence: Two aspects of personality integration. *Journal of Personality and Social Psychology, 68*, 531–543.

Smith, D. S., & Strube, M. J. (1991). Self-protective tendencies as moderators of self-handicapping impressions. *Basic and Applied Social Psychology, 12*, 63–80.

Snyder, C. R., & Smith, T. W. (1982). Symptoms as self-handicapping strategies: The virtues of old wine in a new bottle. In G. Weary & H. L. Mirels (Eds.), *Integration of clinical and social psychology* (pp. 104–127). New York: Oxford University Press.

Thill, E. E. (1993). Age differences in differentiated and undifferentiated conceptions of competence and effeort: Effects on affect and self-handicapping. *International Journal of Psychology, 28*, 845–859.

Urdan, T., Midgely, C., & Anderman, E. M. (1998). The role of classroom goal structure in students' use of self-handicapping strategies. *American Educational Research Journal, 35*, 101–122.

Weiner, B. (1985). An attributional theory of achievement motivation and emotion. *Psychological Review, 92*, 548–573.

Wilson, T. D., & Linville, P. W. (1985). Improving the performance of college freshmen with attributional techniques. *Journal of Personality and Social Psychology, 49*, 287–293.

Zuckerman, M., Kieffer, S., and Knee, C. R. (1998). Consequences of self-handicapping: Effects on coping, academic performances, and adjustment. *Journal of Personality and Social Psychology, 74*, 1619–1628.

## Suggested Reading

Arkin, R. M., & Oleson, K. C. (1998). Self-handicapping. In J. M. Darley & J. Cooper (Eds.), *Attribution and social interaction: The legacy of Edward E. Jones* (pp. 313–371). Washington, DC: American Psychological Association.

Covington, M. V., & Teel, K. M. (1996). *Overcoming student failure: Changing motives and incentives for learning.* Washington, DC: American Psychological Association.

Higgins, R., Snyder, C. R., and Berglas, S. (1990). *Self-handicapping: The paradox that isn't.* New York: Plenum.

Jones, E. E., & Berglas, S. (1978). Control of attributions about the self through self-handicapping strategies: The appeal of alcohol and the role of underachievement. *Personality and Social Psychology Bulletin, 4*, 200–206.

Rhodewalt, F. (1994). Conceptions of ability, achievement goals and individual differences in self-handicapping behavior: On the application of implicit theories. *Journal of Personality, 62*, 67–85.

CHAPTER

7

# The Wisdom of Practice: Lessons Learned from the Study of Highly Effective Tutors

MARK R. LEPPER

*Department of Psychology, Stanford University, California*

MARIA WOOLVERTON

*Department of Pediatrics, Child Development Center,*
*Georgetown University Medical Center, Washington, D. C.*

> One can predict that in a few more years, millions of school children will have access to what Phillip of Macedon's son Alexander enjoyed as a royal prerogative: the personal services of a tutor as well-informed and responsible as Aristotle.
>
> —*Suppes (1966, p. 207)*

As Suppes (1966) notes, for thousands of years, there has been general agreement about the most effective means of teaching children, namely, the individual tutorial. From the ancient Greeks and Romans through the Age of Enlightenment, the children of the rich and powerful (and any others lucky enough to receive any formal instruction) were educated by professional tutors. Even in the midst of the heated debates about the nature of children that characterized 17th- and 18th-century Europe, thinkers as diverse in their

The research reported in this chapter was supported, in part, by Research Grant HD-25258 from the National Institute of Child Health and Human Development to Mark R. Lepper and by a Spencer Foundation Fellowship to Maria Woolverton.

Requests for reprints may be addressed to Mark R. Lepper, Department of Psychology, Jordan Hall—Building 420, Stanford University, Stanford, California 94305–2130 (or, by e-mail, at lepper@psych.stanford.edu).

philosophies as Locke, Hobbes, and Rousseau all agreed on the unsurpassed efficacy of individual tutoring.

Today, as we enter the 21st century, tutoring remains the ideal, the gold standard as it were, of education. In one particularly prominent review of the literature, for example, Benjamin Bloom (1984) documented the major gains in performance that typically result from one-on-one tutoring and suggested that the central task for educational researchers remains the search for other, it is hoped, more practical and cost-effective, instructional techniques that might produce effects on student learning and motivation as powerful as those of personal tutelage. Indeed, even programs in which slightly older students are asked to serve as personal tutors for their younger schoolmates appear to produce substantial gains in both learning and motivation (e.g., Levin, Glass, & Meister, 1984).

At the same time, despite its obvious effectiveness, tutoring has received, until very recently, surprisingly little experimental attention (Wood, Bruner, & Ross, 1976). Presumably, the lack of research interest in tutoring is primarily the result of its high cost, at least as compared with traditional group-oriented instructional methods where single teachers are responsible for teaching 30 or more students. In most public schools, individual tutoring remains a luxury and a rarity. Even today, it is primarily the children of the well-to-do who are able to benefit from individual tutoring, which is paid for by their families, along with a much smaller number of less-advantaged children identified by their schools as requiring exceptional levels of assistance, who receive some individualized instruction as part of various targeted remediation programs (e.g., Clay, 1991; Slavin, Madden, Dolan, & Wasik, 1996).

In the past 10 to 20 years, however, a number of researchers have begun to investigate the process, and not just the results, of tutoring—to examine what makes tutoring such an effective instructional technique. Interestingly, this recent interest has stemmed in large part from the advent of powerful personal computers with the potential, as Suppes had noted in the earliest days of computing, to provide a cost-effective means of providing each child with an individual tutor (e.g., Lajoie & Derry, 1993; Larkin & Chabay, 1992; Lepper & Chabay, 1988; Putnam, 1987; Wenger, 1987). Although there are many ways in which computers are different from people and many things that computers can do better than people, it has seemed to many recent researchers that a better understanding of the dynamics of successful human tutoring might help us to design more effective computer tutors as well (McArthur, Stasz, & Zmuidzinas, 1990; Merrill, Reiser, Merrill, & Landes, 1995).

## BACKGROUND

Certainly, this was true in our own case. Having first become interested in the educational uses of computers as a particularly felicitous laboratory for studying both the determinants of children's intrinsic motivation and the effects of different forms of motivation on children's learning (Lepper, 1985; see also Cordova & Lepper, 1996; Parker & Lepper, 1992), we subsequently came into contact with a variety of earlier efforts by cognitive scientists to use the computational power of the computer to design "intelligent tutoring systems" (Sleeman & Brown, 1982; Wenger, 1987). Generally, these programs seemed well-designed for the efficient transmission of information and feedback to the student, based on that student's current knowledge and misunderstandings of the topic, as assessed by research in cognitive psychology. Indeed, it was often exciting to see these designers building research findings from psychology and education into their programs.

These same programs, however, often seemed to take little account of the affective, motivational, and socioemotional states of the student. Instead, they frequently seemed to presume that the student using these systems would be constantly attentive, highly motivated, and concerned solely with learning as much as possible in as little time as necessary. How else could one explain the existence of tutorial computer programs like the one that sought to correct the fundamental misunderstandings of a struggling remedial student who had asserted that 87 multiplied by 43 yielded 32 with the following pithy commentary:

Your answer is wrong.

Possible causes of error:

1. You multiplied the number in the multiplicand by the number directly beneath it in the multiplier, and you wrote down the carried number, ignoring the units number.

It seemed almost as if programs like this were being designed for robotic, rather than for human, learners—for pupils whose sole mission in life was to improve their task performance as rapidly as possible.

Such assumptions seemed to us unrealistic, especially since these tutoring programs were often explicitly designated as having been designed for use with previously unwilling and unsuccessful students, already identified as requiring remediation in a given area. We began, therefore, to search the educational literature for research on the actual process of tutoring that might help us to highlight the importance of motivational as well as cognitive factors in the tutoring process that we had found missing from the research on computer-based tutors. Surprisingly, although there were clear demonstrations of the overall instructional effectiveness of such techniques, there was virtually no relevant literature on the process of one-to-one human tutoring. In contrast to the many volumes that had been written regarding teaching techniques in the standard classroom, where one teacher must simultaneously seek to instruct and motivate 30 different children who vary in their current levels of achievement and motivation, almost nobody had tried to examine the tutorial process systematically.

Of course, it is possible at a glance to identify several general factors that undoubtedly contribute to the greater effectiveness of tutorials, compared with traditional classroom practices. Most prominently, tutorials provide a venue for learning that is inherently more individualized, more immediate, and more interactive than most common school settings. Let us consider each of these factors, briefly, in turn.

*Individualization.*    First, and more obviously, the tutorial is inherently individualized. In contrast to standard classrooms, in which single teachers must divide their attention and energies across 30 different students, the student in a tutorial session has the complete attention of the tutor. This individualization, in turn, permits the tutor to elicit from each student a much higher level of on-task attention and effort. It is, in addition, a virtual prerequisite for the high levels of both immediacy and interactivity that also characterize the tutorial process.

*Immediacy.*    Thus, in an individual tutorial, both knowledge of results and other forms of feedback and instruction are received by students as, or shortly after, they work on specific problems or activities. Reinforcement for correct work is therefore more effective, and constructive feedback is more likely to be understood and receive attention. Corrections can be made "on-line," and general principles can be related to specific instances at once. This situation is quite unlike much of current formal education in the classroom where homework assignments, papers, and problem sets are often returned with grades and other relevant feedback days or weeks after completion of the work itself.

*Interactivity.*    Similarly, instructional methods in a tutorial are typically more interactive than those in a normal classroom, in the sense that the tutors' choices about what activities to present, what assistance to offer, what encouragement to give, and so forth usually depend heavily on the tutors' careful observations of their students. Both tutors' goals and strategies, in short, depend on information they receive from students (both verbal and nonverbal) and on their perceptions of the current skills and knowledge and the current level of motivation of their tutees. As a result, tasks, feedback, instruction, encouragement, and so on, can all be tailored to the cognitive and motivational profiles and requirements of individual students.

Although these general considerations are of critical importance, our hope was to understand better the more detailed dynamics of successful tutorials. If we wanted to see what more specific factors were critical in producing the substantial gains that individual tutoring seemed capable of producing, however, it appeared we would have to investigate that question ourselves. In the end, we decided to do just that.

## STUDYING "EXPERT" TUTORS

The remainder of this chapter, then, seeks to provide a brief overview of some of the main findings of a set of studies, conducted over the past decade, of what makes individual tutoring such a successful educational method (e.g., Lepper, Aspinwall, Mumme, & Chabay, 1990; Lepper, Drake, & O'Donnell-Johnson, 1997; Lepper & Chabay, 1988; Lepper, Woolverton, Mumme, & Gurtner, 1993; Woolverton, in preparation). Some of these factors, as we shall see, are fairly obvious. Others are less so, though, and become apparent only after detailed observation and careful study. These latter, more subtle factors in the success of the tutorial method, we believe, are often the result of successful tutors trying to accomplish sometimes conflicting cognitive, information-transmittal, versus motivational or affective, goals at the same time, as we describe later in this chapter.

Our studies involved a simple procedure. First, we sought to identify individuals who seemed likely to be highly effective as tutors. We did so by asking a number of schools, teachers, and tutoring agencies to identify for us people whom they considered particularly qualified and highly effective (or likely to be highly effective) as individual tutors. We then interviewed these nominees and, once we had documented that they had indeed had experience in teaching or tutoring in the relevant domain and age range, invited them to participate in our studies by actually serving as a tutor for a number of different students.

These tutoring sessions were videotaped and transcribed for analysis. Learning by the tutees was assessed via traditional written tests on the material covered, which were administered both before and after the tutoring sessions. Motivation was assessed via self-report measures as well as ratings of the videotaped sessions. In addition, tutors were asked to watch the videotapes of their own sessions and to provide a running commentary on what they could recall about what they had been thinking and feeling and what options they had been considering as each session progressed. A number of our best tutors were also interviewed more generally regarding their perceptions and philosophies about tutoring.

To simplify our analytic task somewhat, in all of our studies the topic of study involved some aspect of elementary mathematics, ranging from basic addition to fractions to multistage word problems. Similarly, the students who served as our tutees were all elementary school students who ranged, depending on the topic under study, from first through sixth grade. In most of our studies, as well, the students selected as tutees had been identified by their schools as particularly in need of remedial help on the topic, although we have recently also collected data from one sample of highly successful students who will serve as a contrast group as well.

Highly effective or "expert" tutors were then identified on the basis of their actual degree of observable success, across a number of different tutees, in promoting student learning and motivation. The tutoring sessions conducted by these highly effective tutors were analyzed from a number of perspectives and were contrasted with tutoring sessions conducted by less experienced or by equally experienced but objectively less successful tutors. The goal of our analyses was to begin to identify the goals, strategies, and specific techniques that might contribute to the success of an individual tutorial.

## SOME GENERAL PRELIMINARY FINDINGS

Before we turn to the results of our comparisons between more and less empirically effective tutors, however, there are a number of preliminary findings from this project that will help to contextualize these comparative results. Let us begin by highlighting these general findings, then, if only in capsule form.

### The Tutorial Process

The first "preliminary" finding from our observations of tutorial interactions is that there were, at least in the domain of mathematics, some general commonalities in the nature of the typical tutoring sessions that seemed to be shared by virtually all of our experienced tutors, regardless of their level of relative success. Specifically, there seemed to be in our tutoring sessions a series of recurrent phases, in which the goals and strategies of the tutors characteristically shifted as their students received problems, assistance, feedback, and instruction. Because a knowledge of this "phase structure" of the tutoring sessions will provide a useful background and context for understanding the differences between more and less effective tutors to be considered below, it is worth outlining this structure here.

In particular, once past an initial "introduction" period (in which tutors typically introduced themselves and the topic that was to be studied, and sought to establish some initial rapport with the student), most of the tutoring sessions we observed showed the following recurrent sequence of phases as students worked through a series of problems:

*Problem selection.*    First, the tutors selected a problem for presentation to the student. These selections were based, in large part, on the tutors' diagnoses of their students' current knowledge and (mis)understandings of the material to be covered and on their perceptions of the students' present motivational state. In this initial phase, the tutors' general goal seemed to be to select a problem that would provide either a good learning experience, a motivational boost, and/or an opportunity to gain diagnostic information about the students' current state of knowledge and misconceptions.

*Problem presentation.*   Second, the tutors presented the selected problem to the student, often accompanied by various encouragements, exhortations, admonitions, or problem descriptions. In this presentation phase, the tutors' main aims seemed to be to provide students with helpful information or forewarning about features of the problem and/or to motivate students and encourage their involvement and persistence at the activity.

*Problem solution.*   In the third phase, control shifted somewhat to the tutee, as the student proceeded to try to solve the problem that had been presented by the tutor. During this third phase, typically, tutors sought to provide sufficient scaffolding, assistance, encouragement, and feedback to permit their students to reach a correct solution to the problem. Only very rarely, however, did tutors (once a problem had been presented) actually provide the students directly with correct solutions or explicitly direct them in correct solution procedures.

*Reflection.*   Once the problem had been correctly solved, tutors frequently sought to encourage the student to reflect on the solution process—to articulate the meaning of the problem, to discuss the lessons that had been learned or the steps that had been followed, or to consider the relationship of this problem to other problems or to other contexts.

*Instruction.*   Finally, when necessary, tutors can provide fairly direct instruction about concepts or procedures that the student has not previously encountered. Because our particular tutoring protocols involved primarily remedial students who had already been exposed at some length, and without much success, to didactic instruction on the topics to be covered, this phase proved relatively uncommon in our sample. In other uses of tutoring to present new concepts and procedures, however, such concerns would presumably prove much more crucial and prominent.

## A General Framework

A second crucial background finding is that our best tutors seemed to devote constant and considerable attention to motivating and providing emotional support for students, as well as to simply providing feedback and transmitting information. Indeed, the simultaneous focus of effective tutors on both affective and cognitive factors in the tutoring process is itself one central feature of our general model of expert tutoring. Although space limitations preclude an extended presentation of this analysis, our basic presumption is that highly successful tutors seek to develop and maintain a "working model" of each tutee that encompasses both the current emotional and knowledge states of their students, updating the working model as they gather more information and observe the students progressing through the tutoring session.

Indeed, for purposes of understanding the goals and strategies of excellent tutors, it has proved to us a useful oversimplification to think of these tutors as constructing and maintaining two separate types of diagnostic models of their students.

***Cognitive models.***   The first of these involves a cognitive model that is focused on the student's current state of knowledge/ignorance and on the possible systematic misunderstandings or "bugs" that may characterize that student's understanding of the material. Here we have in mind the sort of diagnostic informational model that has long been assumed and studied by those involved in the design of intelligent tutoring systems (e.g., Burton & Brown, 1979; Sleeman & Brown, 1982; Wenger, 1987).

***Motivational models.***   The second of these, by contrast, involves an affective model that focuses on the student's apparent current level of motivation, attention, interest, and self-confidence in the relevant domain of study. Diagnostic models of this latter sort, concerning student motivation, have received considerably less attention in previous research (del Soldato & du Boulay, 1995; Derry & Potts, 1998; Lepper & Chabay, 1988).

Both of these working models, we presume, are continuously modified and updated during the course of an effective tutoring session, as tutors watch students confront, solve, discuss, and/or fail to master actual problems. Subsequent judgments and decisions about tutorial goals and strategies are then predicted to be, in an interactive and responsive fashion, a joint function of the tutor's models of these two aspects of their students' current functioning. In particular, there are obviously three basic relationships that may exist between the pedagogical implications of a tutor's hypothetically separate models of an individual tutee's present cognitive and present motivational states. At any particular choice point in a tutoring session the implications of a purely cognitive versus a purely motivational analysis may be either entirely congruent with one another, simply independent of each other, or directly in conflict with one another. Each of these three cases, we believe, has different implications for what decision the tutor is likely to make.

Consider, for example, the simple case of a tutor making a decision about what problem to next give a particular student, under these three different conditions:

***Congruent.***   First, the tutor's cognitive versus motivational diagnoses about the student may yield implications for action that are entirely congruent with one another. If the tutor infers (for instance, from the student's immediately prior successful performance on several problems of the same type) that the student both (a) fully understands and (b) feels completely comfortable with a particular type of problem, then the situation is simple. Both cognitive and motivational analyses would suggest that the next problem to be presented should be significantly more difficult than the problem just solved. Moreover, since such a decision follows from both models, we would expect this decision to be an easy one for tutors, and we would expect most tutors to behave in the same fashion when faced with this same situation.

**Independent.**   A second possibility is that either the tutor's cognitive or motivational analysis independently suggests some decision that might have positive effects on one dimension, without any direct effect on the other.[1] If the tutor, for example, believes that the student (a) fully understands the current problems, but (b) is entirely disinterested in the task at hand, the tutor may decide not only to select a more difficult problem, but also to present that problem in a context that is personalized according to the student's interests (e.g., a problem involving sports or music).

**Conflicting.**   Finally, a tutor's cognitive versus motivational analyses may point in precisely opposite directions. Thus, a tutor who feels that the student (a) does not understand the problem well but (b) is nonetheless overconfident and anxious to move to more complex problems may experience a sense of clear conflict, and that tutor's decision may depend on his or her perception of the relative strength and importance of these two competing factors for this particular student. In one such case, we have seen a highly effective tutor deliberately select a problem that the tutor expected would "look" more difficult to the student, without any increase in actual difficulty level; in another instance, we have seen an equally successful tutor choose to present a more difficult problem but with an unusually high level of verbal scaffolding designed to help the student avoid an abject failure. More generally, such cases of direct conflict between the implications of cognitive and motivational diagnoses are predicted to be most likely to prove difficult for tutors, to result in pedagogical "compromises" between efficient information transfer and motivationally supportive pedagogy, and to produce potentially counterintuitive tutoring strategies or techniques. Our discussion below highlights the ways in which truly expert tutors demonstrate these strategies and techniques.

[1]In the long run, of course, any strategies that do have an immediate positive impact on either learning alone or motivation alone should also have positive subsequent effects in both domains. Thus, even under highly controlled experimental conditions, "purely cognitive" factors that demonstrably enhance learning can also be shown to later enhance intrinsic motivation as well (e.g., Bandura & Schunk, 1981). Conversely, "purely motivational" factors that demonstrably enhance intrinsic interest can also be shown to later enhance learning as well (e.g., Cordova & Lepper, 1996).

## THE "EXPERT" TUTOR

A critical finding from our observations of tutorial interactions, then, is that there *are* individuals who do seem to qualify as "expert" or highly effective tutors. Thus, in all of our samples, we were able to identify some tutors who proved empirically effective in promoting both learning and motivation, in all or virtually all of the students with whom they worked. The students tutored by these expert tutors showed, on independent measures of cognition and motivation, clearly greater gains than would have been expected solely on the basis of their initial levels of achievement in the domain.

In fact, by most standards, the progress achieved by our very best tutors in a limited number of individual sessions was often truly remarkable. These most successful tutors were not just effective; they were often superb. At their best, they were able to turn initially resistant, alienated, and seemingly helpless students into interested and excited participants in the learning process. At their best, they were able to help remedial students to progress through what would normally have been weeks or months of curriculum material in a very short time. Moreover, gains in students' learning remained apparent following and outside of the tutoring situation, showing that these gains were not simply the result of differences in the immediate support and scaffolding that tutors provided during the experimental sessions.

Similarly, another important finding was that there did seem to be some commonalities, on at least a number of dimensions, in the goals, strategies, and techniques of those tutors who were highly successful. Indeed, when we compared the various sessions conducted by our best tutors as they each worked with a number of different students, there was a quite surprising level of consistency in their individual approaches across different tutees. Although these top tutors were indeed very responsive to differences among the children they tutored, they did display characteristic styles of instructing and motivating students. Though quick to respond to differences in students, these tutors did so within a basic framework that they established and maintained. Equally important, there were at least some elements of these tutors' approaches that appeared in common across different particular expert tutors, suggesting the potential utility of an analysis of these common elements in the styles of these highly effective individuals.

## THE *INSPIRE* MODEL

With this general background, then, let us turn to some of the more specific strategies and techniques that we found to be especially characteristic of our most effective tutors, as compared with their less effective or less experienced counterparts. Many of our specific findings from these comparisons, we believe, can be summarized in what Lepper, Drake, and O'Donnell-Johnson

(1997) have called the INSPIRE model of tutoring success. This acronym seeks to highlight seven critical characteristics of demonstrably "expert" tutors in our studies: the ways in which our best tutors proved simultaneously Intelligent, Nurturant, Socratic, Progressive, Indirect, Reflective, and Encouraging. Let us then examine each of these specific factors, in turn, in more detail.

## Intelligent

It must seem like a truism to begin by asserting that highly effective tutors are highly knowledgeable and intelligent. Other things being equal, who would ever have argued the opposite? Nevertheless, it may still prove instructive to examine the several sorts of knowledge that our best tutors seem to possess:

*Subject-matter knowledge.*   Certainly excellent teachers in any context must be expected to know thoroughly the material they are teaching. Still, we found ourselves impressed by the depth and breadth of the subject-matter knowledge that our top tutors displayed. For example, compared with their less effective counterparts, our highly effective tutors were more likely to provide relevant historical information about the topic that they thought might be instructive or motivating to students, and they were much more effective in using concrete manipulatives and visual models to help illustrate difficult problems to students. Perhaps most important, these top tutors seemed able to produce a much wider variety of real-world analogies that could be used to help students understand difficult new concepts, such as negative numbers and fractions.

*Subject-specific pedagogical knowledge.*   Equally striking in our tutoring protocols were differences between our most and least effective tutors in what has been called subject-specific pedagogical knowledge. Our best tutors knew, for example, what sorts of problems were most likely to prove especially difficult for students or to elicit particular sorts of errors from them. They even seemed to know which sorts of problems were likely to *appear* more difficult to students even though they were not, and which sorts of problems were likely to *appear* easier to students than they really were.

*General pedagogical knowledge.*   Finally, our best tutors also seemed to show greater general pedagogical knowledge than their peers. Thus, they were more likely both to use and to be able to articulate the variety of instructional and motivational techniques detailed in the following sections.

## Nurturant

At the same time, our best tutors were not simply highly knowledgeable automatons; they were also highly supportive and nurturing of students. At the outset of each tutoring session, for instance, they were more likely to begin by trying to establish some personal rapport with their students—conversing with the students about their interests in and outside of school, their friends and families, their teachers, and the like. Throughout the tutoring sessions, these tutors displayed warmth and concern. They were continuously attentive to their students, they empathized with students' difficulties, and they showed confidence in their students' ability to succeed at the task. Again, although such strategies may sound like they should be intuitive, we did on occasion witness sessions with less effective tutors that resulted in students crying or burying their heads in their hands, despite the fact that such tutors may have come highly recommended by school districts where they served as classroom teachers.

## Socratic

In contrast to our first two features of intelligence and nurturance, which may seem self-evident as desiderata of good tutors, our third feature is potentially more counterintuitive. In particular, our best tutors seem to prefer a Socratic to a more didactic approach, at least when they are working with students who have a history of failure at the topic.

*Questions, not directions.* The first and most obvious feature of our top tutors' Socratic approach can be seen in their constant use of questions, rather than directions or assertions, in working with tutees. Although their questions may often be leading or informative, these tutors try to draw as much as possible from the student and to impose as little as necessary on the student. Indeed, more than 90% of the remarks that our best tutors make are likely to be in the form of questions.

*Hints, not answers.* In a related vein, our most effective tutors also seek to avoid directly giving students answers. Instead they prefer to offer hints or suggestions, to help students take the next step on their own. Moreover, good tutors often persist in this strategy, offering five or six hints in succession if their initial efforts prove unsuccessful in leading students to the correct answer. Indeed, if we did not have clear outcome data establishing the great success of these same tutors, it would be easy to believe that such an initially inefficient strategy might prove quite dysfunctional. Yet it appears that the advantages of this Socratic approach, at least with remedial students, must far outweigh its superficial inefficiency.

*Productive versus nonproductive errors.* Finally, in clear contrast to their less effective counterparts, our best tutors displayed a more highly nuanced and sophisticated understanding of the different types of errors that students may make (Lepper et al., 1997). Whereas our less effective tutors tended to respond in a similar fashion to almost any error that students made, our most effective tutors distinguished different types of errors that had different implications for action by the tutor. At the simplest level, for instance, our best tutors would often simply ignore small errors, especially when these errors did not prevent the tutee from reaching a correct answer, although such errors might also lead these tutors to provide subsequent problems that examined these issues further. Our less successful tutors, however, seemed unable to let any error pass, no matter how trivial or inconsequential.

More important, our best tutors seemed to distinguish between what we might call "productive" and "nonproductive" errors. In particular, to these tutors, some student errors seemed "productive," in the sense that tutors believed that their occurrence would provide good occasions for students, with some subtle guidance from the tutor, to discover their own mistakes in a manner that would promote lasting learning. Such errors were therefore deliberately allowed to occur by the tutors, so that they could then be systematically "debuggged," as described below. By contrast, these tutors also believed that there were other student errors that (a) could be corrected only by a more direct and explicit intervention by the tutor, and (b) if left uncorrected, would lead the student down a dysfunctional path. When "nonproductive" errors of this sort occurred, then, these same excellent tutors were quick to intervene in a more immediate and direct fashion.

## Progressive

Yet a fourth characteristic of our expert tutors concerns the planful and progressive structure they create in the tutoring situation. Aspects of this general approach can be seen in a number of domains, including tutors' selections of problems for presentation to students, their systematic techniques for addressing student errors and misconceptions, and their use of a variety of predictable routines across the tutoring session.

***Problem progression.*** Thus, in contrast to many less effective tutors, our expert tutors clearly plan their tutoring sessions to involve a systematic progression of problem types of increasing difficulty or complexity. Although the rate of progression may vary considerably with different students, these better tutors always begin with problems deliberately selected to allow them to observe and diagnose their students' initial levels of knowledge and misunderstanding. Subsequent problems are then selected that provide opportunities for the correction of any systematic misunderstandings or "bugs" that students have displayed. Once students have proved competent and confident at a given problem level, then, new and more difficult problem types are introduced, and the same cycle of diagnosis, debugging, and increased difficulty is repeated. Surprisingly, our less effective tutors do not regularly use these seemingly self-evident tactics.

*Systematic debugging.* A similar, highly systematic progression is evident, in reverse, in our best tutors' attempts to correct or "debug" students' underlying misconceptions. Here, because these tutors' general goal is to prompt students to discover for themselves the reasons for their errors, excellent tutors who confront students who have made errors that reflect basic misunderstandings routinely begin with very general hints and questions. Only if these initial general prompts fail do these tutors start to become increasingly specific and pointed in their questions and suggestions, until the student attains the desired insight.

*Progressive routines.* Likewise, there is a more general sense in which the tutoring sessions of our most successful tutors are more systematic and progressive than those of our less successful tutors, because our better tutors are generally much more effective in structuring their tutoring sessions through the use of recurring routines. Such routines help to make clear to students the structure of the tutoring session and, in turn, help to focus the students' attention on appropriate issues at different phases of the tutorial. As students internalize this structure, less and less guidance is needed from the tutor to make the tutorial run smoothly.

## Indirect

Closely related to this Socratic stance adopted by our most effective tutors is a fifth characteristic, namely, the indirect style that these tutors typically employ, especially in working with students known to have a history of difficulty in the relevant domain of study. Once again, as with their Socratic approach, it is the strength of tutors' commitment to this style, rather than its existence, which most impressed us in the protocols of our top tutors. These tutors are not just politely indirect with their tutees; they are excruciatingly so, and this indirectness can be seen in both the negative and the positive feedback they provide to students.

*Negative feedback.* Thus, few readers will find it surprising that our highly effective tutors are more likely to avoid overt criticism of their pupils. After all, direct negative feedback of this sort can clearly have deleterious effects on the motivation of students, especially those who have low levels of confidence in their abilities to begin with. What is rather more surprising, however, is that these tutors often manage to avoid *ever* saying *explicitly* that the student has made an error. Rather, in the face of an incorrect problem step or a mistaken answer to a question, these tutors are likely to pose a question that indirectly implies the existence of some error and, sometimes, the location of that error. Their goal is to prompt students into retracing their own steps and "catching" their own errors, while avoiding the negative motivational consequences of pointing explicitly to mistakes and failures on the part of the students.

***Positive feedback.***   Less pervasive, but potentially even more surprising, are our findings concerning the positive feedback that highly successful tutors offer following student successes. For relative to their less successful peers, these top tutors also seem less likely to provide explicit or effusive praise to students, especially praise directed at the person rather than the process of problem solving. Although our less effective tutors appear to believe that frequent and profuse direct praise would prove motivating to their students, our outcome data suggest the opposite—that the adverse effects of turning the tutoring session into a highly evaluative context, at least for students at risk, may outweigh the potential benefits of greater positive reinforcement.

## Reflective

To this point, our description of effective tutors may give the impression that these tutors are focused solely on procedural, as opposed to declarative, knowledge, on learning what, rather than why. Such an impression would be inaccurate, however, because our top tutors also devote considerable effort to encouraging reflection and articulation by students. More than their less effective counterparts, good tutors clearly seek to impart an understanding of underlying general principles, as well as specific procedures and strategies for solving problems.

This commitment to teaching for understanding can be seen in several related aspects of the protocols of highly effective tutors. These more effective tutors are more likely to ask students to articulate what they are learning, to explain their reasoning and their answers, and to generalize or relate their work in the tutoring session to other contexts and problems. At the same time, in keeping with their generally Socratic approach, it is important to emphasize that these tutors do most often attempt first to *elicit* these articulations, explanations, and generalizations from their students. These student-generated reflections may then be shaped and elaborated, if needed. Only when these tutors are convinced that such less direct tactics have proved insufficient, will they directly provide their own explanations or generalizations to their students.

***Articulation.***   Thus, one common characteristic of our best tutors is their penchant for asking students to reflect aloud on what they have just done, immediately after a successful problem solution. In so doing, these tutors seek both to gain information from students about possible misunderstandings that might not have been evident from their solutions to the preceding problem and to help students to be able to understand, at a conceptual level, the operations they had used to solve the problem. Indeed, one particularly successful tutor had students keep a running, written list in their own words of the general ''lessons'' they had learned from the problems they solved during the tutoring session.

**Explanation.**   Similarly, these tutors are also likely to ask students to explain their answers and their procedures, periodically, after successful problem solutions. If, as is often the case, students provide an explanation that is accurate but incomplete, the tutor will elaborate on the student's response, providing a model of a more complete explanation.

**Generalization.**   Likewise, these tutors are also likely to ask students periodically how the work they had just done, or the problem they had just solved, might relate to some other type of problem or to some real-world situation that students would be familiar with and interested in.

## Encouraging

Finally, by describing our best tutors with the term "encouraging," we intend to encompass a wide range of techniques and strategies that our expert tutors employ to keep students interested, attentive, and involved with the topic at hand. These motivational strategies, which have been spelled out in more detail by Lepper et al. (1993), can be seen as falling into five basic categories. These categories reflect five potentially complementary sources of motivation for learning that tutors seek to sustain and increase (Lepper & Malone, 1987; Malone & Lepper, 1987):

**Confidence.**   First, our best tutors are centrally concerned with bolstering students' feelings of competence and mastery, and these concerns are heightened when students begin tutoring sessions with a past history of failure in the classroom and a low level of confidence in their ability in the domain at hand. As noted above, however, our most effective tutors do not simply praise these students more often or more profusely. Rather, their strategies for enhancing students' feelings of competence are considerably more subtle. They frequently emphasize, for instance, the difficulty of the problems they are presenting, implicitly giving students an excuse if they do have difficulty and implicitly increasing the value of success for them if they do succeed.

**Challenge.**   At the same time, our best tutors also do not constantly reassure students about their abilities, even when those students have been selected on the basis of their need for remedial help. Instead, our top tutors are more likely to challenge their students, to goad them into a desire to "show" the tutor just how much they can accomplish. Moreover, in their selection of problems to present and their decisions about how much help to provide on each, these tutors seek to confront students with problems that will be difficult, though not impossible, in the belief that such moderately high levels of challenge will be most effective in motivating students.

***Curiosity.***   Third, our most successful tutors are also more likely to try to pique their students' sense of curiosity, to make them want to find out the answers on their own. These tutors are, for example, more likely to ask students to predict in advance how a current problem might prove similar to, or different from, a previous problem, so that they can see their own expectations confirmed or disconfirmed. Similarly, they may deliberately highlight inconsistencies between different facts or procedures that the student has previously learned in different contexts, to provoke the student to seek some resolution.

***Control.***   In like fashion, our best tutors also seek to provide their students with a sense of personal control in the tutoring situation. Where it is possible to do so without negative instructional consequences, for instance, these tutors offer students choices or comply with their requests.[2] They may also emphasize a student's sense of agency directly, and as noted above, they will generally avoid the sorts of direct didactic methods that would be likely to undermine a learner's feelings of control.

***Contextualization.***   Finally, our top tutors seek to place otherwise purely abstract problems, especially in mathematics, into meaningful and interesting contexts. Students will be more motivated by a problem, these tutors believe, if that problem can be personalized so that students can see its relevance to familiar real-world contexts that they already care about. Likewise, these tutors believe that students will be more motivated to become involved with and to persist at problems that have been embedded in inherently enjoyable and provocative stories or fantasy contexts that make contact with the preexisting interests and knowledge of students.

## SUMMARY

In short, our most effective tutors differ in many ways—in their goals, their strategies, and their specific knowledge and techniques—from their equally experienced, but less successful, counterparts. Nevertheless, the general picture, we hope, is clear: Our best tutors are those who are concerned *simultaneously* with students' learning on the one hand and their motivation on the other. Thus, these tutors do not consider their task to be merely the efficient provision of feedback and information as some early theories of learning might have implied (Lepper & Chabay, 1985). Nor are they willing to sacrifice learning for

[2]Unfortunately, the literature does suggest that students may sometimes make nonoptimal decisions about instructionally critical aspects of their learning if given total control over such factors (Lepper & Malone, 1987; Steinberg, 1989). As one example, children who have had a history of failure in the domain under study will often choose to stick with easier problems at which they are sure they can succeed, at the expense of opportunities for further learning, if they are given the opportunity to choose the problems they will try.

the sake of motivation, as critics of the so-called "self-esteem" movement in the schools have described (Stout, 2000). Rather than "dumbing down" the instructional content by presenting easy problems or preventing student errors in an attempt to preserve students' self-esteem, these tutors demonstrate knowledge of a wide array of systematic techniques, both for presenting information to students and for encouraging student involvement and persistence at a task.

These tutors share a generally Socratic approach, in the sense that they seek to draw as much as possible from the student and to impose as little as possible of themselves on the student. They ask questions, but do not give directions. They offer hints, but avoid giving answers. The feedback they provide students, regularly after failure and sometimes even after success, is typically indirect, to minimize the evaluative pressure of the situation. And, when they are at their best, they are superb, producing both high levels of student interest and attention and extensive learning in a quite limited period.

## IMPLICATIONS

There are many reasons for studying what makes excellent tutors so effective at instructing and motivating their students. From a theoretical perspective, on the one hand, we see the study of individual tutoring sessions as a particularly informative laboratory for studying the dynamics of effective learning in general. In contrast to the vastly more common studies of learning in traditional classrooms, where issues of behavioral control, classroom management, simple time-on-task, and whole-class instruction often dominate discussions, studies of individual tutoring sessions permit us to examine in much greater detail the process of instruction, the types of feedback and assistance that promote learning, and the strategies that most enhance student motivation.

Because we believe in Kurt Lewin's dictum that "there is nothing so practical as a good theory," we believe that the *practical* importance of detailed observations of real-world learning that can contribute to the formation of more effective theories of motivation and instruction should not be underestimated. In addition, studies of the goals and strategies of especially effective tutors should also contribute to the improvement of current educational practices in a number of more immediate and direct ways.

First, such studies can serve as a basis for the design of more effective computer-based tutors. As we noted at the start of this chapter, the past 10 to 15 years have witnessed the development of a variety of computer-based tutors, and many of these programs have been based on considerably oversimplified models of the tutoring process. Traditionally, such programs have featured highly direct and didactic instruction to students, often pointing out each error the student makes, giving the correct answer to the student, describing the misconceptions underlying each error, and explicitly demonstrating correct solution processes. Usually little explicit attention, beyond the inclusion of simple praise statements, is given to attempts to enhance or maintain student interest in the material; instead, an inherently attentive and motivated learner is simply presumed by these programs.

Clearly what highly effective human tutors do when they are at their best is quite different, as we have described above. Although we recognize that there many potentially critical differences between human and computer tutors that may influence the effectiveness of particular tutoring techniques (Lepper & Chabay, 1988), it nonetheless seems evident to us that the effectiveness of many computer tutors might be enhanced by a more complex, research-based model of the determinants of effective tutoring.

Moreover, the same may be true for many of the human tutors who currently work with children. Certainly, we found that even our most effective tutors almost never reported having received any formal training in working with students individually. Instead, most of their courses and student-teaching experiences were focused, quite reasonably, on the more common whole-classroom or small-group instructional settings. Hence, data of the sort collected in our studies may help to provide the basis for designing some systematic training for those who are likely to serve as tutors for our children.[3]

As increasing numbers of even less experienced tutors become involved with children, both through parent or other volunteer tutoring programs at school and through commercial after-school tutoring programs, the need for effective tutor-training programs can only increase. Indeed, the success of formal educational intervention efforts, such as Clay's (1985, 1991) Reading Readiness program and Slavin's Success for All model (Slavin et al., 1996), that include the provision of periodic access to individual tutors for all students having academic problems, has provided a considerable further impetus to the regular use of human tutors in schools here and abroad.

Similarly, the detailed study of the techniques and strategies of expert adult tutors may even have implications for programs that seek to involve other students as tutors for younger, or less capable, peers (e.g., Fitz-Gibbon, 1977; Graesser, Bowers, Hacker, & Person, 1997)—programs that have been identified as perhaps the single most cost-effective intervention that our schools could implement with minimal difficulty tomorrow (e.g., Levin et al., 1984). Plainly, there will be many respects in which the dynamics of cross-age tutoring will necessarily differ from those of adult tutoring, for we certainly cannot expect young students to develop the same levels of knowledge and expertise as their older counterparts. Nonetheless, an increased understanding of effective tutoring methods may help us to create better structures, materials, and training procedures for students who are to serve as tutors in such cross-age tutoring programs.

[3]Yet one further domain in which tutoring may become increasingly available in the future involves individual tutoring offered via the Internet. In this theoretically interesting setting, individual tutors virtually interact with individual students in real time, with a shared computer display serving as a ''white board'' that both parties can see and use.

Finally, if we consider the study of expert tutorials more generally, as a laboratory for the study of highly effective learning, there may even be lessons to be learned for traditional classroom practices as well. When we consider the truly extensive efforts devoted by our best tutors to maintaining students' motivation, along with their general commitment to Socratic and inquiry-based strategies, the contrast with many traditional classroom practices seems striking. Instead, the goals and strategies of our expert tutors seem much closer to those of classroom teachers who seek to integrate into their classrooms the use of inherently interesting and demonstrably meaningful "projects" and other discovery-oriented educational techniques (e.g., Bruner, 1966; Edwards, Gandini, & Foreman, 1993; Katz & Chard, 1989; Lampert, 1986). In this respect, perhaps the most general lesson to emerge from our studies of highly successful tutors is that encompassed in the ancient proverb about the process of truly effective learning:

I hear and I forget. I see and I remember. I do and I understand.

## Teachers' Questions and Answers

**Q:**   I have two related questions. First as a teacher, I truly believe those characteristics described in your chapter do make effective tutors and teachers. However, oftentimes when a teacher uses the kind of strategies described in your chapter (Socratic, inquiry-based, indirect positive feedback, etc.), these tend to be received by students (especially those who are not very successful) with some resistance, especially at the beginning. Was this observed in your studies? What can be done to minimize this response from students? Were there any differences in reactions between remedial and successful students?

Second, I wonder if there were any observed differences when using indirect positive feedback among remedial versus successful students or with students of different ages? Although I have found indirect feedback to be the most effective, as a teacher one of the hardest things for me is to achieve a balance with respect to positive feedback—not enough, too much, too direct, too indirect. Any suggestions on how to achieve this balance?

**A:**   You raise really important questions about what is perhaps the most complex aspect of our expert tutors' strategies, namely, their generally indirect and Socratic style. As your questions suggest, the use of this approach may sometimes require art, as well as science.

A first issue concerns students' possible resistance to such techniques, especially at the outset. Although we did not see much of this response in the tutoring sessions we observed, we have seen this sort of resistance in many other settings. We think that it occurs primarily when students are trying simply to "get through" the material as quickly as possible and therefore see an indirect approach, relying on hints and questions rather than answers and directions, as inefficient and likely to prolong a tutoring or teaching situation.

This problem typically takes a different form for remedial versus successful students. For remedial students, resistance usually stems from a desire just to get through as quickly as possible, without any concern for actually learning the material. Hence, they would prefer it if they were just given the answers so that they can leave a situation they find an embarrassing reminder of their lack of competence in a domain. For more successful students, in contrast, this same response can occur for slightly different reasons, when they feel that they understand things well, but have simply forgotten (or never learned) some specific point that is now preventing them from going forward. Again in this situation, indirect techniques may be seen as simply slowing these good students down.

The hard part, of course, is how to prevent this reaction. We think there may be three reasons why we did not see this response very often in the tutoring sessions we studied. First, the sessions were a fixed length, so that there was no possibility of exiting the situation more quickly by simply "taking dictation" from the tutor. Second, our best tutors seemed to be very effective in using a variety of techniques to convince even the most problematic students that they really could learn the material, despite their past difficulties. Third, these tutors also seemed to find ways of making their students want to learn. Of the many techniques that we saw, perhaps the most striking was the ability of many of these tutors to make the tutoring session into a sort of game for students. Most generally, we think that students will generally accept these techniques once a good relationship has been established between teacher and student.

Finally, as you note, there certainly is a difficult balancing act that teachers using these techniques must negotiate, especially when it comes to the use of praise and positive feedback. Unfortunately, there is no simple answer to this one. On the one hand, feedback has to be clear: students must know when their responses are right and when they are wrong. On the other hand, praise must always be credible. In our sessions, tutors who praised remedial students who had succeeded at very simple problems as having "a great math mind" or being "a real whiz" clearly did not achieve the goals they had intended, as the incredulous looks on their students' faces plainly indicated. On the other hand, if there is not already a positive relationship between tutor and student, the tutor may need to make more use of explicit praise, and overt statements of confidence in the student's ability, at the start of a session, to build student confidence that the tutor is on his or her side.

**Q:**    At the private school where I work, a fair number of teachers do not have an education degree. However, they do have advanced degrees in their subject areas and are excellent teachers. One of the characteristics of highly effective tutors mentioned in your chapter was their high general pedagogical knowledge. Did this knowledge come from having taken courses in the field of education or from experience? Did most of these highly effective tutors have formal education training? From the standpoint of school administrators who very often have to read resumes of prospective teachers to decide which candidate will be hired, which if either of the two, subject-matter or pedagogical knowledge, seemed a more critical component of a highly effective teacher in the modern classroom?

**A:** In our sample, all of our tutors, the best and the worst alike, had had formal training in education, because that was one of the criteria by which we chose them. At the same time, in interviews, none of our tutors remembered ever receiving much training in one-to-one, as opposed to whole-class or small-group, situations. They seemed to think, therefore, that most of what they knew about tutoring they had learned by experience.

Obviously principals are often faced with choices among candidates with different sorts of credentials and training, in specific subjects versus general education, and this is an important issue. To be asked whether subject-matter expertise or general pedagogical expertise is more important, though, seems difficult. In the work of our best tutors, the two seem so intertwined that it is like asking whether a person's right leg or left leg is more important to walking. If we had to guess, we would say that it probably depends somewhat on the grade level of the students and the nature of the topic: that the more advanced the students and the more complex the topic, the more critical specific subject-matter knowledge is likely to be.

## Acknowledgments

These projects benefited greatly from the contributions of many collaborators, including Lisa Aspinwall, Ruth Chabay, Michael Drake, Jean-Luc Gurtner, Donna Mumme, and Teresa O'Donnell-Johnson. The authors are deeply indebted to all of them.

## References

Bandura, A., & Schunk, D. (1981). Cultivating competence, self-efficacy, and intrinsic interest through proximal self-motivation. *Journal of Personality and Social Psychology, 41*, 586–598.

Bloom, B. S. (1984). The 2–sigma problem: The search for methods of group instruction as effective as one-to-one tutoring. *Educational Researcher, 13*, 4–16.

Bruner, J. S. (1966). *Toward a theory of instruction.* New York: Norton.

Burton, R. R., & Brown, J. S. (1979). An investigation of computer coaching for informal learning activities. *International Journal of Man–Machine Studies, 11*, 5–24.

Clay, M. M. (1985). *The early detection of reading difficulties.* Portsmouth, NH: Heinemann.

Clay, M. M. (1991). *Becoming literate: The construction of inner control.* Portsmouth, NH: Heinemann.

Cordova, D. I., & Lepper, M. R. (1996). Intrinsic motivation and the process of learning: Beneficial effects of contextualization, personalization, and choice. *Journal of Educational Psychology, 88*, 715–730.

del Soldata, T., & du Boulay, B. (1995). Implementation of motivational tactics in tutoring systems. *Journal of Artificial Intelligence in Education, 6*, 337–378.

Derry, S. J., & Potts, M. K. (1998). How tutors model students: A study of personal constructs in adaptive tutoring. *American Educational Research Journal, 35,* 65–99.

Edwards, C., Gandini, L., & Forman, G. (1993). *The hundred languages of children: The Reggio Emilia approach to early childhood education.* Norwood, NJ: Ablex.

Fitz-Gibbon, C. R. (1977). *An analysis of the literature of cross-age tutoring.* Washington, DC: National Institute of Education. (ERIC Document Reproduction Service No. ED 148 807)

Graesser, A. G., Bowers, C., Hacker, D. J., & Person, N. (1997). An anatomy of naturalistic tutoring. In K. Hogan & M. Pressley (Eds.), *Scaffolding student learning: Instructional approaches and issues* (pp. 145–184). New York: Brookline Books.

Katz, L. G., & Chard, S. C. (1989). *Engaging children's minds: The project approach.* Norwood, NJ: Ablex.

Lajoie, S. P., & Derry, S. J. (Eds.) (1993). *Computers as cognitive tools.* Hillsdale, NJ: Erlbaum.

Lampert, M. (1986). Knowing, doing, and teaching multiplication. *Cognition and Instruction, 3,* 305–342.

Larkin, J. H., & Chabay, R. W. (Eds.) (1992). *Computer-assisted instruction and intelligent tutoring systems: Shared goals and complementary approaches.* Hillsdale, NJ: Erlbaum.

Lepper, M. R. (1985). Microcomputers in education: Motivational and social issues. *American Psychologist, 40,* 1–18.

Lepper, M. R., Aspinwall, L., Mumme, D., & Chabay, R. W. (1990). Self-perception and social perception processes in tutoring: Subtle social control strategies of expert tutors. In J. M. Olson & M. P. Zanna (Eds.), *Self-inference and social inference: The Ontario symposium* (Vol. 6, pp. 217–237). Hillsdale, NJ: Erlbaum.

Lepper, M. R., & Chabay, R. W. (1985). Intrinsic motivation and instruction: Conflicting views on the role of motivational processes in computer-based education. *Educational Psychologist, 20,* 217–230.

Lepper, M. R., & Chabay, R. W. (1988). Socializing the intelligent tutor: Bringing empathy to computer tutors. In H. Mandl & A. M. Lesgold (Eds.), *Learning issues for intelligent tutoring systems* (pp. 242–257). Chicago: Springer-Verlag.

Lepper, M. R., Drake, M., & O'Donnell-Johnson, T. M. (1997). Scaffolding techniques of expert human tutors. In K. Hogan & M. Pressley (Eds.), *Scaffolding student learning: Instructional approaches and issues* (pp. 108–144). New York: Brookline Books.

Lepper, M. R., & Malone, T. W. (1987). Intrinsic motivation and instructional effectiveness in computer-based education. In R. E. Snow & M. J. Farr (Eds.), *Aptitude, learning, and instruction: III. Conative and affective process analysis* (pp. 255–286). Hillsdale, NJ: Erlbaum.

Lepper, M. R., Woolverton, M., Mumme, D. L., & Gurtner, J. (1993). Motivational techniques of expert human tutors: Lessons for the design of computer-based tutors. In S. P. Lajoie & S. J. Derry (Eds.), *Computers as cognitive tools* (pp. 75–105). Hillsdale, NJ: Erlbaum.

Levin, H. M., Glass, E., & Meister, G. (1984). *A cost–effectiveness analysis of four educational interventions* (IFG Project Report 84–A11). Stanford, CA: Institute for Research on Educational Finance and Governance.

Malone, T. W., & Lepper, M. R. (1987). Making learning fun: A taxonomic model of intrinsic motivations for learning. In R. E. Snow & M. J. Farr (Eds.), *Aptitude, learning, and instruction: III. Conative and affective process analysis* (pp. 223–253). Hillsdale, NJ: Erlbaum.

McArthur, D., Stasz, C., & Zmuidzinas, M. (1990). Tutoring techniques in algebra. *Cognition and Instruction, 7,* 197–244.

Merrill, D. C., Reiser, B. J., Merrill, S. K., & Landes, S. (1995). Tutoring: Guided learning by doing. *Cognition and Instruction, 13,* 315–372.

Parker, L. E., & Lepper, M. R. (1992). Effects of fantasy contexts on children's learning and motivation: Making learning more fun. *Journal of Personality and Social Psychology, 62,* 625–633.

Putnam, R. T. (1987). Structuring and adjusting content for students: A study of live and simulated tutoring of addition. *American Educational Research Journal, 24,* 13–48.

Slavin, R. E., Madden, N. A., Dolan, L. J., & Wasik, B. A. (1996). *Every child, every school: Success for all.* Thousand Oaks, CA: Corwin.

Sleeman, D., & Brown, J. S. (Eds.) (1982). *Intelligent tutoring systems*. New York: Academic Press.

Steinberg, E. R. (1989). Cognition and learner control: A literature review, 1977–1988. *Journal of Computer-Based Instruction, 16*, 117–121.

Stout, M. (2000). *The feel-good curriculum: The dumbing down of America's kids in the name of self-esteem.* Cambridge, MA: Perseus Books.

Suppes, P. (1966). The uses of computers in education. *Scientific American, 215*, 206–221.

Wenger, E. (1987). *Artificial intelligence and tutoring systems*. Los Altos, CA: Morgan Kaufmann.

Wood, D. J., Bruner, J. S., & Ross, G. (1976). The role of tutoring in problem solving. *Journal of Child Psychology and Psychiatry, 17*, 89–100.

Woolverton, M. (In preparation). Observational studies of effective tutoring practices.

CHAPTER

8

# Students' Motivation During the Middle School Years

ALLAN WIGFIELD

*University of Maryland, College Park, Maryland*

JACQUELYNNE S. ECCLES

*University of Michigan, Ann Arbor, Michigan*

The early adolescent developmental period is one in which individuals experience many changes, including the biological changes associated with puberty, important changes in relations with family and peers, and the social and educational changes resulting from transitions from elementary to junior high school and junior high school to high school (see Eccles & Wigfield, 1997; Wigfield, Eccles, & Pintrich, 1996). Different theorists (e.g.; Eccles & Midgley, 1989; Hill & Lynch, 1983; Midgley & Edelin, 1998) have proposed that these changes have significant impact on a variety of developmental outcomes. Many children make these changes relatively easily. Others, however, have difficulty with one or another of these changes and as a result are at risk for various negative outcomes. We focus in this chapter on changes in early adolescents' motivation and self-concepts, and how changes in these characteristics are influenced by different experiences in middle schools. A special focus of this chapter is on gender differences in motivation and self-concept at early adolescence. We begin the chapter with a brief discussion of some of the important biological and cognitive changes that occur during early

The writing of this chapter was supported in part by a grant from the University of Maryland's General Research Board to Allan Wigfield and by Grant HD17553 from the National Institute for Child Health and Human Development to Jacquelynne S. Eccles, Allan Wigfield, Phyllis Blumenfeld, and Rena Harold. The views expressed are solely the responsibility of the authors.

adolescence, to provide background for our discussion of changes in children's self-concepts and motivation.

## BIOLOGICAL AND COGNITIVE CHANGES AT EARLY ADOLESCENCE

The biological changes associated with puberty are the most dramatic ones that individuals experience during their lifetimes (outside of prenatal development), and these changes have been used to characterize the early adolescent period as a period of "storm and stress," where there is a great deal of conflict between children, parents, and teachers (e.g., Blos, 1979; Hall, 1904). We have heard teachers (and parents) say that "If we could just lock kids up for those years things would be fine"! While it is undeniable that major physical changes occur during early adolescence, many researchers now believe that the characterization of this period as one of storm and stress is an overstatement (see, for example, Dornbusch, Petersen, & Hetherington, 1991). Yet Lerner, Entwisle, and Hauser (1994) again used the term "crisis" in their description of the state of contemporary American adolescents. Whether or not adolescents are in crisis, the biological changes they go through do have many influences on their thinking and behavior.

Because these changes occur at different times for boys and girls their impact on each sex differs (see Malina, 1990). There is some consensus that for boys early maturity is advantageous, particularly with respect to their participation in sports activities (see Malina, 1990) and social standing in school (Petersen, 1985). For girls early maturity can be problematic, as they will be the first to experience pubertal changes and thus can feel "out of sync" with their agemates (see Petersen, 1988; Simmons & Blyth, 1987; Stattin & Magnusson, 1990). In fact, Simmons and her colleagues report that early-maturing girls have the lowest self-esteem and the most difficulty adjusting to school transitions, particularly the transition from elementary to junior high school (e.g., Simmons, Blyth, Van Cleave, & Bush, 1979). Because girls enter puberty earlier than boys do, they are more likely to be coping with pubertal changes at the same time they make the middle-grade school transition than are boys, and thus are more likely to face multiple transitions simultaneously. Like early-maturing girls, later-maturing boys also may have some difficulties due to their physical development being out of synchrony with their agemates.

One important educational implication of this work concerns the issue of timing for the transition from elementary to secondary school. Many researchers and educational policy analysts urged that middle-grade school should begin earlier, so that students make the school transition before they enter puberty, and many school districts have followed this advice. Middle school now often encompasses sixth through eighth grade, rather than seventh through ninth grade. Others have argued that a K–8 organizational structure may be most beneficial to early adolescents. There is increasing awareness among educators that this is a unique developmental phase that requires careful structuring of educational environments (see further discussion later).

A great deal has been written about how children's thinking changes during the adolescent years (e.g., see Byrnes, 1988; Keating, 1990). For our purposes the most important changes to note are the increasing ability of children to think abstractly, consider the hypothetical as well as the real, engage in more sophisticated and elaborate information processing strategies, consider multiple dimensions of a problem at once, and reflect on oneself and on complicated problems (see Keating, 1990, for more complete discussion). Abstract thought and hypothetical thinking are hallmarks of Piaget's formal operations stage, the stage that he and his colleagues stated should emerge during adolescence (e.g., Piaget & Inhelder, 1973). Currently there is much debate about when exactly these kinds of cognitive processes emerge, and many researchers now question whether the emergence of these processes reflects global stage-like changes in cognitive skills as described by Piaget. However, most theorists do agree that these kinds of thought processes are more characteristic of adolescents' cognition than of younger children's cognition (e.g., see Fischer, 1980; Moshman, 1998).

Along with their impact on children's learning, these changes in children's thinking have important implications for individuals' self-concepts and motivation. Theorists such as Erikson (1963) and Harter (1990) view the adolescent years as a time of substantial change in children's self-concepts, as they consider what possibilities are available to them and try to come to a deeper understanding of themselves. These sorts of self-reflections require the kinds of higher-order cognitive processes just discussed. With motivation increasingly conceived in cognitive terms these changes also have implications for early adolescents' motivation.

## CHANGES IN SELF-CONCEPT AND MOTIVATION DURING EARLY ADOLESCENCE

### Self-Concept and Identity Development During Early Adolescence

As just noted, adolescence has long been thought to be a time of great change in children's self-concepts. Erikson (1963), in his ground breaking work, characterized adolescence as the time in which individuals searched for their identity, either finding it or sinking into role confusion. More recently, Harter (1990, 1998) discussed how during middle adolescence the self-concept is both less integrated and more unstable than at earlier or later periods, and that perceived inconsistencies or conflicts in one's characteristics were a source of great concern during middle adolescence (see also Rosenberg, 1986;

Simmons & Blyth, 1987). Thus like Erikson, Harter proposed that a major task of adolescence is to integrate the disparate aspects of self.

One hallmark of recent research on adolescents' self-concepts is that researchers have focused on particular aspects of self-concept rather than just measuring individuals' general sense of themselves. They have developed measures of self-concept that have better psychometric properties than earlier scales. How the self organizes and regulates behavior also has been a major focus of recent work.

Markus and her colleagues (e.g., Markus & Nurius, 1986; Markus & Wurf, 1987) discussed how the self organizes and regulates behavior. They argued that individuals take information about the self and organize it into coherent frameworks that they call "self-schemas." For instance, students have a sense of themselves in the role of student, Markus and Nurius would call these self beliefs a "student self-schema." These self-schemas have a strong role in determining the goals we have, directing our behavior, and evaluating information we receive about ourselves. Those with strong student self-schemas are likely to do better in school and continue their educational pursuits. Markus also discussed how our self-concepts relate to our future activities, using the term "possible selves" to discuss the images we have of what we want to be in the future. The possible self notion is of course particularly germane to adolescents, because it is a period in which individuals explore different possibilities for themselves and begin to determine which roles are best and most appropriate for them.

Marsh and his colleagues have done a great deal of empirical work to examine the structure of self-concept, using Shavelson, Hubner, and Stanton's (1976) model of the self-concept as the theoretical basis for their work. They developed scales to measure children's self-concepts in many different activity domains, including both academic and nonacademic activities. Extensive factor analytic work with these scales has shown, first, there are clearly separate dimensions of self-concept even in very young children (see also Eccles, Wigfield, Harold, & Blumenfeld, 1993). Second, during middle childhood and early adolescence children's self-concepts appear to be organized hierarchically (e.g., Marsh, 1990; Marsh & Shavelson, 1985), with specific aspects of self-concept at the bottom of the hierarchy (e.g., math self-concept) and global self-concept at the top. Interestingly, during later adolescence there is less evidence for a hierarchical self-concept. These findings suggest an intriguing pattern in self-concept development across childhood and adolescence, from differentiated and hierarchical to differentiated into quite distinct components.

Harter (1982, 1990) also has done extensive work on the structure of children's and adolescents' self-concepts. Her work also has shown that children's self-concepts are multidimensional and increase in complexity during adolescence. In addition to her work on the structure of self-concept Harter has focused on the nature of some important self-processes during adolescence. For example, she and her colleagues examined adolescents' sense of whether they could express their "true" selves or were not able to do so, in different settings. They have found that adolescents who hide their "true" selves do so because they think others devalue their true selves, because they want to make a good impression on others, or because they want to fit in. Adolescents who think others devalue their true selves have the lowest self-esteem (see Harter, 1998; Harter, Waters, & Whitesell, 1997, for further discussion). Adolescents believing they must receive approval from others before they can approve themselves also tend to have lower self-esteem.

The issue of how self-esteem changes at early adolescence has been an important concern of various researchers (see Harter, 1998). Self-esteem often is defined as one's overall self-evaluation. Self-esteem changes in important ways at early adolescence. Simmons, Rosenberg, and Rosenberg (1973) showed that following the transition to junior high school early adolescents' general self-esteem is lower and less stable and their self-consciousness, higher. However, there has been some debate about how prevalent these negative changes in general self-esteem are. In our work (Eccles, Wigfield, Flanagan, Miller, Reuman, & Yee, 1989; Wigfield, Eccles, Mac Iver, Reuman, & Midgley, 1991), children's self-esteem was lowest immediately after the transition into junior high school in seventh grade, but increased during students' seventh grade year. In their longitudinal work Blyth, Simmons, and Carlton-Ford (1983) and Simmons et al. (1979) found that for most children, self-esteem scores increase across middle adolescence (see also Dusek & Flaherty, 1981; O'Malley & Bachman, 1983). In Simmons and Blyth's work, white girls who make the transition to junior high school are the only group to show consistent evidence of declines in self-esteem. Eccles and her colleagues (Eccles & Midgley, 1989) and Simmons and her colleagues (Blyth et al., 1983; Simmons, Rosenberg, & Rosenberg, 1973; Simmons & Blyth, 1987) have postulated that these changes in early adolescents' self-beliefs are due in part to changes in the school environment that occur following the transition to junior high; these changes are discussed in more detail later.

Determining which specific components of children's self-concepts relate most strongly to their overall self-esteem or self-worth at different ages has been an important research topic. Harter (1986) found that during the elementary school years and adolescence, perceptions of physical appearance and social acceptance relate most strongly to children's feelings of self-worth (see Harter, 1990). These findings probably will come as no surprise to teachers and others working with early adolescents. Social status and physical appearance often seem to be much more important to adolescents than things like school success. The great changes in physical appearance occurring at this time likely are a major reason why adolescents are so concerned about their appearance.

A more difficult issue is determining exactly *how* the specific aspects of self-concept may influence general self-worth. Harter (1990) proposed that individuals' general self-worth is determined in part by the synchrony between their sense of competence at different activities and the importance of those activities to them. Doing well in activities that are important should foster positive general self-worth. Harter has found support for this notion in her empirical work; children believing they are good at activities they think are important have more positive general self-worth than do children who believe certain activities are important but do not think they are competent at those activities.

This issue also has very important implications for students' school engagement. To the extent that adolescents' do well in school and believe it is important, they should remain engaged in academic activities. If either their performance decreases or they begin to decide that school is not important, then their engagement will decrease. One of the challenges for middle school educators is that the perceived importance of school often decreases during adolescence because many adolescents begin to see social activities as more important to them at this time, and like those activities much more than academic tasks (see Eccles et al., 1989; Wigfield et al., 1991). We return to this issue later.

## Changes in Early Adolescents' Achievement Motivation

Work on motivation and achievement-related beliefs has flourished in the last 25 years (see Eccles, Wigfield, & Schiefele, 1998; Pintrich & Schunk 1996, for review). Many researchers studying motivation have taken the broad perspective that it is children's *interpretations* of their achievement outcomes that are critical mediators of subsequent achievement behavior; therefore, students' beliefs about themselves and their achievement have been a major focus of research. Students' purposes for engaging in achievement activities also have received a great deal of attention; constructs concerned with these purposes include students' goals, and their valuing of achievement activities.

To organize the proliferation of motivation constructs, Eccles et al. (1998) proposed that they can be thought of in terms of two major questions students can ask themselves. One question is "Can I succeed on this task or activity?" Constructs related to this question include students' competence-related beliefs such as self-efficacy (Bandura, 1997; Stipek & Mac Iver, 1989), their attributions (or explanations) for success and failure (Weiner, 1985), and their perceptions of control over outcomes (Skinner, Zimmer-Gembeck, & Connell, 1998). In general, when students have high self-efficacy, the belief that they can control their achievement outcomes, and internal attributions for their success, they tend to be more positively motivated and perform better on different achievement tasks and activities (see Eccles et al., 1998, for complete review; see also Chapter 2 by Pajares and Schunk in this volume for further discussion of some of these constructs).

The second question is "Why do I want to do this activity?", a question having to do with the purposes for which students engage in academic activities. This question is crucial to motivation. Even if individuals believe they can succeed on a task or activity, they may not engage in it if they have no clear purpose for doing so. Constructs related to this question include students' valuing of achievement, goals for achievement, and intrinsic and extrinsic motivation. Eccles, Adler, Futterman, Goff, Kaczala, Meece, and Midgley (1983) defined three main aspects of children's valuing of achievement: their interest in the activity, its usefulness to them, and its relative importance to them. They found that students' valuing of achievement relates strongly to their choices of which activities to continue to do (Eccles et al., 1983; Meece, Wigfield, & Eccles, 1990). For example, when students value math they are more likely to keep taking math courses, when they have choices about which courses to take.

Researchers studying achievement goals initially focused on two major goal orientations. One goal orientation concerns individuals' desire to learn new things and master material; this orientation has been called a task mastery or learning goal orientation by different researchers (Ames, 1992; Dweck & Leggett, 1988; Nicholls, 1984). The second orientation concerns individuals' desires to outperform others and receive favorable evaluations of their performance; this orientation is termed ego or performance goal orientation. Recently researchers have explored dual aspects of the performance orientation, dividing it into performance-approach and performance-avoidance goals (see Pintrich, 2000). Performance-approach goals include things like wanting to do better than others. Performance-avoidance goals are things like not wanting to appear stupid. Students adopting a performance-approach orientation tend to be more strongly motivated for achievement activities than do students adopting a performance-avoidance orientation (Elliot & Harackiewicz, 1996).

Intrinsic motivation refers to doing an activity out of interest and personal engagement in it, whereas extrinsic motivation means doing an activity to receive a reward or some other kind of recognition (see Chapter 4 by Deci and Ryan in this volume). Researchers assessing these constructs have found that when students hold mastery goals, performance-approach goals, are intrinsically motivated, and highly value achievement they will achieve better and be more engaged in learning activities.

Researchers looking at how these beliefs, goals, and values change during early adolescence and adolescence often have found that adolescents' motivation declines during this period (see Anderman & Maehr, 1994; Eccles et al., 1998, for review). Specifically, early adolescents have lower perceptions of their competence for different school subjects than do their younger peers (Eccles et al., 1989; Marsh, 1989; Wigfield et al., 1991). Many early adolescents become more anxious about school in general and mathematics in particular (Brush, 1980; Harter, Whitesell, & Kowalski, 1992). Students' valuing of different school subjects often declines as they move through school, with the declines especially marked across the transition to middle school (Eccles et al., 1989; Wigfield et al., 1991), Their intrinsic motivation for learning often decreases (Harter, 1981; Harter et al., 1992). Students often focus more on performance goals as they get older, at the expense of task mastery goals (Anderman & Midgley, 1997; Midgley, Anderman, & Hicks, 1995).

Researchers have explained these changes in two major (and complementary) ways. One explanation focuses on cognitive and other changes within the individual. As children mature cognitively and receive increasing amounts of evaluative feedback, they come to understand more clearly their relative level of performance and what the evaluative feedback means (see Stipek & Mac Iver, 1989, for further discussion). As one illustration of this process, when asked how good they are in reading, most first grade children think they are one of the best in the class. Later in elementary school fewer children believe this (see Nicholls, 1979). The second explanation acknowledges these individual changes, but focuses more on the kinds of experiences children have in school as the reason for the declines in motivation. A major premise of this explanation is that when schools focus too much on ability evaluations, social comparison between students, and performance goals, many students' sense of competence, intrinsic motivation, and mastery goal orientation will decrease. The particular ways in which the transition from elementary school to middle school can produce these effects is the topic of the next section.

## THE MIDDLE-GRADE SCHOOL TRANSITION AND STUDENT MOTIVATION

### The Transition to Traditional Junior High Schools

Traditional junior high schools (and middle schools) differ structurally in important ways from elementary schools. Most junior high schools are substantially larger than elementary schools, because they draw students from several elementary schools. As a result, students' friendship networks often are disrupted as they attend classes with students from several different schools. Students also are likely to feel more anonymous because of the large size of many middle schools. Instruction is likely to be organized and taught departmentally. Thus junior high school teachers typically teach several different groups of students each day and are unlikely to teach any particular students for more than one year. This departmental structure can create a number of difficulties for students. One is that the curriculum often is not integrated across different subjects. A second is that students typically have several teachers each day with little opportunity to interact with any one teacher on any dimension except the academic content of what is being taught and disciplinary issues. Finally, family involvement in school often declines during the middle school years.

Researchers also have discussed how in traditional junior high schools and middle schools, classroom and school environments change away from practices that foster mastery goals and intrinsic motivation and focus instead on practices that promote a performance goal orientation in students (Eccles & Midgley, 1989; Maehr & Midgley, 1996; Wigfield et al., 1996). Such practices also can contribute to the decline in students' academic competence beliefs, interest, and intrinsic motivation discussed earlier. We focus here on several particular changes in teacher–student relations and social organizations of classrooms and schools. The first is changes in *authority relationships*. Middle school classrooms, as compared with elementary school classrooms, are characterized by a greater emphasis on teacher control and discipline and fewer opportunities for student decision making, choice, and self-management (e.g., Midgley & Feldlaufer, 1987; Moos, 1979). These practices can reduce students' sense of control and autonomy.

Second, traditional middle school classrooms, as compared with elementary school classrooms, often are characterized by *less personal and positive teacher–student relationships* (see Eccles & Midgley, 1989). For example, Trebilco, Atkinson, and Atkinson (1977) found that students reported less favorable interpersonal relations with their teachers after the transition to secondary school than before. Similarly, Feldlaufer, Midgley, and Eccles (1988) found that both students and observers rated junior high school math teachers as less friendly, less supportive, and less caring than the teachers these same students had one year earlier in the last year of elementary school. Positive and emotionally warm relations with teachers relate to students' motivation and adjustment in the classroom (Wentzel, 1997).

Third, the shift to middle school is associated with systematic changes in the *organization of instruction*, such as increases in practices such as having the entire class working together, and between classroom ability grouping (see Eccles & Midgley, 1989). Such changes are likely to increase social comparison, concerns about evaluation, and competitiveness, all of which could foster an ego goal orientation and a stronger focus on perceived competence (see Rosenholtz & Simpson, 1984). In addition, under these learning conditions children doing less well in school will be more likely to begin to doubt their competence.

Fourth, junior high school teachers often feel less effective as teachers, especially for low-ability students. This was one of largest differences we found between sixth and seventh grade teachers in the Michigan Study of Adolescent Life Transitions. Seventh grade teachers in these junior high schools reported much lower confidence in their teaching efficacy than did the sixth grade elementary school teachers in the same school districts (Midgley, Feldlaufer, & Eccles, 1988). Others have reported similar results. Alexander and George (1981) found that teachers in traditional junior high schools had a lower sense of their teaching efficacy than did teachers in a more innovative middle-grade school.

Several studies have documented the impact of teacher efficacy on student beliefs, attitudes, motivation, and achievement. Alexander and George (1981), in the study just mentioned, found that teachers in the more innovative middle-grade schools had higher expectancies for student success and also were more likely to take personal responsibility for student failure than were the junior high school teachers. Ashton (1985) found that teachers' sense of efficacy relates positively to high school students' performance on math and language arts achievement test scores. More efficacious teachers also were more encouraging and supportive of students.

Fifth, despite what one might expect given what we know about cognitive development at this age, there is evidence that classwork during the first year of junior high school requires lower-level cognitive skills than classwork at the elementary level. One rationale often given for the large, departmentalized junior high school system is its efficiency in providing early adolescents with higher-level academic work and more varied academic courses taught by specialists in their fields (see Clark & Clark, 1993). It is argued that the early adolescents are ready for more formal instruction in the various subject areas. Two assumptions are implicit in this argument. First, it is assumed that more formal, departmentalized teaching is conducive to the learning of more advanced cognitive processes. Second, it is assumed that children in junior high school are undertaking learning tasks that require advanced (or higher-order) thinking in their departmentalized courses. Both of these assumptions have been questioned. For example, in an observational study of 11 junior high school science classes, only a very small proportion of tasks required higher-level creative or expressive skills; the most frequent activity involved copying answers from the board or textbook onto worksheets (Mergendoller, Marchman, Mitman, & Packer, 1988). Similarly, Walberg, House, and Steele (1973) rated the level of complexity of student assignments across grades 6 to 12 according to Bloom's taxonomy of educational objectives. The proportion of low-level activities peaked at grade 9, the first year after the students in this district made the transition into secondary school. Thus, although the students have been led to believe that they are moving to a more challenging school environment, they may well find themselves in classes that are reviewing the material they learned in elementary school, and as will be discussed next, they are likely to be given lower grades for their work. As we shall see below, this experience is not likely to facilitate their motivation.

Sixth, junior high school teachers appear to use a higher standard in judging students' competence and in grading their performance than do elementary school teachers (see Eccles & Midgley, 1989). There is no stronger predictor of students' sense of competence than the grades they receive. If grades change, then we would expect to see a concomitant shift in the adolescents' self-perceptions and academic motivation. There is evidence that junior high school teachers use stricter and more social comparison-based standards than elementary school teachers to assess student competency and to evaluate student performance, leading to a drop in grades for many early adolescents as they make the junior high school transition. For example, Simmons and Blyth (1987) found a greater drop in grades between sixth and seventh grade for adolescents making the junior high school transition at this point than for adolescents enrolled in K–8 schools.

The decline in grades is not matched by a decline in the adolescents' scores on standardized achievement tests, suggesting that the decline reflects a change in grading practices rather than a change in the rate of the students' learning (Kavrell & Petersen, 1984). Imagine what this decline in grades might do to early adolescents' sense of competence, especially in light of the fact that the material is not likely to be more intellectually challenging. Indeed, even controlling for a youth's performance prior to the school transition, the magnitude of the grade drop following the transition into either junior high school or middle school is a major predictor of dropping out of school (Simmons & Blyth, 1987).

Finally, as noted above, peer networks are disrupted when children change schools. Many times friends are separated from one another, and it takes some time for children to reestablish social networks. Wigfield et al. (1991) found that children's sense of social competence was lowest immediately after the transition to junior high school, in comparison to before the transition or later in junior high school. Such disruptions could influence children's academic motivation as well.

In summary, traditional junior high schools and middle schools have a variety of organizational characteristics and classroom practices that have negative effects on students' competence beliefs, mastery goals, and intrinsic motivation for learning. Eccles and Midgley (1989) argued that a main reason these practices have a negative impact is that they are developmentally inappropriate for early adolescents. At a time when the children are growing cognitively and emotionally, desiring greater freedom and autonomy, and focusing on social relations, they experience teaching practices like those just described that do not fit well with the developmental characteristics of early adolescents. Therefore, for many early adolescents these practices contribute to the negative change in students' motivation and achievement-related beliefs. What has been done about these problems? That is the topic of the next section.

## Middle School Reform Efforts and Student Motivation

Based in part on the research just reviewed, proposals by middle school experts, and the *Turning Points* report written by the Carnegie Council on Adolescent Development, middle schools across the country have begun to change greatly (see Alexander & George, 1981; Carnegie Council on Adolescent

Development, 1989; Clark & Clark, 1993; Irvin, 1992; Midgley & Edelin, 1998). There is growing consensus about what kinds of changes should be made in middle-grade schools (Lipsitz, Mizell, Jackson, & Austin, 1997). One structural change adopted in many school districts has been to move the transition to middle school from after to before sixth grade, in part so that fewer students would experience pubertal changes at the same time they underwent the middle school transition. This change on its own accomplishes little; what is more important is changing school organization and instructional practices in systematic ways (Mac Iver & Epstein, 1993). Both the Carnegie Council on Adolescent Development and the National Middle Schools Association have made recommendations for how middle schools should be changed; a summary of their recommendations is presented in Table 1. As can be seen in the table, there is much overlap between the two sets of recommendations.

**TABLE 1**
**Recommendations for Restructuring Educational Practices in Middle-Grade Schools**

Recommendations from the Carnegie Council on Adolescent Development

1. Turn large schools into smaller learning communities.
2. All students should receive a common core of high-level knowledge.
3. All students should be given the opportunity to succeed.
4. Teachers and administrators should be empowered to make important decisions.
5. Middle-grade teachers should receive special preparation for teaching at the middle school level.
6. Early adolescents' fitness and health should be enhanced to enhance their academic performance.
7. Families should be reengaged in middle schools.
8. Connections between schools and communities need to be built.

Recommendations from the National Middle School Association

1. Middle school educators should be knowledgeable about young adolescents.
2. The middle school curriculum should be balanced and responsive to the needs of young adolescents.
3. There should be a range of organizational arrangements in middle schools.
4. Instructional strategies should be varied.
5. There should be full exploratory programs in different schools.
6. Comprehensive advising and counseling should be provided for all students.
7. All students should make continuous progress.
8. Evaluation procedures should be compatible with the nature of young adolescents.
9. Teachers should have time for cooperative planning.
10. Each middle school should have a positive school climate.

Many of these recommendations have strong appeal for those interested in developmentally appropriate education for early adolescents. Indeed, several focus directly on the special nature of the early adolescence age period and how teachers need to be prepared specifically for working with this age group. From our perspective as developmental psychologists such recommendations are particularly important. Early adolescence is a unique developmental period in many respects, and designing educational programs to fit the developmental needs of early adolescents can facilitate students' learning and adjustment (see Eccles & Wigfield, 1997).

We also believe recommendations that increase the sense of community in middle schools are particularly important. A good example of this are the recommendations focusing on replacing department structures with teams of teachers working with the same group of students. This practice allows groups of teachers to spend more time with the same group of adolescents, thus getting to know them better. It also allows for greater integration across the curriculum. Teachers serving as advisors and counselors has become more prevalent, so that adolescents can develop relationships with adults other than their parents. To create smaller learning communities in often-large middle schools, "schools within schools" have been created, in part through the teaming approach just discussed. This is particularly likely to occur for the youngest group in a middle school, be they fifth graders, sixth graders, or seventh graders. Cooperative learning practices are used more frequently, in part to reduce the use of ability grouping or tracking. Such practices, when implemented appropriately, enhance relations between teachers and students and have been shown to be effective in enhancing student engagement and learning (Arhar, 1997; Lee, Bryk, & Smith, 1993).

We also find very important the recommendations focusing on the need to engage more fully families and communities in middle schools. A great deal of research indicates that when parents are involved in their children's education children's achievement and motivation in school are enhanced (see Brough, 1997; Epstein, 1987). Yet many parents are not involved in their children's education or at the schools, and the involvement that does occur often declines once children reach middle school. Reasons parents are not involved include responsibilities at work, lack of time, poor communication from the school, and (at times) a sense of not being wanted in the school. Brough (1997) described a variety of ways in which middle schools can increase parental involvement, including better communication about school activities, regular communication from teachers about what is occurring in their classrooms, active solicitation of parental involvement, and encouragement of home–school partnerships. The increased parental involvement resulting from such efforts can facilitate students' engagement and learning.

How many middle schools have adopted such changes? Mac Iver and Epstein (1993) reported results of a study of teaching practices in middle schools across the country. They found that many school districts have not adopted the "school within a school" approach for making middle schools seem smaller. Forty percent of middle schools use tracking for math and English, and 20% use it for all subjects. Seventy five percent of schools have advising periods for students, although Mac Iver and Epstein noted that many of these are used primarily for school business, such as attendance taking and announcements, rather than for "true" advising and counseling. Close to 40% of middle schools reported using some kind of interdisciplinary teaming, but few of these schools allowed for team planning periods. Only 10% of the schools have teaming programs that allow teachers regular times for planning their academic programs. It should be clear from these data that implementation of the recommendations is occurring slowly. Mac Iver and Epstein asked principals to forecast how their schools would change over the next few years. Principals were most likely to mention teaming with planning periods, students assigned to the same advisory teacher for the entire time they are in middle school, flexible scheduling, and greater use of cooperative learning.

Lipsitz and her colleagues (1997) discussed middle school reform efforts across the country. They focused in particular on three sets of middle schools in Illinois, Michigan, and Indiana in which reform efforts in line with the recommendations included in Table 1 have been undertaken in meaningful ways. Felner, Jackson, Kasak, Mulhall, Brand, and Flowers (1997) reported systematic evaluations of the schools in the Illinois network. They conducted longitudinal studies in schools implementing fully the recommendations from the Carnegie Council, comparing them with schools implementing the recommendations to a degree and not at all. The comparison schools were matched carefully on demographic and other characteristics. Felner et al. obtained measures of students' achievement, school attitudes, and behavior problems. Preliminary analyses indicate that schools in which the implementation has been fullest have higher achieving students. Students in these schools report higher self-esteem and fewer worries about bad things happening to them in schools, and teachers report fewer behavior problems. These results provide encouraging support for the efficacy of the reform efforts. One crucial point made by Felner et al. is that comprehensive reform is what needed. Schools in which one or two of the recommendations have been implemented and schools in which the implementation of several recommendations has proceeded slowly have not been as successful. Unfortunately, as noted above many schools are just beginning to implement change or are doing so selectively.

In summarizing middle school reform efforts Midgley and Edelin (1998) argued that many middle schools have improved the climate of their school, particularly relations between teaches and students, but fewer have changed their instructional practices. They argued for the need for both kinds of changes to occur for reform to occur more completely and, therefore, for adolescents' achievement and motivation to improve. Their position thus is similar to that of Felner et al. (1997): full implementation of reforms is needed to affect student outcomes. They further discussed how some have suggested that the focus on improving teacher – student relations has come at the expense of improving academics, and stated strongly that it is not necessary to view these two aspects of change as competing with one another. Both are necessary to do, and can be done together.

What about students' motivation in reformed middle schools? Unfortunately there is not yet a great deal of information about how reform efforts have affected students' motivation. Felner and his colleagues measured self-esteem, but not the different aspects of motivation we have discussed in this chapter. Some researchers have assessed motivation in their work in reformed middle schools, and we close this section by discussing their work. Mac Iver and his colleagues began a middle school reform effort that they call Talent Development middle schools (see Mac Iver, Mac Iver, Balfanz, Plank, & Ruby, 2000; Mac Iver & Plank, 1997, for a summary). This project is focused on reforming middle schools that serve early adolescents who are at risk because of the backgrounds from which they come. The program involves the implementation of many of the recommendations discussed in this section: detracking the schools, using cooperative learning extensively, team teaching, offering a challenging core curriculum (including algebra) to all students, and providing advising services. The program began in a few schools in Philadelphia, and is spreading to other areas of the country. Results to date for both achievement and motivational outcomes are encouraging. Students in the Talent Development schools gained more in mathematics and reading achievement than did students in matched control schools. Mac Iver and colleagues measured several motivation outcomes, including students' perceptions of their effort, sense of ability, and valuing of school learning, and students in the Talent Development schools were more positive in these aspects of motivation. They also perceived their teachers as more caring.

Maehr and Midgley (1996) presented an account of their collaborative effort to change the culture organization of a middle school using principles from achievement goal theory. Through collaborations with teachers and school administrators different practices in the school were changed to facilitate mastery rather than ability-focused goal orientations. The specific basis for the change was Ames' TARGET program. Ames (1992) discussed how classroom grouping and other practices influence students' achievement goal orientations and other aspects of motivation. Ames, following Epstein (1988), focused on the following aspects: classroom tasks, authority structure, recognition, grouping, evaluation, and time, using the acronym TARGET to describe them. Each of these aspects can influence whether students develop a task mastery or performance goal orientation. In describing these influences we focus on practices that facilitate a mastery goal orientation. *Tasks* that are diverse, interesting, and challenging foster students' mastery goals, as do tasks students think they have a reasonable chance to complete. When the *authority* in classrooms is structured such that students have opportunities to participate in decision making and take responsibility for their own learning, they are more mastery oriented. *Recognition* of student effort instead of only ability and giving all students a chance to achieve recognition (rather than just the "best" students) foster task-involved goals. Mastery goals are fostered when cooperative *grouping* is used and students have opportunities to work with a heterogeneous mix of students. When teachers *evaluate* students' progress and mastery rather than just their outcomes, and provide students opportunities to improve, then mastery goal orientations are more likely. Finally, *time* refers to how instruction is paced. Crucial things for fostering mastery goals are varying the amounts of time available for different students to complete their work and helping students learn to plan their own work schedule and organize how they progress through the work. Ames (1992) argued cogently that such practices will allow more students to remain positively motivated in the classroom, in that they will have more positive competence beliefs and task-involved goals (see also Stipek, 1996).

The school – university team worked extensively in one elementary school and one middle school to restructure the schools toward a focus on mastery goal; they spent 3 years in each school. The schools were in a working class community in the Middle West. The researchers met extensively with teachers and administrators at the school to develop collaborative working relationships. Together with the teachers and administrators they developed plans for reorganization and implementation of the plans. At the middle school they focused on creating teams of teachers, "schools within the school," and changing the student recognition patterns.

Maehr and Midgley's account of the process of attempting to reorganize the school is fascinating. They were able to work with teachers at the elementary school and implement agreed-on changes much more easily than they were at the middle school. At the middle school there were many difficult issues that the researchers encountered throughout the process. These included some teachers' (especially the math teachers) resistance to change, particularly with respect to doing away with grouping, difficulties in adjusting the rigid middle school bell schedule to accommodate teaming and flexible class scheduling, and parents' objections that their high-achieving students did not receive enough recognition. These difficulties illustrate the continuing challenges inherent in school reform efforts.

What kinds of effects did the changes have? Despite the difficulties in implementing some of the proposed changes at the middle school level, the changes appear to have had positive effects on students' motivation. Anderman, Maehr, and Midgley (1999) reported results of analyses obtained from students in elementary and middle schools, in both the collaborating middle school, and a comparison middle school in which the changes did not occur. Indeed, in the comparison school competition and ability grouping were emphasized. There were few differences in students' motivation during elementary school. Following the transition to middle school students in the comparison school had stronger performance goals and extrinsic goals for learning. These students also perceived a stronger emphasis in their school on performance goals. These shifts in students' motivation did not occur for the students in the collaborating school.

In summary, reform efforts organized by a guiding set of principles are underway in middle schools across the country. However, despite the call for these changes and agreement on the principles to guide change, many middle schools have been slow to adopt them or have not changed at all. There is an urgent need for these reform efforts to move ahead. Evidence from schools adopting the recommended changes suggests students' motivation is enhanced in these middle schools; thus the decline in student motivation that we have been discussing is not inevitable. This evidence is still sketchy, however; much more work is needed on how middle school reform efforts are influencing students' motivation along with their achievement.

## GENDER DIFFERENCES IN MOTIVATION AND SELF-CONCEPT AT EARLY ADOLESCENCE

In our discussion of change in motivation and self-concept we have discussed overall change. An important question is whether the changes occur in similar ways for all children. In our own work we have been interested particularly in sex differences in children's motivation. Though sex-typing itself occurs in the preschool years (see Ruble & Martin, 1998), several researchers have suggested that engaging in gender-role appropriate activities may become quite important to early adolescents, as they try to conform more to gender-role stereotypes once they enter puberty (Eccles, 1987; Hill & Lynch, 1983). Hill and Lynch labeled this phenomenon "gender-role intensification." This phenomenon may lead early adolescents to have less positive beliefs and be less involved in activities that they see as less appropriate to their own gender. For instance, girls who believe that math is not appropriate for females, and who wish to conform to perceived feminine roles, may decide to discontinue taking math when that possibility becomes available, even if they are doing very well in math.

Regarding the motivation constructs we have discussed in this chapter, there are many gender differences in children's competence beliefs for activities in different domains (see Wigfield, Battle, Solomon, & Eccles, 2002, for more detailed discussion). These differences are intriguing in light of evidence that actual achievement and test score differences between boys and girls are decreasing. In an important article Linn and Hyde (1989) presented a meta-analysis of work on sex differences in verbal, mathematics, and science aptitude test performance They concluded that sex differences in verbal ability now are negligible; differences in quantitative skills show that girls' computation skills are better at all ages and boys do better on mathematics conceptual "word" problems in high school, though again these differences have decreased in the past 15 years; and differences in science knowledge and process still favor boys, though they also are decreasing and appear to reflect experiential differences between boys and girls in science.

Despite these findings, gender differences in self-perceptions and values remain. In our work adolescent boys have higher competence beliefs for sports and math than do adolescent girls, and the girls have higher competence beliefs for English (see Eccles et al., 1983, 1989; Wigfield, et al., 1991). Marsh (1989) also reported many gender differences in response to his self-concept scales, though he noted that the gender differences explain only about 1% of the variance in responses. As in our work, boys' math self-concept of ability scores are higher than those of girls, whereas girls' scores are higher for verbal/reading and general school subscales. Interestingly, there are few age × sex interactions in children's and adolescents' responses to our measures or those of Marsh, suggesting that the gender differences neither increase nor decrease in magnitude across age. A recent longitudinal study has found similar declines in boys' and girls' competence beliefs across grades 1 through 12 (Jacobs, Hyatt, Eccles, Osgood, & Wigfield, in press).

We also have found differences in boys' and girls' valuing of different tasks (assessing the different components of achievement values described earlier). Girls value English and reading more than boys do. Interestingly, during middle school there are no differences in the valuing of math (Eccles et al., 1989; Wigfield et al., 1991). Though it is encouraging that boys and girls like math similarly and think it equally important, the fact that girls have less positive views of their ability in math could be problematic. The doubts girls have about their math ability likely leads them to be less likely to continue taking math courses as math becomes more difficult. Although there currently are few course enrollment differences between boys and girls in high school, substantial differences remain at the college level. Boys' devaluing of reading also is problematic, because of the importance reading plays in so many academic endeavors.

Researchers also have examined sex differences in self-esteem, and discussed whether girls' self-esteem becomes less positive than boys' self-esteem during early adolescence. Rosenberg (1986) suggested that girls are more affected by the physical changes occurring at puberty and thus their self-concepts are more volatile than those of boys during this period. Simmons and Blyth (1987) found that the junior high transition had a negative effect only on girls' self-esteem; our own work did not replicate this finding (Eccles et al., 1989; Wigfield et al., 1991). However, in our studies (e.g., Eccles et al., 1989; Wigfield et al., 1991) and those of others, boys report higher self-esteem than do girls during the early adolescence period (e.g., Blyth et al., 1983; Marsh, 1989; Simmons et al., 1979). We are unsure whether this finding reflects "true" gender differences in self-esteem or response bias, as boys tend to be more self-congratulatory than girls in their responses to self-report measures, while girls may be more modest in their self-reports.

Various authors have argued that early adolescence is a particularly challenging time for girls' self-development as they come to terms with their roles in society. Gilligan and her colleagues have written extensively about this topic (e.g., Gilligan, 1982, 1993; Gilligan, Lyons, & Hammer, 1989), discussing how many girls lose their "voice" at early adolescence. They postulated that this occurs because as they mature, girls learn that females' roles in our society are limited and that the stereotype is for women to be pleasing to others, unassertive, and quiet. Further, Gilligan and others have argued that relations with others are primary to adolescent females and women, leading them to be strongly motivated to preserve positive relations with others. Still others have posited that schools are biased in ways that favor boys' expression of their voices and the suppression of girls' voices (American Association for University Women, 1992). As a result of these changes adolescent girls may suppress their true views of things to maintain relations with others and conform to the cultural stereotype; hence they lose their voice. Gilligan based her conjectures on interviews with adolescent girls in different settings.

Gilligan's work has been influential, influencing views expressed in the popular press describing the difficulties many adolescent girls face (e.g., Pipher, 1994). Although Gilligan's interviews provide some support for her views, Harter, Waters, and Whitesell (1997) argued recently that there is not a lot of documentation for the claim that many females lose their voices at early adolescence. They also suggested that there is a great deal of overlap between boys and girls on a variety of self-related constructs relevant to this issue. In an intriguing series of studies they examined both boys' and girls' voice at early adolescence, as measured by a questionnaire they developed. The questionnaires asked the adolescents they extent to which they felt they could express their opinions and beliefs in different situations. One issue they examined was which relational context the adolescents felt they were able to express their voice. Both boys and girls felt they were freer to express themselves with their peers than with teachers or parents, a finding that perhaps is not surprising.

Harter and her colleagues also have looked at how expression of voice varies by age and gender and gender-role orientation. In cross-sectional studies they have found no evidence for a decline in girls' expression of voice across 6th through 12th grades; this result conflicts with the idea that girls' voices are silenced at early adolescence. Further, in both middle and high school there were no gender differences in voice. However, there were gender-role differences in certain relational contexts. Feminine girls were less expressive in school than were androgynous girls, especially with male classmates. With parents and close friends, however, there were no differences between these groups.

This work suggests that Gilligan's claims about loss of voice at adolescence for girls are too broad; if voice is lost at adolescence it appears to be for a subset of girls, those who endorse a traditionally feminine sex-role orientation. The different methodologies used in Gilligan's and Harter's work perhaps make direct comparisons difficult. However, we concur with Harter and colleagues that Gilligan's conclusions about voice likely are too general. In future research perhaps new methodologies can be developed to reconcile these conflicting findings.

Hoff Sommers (2000) recently published an even stronger critique of Gilligan's work in the *Atlantic Monthly*, criticizing the methodologies used by Gilligan and arguing that little of her work has received strong peer review. She argued further that boys really are the ones at greater risk, reviewing evidence that boys have lower grades in school, are more likely to drop out, are less likely to attend college, and are much more likely to be diagnosed as learning disabled or having attention deficit disorder, among other things. She concluded that the concern about girls is misplaced and that schools really should worry more about boys. Although some of her critiques of Gilligan's work are justified and her points about the difficulties many boys face are well-taken, it is perhaps unfortunate that this debate is being cast in this way. Rather than arguing either that boys have problems and girls do not, or girls have problems and boys do not, it seems that some members of each gender experience challenges that need attention in school. These challenges are quite different, and so as a result the same solutions will not work for each. For instance, many boys' performance in reading needs to be enhanced for them to achieve better in school. The need for greater participation by girls in mathematics and science-related careers also seems essential, particularly as more and more of the high-paying positions generated by the "new economy" require these skills. It therefore does not seem appropriate to focus primarily on either gender, but rather to deal with the separate issues that each gender group faces.

In sum, despite evidence that males' and females' performance in math and English is becoming more similar, gender differences in competence beliefs and values regarding these subjects remain. At early adolescence girls appear to have lower self-esteem than boys do. The question of whether the transition to middle school has stronger negative effects on girls than on boys has received some support in the literature, but the evidence is not always consistent with this view. And although some girls may lose voice at adolescence, the claim that most girls do so appears to be too sweeping. Many boys also experience difficulties in adjusting to school and performing well in certain subjects. To connect this work to that reviewed in the previous section, researchers should examine how middle school reform efforts impact motivation and self-esteem of both boys and girls, to see what kinds of impact these reforms are having on both groups.

To conclude, we have reviewed work on how motivation and self-concept change at early adolescence, discussing how aspects of school and classroom environment can produce the observed changes. We also discussed the still nascent work on how middle school reform efforts are influencing early adolescents' motivation and self-esteem. These reforms appear very promising, and results of some of the early evaluations of their effects have been quite positive. Continuing such work is a priority for the new millennium.

## Teachers' Questions and Answers

**Q:** I teach in a large middle school where we try to arrange things to accommodate the large numbers of students. For example, to deal with the problem of moving so many kids through their day without overcrowding the cafeteria we use things like different bell schedules for different subject departments. But I wonder if such practices only create more distractions for students.

**A:** A number of the recommendations for change would seem to be especially important in large middle schools. Research increasingly has shown that when a sense of community and belonging is present in schools, students are more engaged and achieve better. This sense of community is more likely to be lacking in very large schools, as students likely often feel lost in the crowd in these schools. Creating smaller learning communities, organizing instruction by teams rather than departments, and providing other ways to connect students to these schools seems crucial in these kinds of institutions. With smaller learning communities and teams of teachers, bell schedules could be adjusted within the teams. Doing so may be more challenging than in smaller schools, but it might be even more important and provide stronger benefits.

**Q:** I am worried that my students are being damaged by our current practice of giving them so many high-stakes tests throughout the year. I'm particularly worried that the lower scoring and anxious students are losing motivation as a result. Does any research document this and provide ideas on how to combat these effects?

**A:** Many motivation theorists and researchers are quite concerned about the impact of high-stakes testing on students' motivation, and think that such testing can undermine many students' motivation. Two particular concerns are what will happen to anxious students and to those performing poorly. Anxious students often are quite stressed by tests, and their level of stress increases as the stakes of testing are raised. Low achievers likely fail many items on the tests, making it more likely that they will doubt their abilities. I don't think systematic work has been done yet to determine exactly what the effects of high-stakes testing on motivation are, but certainly for both these kinds of students they are not likely to be positive. To support students, a number of things can be done. One is to help anxious students deal with the pressures of testing by giving them ideas about how to approach the test (e.g., doing the ones you can first, not dwelling too much on items that pose serious challenges for students, giving students ways to relax while they are taking tests). Lower-achieving students who feel like giving up may be less likely to do so if they experience success in other tasks and activities in school. Emphasizing to them the importance of effort and use of good strategies while working on the tests may help them avoid the sense that they simply lack ability.

**Q:**   If students lose self-esteem when they go through middle school, should we be taking steps to bolster it? If so, might this detract from our efforts to boost their achievement?

**A:**   Fostering a positive sense of self-esteem in students is a worthy goal at all levels of education, because high self-esteem relates to a number of important mental health and other outcomes. However, the development of a positive sense of self in school needs to be done in the context of legitimate accomplishments; students' sense of themselves needs to be grounded in this way. Students' self-esteem (and other aspects of their beliefs about themselves) need to have a stronger foundation than simply being told they are great. A sense of self that is not based in accomplishments can be hollow, and may crumble when challenges are faced.

Efforts to enhance self-esteem and efforts to increase academic rigor and performance need not be in opposition. As Midgley and Edelin (1998) noted, efforts to improve the climate of school, students' sense of belonging there, and their self-esteem are crucial parts of middle school reform efforts. Efforts to increase academic rigor and student achievement also are central to reform. The two can be complementary rather than in opposition to each other, and indeed should be complementary.

# References

Alexander, W., & George, P. (1981). *The exemplary middle school.* New York: Holt, Rinehart, Winston.

American Association for University Women (1992). *How schools shortchange girls* (report). American Association of University Women's Educational Foundation.

Ames, C. (1992). Classrooms: Goals, structures, and student motivation. *Journal of Educational Psychology, 84,* 261–271.

Anderman, E. M., & Maehr, M. L. (1994). Motivation and schooling in the middle grades. *Review of Educational Research, 64,* 287–309.

Anderman, E. M., Maehr, M. L., & Midgley, C. (1999). Declining motivation after the transition to middle school: Schools can make a difference. *Journal of Research and Development in Education, 32,* 131–147.

Anderman, E. M., & Midgley, C. (1997). Changes in achievement goal orientations, perceived academic competence, and grades across the transition to middle-level schools. *Contemporary Educational Psychology, 22,* 269–298.

Arhar, J. (1997). The effects of interdisciplinary teaming on teachers and students. In J. L. Irvin (Ed.), *What current research says to the middle level practitioner* (pp. 49–56). Columbus, OH: National Middle School Association.

Ashton, P. (1985). Motivation and the teacher's sense of efficacy. In C. Ames & R. Ames (Eds.), *Research on motivation in education* (Vol. 2, pp. 141–171). Orlando, FL: Academic Press.

Bandura, A. (1997). *Self-efficacy: The exercise of control.* San Francisco: Freeman.

Blos, P. (1979). *The adolescent passage.* New York: International Universities Press.

Blyth, D. A., Simmons, R. G., & Carlton-Ford, S. (1983). The adjustment of early adolescents to school transitions. *Journal of Early Adolescence, 3*, 105–120.

Brough, J. A. (1997) Home-school partnerships: A critical link. In J. L. Irvin (Ed.), *What current research says to the middle level practitioner* (pp. 265–274). Columbus, OH: National Middle Schools Association.

Brush, L. (1980). *Encouraging girls in math.* Cambridge, MA: Abt.

Byrnes, J. B. (1988). Formal operations: A systematic reformulation. *Developmental Review, 8*, 1–22.

Carnegie Council on Adolescent Development (1989). *Turning points: Preparing American youth for the 21st century.* New York: Carnegie Corporation.

Clark, S. N., & Clark, D. C. (1993). Middle level school reform: The rhetoric and the reality. *Elementary School Journal, 93*, 447–460.

Dornbusch, S. M., Petersen, A. C., & Hetherington, E. M. (1991). Projecting the future of research on adolescence. *Journal of Research on Adolescence, 1*, 7–18.

Dusek, J. B., & Flaherty, J. F. (1981). The development of the self-concept during the adolescent years. *Monographs of the Society for Research in Child Development, 46* (4, Serial No. 191).

Dweck, C. S., & Leggett, E. L. (1988). A social-cognitive approach to motivation and personality. *Psychological Review, 95*, 256–273.

Eccles, J. S. (1987). Gender roles and women's achievement-related decisions. *Psychology of Women Quarterly, 11*, 135–172.

Eccles, J., Adler, T. F., Futterman, R., Goff, S. B., Kaczala, C. M., Meece, J., & Midgley, C. (1983). Expectancies, values and academic behaviors. In J. T. Spence (Ed.), *Achievement and achievement motives* (pp. 75–146). San Francisco: Freeman.

Eccles, J. S., & Midgley, C. (1989). Stage – environment fit: Developmentally appropriate classrooms for young adolescents. In C. Ames & R. Ames (Eds.), *Research on motivation in education* (Vol. 3, pp. 139–186). San Diego: Academic Press.

Eccles, J. S., & Wigfield, A. (1997). Early adolescent development. In J. L. Irvin (Ed.), *What current research says to the middle level practitioner* (pp. 15–29). Columbus, OH: National Middle Schools Association.

Eccles, J., Wigfield, A., Harold, R., & Blumenfeld, P. (1993). Age and gender differences in children's self and task perceptions during elementary school. *Child Development, 64*, 830–847.

Eccles, J. S., Wigfield, A., Flanagan, C., Miller, C., Reuman, D., & Yee, D. (1989). Self-concepts, domain values, and self-esteem: Relations and changes at early adolescence. *Journal of Personality, 57*, 283–310.

Eccles, J. S., Wigfield, A., & Schiefele, U. (1998). Motivation to succeed. In W. Damon (Series Ed.) & N. Eisenberg (Vol. Ed.), *Handbook of child psychology* (5th ed., Vol. 3, pp. 1017–1095). New York: Wiley.

Elliott, A. J., & Harackiewicz, J. M. (1996). Approach and avoidance goals and intrinsic motivation: A mediational analysis. *Journal of Personality and Social Psychology, 70*, 461–475.

Epstein, J. (1987). Parent involvement: What research says to adminstrators. *Educational and Urban Society, 19*, 119–136.

Epstein, J. L. (1988). Effective schools or effective students? Dealing with diversity. In R. Haskins & D. MacRae (Eds.), *Policies for America's public schools: Teacher equity indicators.* Norwood, NJ: Ablex.

Erikson, E. H. (1963). *Childhood and society.* New York: Norton.

Feldlaufer, H., Midgley, C., & Eccles, J. S. (1988). Student, teacher, and observer perceptions of the classroom environment before and after the transition to junior high school. *Journal of Early Adolescence, 8*, 133–156.

Felner, R. D., Jackson, A. W., Kasak, D., Mulhall, P., Brand, S., & Flowers, N. (1997). The impact of school reform for the middle years: Longitudinal study of a network engaged in Turning Points-based comprehensive school transformation. *Phi Delta Kappan, 78*, 528–532, 541–550.

Fischer, K. (1980). A theory of cognitive development: The control and construction of hierarchies of skills. *Psychological Review, 87*, 477–531.

Gilligan, C. (1982). *In a different voice: Psychological theory and women's development.* Cambridge, MA: Harvard University Press.

Gilligan, C. (1993). Joining the resistance; Psychology, politics, girls, and women. In L. Weis & M. Fine (Eds.), *Beyond silenced voices* (pp. 143–168). Albany: State University of New York Press.

Gilligan, C., Lyons, N., & Hammer, T. J. (1989). *Making connections.* Cambridge, MA: Harvard University Press.

Hall, G. S. (1904). *Adolescence: Its psychology and its relations to anthropology, sex, crime, religion, and education.* New York: Appleton.

Harter, S. (1981). A new self-report scale of intrinsic versus extrinsic orientation in the classroom: Motivational and informational components. *Developmental Psychology, 17,* 300–312.

Harter, S. (1982). The perceived competence scale for children. *Child Development, 53,* 87–97.

Harter, S. (1986). Processes underlying the construction, maintenance and enhancement of the self-concept in children. In J. Suls & A.C. Greenwald (Eds.), *Psychological perspectives on the self* (Vol. 3, pp. 137–181). Hillsdale, NJ: Erlbaum.

Harter, S. (1990). Processes underlying adolescent self-concept formation. In R. Montemayor, G. R. Adams, & T. P. Gullotta (Eds.), *From childhood to adolescence: A transitional period?* (pp. 205–239). Newbury Park, CA: Sage.

Harter, S. (1998). The development of self-representations. In W. Damon (Series Ed.) & N. Eisenberg (Vol. ed.), *Handbook of child psychology* (5th ed., Vol. 3, pp. 553–618). New York: Wiley.

Harter, W., Waters, P. L., & Whitesell, N. R. (1997). Lack of voice as a manifestation of false self-behavior among adolescents: The school setting as a stage upon which the drama of authenticity is enacted. *Educational Psychologist, 32,* 153–174.

Harter, S., Whitesell, N., & Kowalski, P. (1992). Individual differences in the effects of educational transitions on children's perceptions of competence and motivational orientation. *American Educational Research Journal, 29,* 777–808.

Hill, J. P., & Lynch, M. E. (1983). The intensification of gender-related role expectations during early adolescence. In J. Brooks-Gunn & A. C. Petersen (Eds.), *Girls at puberty* (pp. 201–228). New York: Plenum.

Irvin, J. L. (Ed.) (1992). *Transforming middle level education: Perspectives and possibilities.* Boston: Allyn & Bacon.

Jacobs, J., Hyatt, S., Eccles, J. S., Osgood, D. W., & Wigfield, A. (in press). The ontogeny of children's self-beliefs: Gender and domain differences across grades one through 12. *Child Development.*

Kavrell, S. M., & Petersen, A. C. (1984). Patterns of achievement in early adolescence. In M. L. Maehr (Ed.), *Advances in motivation and achievement* (Vol. 4, pp. 1–35). Greenwich, CT.: JAI Press.

Keating, D. P. (1990). Adolescent thinking. In S. S. Feldman & G. R. Elliott (Eds.), *At the threshold: The developing adolescent* (pp. 54–89). Cambridge, MA: Harvard University Press.

Lee, V. E., Bryk, A. S., & Smith, J. B. (1993). The organization of effective secondary schools. In L. Darling-Hammond (Ed.), *Review of research in education* (pp. 171–267). Washington DC: American Educational Research Association.

Lerner, R., M., Entwisle, D. R., & Hauser, S. T. (1994). The crisis among contemporary American adolescents: A call for the integration of research, policies, and programs. *Journal of Research on Adolescence, 4,* 1–4.

Linn, M. C., & Hyde, J. S. (1989). Gender, math, and science. *Educational Researcher, 18,* 17–27.

Lipsitz, J., Mizell, M. H., Jackson, A. W., & Austin, L. M. (1997). Speaking with one voice: A manifesto for middle-grades reform. *Phi Delta Kappan,* 533–540.

Mac Iver, D. J., & Epstein, J. L. (1993). Middle grades research: Not yet mature, but no longer a child. *Elementary School Journal, 93,* 519–533.

Mac Iver, D. J., Mac Iver, M. A., Balfanz, R., Plank, S. B., & Ruby, A. (2000). Talent development middle schools: Blueprints and results for a comprehensive whole-school reform model. In M. G. Sanders (Ed.), *Schooling students placed at risk* (pp. 261–288). Mahwah, NJ: Erlbaum.

Mac Iver, D. J., & Plank, J. B. (1997). Improving urban schools: Developing the talents of students placed at risk. In J. L. Irvin (Ed.), *What current research says to the middle level practitioner* (pp. 243–256). Columbus, OH: National Middle School Association.

Maehr, M. L., & Midgley, C. (1996). *Transforming school cultures.* Boulder, CO: Westview Press.

Malina, R. M. (1990). Physical growth and performance during the transitional years (9–16). In R. Montemayor, G. R. Adams, & T. P. Gullotta (Eds.), *From childhood to adolescence: A transitional period* (pp. 41–62). Newbury Park, CA: Sage.

Markus, H., & Nurius, P. (1986). Possible selves. *American Psychologist, 41*, 954–969.

Markus, H., & Wurf, E. (1987). The dynamic self-concept: A social psychological perspective. *Annual Review of Psychology, 38*, 299–337.

Marsh, H. W. (1989). Age and sex effects in multiple dimensions of self-concept: Preadolescence to early adulthood. *Journal of Educational Psychology, 81*, 417–430.

Marsh, H. W. (1990). The structure of academic self-concept: The Marsh/Shavelson model. *Journal of Educational Psychology, 82*, 623–636.

Marsh, H. W., & Shavelson, R. (1985). Self-concept: Its multifaceted hierarchical structure. *Educational Psychologist, 20*, 107–123.

Meece, J., Wigfield, A., & Eccles, J. (1990). Predictors of math anxiety and its influence on young adolescents' course enrollment intentions and performance in mathematics. *Journal of Educational Psychology, 82*, 60–70.

Mergendoller, J. R., Marchman, V. L., Mittman, A. L., & Packer, M. J. (1988). Task demands and accountability in middle-grade science classes. *Elementary School Journal, 88*, 251–265.

Midgley, C., Anderman, E., & Hicks, L. (1995). Differences between elementary school teachers and students: A goal theory approach. *Journal of Early Adolescence, 15*, 90–113.

Midgley, C., & Edelin, K. C. (1998). Middle school reform and early adolescent well-being: The good news and the bad. *Educational Psychologist, 33*, 195–206.

Midgley, C., & Feldlaufer, H. (1987). Students' and teachers' decision-making fit before and after the transition to junior high school. *Journal of Early Adolescence, 7*, 225–241.

Midgley, C., Feldlaufer, H., & Eccles, J. S. (1988). The transition to junior high school: Beliefs of pre- and post-transition teachers. *Journal of Youth and Adolescence, 17*, 543–562.

Moos, R. H. (1979). *Evaluating educational environments*. San Francisco, CA:. Jossey-Bass.

Moshman, D. (1998). Cognitive development beyond childhood. In W. Damon (Series Ed.) & R. Siegler (Vol. Ed.) *Handbook of child psychology* (5th ed., Vol. 2, pp. 947–978). New York: Wiley.

Nicholls, J. G. (1979). Quality and equality in intellectual development: The role of motivation in education. *American Psychologist, 34*, 1071–1084.

Nicholls, J. G. (1984). Achievement motivation: Conceptions of ability, subjective experience, task choice, and performance. *Psychological Review, 91*, 328–346.

O'Mally, P. M., & Bachman, J. C. (1983). Self-esteem changes and stability between ages 13 and 23. *Developmental Psychology, 19*, 257–268.

Petersen, A. (1985). Pubertal development as a cause of disturbance: Myths, realities, and un-answered question. *Genetic, Social and General Psychology Monographs, 111*, 205–232.

Petersen, A. (1988). Adolescent development. *Annual Review of Psychology, 39*, 583–607.

Piaget, J., & Inhelder, B. (1973). *Memory and intelligence*. London: Routledge & Kegan Paul.

Pintrich, P. R. (2000). The role of goal orientation in self-regulated learning. In M. Boekarts, P. R. Pintrich, & M. Zeidner (Eds.), *Handbook of self-regulation: Theory, research, and applications.* San Diego: Academic Press.

Pintrich, P. R , & Schunk, D. H. (1996). *Motivation in education: Theory, research, and applications.* Englewood Cliffs, NJ: Prentice–Hall.

Pipher, M. (1994). *Reviving Ophelia: Saving the selves of adolescent girls*. New York: Ballantine.

Rosenberg, M. (1986). Self-concept from middle childhood through adolescence. In J. Suls & A. G. Greenwald (Eds.), *Psychological perspectives on the self* (Vol. 3, pp. 107–136). Hillsdale, NJ: Erlbaum.

Rosenholtz, S. J. & Simpson, C. (1984). The formation of ability conceptions: Developmental trend or social construction? *Review of Educational Research, 54*, 301–325.

Ruble, D. N., & Martin, C. L. (1998). Gender development. In W. Damon (Series Ed.) & N. Eisenberg (Vol. Ed), *Handbook of child psychology* (5th ed., Vol. 3, pp. 933–1016). New York: Wiley.

Shavelson, R., J., Hubner, J. J., & Stanton, G. C. (1976). Self-concept: Validation of construct interpretations. *Review of Educational Research, 46*, 407–441.

Simmons, R. G., & Blyth, D. A. (1987). *Moving into adolescence: The impact of pubertal change and school context.* Hawthorn, NY: Aldine de Gruyler.

Simmons, R. G., Blyth D. A., Van Cleave, E. F., & Bush, D. (1979). Entry into early adolescence: The impact of school structure, puberty, and early dating on self-esteem. *American Sociological Review, 44*, 948–967.

Simmons, R. G., Rosenberg, M. F., & Rosenberg, M. C. (1973). Disturbance in the self-image at adolescence. *American Sociological Review, 38*, 553–568.

Skinner, E. A., Zimmer-Gembeck, M. J., & Connell, J, P. (1998). Individual differences and the development of perceived control. *Monographs of the Society for Research in Child Development, 63* (Serial No. 254).

Sommers, H. (2000). The war against boys. *Atlantic Monthly, 285* (3), 59–74.

Stattin, H., & Magnusson, D. (1990). *Pubertal maturation in female development.* Hillsdale, NJ: Erlbaum.

Stipek, D. (1996). Motivation and instruction. In D. Berliner & R. Calfee (Eds.), *Handbook of educational psychology* (pp. 85–113). New York: Macmillan.

Stipek, D., & Mac Iver, D. (1989). Developmental change in children's assessment of intellectual competence. *Child Development, 60*, 521–538.

Trebilco, G. R., Atkinson, E. P., & Atkinson, J. M. (1977, November). *The transition of students from primary to secondary school.* Paper presented at the annual conference of the Australian Association for Research in Education, Canberra.

Walberg, H. J., House, E. R., & Steele, J. M. (1973). Grade level, cognition, and affect: A cross-section of classroom perceptions. *Journal of Educational Psychology, 64*, 142–146.

Weiner, B., (1985). An attributional theory of achievement motivation and emotion. *Psychological Review, 92*, 548–573.

Wentzel, K. R. (1997). Students motivation in middle school: The role of perceived pedagogical caring. *Journal of Educational Psychology, 89*, 411–419.

Wigfield, A., Battle, A., Solomon, L., & Eccles, J. S. (2002). Sex differences in motivation, self-concept, career aspirations, and career choice: Implications for cognitive development. In A. McGillicuddy-DelLisi & R. DeLisi (Eds.), *Biology, sociology, and behavior: The development of sex differences in cognition.* Greenwich, CT: Ablex.

Wigfield, A., Eccles, J., Mac Iver, D., Reuman, D., & Midgley, C. (1991). Transitions at early adolescence: Changes in children's domain-specific self-perceptions and general self-esteem across the transition to junior high school. *Developmental Psychology, 27*, 552–565.

Wigfield, A., Eccles, J. S., & Pintrich, P. R. (1996). Development between the ages of 12 and 25. In D. Berliner & R. Calfee (Eds.), *Handbook of educational psychology* (pp. 148–185). New York: Macmillan.

CHAPTER

9

# Self-Efficacy and Self-Regulated Learning: The Dynamic Duo in School Performance

PAMELA J. GASKILL AND ANITA WOOLFOLK HOY

*The Ohio State University, Columbus, Ohio*

On an early autumn morning the second graders cheerily exchange greetings as they enter their classroom, hang up their jackets, and prepare to start their day. Dan immediately goes to his desk and looks toward the chart that poses the "problem of the day," a challenging mathematical activity the children routinely do when they arrive each morning. He pulls out his math journal, and begins to read the problem and contemplate his solution. Chris, on the other hand, walks around the classroom awhile before going to his desk. When finally seated, he pulls out a toy dinosaur to examine. Seeing the other children at his table working in their math journals, he half-heartedly retrieves his journal from his desk and glances briefly at the Problem of the Day chart. He never actually gets around to writing anything down.

Dan and Chris are real students. Their names have been changed, but they are actual second graders. Although they are equally intelligent boys, there is a vast difference in their approaches to academic tasks and, as a result, a widening difference in their levels of academic attainment as well. What is it that has created this dichotomy? What can his teachers do to ensure that Dan will continue with his positive level of engagement? What can be done to encourage Chris to become more successfully engaged?

Scenarios such as the above are a daily occurrence in classrooms. These questions about student differences have intrigued and perplexed parents, teachers, and researchers alike as long as there has been formal education. The answers are not simple. Individual differences have many bases, including personality traits, ability, experience, family and personal expectations, and environmental factors. All of these factors interact to influence motivation, an integral part of students' school performance. But increasing evidence suggests that an additional factor, adults' and children's beliefs about their ability to perform a task, exerts a powerful influence over their motivation for that task. According to Bandura et al. (1996), "Among the mechanisms of personal agency, none is more central or pervasive than people's beliefs in their capabilities to exercise control over their level of functioning and environmental demands" (p. 1026). The construct of *self-efficacy* has thus emerged as a strong predictor of behavior.

## SELF-EFFICACY

Just what is self-efficacy? Perceived self-efficacy refers to individuals' beliefs about their ability to execute a particular performance (Bandura, 1986). Many people assume self-efficacy is the same as self-concept or self-esteem, but it is not. Self-efficacy is distinct from other conceptions of self in that it involves judgments about capabilities *specific to a particular task*. Pajares (1997) defines self-efficacy as "a context-specific assessment of competence to perform a specific task" (p. 15). Self-concept is a more global construct that contains many perceptions about the self, including self-efficacy. Self-concept is developed as a result of external and internal comparisons, using other people or other aspects of the self as frames of reference. But self-efficacy focuses on ability to successfully accomplish a particular task with no need for comparisons: the question is can *I* do it, not would others be successful (Marsh, Walker, & Debus, 1991). Also, efficacy beliefs are strong predictors of behavior, but self-concept has weaker predictive power (Bandura, 1997).

Compared with self-esteem, self-efficacy is concerned with judgments of personal capabilities; self-esteem is concerned with judgments of self-worth. Self-esteem and self-efficacy are not perfectly correlated. It is possible to feel highly efficacious in one area and still not have a high level of self-esteem, or vice versa. For example, you may have low self-efficacy for singing, but your self-esteem would not be affected if your life did not require singing. But if you were a teacher and your self-efficacy for teaching started dropping after several bad experiences, it is likely that your self-esteem would suffer too. So self-efficacy for a particular task affects self-esteem only if the person *values* that task.

## Sources of Self-Efficacy

Bandura identified four sources of efficacy expectations: mastery experiences, physiological and emotional arousal, vicarious experiences, and verbal persuasion. *Mastery experiences* are our own direct experiences—the most powerful source of efficacy information. Successes raise efficacy beliefs whereas failures lower efficacy. Level of *arousal* affects efficacy, depending on how the arousal is interpreted. As you face a task, are you anxious and worried (lowers efficacy) or excited and "psyched" (raises efficacy) (Bandura, 1997; Pintrich & Schunk, 2002).

In *vicarious experiences*, accomplishments are modeled by someone else. The more closely you identify with the model, the greater the impact on efficacy. When the model performs well, your efficacy is enhanced, but when the model performs poorly, efficacy expectations decrease. Although mastery experiences generally are acknowledged as the most influential source of efficacy beliefs in adults, Keyser and Barling (1981) found that children (sixth graders in their study) rely more on modeling than mastery as a source of self-efficacy information. Similar peers (similar in age, competence, and in certain situations, gender) make the most powerful models (Schunk, 2000).

*Verbal persuasion* may be a "pep talk" or specific performance feedback. Verbal persuasion alone cannot create enduring increases in self-efficacy, but a persuasive boost in self-efficacy can lead an individual to make an effort, attempt new strategies, or try hard enough to succeed (Bandura, 1982). Verbal persuasion can counter occasional setbacks that might have instilled self-doubt and interrupted persistence. The potency of persuasion depends on the credibility, trustworthiness, and expertise of the persuader (Bandura, 1986).

Examples might be helpful in explaining each of the four sources of efficacy. If a student earns a perfect score on a spelling test, that mastery attainment will increase his efficacy for getting a perfect score on the next spelling test. After watching one of her classmates correctly solve a two-digit subtraction problem, a vicarious or modeling experience, a second grader may raise her belief that she can solve a similar problem. A teacher's words of encouragement such as "You figured out all of the words on that page by yourself! I'll bet you can read the next page just as well" can influence the student's efficacy for successfully reading a page of similar difficulty. On the other hand, efficacy sources can also be negative. If a student has a strong physiological reaction to a task, such as a pounding heart and sweaty palms as she begins to give an oral report, she may conclude that report giving is a difficult task that she cannot perform successfully. Each of the four sources may either raise or lower self-efficacy judgments, depending on the interpretations made by a particular individual in a particular situation.

## Impact of Efficacy Beliefs

Highly efficacious students tend to select more challenging tasks, put forth more effort to successfully accomplish tasks, and persist longer when tackling difficult tasks (Bandura, 1997; Schunk, 1990). Students with low levels of efficacy may choose only easy tasks or avoid a task altogether, apply minimal effort, and give up easily. Even when students have the same level of academic skills, those with higher self-efficacy for the task perform better on schoolwork (Zimmerman, 1995).

Self-efficacy would be one of the first factors to consider in explaining Dan's and Chris' approaches to the Problem of the Day, as well as the differences in their overall school performance. What might have caused these two boys to form such contrasting sets of beliefs about their abilities for school success? The similarities between Dan and Chris are striking in many respects. Both boys are being raised by their mothers in single-parent homes. Both have one sister, 3 years older, and no younger siblings in the home. Their sisters are conscientious and capable students. Both Chris and Dan are bright and articulate, have pleasant personalities, are polite and cooperative, and are well-liked by their peers.

There is, however, an important difference between the two boys. Chris has a physical disability that resulted in several surgeries since his birth, frequent bouts of illness, and some physical limitations. From a very early age, he lagged in physical development and stature. It is reasonable to assume that many expectations were lowered for Chris in light of the physical struggles he faced. Although his physical disabilities had no direct impact on his mental ability, it is quite possible that his self-belief system was strongly influenced by related consequences. It is likely that Chris began to get early messages, both at home and later at school, that it was acceptable for his performance level to be less than that of students with no disability.

Compared with many students with low levels of efficacy for school performance, Chris's case is more understandable and maybe even predictable. Regardless of the causes, however, it is important for teachers to do whatever they can to facilitate development of positive levels of self-efficacy in all of their students. Clearly, any courses of action that enhance children's efficacy could improve their odds for achieving success.

## Importance of the Primary Grades

Children entering first grade already show a wide range of individual differences. And yet, because their self-beliefs for school success and their efficacy for cognitive learning are so undeveloped, they undoubtedly are at their most malleable stage because efficacy is most malleable early in the learning experience (Bandura, 1997). After third grade, academic work becomes increasingly demanding. What happens to students in the first few years of school will lead them to develop self-beliefs that will become increasingly stable as they confront more demanding work. "Because of the formative aspect of these early school years and this shift in academic expectations beyond third grade, many preventive programs define kindergarten through third grade as the window in which children build the foundations of successful school careers" (Perry & Weinstein, 1998, p. 178).

Even though the foundation for future success or failure is built in the primary grades, relatively little research directly explores self-efficacy under fourth grade. Some educational psychologists suggest that children in the early grades rarely reflect on their own performance (Paris & Newman, 1990). Children do, however, construct implicit beliefs and concepts about their abilities; these beliefs mediate their learning. Early on, children develop their personal theories of schooling, often based on social interactions in the classroom, that influence their actions at school and either foster or impede academic achievement. Besides beliefs about their academic abilities, they also form beliefs about the nature of academic tasks, cognitive strategies, social dispositions of others, and expectations for their own success. These ideas develop concurrently as children progress through formal education (Paris & Newman, 1990). There are cumulative effects as children move from the primary grades into the intermediate grades.

## Characteristics of Young Children That Affect Efficacy Judgments

If preschool and primary teachers are serious about promoting self-efficacy beliefs, it is important that the teachers have a basic understanding of young children's common characteristics and conceptions about competence. The following sections describe several of these characteristics and conceptions.

### Modeling: Social and Cognitive Comparisons

Watching other children and comparing themselves with their peers provide important information as children begin to make self-judgments. As children mature, they become increasingly discriminating in their use of comparative efficacy information. Around age 6, children begin to realize that the most informative comparisons are made with others who are like themselves but slightly better (Bandura, 1986). So primary grade children are becoming more skilled at making accurate judgments about their abilities by comparing themselves with other young children.

Cognitive modeling can be used to increase children's skills in making efficacy judgments. In cognitive modeling, individuals think aloud as they solve problems or make judgments so that their thought processes are observable (Meichenbaum & Asarnow, 1979). Both the student who is doing the cognitive modeling and the observers can benefit from this strategy. For example, a student might be required to talk through the steps used to solve a word problem in math. During this modeling process, the teacher or a peer tutor can point out all of the steps that the student is performing correctly, thus highlighting mastery experience. The student can be encouraged to attempt difficult steps with support and coaching from the teacher or a peer (verbal persuasion), and given feedback along the way that notes how the student's effort leads to success and how success reflects ability. By reviewing how the student handled the task and overcame difficulties to succeed, teachers help students learn to interpret and integrate efficacy information (from mastery experience, verbal persuasion, or other sources) on future tasks that are similar. Children who observe the model will learn how to use relevant cues for assessing their own ability to perform the task successfully.

## Attention to Immediate Outcomes and Efficacy Accuracy

Piaget's (1963, 1970) work on cognitive and perceptual development demonstrated that children of about 6 and younger were unable to focus on more than one dimension of a problem or situation at a time. Bandura (1986) suggested that this limitation causes young children to rely on immediate and conspicuous outcomes for their self-appraisals. A note written on a first or second grader's paper telling her that her writing is messy may not be helpful for improvement of her writing or for her efficacy for neat handwriting. Monitoring her writing and reminding her to make sure that her lines do not go below the baseline on her writing paper and noting how much neater her writing looks when she stops on the line provide concrete cues both about how she can improve the appearance of her handwriting and how she can judge the writing she does on her own in the future. When one new handwriting technique is mastered, another can then be introduced.

Another reason why children are less accurate in their efficacy judgments than adults may be because the children are less advanced in their cognitive development. As they mature, children develop their abilities to consider increasingly complex data and use greater logical reasoning to make efficacy judgments. For example, Kaley and Cloutier (1984) found that efficacy estimates of fifth and ninth graders predict their behavior more accurately than the efficacy estimates of first graders predict these younger students' actions. We have found, however, that when students are given a concrete task at the appropriate developmental level, second graders can make quite accurate efficacy predictions (Gaskill, 2000).

## Misconceptions: Equating Social and Academic Abilities

Investigations of young children's early beliefs about their competence reveal some surprising misconceptions. Most of the misconceptions are related to the children's limited cognitive development. To encourage early positive effi-cacy beliefs rather than undermine them, it is important for teachers to be aware of some of the differences between the ways that younger children and older children interpret information about their competence. Let us consider a few of these differences and misconceptions.

One of the striking misconceptions is that young children often confuse academic ability and social behavior. When Stipek and Tannatt (1984) asked preschoolers to tell which of their classmates were smart, more than half of them mentioned children who behaved appropriately by staying in their seats, obeying the teacher, and not teasing others. Blumenfeld, Pintrich, Meece, and Wessels (1981, 1982) found that first graders believed that the children who shared were average or smart, and those who received criticism were less capable. These young students were unable to separate behavioral from academic feedback. They related being smart to paying attention, finishing work, and not fooling around; they felt more guilty about inappropriate behav-ior than fifth graders did. Stipek and Tannatt (1984) found that kindergarten through third grade children were significantly more likely to refer to work habits than preschool children when assessing their ability, although this may be a socially constructed belief based on teacher emphasis on effort.

## Interpretations of Teacher Actions

There also may be developmental differences in how children use praise and blame as cues about competence. For example, Barker and Graham (1987) found that 5-year-olds perceived praised students to be more able and blamed students to be less competent when compared with students who received neutral feedback. The result reversed as students got older: praised students were seen as less able and blamed students as more competent. Older children may see criticism as a signal from the teacher that the criticized student has the ability to do better, whereas praise can communicate, "You poor child, you did well considering your limited abilities." Brophy (1985) calls this "praise as a consolation prize" for failing.

A similar age-related difference is associated with strategies used by chil-dren to interpret the meanings of their teachers' actions, including teacher attention and expressions of liking or warmth. For example, 6- and 7-year-old students believed that a student who was hugged by his teacher was smarter than an unhugged student, but 10- and 11-year-olds reached the exact oppos-ite conclusion (Lord, Umezaki, & Darley, 1990). That is, the older children interpreted the hugs as a sign of sympathy, indicating that the teacher did not believe the hugged child had the ability to perform as well as the unhugged child. By the same token, Graham and Barker (1990) found that when teachers gave unsolicited help to students, it signaled that the receiving children were less smart and less likely to be successful in the future.

## Effort and Ability Beliefs

As described by Dweck (Chapter 4 in this volume), adults use two basic concepts of ability. An entity view of ability assumes that ability is a *stable, uncontrollable* trait—a characteristic of the individual that cannot be changed. According to this view, some people have more ability than others, but the amount each person has is set. An incremental view of ability, on the other hand, suggests that ability is *unstable and controllable*—"an ever-expanding repertoire of skills and knowledge" (Dweck & Bempechat, 1983, p. 144). By hard work, study, or practice, knowledge can be increased and thus ability can be improved.

Young children tend to hold an exclusively incremental view of ability: ability can be improved by effort because hard work *is* high ability (Nicholls & Miller, 1984). Thus through the early elementary grades, most students believe that effort is the same as intelligence. Students who work harder are seen as more capable, a phenomenon labeled the "halo schema" (Kun, 1977). If you fail, you are not smart and you did not try hard; if you succeed, you must be a smart, hard worker (Stipek, 2002). Equating effort and ability can be seen as a positive belief because all children can perceive of themselves as capable as long as they try hard. The emphasis on effort by young children requires less continuous comparison with others: you know that you are capable as long as you are working hard. Thus ability is more under the individual's control (Rosenholtz & Simpson, 1984).

Unfortunately, cognitive growth—along with all its positive effects—brings negatives as well. Children of 11 or 12 begin to differentiate among effort, ability, and performance. Thus fifth and sixth grade students begin to infer that having to exert more effort must reflect less ability: if you were really smart you would not have to work hard at all (Lord et al., 1990). So older students may protect their self-esteem about ability by avoiding the appearance of working hard, a strategy that will undermine learning and thus diminish self-efficacy in the long run.

Another advantage of maintaining the incremental view that intelligence is malleable and that effort improves ability is the adoption of learning goals (Dweck, 1986; Chapter 4 in this volume). Children with learning goals try to increase their competence and to understand or master something new, whereas children with performance goals focus on making good impressions or avoiding negative judgments of their ability. Working toward learning goals is characterized by seeking challenge and persisting when confronted with obstacles, but embracing performance goals results in low persistence and avoiding challenge.

What can we conclude as teachers? Because children in the primary grades naturally take the incremental view, helping them to maintain that view as long as possible is important for the development of positive self-efficacy (Nicholls, 1978; Schunk, 1983). Unfortunately, as children progress through the grades, they increasingly conceive of ability as a stable and inherent trait and they sometimes see effort as signaling low ability, due in part to the social comparisons that permeate school testing and grading practices. If students judge their own ability to be inferior and avoid effort because it signals low ability, efficacy beliefs are impaired.

We have covered many possibilities for helping young children to raise their judgments of academic efficacy. Knowing how to seamlessly embed efficacy information into routine classroom instruction is an important teacher tool. Let us take a look at some strategies that were used to improve Chris' efficacy for the Problem of the Day activity. First of all, it was necessary for Chris to encounter some positive experiences with the task in a supportive climate. At the beginning of each math class, the procedure was to go over the day's problem together and have students share different ways in which they were able to solve the problem. Chris was able to see his peers model and discuss their solutions, an important vicarious experience.

In addition, the teacher sometimes asked Chris and other students who had been unable to solve a problem to think about which of the demonstrated solutions they would choose for themselves. In this way they were able to contribute to the class discussions. They were observed and scaffolded as necessary as they then added their solution to their otherwise empty journal page. The teacher provided feedback that focused on the skills that they already had and were able to apply to the process. At the same time, the teacher observed these students for areas of weakness that needed to be addressed in upcoming math lessons. Efforts were always made to keep the climate of the classroom warm and encouraging for all students, not focusing unusual levels of attention on the unsuccessful students, but at the same time acknowledging their ability to solve the problem successfully.

Students like Dan who had successfully solved the problem earlier in the day were encouraged to think about alternative solutions or ones that they thought might be better than their originals. In this way all students' were being challenged by the Problem of the Day activity. Dan began to challenge himself by coming up with several solutions in the hope of finding ones that no one else would think of, while Chris began to believe that he could successfully participate in the activity, This higher level of efficacy for the task led Chris to more ready engagement on his arrival in the morning. This engagement was a necessary part of skill development that would lead him toward an upward spiral of math success.

For teachers, knowing the sources of self-efficacy judgments and the unique beliefs and misconceptions of children is only half the picture, however, because maintaining efficacy beliefs requires successful actions. As early as the primary grades, teachers should begin to help students to develop *strategies* that will help them to be in control of their academic behavior. This control will increase their odds of success with school tasks and keep self-efficacy and ability judgments from eroding. For the remainder of this chapter we focus on the strategies that will help students to become self-regulated learners, in control of their own academic lives.

## SELF-REGULATED LEARNING

Self-efficacy beliefs and self-regulated learning strategies are interdependent. Both require the presence of specific cognitive capacities, including the ability to set goals, self-monitor, reflect, and make judgments. Both also support personal agency or control. Examining the self-regulated learning skills of primary-aged children is essential for understanding the maintenance of self-efficacy.

What do self-regulated learners look like? They, like Dan in the opening section of this chapter, "approach educational tasks with confidence, diligence, and resourcefulness..., are aware when they know a fact or posses a skill..., (and) proactively seek out information when needed and take the necessary steps to master it" (Zimmerman, 1990, p. 4). Metacognitively, they plan, set goals, organize, self-monitor, and self-evaluate. Motivationally, they take responsibility for successes and failures, are intrinsically interested in the task, and have high self-efficacy, which together lead to greater effort and persistence. Behaviorally, they seek out help and advice, create optimal learning environments, self-instruct, and self-reinforce. Throughout the entire self-regulation process they monitor progress, react, and adapt. This self-oriented feedback loop is at the heart of self-regulated learning. These learners demonstrate self-as-agent as they integrate the cognitive and metacognitive aspects of "skill" with the internalized desire associated with "will" (McCombs & Marzano, 1990).

Thus, in self-regulated learning (SRL), the student must incorporate a combination of cognitive, metacognitive, motivational, and behavioral processes to attain the highest possible level of achievement (Zimmerman & Kitsantas, 1997).

## Interactions between Self-Regulation and Self-Efficacy

There are two areas of interaction between the development of self-regulated learning strategies and the development of self-efficacy beliefs. First, a student's level of self-efficacy predicts her or his use of cognitive strategies and self-regulation. Use of these strategies then predicts academic achievement (Zimmerman, 1995). This creates a reciprocal relationship, for as students increase their use of learning strategies and their academic performance improves, their academic self-efficacy increases. Self-efficacy perceptions, then, are both a reason to learn and an outcome of learning (Zimmerman, 1990).

Second, both self-regulated learning and self-efficacy judgments require a similar series of cognitive and metacognitive processes, including self-observation, self-judgment, and self-reaction. This process of monitoring strategies and beliefs may be the most significant defining feature of the dynamic duo of self-efficacy and self-regulated learning. Monitoring progress is the critical behavior necessary for making self-judgments. To be motivated by a discrepancy between "where you are" and "where you want to be," you must have an accurate sense of where you are and how far you have to go. If they judge that current efforts have fallen short of the goal, self-regulated learners can exert more effort or even try another strategy. Thus reactions to goal progress motivate behavior (Bandura, 1986). If self-regulated learners see their progress toward a goal as acceptable, not only do they anticipate the satisfaction of reaching the goal, they also feel enhanced self-efficacy and motivation. Deliberate attention to our behavior informs and motivates (Zimmerman, 1990). Young children have difficulty detecting their own errors and monitoring progress, but training can improve their ability to regulate their own strategies (Paris & Lindauer, 1982).

## IMPLICATIONS FOR TEACHERS

The previous discussion described the links between the development of self-efficacy and self-regulated learning. In the following sections we examine what teachers can do to foster self-efficacy for preschool and primary grade children and then turn to instructional approaches that build self-regulated learning.

## Preschool Children

Two elements—adult expectations and feedback and children's task selection—interact to enhance the development of cognitive and social skills that are a foundation for an emerging sense of efficacy in preschool children. For our purposes we will isolate some of these contexts and behaviors to discuss them as separate entities, even though the factors likely work together.

### Reactions to Adults' Expectations and Feedback

In studies of toddlers and preschoolers, Stipek, Recchia and McClintic (1992) assessed reactions to success and failure, the effects of praise on children's reactions to success, and the nature of standards for success set by these young children. Toddlers younger than 22 months displayed positive emotional reactions to success, but there was no negative analog; these toddlers simply changed goals at the first signs of difficulty so they seldom experienced failure. Even though older toddlers recognize and respond to external approval, they do not require praise to feel positive about mastery experiences. Instead, an "intrinsic, mastery-oriented motivational system predominates throughout the preschool years" (Stipek et al., 1992, p. 73). Preschoolers are able to maintain this mastery system in part because, like toddlers, they can change goals or tasks in their lives outside school, thus avoiding failure situations.

By age 2, children become distressed about failing to meet adult standards in achievement contexts. Frustration, anger, discouragement, and other negative emotional reactions could result when adults impose unachievable goals or remain rigid in their expectations. Children who frequently experience these adult demands may become wary of achievement contexts before they ever enter school because achievement is associated with such negative emotions.

## Task Selection

Stipek et al. (1992) report on studies showing that even children as young as 2 appear to be more motivated and persistent when tackling tasks they have chosen for themselves. When mothers interfered by limiting their child's choice and initiative, the children were less motivated to stay on task and generally showed less positive emotions. Results from an anthropological study comparing 4-year-olds from two cultural communities (Tudge & Putnam, 1997) suggest that professional parents are more likely than parents of lower socioeconomic status to set goals of independence and control over their environment for their children. Children in the professional group were much more likely to initiate activities and to maintain their involvement in activities, becoming more self-directed even at this early age.

Again, teachers can take heed of these findings. Young children need to be able to initiate their own activities when possible, with the flexibility to change tasks as necessary to avoid failure. Rigid expectations from adults should be avoided.

## Developing Self-Efficacy in the Primary Grades

In this section we focus on the aspects of classrooms that support student success and thus encourage positive self-efficacy judgments. Keeping in mind the four sources of information that influence self-efficacy judgments —vicarious experience, verbal persuasion, physiological states, and mastery experience—we discuss classroom features most likely to provide the greatest impact from each of these sources. We know that there are major differences in self-beliefs and cognitive development along the continuum from kindergarten to third grade. Still we will identify some general classroom features that we believe can positively impact many, if not all, students.

This list of suggestions is by no means new to either parents or practitioners, although to our knowledge it is the first attempt at identifying how classroom activities and climate align with the framework of self-efficacy development.

Even though we have separated these four areas of influence for the sake of our discussion, clearly there are inevitable interactions among them in the classroom. Children derive their self-efficacy information from varying combinations of the four sources, but even then individual cognitive judgments and interpretations of the information ultimately determine the level of self-efficacy.

## Facilitating Useful Vicarious or Observational Experiences

Because young children rely so heavily on modeling cues, this source of information should be made available as frequently as possible. Children use modeling of similar others as a basis of comparison for their own performance either to raise or to lower their self-efficacy. Watching like models successfully perform a task motivates a child to do the same. However, if the observer fails to perform the task successfully after watching a model, gains in self-efficacy will be negated. Some ideas for primary grade classroom teachers to use to incorporate modeling experiences include:

- Allow peer models to demonstrate a task, verbalizing their thoughts and reasoning as they perform.
- Encourage peer tutoring when appropriate. Figure 1 is a checklist for guiding students in peer tutoring situations. Young children need to be taught how to be a good tutor and then supported in their efforts. The checklist provides visual cues about how to be a good tutor.
- Provide children with comparative information that focuses on behaviors that support learning: "Look at the way Rhonda keeps her numbers in a line up and down so she doesn't get mixed up in her addition."
- Incorporate cooperative learning activities with partners or small groups, establishing goals and expectations for the group prior to their task. See Aronson (Chapter 10 in this volume) for information about one form of cooperative learning, the jigsaw method.
- Use flexible grouping for small group instruction to avoid labeling individuals. Form and reform groups on the basis of students' *current performance* in the subject being taught and change group placement frequently when students achievement changes. Discourage comparisons between groups and encourage students to develop a whole-class spirit. Avoid naming ability groups ("tigers," "sorcerers," "hurricanes," etc.); save the names for mixed-ability or whole-class teams. Organize and teach groups so that low-achieving students get appropriate extra instruction, not just the same material again.

## Making Use of Verbal Persuasion

We include all types of verbal feedback as sources of verbal persuasion. Some guidelines include:

**Written Prompts: A Peer-Tutoring Checklist**
By using this checklist, students are reminded how to be effective tutors. As they become more proficient, the checklist may be less necessary.

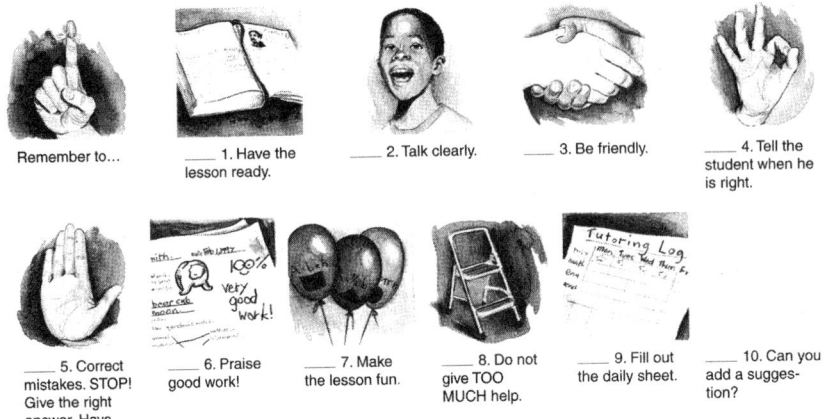

Remember to...

_____ 1. Have the lesson ready.

_____ 2. Talk clearly.

_____ 3. Be friendly.

_____ 4. Tell the student when he is right.

_____ 5. Correct mistakes. STOP! Give the right answer. Have the student do it.

_____ 6. Praise good work!

_____ 7. Make the lesson fun.

_____ 8. Do not give TOO MUCH help.

_____ 9. Fill out the daily sheet.

_____ 10. Can you add a suggestion?

**FIGURE 1**

A checklist for guiding students in peer tutoring situations. From *Achieving Educational Excellence: Behavioral Analysis for School Personnel* (Figure, p. 89), by B. Sulzer-Azaroff and G. R. Mayer, 1994, San Marcos, CA: Western Image, P.O. Box 427. Copyright 1994 by Beth Sulzer-Azaroff and G. Roy Mayer. Reprinted by permission of the authors.

- Be aware of children's actual ability to succeed when giving encouragement. Do not say, "You can do that problem—it's easy." Instead, suggest that "You might be able to get this one if you take your time and line up the numbers."
- Provide attributional feedback that focuses on effort: "Your hard work is paying off" or "I'm glad you did this last revision—your story uses more describing words now."
- Use constructive feedback to enhance future performance. It is more helpful to tell children *why* they are wrong so they can learn more appropriate strategies (Bangert-Drowns, Kulik, Kulik, & Morgan, 1991). Without such feedback, they are likely to make the same mistakes again. Yet this type of feedback is rarely given. In one study, only about 8% of the teachers noticed a consistent type of error in a student's arithmetic computation and informed the student (Bloom & Bourdon, 1980). What are the identifying characteristics of effective written feedback? Working with sixth grade teachers, Elawar and Corno (1985) found that feedback was dramatically improved when the teachers used these four questions as a guide: "What is the key error? What is the probable reason the student made this error?

How can I guide the student to avoid the error in the future? What did the student do well that could be noted?" (p. 166).

• Use only sincere praise as children can see through empty praise.

Let us look at teacher praise and reinforcement more closely. Positive results occur when teachers carefully and systematically praise their students. Unfortunately, praise is not always given appropriately and effectively. Merely "handing out compliments" will not improve behavior. To be effective, praise must (1) be contingent on the behavior to be reinforced, (2) specify clearly the behavior being reinforced, and (3) be believable (O'Leary & O'Leary, 1976). In other words, the praise should be sincere recognition of a well-defined behavior so students understand what they did to warrant the recognition. Teachers who have not received special training often violate these conditions (Brophy, 1981).

Brophy's extensive review of praise suggests several guidelines for teachers: Be clear and systematic in giving praise. For example, be sure the student understands the specific action or accomplishment that is being praised. Say, "You returned this book on time and in good condition," not "You were very responsible," Recognize genuine accomplishments. Tie praise to students' improving competence or to the value of their accomplishment. For example, say, "I noticed that you double-checked all your problems. Your score reflects your. careful work." Set standards for praise based on individual abilities and limitations. Focus the student's attention on his or her own progress, not on comparisons with others' achievements. Attribute the student's success to effort and ability so the student will gain confidence that success is possible again. Ask students to describe the problems they encountered and how they solved them. Do not give undeserved praise to students simply to balance failures. It is seldom consoling and calls attention to the student's inability to earn genuine recognition.

## Controlling the Classroom for Positive Physiological States

Teachers need to work at keeping the level of arousal right for the task at hand. If students are going to sleep, energize them by introducing variety, piquing their curiosity, surprising them, or giving them a brief chance to be physically active. Learn about their interests and incorporate interests into lessons and assignments. If arousal is too great, and students become anxious, consider these strategies for reducing anxiety:

• Use competition carefully. Monitor activities to make sure no students are being placed under undue pressure. During competitive games, make sure all students involved have a reasonable chance of succeeding.

• Avoid situations in which highly anxious students will have to perform in front of large groups. Ask anxious students questions that can be answered with a simple yes or no or some other brief reply. Give anxious students practice in speaking before smaller groups.

• Make sure all instructions are clear. Uncertainty can lead to anxiety. Write test instructions on the board or on the test itself instead of giving them orally. Check with students to make sure they understand. Ask several students how they would do the first question or an exercise or the sample question on a test. Correct any misconceptions. If you are using a new format or starting a new type of task, give students examples or models to show how it is done.

• Avoid unnecessary time pressures and remove some of the pressures from major tests and exams. Teach test-taking skills; give practice tests; provide study guides. Develop alternatives to written tests. Try oral, open-book, or group tests. Have students do projects, organize portfolios of their work, make oral presentations, or create a finished product.

Because negative thoughts and fears can lower perceptions of ability and contribute to inadequate performances, strive to maintain a classroom environment that creates a positive, caring emotional tone. Here are a few ideas. Maintain a humanistic classroom approach rather than a custodial approach. Emphasize rights and responsibilities rather than rules and regulations. Teach students to assess their own work by providing models and rubrics. Recognize students when they are appropriately self-critical. Avoid competition between students but foster cooperation. Emphasize understanding and learning rather than focusing on right answers. For example, encourage revisions and rewrites rather than grading the only attempt. Use efficient classroom management and organization. Many students become stressed when they do not know what to do or when the class is disruptive. Display a sense of humor, enthusiasm, and warmth toward students and incorporate their ideas and interests into class activities.

## Providing Opportunities for Mastery Experience

All students want to be successful, although some have built up defense mechanisms because of previous failures. Guaranteeing successful mastery experiences for all children in a classroom is a weighty endeavor, but one well worth the effort. Some guidelines for teachers include:

• Provide a variety of activities for children with various learning styles, enabling all children to experience success.

• Create daily routines so that children have a sense of expectation and control over their environment. Signal the routines with a daily schedule or other cues so that all students are reminded and know what to do or where to go next.

• Ensure that learning tasks are on an appropriate level for all students. This requires both an intimate knowledge of each student's performance level in each subject domain along with the creation of individualized tasks as necessary.

- Create opportunities for students to experience the "practice effect" by providing familiar tasks to improve their performance.
- Plan instructional activities that are interesting, hands-on, and related to real life.
- Provide instructional support as necessary to guarantee student success.
- Help students to maintain incremental views of intelligence and adopt learning goals rather than performance goals. For example, remove performance pressures by giving feedback and then allowing students to redo and improve work, use portfolios so that students see their own progress, periodically revisit earlier assignments to show students how much they have learned, recognize creativity and partially correct answers, not just perfect papers, and avoid comparing students with each other. See Dweck (Chapter 4 in this volume) for other ideas.
- Teach cognitive and metacognitive skills such as planning, monitoring, and goal setting.
- Teach specific self-regulatory strategies that will impact student performance, such as help seeking, maintaining task focus and attention, applying memory strategies, managing time, and organizing.

This emphasis on teaching the self-regulatory skills leads to our final consideration, developing self-regulated learning in young students. How can you address this goal directly?

## Developing Self-Regulated Learning in Primary Grade Children

Developing strategies that will enable young learners to act as agents for achieving their own success is an important way to enhance their self-efficacy. As Bandura (1997) states:

> It is easier to instill beliefs of personal efficacy if the instruction and informative feedback center on mastery of strategies that enable one to achieve progress rather than only on level of performance attainments. Knowing the means for becoming adept in given endeavors instills a sense of personal control over one's development. (p. 182)

In other words, students must be given some tools that will increase their odds of succeeding if their efficacy is to spiral upward along with their improving learning skills. They need not only the "will" to succeed but the "skill" as well. Although all learners use SRL strategies to some extent, self-regulated learners take it a step further by recognizing the connections between their strategy use and their success. In addition self-regulated learners systematically use these strategies to reach their academic goals. Now we turn to the important question. How can teachers help young children develop self-regulated learning?

## Development of Self-Regulation

Over the past two decades there has been substantial research that documents young children's development of learning strategies. From approximately 5 to 12 years of age children acquire a diverse range of cognitive strategies, including focusing attention, monitoring understanding during reading, and planning study time (Paris, Newman, & McVey, 1982). Zimmerman and Martinez-Pons (1988) developed a list of 14 self-regulated learning strategies, specific to a school context, that have been used with high school and middle school students. Among strategies that are more readily available to younger students, particularly if given training and a rationale for their use, are attention monitoring or maintaining task focus, self-verbalization, help seeking, memory and metamemory skills, time planning and management, and goal setting.

Research is also showing that the schooling experience is a powerful shaper of skills, such as memory skills, in young children. Morrison, Smith, and Dow-Ehrensberger (1995) cite major differences in cross-cultural studies between schooled and unschooled children in the growth of memory skills, among other things. In a study of their own they looked at the growth of memory and language skills of students clustered around their school district's cutoff date for entrance age, comparing the students who just make the cutoff to begin school with those who just missed. They concluded that the shift in children's cognitive functioning between the ages of 5 and 7 is "almost exclusively a product of schooling and related experiences, at least in the limited area of memory development studied" (p. 795). The powerful message for educators is that it is their responsibility to provide these experiences for the students in their care.

## Instructional Principles

Even though educational psychologists differ in their opinions about how self-regulated learning develops in children (see Winne 1995, 1997), they do agree on some instructional principles. If these principles, in fact, lead to the development of SRL, they should also similarly enhance development of increased self-efficacy for the strategies executed.

- Provide a wide range of opportunities in the form of diverse tasks so that students can experience success and learn that effort pays off.
- Allow practice of new skills to the point of overlearning before introducing and expecting SRL strategies.
- Encourage the epistemological beliefs that learning is difficult and requires effort and that knowledge is rarely absolute.
- Help students to understand the utility of newly acquired strategies and conceptual knowledge.
- Introduce learning and practice of several new procedures at once. Interspersal of practice may increase durable knowledge.

- Make sure strategy execution during practice is easy.
- Help students to improve monitoring awareness, possibly by prompts to monitor daily lessons.

Perhaps even more basic than these principles are such early self-regulated learning skills as focusing attention, maintaining task focus through to completion, seeking help as needed, and strategies related to task initiation. It was just such strategies that were effective in improving Chris' math performance. Through the modeling provided by successful students, Chris began to regulate his ability to follow the daily routine of the problem solving task by going directly to his seat, getting his materials ready, and focusing his attention on the problem. As his efficacy for successful solution improved because of his scaffolded experiences during math class, his motivation to engage improved accordingly. It was the combination of both improved efficacy and acquisition of the strategies that provided the necessary interactions to make the gradual advancements.

Sometimes we forget that students do not all come to school with the basic strategies that guide successful learning. Primary grade teachers must identify the needs of struggling students and offer very fundamental guidance if they are to move forward. For example, it was necessary to point out to Chris that the other students were hanging up their jackets, going directly to their seats, and getting their journals out. The type of persuasion that gives an initial boost to get started is sometimes all that is needed to promote active engagement. Fundamental strategies for a specific task, such as beginning by reading through the problem, may need to be pointed out to some students. Helping students to develop an awareness of the need for an action must be accompanied by a personal commitment to the action (e.g., I ought to do this and I can do it). How do we accomplish this? We go back to the same four sources that provide information for efficacy beliefs: mastery experiences, modeling, persuasion, and physiological reactions. The influence of self-efficacy and feelings of agency are clearly intertwined with the process of self-regulation (Paris & Newman, 1990).

Perhaps self-regulation should be viewed more as an attitude than as a set of behaviors. Teachers may best promote development of self-regulated learning by bearing in mind that the overarching goal of self-regulated learning is the transfer of control from others to the self (Paris & Newman, 1990). While very little research has examined SRL in natural classroom settings (Perry, 1998), certain classroom climates are more conducive to the transfer of control to the self. Perry (1998) specifically lists the advantage of child-centered versus teacher-centered classrooms, open task structures that allow children opportunities to select materials that are personally meaningful and at an appropriate level, and process approaches as opposed to skills-oriented models.

The teachers' own efficacy perceptions also play a fundamental role in the execution of these classroom practices that can help to lead students to achieve success. Teachers with a high sense of personal efficacy are more likely to believe that they can make a difference and demonstrate the necessary effort and persistence necessary to do so (Woolfolk & Hoy, 1990).

## CONCLUSION

The first author has taught second grade for more than 20 years and has had experience teaching preschool and students with learning disabilities as well. Chris and Dan are not hypothetical students but very real boys in her class (their names have been changed). Although the causes for their differences in performance cannot be fully established, Gaskill's experiences suggest that the answer lies in the students' beliefs about their own ability to perform. As a matter of fact, by gradually leading Chris to more successful experiences, in just a few months' time he already showed signs of improvement. As with Chris, Gaskill has seen firsthand evidence of self-efficacy and more global self-beliefs at work with many, if not all, students.

We believe that self-efficacy plays a mediating role in learning, even in the primary classroom. Although researchers have looked in depth at many of the topics listed in our guidelines, there is a dearth of research that specifically links these topics to the development of self-efficacy in young children. We encourage teachers to conduct their own action research studies of the effectiveness of the ideas and guidelines in this chapter. Of course these will not be easy tasks. But in our minds, based on our combined experience in working with young children and exploring the extensive mediating effect of self-efficacy in adults, there are few more exciting and fruitful endeavors. It is our hope that more research with children of this age group will lead to a fuller and deeper understanding of the exact nature of these beliefs to provide all children with a positive and exciting start in their quest for life-long learning.

## Teachers' Questions and Answers

**Q:**   What is the parents' role in encouraging self-efficacy in their children prior to and during their transition to school?

**A:**   Parental influence, a primary force in many aspects of child develop-ment, plays a key role in shaping children's earliest self-beliefs. Beginning in infancy, family processes that lead to improved levels of perceived control, competency, and autonomy are key factors. Bronson (2000) identified some specific behaviors that are associated with motivation for control and mastery in young children, conditions supportive of future positive efficacy beliefs. These include relating to children in caring and emotionally supportive ways, being responsive to children's activities and communications, giving consist-ent but not rigid responses that help them understand appropriate and valued behaviors, using inductive guidance strategies that point out cause and effect, encouraging responsibility and independence, and teaching problem-solving strategies to increase their independence. Children's adaptation to school in the first few years is influenced by the "fit" between the home and the school. Parenting styles, disciplinary methods, and engagement in educational activities that are close to those encountered in the school setting are more likely to facilitate adaptation to school. Parent expectations of their children's performance are also potent influences.

**Q:**   Is there research describing the development of self-efficacy and self-regulation in reading and writing?

**A:**   Yes, there is exciting research that has examined what excellent teachers do in the early grades to encourage self-regulated learning during literacy activities. For example, Nancy Perry and her colleagues (Perry, 1998; Perry & VandeKamp, 2000) have studied classroom contexts that support the development of self-regulated learning. Teachers in supportive classrooms engage students in open-ended reading and writing activities; offer students choices about books, topics, or activities; allow students to control the challenge or difficulty of assignments; give students opportunities to evaluate their own work and the work of others; emphasize personal progress rather than social comparisons; and help students interpret errors as opportunities to learn.

**Q:**   Is there an age when it is "too late" to intervene to teach self-regulation, and if not, what can teachers do to help older students?

**A:**   It is never too late to become more self-regulating—corporate trainers who teach time management and goal-setting skills help adults to better organize their lives and thus become more self-regulating. But the longer students go in school without the skill and will to be self-regulated, the more discouraged they can become. The spiral up from self-regulation to higher self-efficacy to greater self-regulation can become a spiral down to learned helplessness, especially for students who face physical, emotional, or intellectual challenges. The principles are the same at any age, but the applications vary. Goal setting and monitoring progress is especially powerful, as many people know who struggle to change their own unhealthy habits. Moving in small steps, then adding requirements as skills and confidence increase, can be useful. Helping students of any age to evaluate their own work and see the good as well as the "needs improvement" can give the students a sense of power to change. Often portfolios are helpful in recording and reflecting on growth and setting goals for the future. Something as simple as teaching middle school students how to use a daily planner to organize assignments can be a start. Or students might develop power point presentations for each other on how to tackle larger assignments to make them manageable and how to seek appropriate help when needed.

# References

Bandura, A. (1982). Self-efficacy mechanism in human agency. *American Psychologist, 37*, 122–147.

Bandura, A. (1986). *Social foundations of thoughts and action: A social cognitive theory.* Englewood Cliffs, NJ: Prentice–Hall.

Bandura, A. (1989). Regulation of cognitive processes through perceived self-efficacy. *Developmental Psychology, 25*, 729–735.

Bandura, A. (1997). *Self-efficacy: The exercise of control.* New York: Freeman.

Bandura, A., Barbaranelli, C., Caprara, G. V., & Pastorelli, C. (1996). Multifaceted impact of self-efficacy beliefs on academic functioning. *Child Development, 67*, 1206–1222.

Bandura, A., & Cervone, D. (1983). Self-evaluation and self-efficacy mechanisms governing the motivational effects of goal systems. *Journal of Personality and Social Psychology, 45*, 1017–1028.

Bangert-Drowns, R. L., Kulik, C. C., Kulik, J. A., & Morgan, M. T. (1991). The instructional effect of feedback in test-like events. *Review of Educational Research, 61*, 213–238.

Barker, G. P., & Graham, S. (1987). Developmental study of praise and blame as attributional cues. *Journal of Educational Psychology, 79*, 62–66.

Bloom, R., & Bourdon, L. (1980). Types and frequencies of teachers' written instructional feedback. *Journal of Educational Research, 74*, 13–15.

Blumenfeld, P. C., Pintrich, P. R., Meece, J., & Wessels, K. (1982). The formation and role of self-perceptions of ability in elementary classrooms. *Elementary School Journal, 82*, 401–420.

Blumenfeld, P. C., Pintrich, P. R., Meece, J., & Wessels, K. (1981). *Age and sex differences in the impact of classroom experiences on self-perception.* Paper presented at the annual meeting of the Society for Research in Child Development, Boston.

Bronson, M. (2000). *Self-regulation in early childhood: Nature and nurture.* New York: Guilford Press.

Brophy, J. E. (1981). Teacher praise: A functional analysis. *Review of Educational Research, 51*, 5–21.

Brophy, J. E. (1985). Teacher–student interaction. In J. Dusek (Ed.), *Teacher expectancies.* Hillsdale, NJ: Erlbaum.

Dweck, C. (1986). Motivational processes affecting learning. *American Psychologist, 41*, 1040–1048.

Dweck, C., & Bempechat, J. (1983). Children's theories on intelligence: Consequences for learning. In S. Paris, G. Olson, & W. Stevenson (Eds.), *Learning and motivation in the classroom* (pp. 239–256). Hillsdale, NJ: Erlbaum.

Elawar, M. C., & Corno, L. (1985). A factorial experiment in teachers' written feedback on student homework: Changing teacher behavior a little rather than a lot. *Journal of Educational Psychology, 77*, 162–173.

Gaskill, P. (2000). *Effects of a memory strategy on second-graders' self-efficacy.* Paper presented at the annual meeting of the American Psychological Association, Washington, DC.

Graham, S., & Barker, G. P. (1990). The down side of help: An attributional–developmental analysis of helping behavior as a low-ability cue. *Journal of Educational Psychology, 82*, 7–14.

Kaley, R., & Cloutier, R. (1984). Developmental determinants of self-efficacy predictiveness. *Cognitive Therapy and Research, 3*, 643–656.

Keyser, V., & Barling, J. (1981). Determinants of children's self-efficacy beliefs in an academic environment. *Cognitive Therapy and Research, 5*, 29–40.

Kun, A. (1977). Development of the magnitude-covariation and compensation schemata in ability and effort attributions of performance. *Child Development, 48*, 862–873.

Lord, C. G., Umezaki, K., & Darley, J. M. (1990). Developmental differences in decoding the meanings of the appraisal actions of teachers. *Child Development, 61*, 191–200.

Marsh, H., Walker, R., & Debus, R. (1991). Subject-specific components of academic self-concept and self-efficacy. *Contemporary Educational Psychologist, 25*, 51–69.

McCombs, B. L., & Marzano, R. J. (1990). Putting the self in self-regulated learning: The self as agent in integrating skill and will. *Educational Psychologist, 25*, 51–69.

Meichenbaum, D., & Asarnow, J. (1979). Cognitive-behavioral modification and metacognitive development: Implications for the classroom. In P. C. Kendall & S. D. Hollon (Eds.), *Cognitive-behavioral interventions: Theory, research, and procedures* (pp. 11–35). New York: Academic Press.

Morrison, F., Smith, L., & Dow-Ehrensberger, M. (1995). Education and cognitive development: A natural experiment. *Developmental Psychology, 31*, 789–799.

Nicholls, J. G. (1978). The development of concepts of effort and ability, perceptions of academic attainment, and the understanding that difficult tasks require more ability. *Child Development, 49*, 800–814.

Nicholls, J. G., & Miller, A. (1984). Development and its discontents: The differentiation of the concept of ability. In J. G. Nicholls (Ed.), *Advances in motivation and achievement: Vol. 3. The development of achievement motivation* (pp. 185–218). Greenwich, CT: JAI.

O'Leary, S., & O'Leary, K. (1976). Behavior modification in the schools. In H. Leitenberg (Ed.), *Handbook of behavior modification and behavior therapy.* Englewood Cliffs, NJ: Prentice–Hall.

Pajares, F. (1997). Current directions in self-efficacy research. In M. L. Maehr & P. R. Pintrich (Eds.), *Advances in motivation and achievement* (Vol. 10, pp. 1–49). Greenwich, CT: JAI Press.

Paris, S. G., & Lindauer, B. K. (1982). The development of cognitive skills during childhood. In B. Wolman (Ed.), *Handbook of develpmental psychology.* Englewood Cliffs, NJ: Prentice–Hall.

Paris, S., Newman, R., & McVey, K. (1982). Learning the functional significance of mnemonic actions: A microgenetic study of strategy acquisition. *Journal of Experimental Child Psychology, 34*, 490–509.

Paris, S. G., & Newman, R. S. (1990). Developmental aspects of self-regulated learning. *Educational Psychologist, 25*, 87–102.

Perry, N. (1998). Young children's self-regulated learning and contexts that support it. *Journal of Educational Psychology, 90*, 715–729.

Perry, N., & Weinstein, R. (1998). The social context of early schooling and children's school adjustment. *Educational Psychologist, 33*, 177–194.

Perry, N. E., & VandeKamp, O. K. (2000). Creating classroom contexts that support young children's development of self-regulated learning. *International Journal of Educational Research, 33*, 821–843.

Piaget, J. (1963). *Origins of intelligence in children.* New York: Norton.

Piaget, J. (1970). Piaget's theory. In P. Mussen (Ed.), *Handbook of child psychology* (3rd ed.). New York: Wiley.

Pintrich, P. R., & Schunk, D. H. (2002). *Motivation in education: Theory, research, and applications* (2nd ed.). Columbus, OH: Merrill/Prentice–Hall.

Rosenholtz, S. J., & Simpson, C. (1984). The formation of ability conceptions: Developmental trend or social construction? *Review of Educational Research, 54*, 31–63.

Schunk, D. H. (1983). Ability versus effort attributional feedback: Differential effects on self-efficacy and achievement. *Journal of Educational Psychology, 75*, 848–856.

Schunk, D. H. (1984). Enhancing self-efficacy and achievement through rewards and goals: Motivational and informational effects. *Journal of Educational Psychology, 78*, 29–34.

Schunk, D. H. (1990). Goal setting and self-efficacy during self-regulated learning. *Educational Psychologist, 25(1)*, 71–86.

Schunk, D. (2000). *Learning theories: An educational perspective* (3rd ed.). Columbus, OH: Merrill/Prentice–Hall.

Stipek, D., & Tannatt, L. (1984). Children's judgments of their own and their peers' academic competence. *Journal of Educational Psychology, 76*, 75–84.

Stipek, D., Recchia, S. & McClintic, S. (1992). Self-evaluation in young children. *Monographs of the Society for Research in Child Development, 57*, 1–83.

Stipek, D. J. (2002). *Motivation to learn* (4th ed.). Boston: Allyn & Bacon.

Tudge, J., & Putnam, S. (1997). The everyday experiences of North American preschoolers in two cultural communities: A cross-disciplinary and cross-level analysis. In J. Tudge, M. Shanahan, & J. Valsiner (Eds.), *Comparisons in human development: Understanding time and context* (pp. 252–281). New York: Cambridge University Press.

Winne, P. (1995). Inherent details in self-regulated learning. *Educational Psychologist, 30*, 173–187.

Winne, P. (1997). Experimenting to bootstrap self-regulated academic learning. *Journal of Educational Psychology, 89*, 397–410.

Woolfolk, A. E., & Hoy, W. K. (1990). Prospective teachers' sense of efficacy and beliefs about control. *Journal of Educational Psychology, 82,* 81–91.

Zimmerman, B., & Martinez-Pons, M. (1988). Construct validation of a strategy model of student self-regulated learning. *Journal of Educational Psychology, 80,* 284–290.

Zimmerman, B. J. (1989). A social cognitive view of self-regulated academic learning. *Journal of Educational Psychology, 81,* 329–339.

Zimmerman, B. J. (1990). Self-regulated learning and academic achievement: An overview. *Educational Psychologist, 25,* 3–17.

Zimmerman, B. J. (1995). Self-efficacy and educational development. In A. Bandura's (Ed.), *Self-efficacy in changing societies.* New York: Cambridge University Press.

Zimmerman, B. J., Bandura, A., & Martinez-Pons, M. (1992). Self-motivation for academic attainment: The role of self-efficacy beliefs and personal goal setting. *American Educational Research Journal, 29,* 663–676.

Zimmerman, B. J., & Kitsantas, A. (1997). Developmental phases in self-regulation: Shifting from process goals to outcome goals. *Journal of Educational Psychology, 89,* 29–36.

# Building Empathy, Compassion, and Achievement in the Jigsaw Classroom

ELLIOT ARONSON

*Distinguished Visiting Professor, Stanford University, Stanford, California*

In their remarkable little book, *The Children are Watching*, educators Ted and Nancy Sizer suggest that the classroom curriculum constitutes only a small part of what a youngster actually learns in school. Students pay close attention to and learn from just about everything that happens in and around their school. For example, if the building is drafty, has broken windows, unswept floors, grimy walls, cracked linoleum, and leaky toilets, the students get the message that the adult community does not care a lot about their education. I would add that, by the same token, students may learn as much from the style or process in which information is conveyed as they do from the information itself.

I hasten to explain. It goes without saying that there are a great many ways to convey information to students. Let us say we want the students to learn about World War II. The teacher can create two or three lectures about the causes and consequences of that war. Alternatively, the students can simply read the basic facts about World War II in a textbook. As a third alternative, the teacher can assign students to do their own research in the library, or have students interview people who served in the military or lived through the war period in the United States, Europe, and Asia. The teacher might require students to work individually or in groups. To demonstrate what they have learned, students might take a test, write a term paper, or give an oral presentation to the entire class. The teacher might also run the class as if it were a quiz show where he or she asks questions and the students show their quickness and mastery of the subject by raising their hands as soon as they know the answer.

Each of these methods of conveying and retrieving information sends its own special message to students. Some of these messages may be unintended. Teachers who lecture send the message that they are an expert source of information and that the things that they know are the important things to learn. Teachers who dispatch students to the library send the message that it is useful for students to become skillful researchers as well as to learn about the topic at hand. Teachers who require students to interview a war veteran convey the implicit message that not all important information is contained in books or conveyed by people in the teaching profession. Teachers who run their class like a quiz show or contest indicate that quickness, assertiveness, and competitiveness are important aspects of the learning endeavor—and perhaps of life itself.

The point is that the learning students derive from the process of their educational experience is powerful indeed. In classes where students are expected to raise their hands as soon as they know the answer and take tests graded on a curve, the process encourages students to compete individually against each other. The implicit message is that the other students are competitors for scarce resources. It would not be surprising, then, if this process were to create tension among peers and tended to discourage trust or friendship among youngsters who were not already friends beforehand.

In American schools, this kind of competitive process is the predominant method employed in most classrooms most of the time. High school students who have gone through several years of participation in such a competitive process are likely to view the world (both inside and outside of school) as one gigantic game of musical chairs, as a dog-eat-dog place where the prizes go to those who are quickest, or strongest, or most aggressive, or most charming, or most athletic. Such a process may implicitly encourage students to look for weaknesses or flaws in their peers—to find reasons for excluding or taunting those who falter, or seem different, or socially awkward and to think of them as weird or as losers.

This may be a major reason why research reveals that most American high schools are clique-driven and exclusionary. Even casual observation of the social climate of the typical high school reveals a clear hierarchy of who is in and who is out that is remarkably similar in all parts of the country. In most high schools, the youngsters at the top of the social pyramid are athletes (especially football players), cheerleaders, class officers, attractive women, and "regular guys." Near the bottom of the social pyramid are those youngsters who are the "wrong" race or the "wrong" ethnic group; dress differently; are too short, too tall, too thin, too fat, too "nerdy", or just do not fit in easily. Interviews with high school students in all parts of the country indicate that just about every student in a given school can name the hierarchy of in-groups and out-groups and can identify where each of their classmates can be placed in that hierarchy (Aronson, 2000; Gibbs & Roche, October 1999; Lewin, 1999; Townsend, 1999).

Those youngsters in the relatively small in-group want to differentiate themselves from the losers. They do not associate with them, sometimes they tease or taunt them; occasionally they bully them. In most cases, those near the bottom of the social pyramid suffer in silence, retreating further and further from the mainstream. The more they are ignored, excluded, or taunted, the further away they drift. For a great many youngsters, the high school atmosphere is extremely unpleasant. For some, it is a living hell. Given this kind of social atmosphere, and given the fact that teenagers spend almost half their waking hours embedded in that atmosphere, it should not be surprising that occasionally, some of these students go over the edge—doing serious damage to themselves or others. The most recent statistics are chilling: One of five teenagers has seriously contemplated suicide; one of ten has made an attempt at suicide (Goldberg & Connelly, 1999).

In recent years, when we think of students going over the edge and doing serious damage to themselves or others, we are immediately reminded of Columbine High School in Littleton, Colorado. You will recall that, in April of 1999, two students, Eric Harris and Dylan Klebold, armed with an arsenal of guns and explosives, went on a rampage, killing a teacher and 12 of their fellow students before turning their guns on themselves. While tragic events of this sort are not everyday occurrences, they are not as rare as we would like to believe. At the turn of the century, there were nine rampage killings in high schools and junior high schools in a period of 18 months.

What is to be done? How does a society protect its students from these senseless killings? In the aftermath of a horrendous event like the Columbine massacre, we are tempted to look for instant solutions before we fully understand the cause of the problem. Thus, following the Columbine massacre, Congress voted to tack onto the crime bill an amendment giving states the right to allow the display of the Ten Commandments on school walls and bulletin boards. In the interest of making schools safer, there was a rush to install metal detectors. School administrators have also asked students to report other students who threaten violence or who even seem different (dress strangely, keep to themselves, and so on). Some school officials have ordered personality tests to be administered to all students—tests aimed at profiling those students who might be most apt to go on a murderous rampage.

Some of these interventions are silly. Others are harmful. Still others, while harmless, miss the point by a wide margin. Here, I would like to make a distinction between root cause solutions and what I like to call "pump handle" solutions. Here is what I regard as the defining example of this distinction. In 1854, Dr. John Snow, England's leading epidemiologist, was charged with the task of stanching a cholera epidemic that was devestating London. Dr. Snow needed to act quickly. He first determined that most of the cases of cholera clustered around a particular well near the center of the city. But he made no attempt to educate the local residents or to convince them that it might be dangerous to drink from that well. He simply removed the pump handle so that water could no longer be drawn from it. It worked. In many respects it was a perfect solution—for that particular epidemic, in that particular place, at that particular time.

But Dr. Snow did not stop with this measure. After ending the immediate threat, he proceeded to do some systematic sleuthing, trying to get at the root cause of the epidemic. That is, he raised the scientific question: Why was that particular well contaminated and not others? Within a few months, he was able to conclude with a high degree of certainty that the contamination was caused by fecal matter from nearby latrines leaking into the water supply being tapped by the well. This discovery led to legislation requiring latrines to be built at a reasonable distance from wells. By getting at the root cause of the problem, Dr. Snow succeeded in preventing future epidemics not only in London but throughout England and, eventually, throughout the entire civilized world.

With this in mind, let us take a close look at the solutions to the school shootings proposed by policymakers:

1. Posting the Ten Commandments. This intervention may be politically expedient, because it creates the illusion that Congress is doing something; but, as public policy, it is pathetically feeble. Needless to say, the Ten Commandments is a magnificent code of ethics; but posting it on a school's bulletin board will have very little impact on the behavior of any students hell-bent on murdering their classmates. Every high school student knows about the Ten Commandments. I am reasonably certain that most could even recite the most relevant items on the list. They know they are not supposed to kill or steal. They know they are supposed to honor their fathers and their mothers. They probably even know they are not supposed to mention God's name in vain, although my guess is that few are certain what that one means. But being able to recite the Ten Commandments and living by the Ten Commandments are two very different things. Those students who already have a moral compass have no need of posters to remind them that one should not kill or steal. Those who do not have a moral compass will not be prevented from killing or stealing by seeing a piece of paper tacked to the wall.

2. Metal Detectors. There is no doubt in my mind that installing metal detectors in every entrance to every school in the country will reduce killings, but it is far from ideal. The downside of this action is that it makes the school seem like a scary place and suggests that, as a society, we cannot trust our own kids not to kill each other. Moreover, installing metal detectors is far from a perfect pump-handle solution. It would not make the schools perfectly safe. If teenagers with grievances and guns are motivated to shoot their fellow

students, they can easily accomplish their mission without even entering the school building. For example, in Jonesboro, Arkansas, the shooters fired on their classmates from behind trees surrounding the school after first luring their victims out of the building by setting off the school's fire alarm. Metal detectors do not get anywhere near the root of the problem; needless to say, the cause of the recent rash of school shootings is not the lack of metal detectors in schools.

3. Profiling Potential Troublemakers. Identifying the youngsters who are loners, different, or awkward either by asking other students to point them out and turn them in or by forcing them to take some sort of personality test will not solve the problem. Indeed, singling out these youngsters—the very youngsters who are most hurt by having been excluded—is likely to exacerbate the root problem by increasing their level of exclusion. Moreover, personality tests simply are not as accurate or as precise as the general public thinks they are. Using such tests in an attempt to identify troubled youngsters will undoubtedly target a great many who are not troubled at all, while allowing some seriously troubled individuals to slip by undetected.

## TAKING A CLOSE LOOK AT THE
## CLASSROOM ATMOSPHERE

I should point out one obvious fact: Young mass murderers are not shooting people in their neighborhood, or in the local video arcade, or in the fast food outlet. They kill their classmates and teachers, and sometimes themselves, in or around the school building itself. Looking for root causes in individual pathology is an approach that seems sensible on the surface but it does not get to the root of the problem. What is it about the atmosphere in the schools themselves that makes these young people so desperate, diabolical, and callous? Why do they seek revenge, or a twisted notion of turning humiliation into pride, by shooting their classmates? In what ways have they felt rejected or, humiliated at school? Are schools doing the best they can to develop students' characters as well as their intellects? Can schools do better at creating inclusive, caring communities with positive role models for students?

As suggested earlier, my observations of the typical classroom atmosphere suggest that it is highly likely that the perpetrators were reacting in an extreme and pathological manner to a general school atmosphere—an atmosphere of exclusion—that many if not most of the student body find unpleasant, distasteful, difficult, and even humiliating (Aronson, 2000).

My observations receive strong support from the way high school students from all parts of the country reacted to the tragic events in Littleton. Shortly after the Columbine massacre, a search of the Internet revealed powerful feelings being expressed by large numbers of teenagers. The overwhelming majority fairly crackled with expressions of anguish and unhappiness, describing how awful it feels to be rejected and taunted by their more popular classmates. Several weeks before the contents of the Harris/Klebold videotapes were released, many of the writers were convinced that Harris and Klebold must have had similar experiences of rejection and exclusion. I hasten to add that none of these teenagers condoned the shootings; yet their Internet postings revealed a surprisingly high degree of understanding and empathy for the suffering that Harris and Klebold must have endured. While none of the students posting their comments on the Internet had any intention of following the lead of Harris and Klebold, some admitted that they had had fantasies of doing similar things. That should make us sit up and take notice, not so that we can track down those kids and hospitalize them, but rather, to try to figure out how to improve the atmosphere of the school so that youngsters might become prone to have such violent fantasies.

## CHANGING THE CLASSROOM ATMOSPHERE

Our policymakers framed the question in the context of the Columbine massacre: How can we prevent such events in the future? But, as implied above, the question is a far broader one. How can we change the process of the typical classroom so that our schools can transform themselves into more humane social environments for all students? The general answer is to change the dynamic of the classroom from dog-eat-dog competition to a more cooperative, more caring one. Easier said than done. Many schools have actively attempted to counteract the negative influences of excessive competition by asking kids to try to cooperate with one another. It would be hard to find a preschool or elementary school that did not actively encourage children to share, to work harmoniously with their peers, and to behave respectfully and cooperatively with one another. Many elementary schools now have students sit in small groups at tables, rather than in rows of individual desks.

But simply assigning students to work together in groups to produce a joint report does not guarantee true cooperation. Unstructured attempts to encourage cooperation in the classroom usually fail to accomplish their ultimate goal and might even backfire if not carefully designed. Most often the group dynamics of an unstructured "cooperative" situation mirror the larger competitive classroom dynamic. The one or two most able or most motivated students put themselves forward to do most of the work while simultaneously resenting the fact that they are carrying the load for the entire group. And the less able or less motivated students end up doing little, learning little, and feeling inadequate. These so-called cooperative groups are cooperative in name only.

## THE JIGSAW CLASSROOM

The problem with cooperative learning assignments is not that they do not work. It is that they need to be carefully designed and rigorously structured for them have the intended effect. One successful model, with a three-decade track record, is the jigsaw classroom. Jigsaw is a specific type of group learning experience wherein each student must cooperate with his or her peers to achieve his or her individual goals. Just as in a jigsaw puzzle, each piece—each student's part—is essential for the production and full understanding of the final product. If each student's part is essential, then each student is essential; and that is precisely what makes this strategy so effective.

Here is how it works: The students in a history class, for example, are divided into small groups of five or six students each. Suppose their task is to learn about World War II. In one jigsaw group let us say that Sara is responsible for researching Hitler's rise to power in pre-war Germany. Another member of the group, Steven, is assigned to cover concentration camps; Pedro is assigned Britain's role in the war; Melody is to research the contribution of the Soviet Union; Willie will handle Japan's entry into the war; Clara will read about the development of the atom bomb.

Eventually each student will come back to his or her jigsaw group and will try to present a vivid, interesting, well-organized report to the group. The situation is specifically structured so that the only access any member has to the other five assignments is by listening intently to the report of the person reciting. Thus, suppose Steven does not like Pedro and thinks Sara is a nerd. If he heckles them, or tunes out while they are reporting, he cannot possibly do well on the exam that follows.

To increase the probability that each report will be factual and accurate, the students doing the research do not immediately take it back to their jigsaw group. After doing their research, they must first meet with the other students (one from each of the jigsaw groups) who had the identical assignment. For example, those students assigned to the atom bomb topic will meet together to work as a team of specialists, gathering information, discussing ideas, becoming experts on their topic, and rehearsing their presentations. We call this the "expert" group. It is particularly useful for those students who might have initial difficulty learning or organizing their part of the assignment, for it allows them to benefit from paying attention to and rehearsing with other "experts," to pick up strategies of presentation, and generally to bring themselves up to speed.

After this meeting, when each presenter is up to speed, the jigsaw groups reconvene in their initial heterogeneous configuration. The atom bomb expert in each group teaches the other group members what she has learned about the development of the atom bomb. Each student in each group educates the whole group about his or her specialty. Students are then tested on what they have learned from their fellow group members about World War II.

What is the benefit of the jigsaw classroom? First and foremost, it is a remarkably efficient way to learn the material. Our research shows that elementary school students learn the material faster and perform significantly better on objective exams than a control condition of students learning the same material in more traditional classrooms (Aronson, Stephan, Sikes, Blaney, & Snapp, 1978; Aronson & Patnoe, 1997; Lucker, Rosenfield, Sikes, & Aronson, 1977). But even more important, in terms of the present discussion, the jigsaw process encourages listening, engagement, and empathy by giving each member of the group an essential part to play in the academic activity. Group members must work together as a team to accomplish a common goal; each person depends on all the others. No student can achieve his or her individual goal (learning the material, getting a good grade) unless everyone works together well as a team. Group goals and individual goals complement and bolster each other. This "cooperation by design" facilitates interaction among all students in the class, leading them to come to value each other as contributors to their common task (Aronson, 2000; Aronson & Patnoe, 1997).

My graduate students and I invented the jigsaw strategy in Austin, Texas, in 1971. We invented jigsaw as a matter of absolute necessity to help defuse a highly explosive situation. The city's schools had recently been desegregated and, because Austin had always been residentially segregated, white youngsters, African-American youngsters, and Hispanic youngsters found themselves in the same classrooms for the first time in their lives. Within a few weeks, long-standing suspicion, fear, distrust, and antipathy between groups produced an atmosphere of turmoil and hostility, exploding into interethnic fistfights in corridors and schoolyards across the city. The school superintendent called me in to see if my students and I could possibly do something to help students learn to get along with one another. After observing what was going on in classrooms for a few days, we concluded that intergroup hostility was being exacerbated by the competitive environment of the classroom.

In every single classroom, the students worked individually and competed against each other for grades. Here is a description of a typical fifth grade classroom we observed:

> The teacher stands in front of the class, asks a question, and waits for the children to indicate that they know the answer. Most frequently, six to ten youngsters raise their hands. But they do not simply raise their hands; they lift themselves a few inches off their chairs and stretch their arms as high as they can in an attempt to attract the teacher's attention. To say they are eager to be called on is an incredible understatement. Several other students sit quietly with their eyes averted, as if trying to make themselves invisible. These are the ones who don't know the answer. Understandably, they are trying to avoid eye contact with the teacher because they do not want to be called on.
>
> When the teacher calls on one of the eager students, there are looks of disappointment, dismay, and unhappiness on the faces of the other students who were avidly raising their hands but were not called on. If the selected student comes up with the right answer, the teacher smiles, nods approvingly, and goes on to the next question. This is a great reward

for the child who happens to be called on. At the same time that the fortunate student is coming up with the right answer and being smiled upon by the teacher, an audible groan can be heard coming from the children who were striving to be called on but were ignored. It is obvious they are disappointed because they missed an opportunity to show the teacher how smart and quick they are. Perhaps they will get an opportunity next time. In the meantime, the students who didn't know the answer breathe a sigh of relief. They have escaped being humiliated this time.

On interviewing several of the teachers we learned that virtually all of them started the school year with a determination to treat every student equally and encourage all to do their best, but the students quickly sorted themselves into different groups. The "winners" were the bright, eager, highly competitive students who fervently raised their hands, participated in discussions, and did well on tests. Understandably, the teacher felt gratified that these students responded to her teaching. She praised and encouraged them, continued to call on them, and depended on them to keep the class going at a high level and at a reasonable pace.

Then there were the "losers." At the beginning, the teacher called on them occasionally, but they almost invariably did not know the answer, or were too shy to speak, or could not speak English well. They seemed embarrassed to be in the spotlight; some of the other students made snide comments—sometimes under their breath, occasionally out loud. Because the schools in the poorer section of town were substandard, the African-American and Mexican-American youngsters had received a poorer education prior to desegregation. Consequently, in Austin, it was frequently these students who were among the losers. This tended unfairly to confirm the unflattering stereotypes that the white kids had about minorities. They considered them stupid or lazy. The minority students also had preconceived notions about white kids: they were pushy showoffs and teacher's pets. These stereotypes were also confirmed by the way most of the white students behaved in the competitive classroom.

After a while, the typical classroom teacher became discouraged in trying to engage the students who were not doing well. She also felt it was kinder not to call on them and expose them to ridicule by the other students. In effect, she made a silent pact with the "losers"; she would leave them alone as long as they were not disruptive. Without really meaning to, she gave up on these students, and so did the rest of the class. Without really meaning to, the teacher contributed to the difficulty the students were experiencing. After a while, these students tended to give up on themselves as well—perhaps believing that they *were* stupid, because they sure weren't getting it.

It required only a few days of intensive observation and interviews for us to have a pretty good idea of what was going on in these classrooms. We realized that we needed to do something drastic to shift the emphasis from a relentlessly competitive atmosphere to a more cooperative one. It was in this context that we invented the jigsaw strategy. One of our first interventions was with fifth graders. First we helped several fifth grade teachers devise a cooperative jigsaw structure for the students to learn about the life of Eleanor Roosevelt. We divided the students into small groups, diversified in terms of race, ethnicity, and gender, making each student responsible for a certain portion of Roosevelt's biography. Needless to say, at least one or two of the students in each group were already viewed as "losers" by their classmates.

Carlos was one such student. Carlos was very shy and feeling insecure in his new surroundings. English was his second language. He spoke it quite well, but with a slight accent. Try to imagine his experience: After attending an inadequately funded, substandard neighborhood school consisting entirely of Hispanic students, like himself, through the fourth grade, he was suddenly bussed across town to the middle class area of the city and catapulted into a class with Anglo students who spoke English fluently, seemed to know much more than he did about all the subjects taught in the school, and were not reluctant to let him know it.

When we restructured the classroom so that students were now working together in small groups, initially, this was terrifying to Carlos. For now, he should no longer slink down in his chair and hide in the back of the room. The jigsaw structure made it necessary for him to speak up when it was his turn to recite. Although he had gained a little added confidence by rehearsing together with others who were also studying Eleanor Roosevelt's work with the United Nations, he was understandably reticent to speak when it was his turn to teach the students in his jigsaw group. He blushed, stammered, and had difficulty articulating the material that he had learned. Skilled in the ways of the competitive classroom, the other students were quick to pounce on Carlos' weakness and began to ridicule him.

One of my research assistants was observing that group and heard some members of Carlos' group make comments such as, "Aw, you don't know it, you're dumb, you're stupid. You don't know what you're doing. You can't even speak English." Instead of admonishing them to "be nice" or "try to cooperate," she made one simple but powerful statement. It went something like this: "Talking like that to Carlos might be fun for you to do, but it's not going to help you learn anything about what Eleanor Roosevelt accomplished at the United Nations—and the exam will be given in about 15 minutes." What my assistant was doing was reminding the students that the situation had changed. The same behavior that might have been useful to them individually in the past, when they were competing against each other, was now going to cost them something very important: the chance to do well on the upcoming exam.

Needless to say, old, dysfunctional habits do not die easily. But they do die. Within a few days of working with jigsaw, Carlos' groupmates gradually realized that they needed to change their tactics. It was no longer in their own best interest to rattle Carlos; he was not the enemy, he was on their team. They needed him to perform well to do well themselves. Instead of taunting him and putting him down, they started to gently ask him questions. But how? What kind of questions? In effect, they had to put themselves in Carlos' shoes to find a way to ask questions that did not threaten him but could facilitate his reciting in a clear and understandable manner. After a week or two, most of Carlos's group-mates developed into skillful interviewers, asking him relevant questions to elicit the vital information from him. They became more patient, figured out the most effective way to work with him, helped him out, and encouraged him. The more they encouraged Carlos, the more he was able to relax; the more he was able to relax, the quicker and more articulate he became. Carlos's groupmates began to see him in a new light. He became transformed in their minds from a "know-nothing loser who can't even speak English" to someone they could work with, someone they could appreciate, maybe even someone they could like. Moreover, Carlos began to see *himself* in a new light, as a competent, contrib-uting member of the class who could work with others from different ethnic groups. His self-esteem grew and as it grew, his performance improved even more; and as his performance continued to improve, his groupmates continued to view him in a more and more favorable light.

Within a few weeks, the success of the jigsaw was obvious to the classroom teachers. They spontaneously told us of their great satisfaction with the way the atmosphere of their classrooms had been transformed. Adjunct visitors (such as music teachers and the like) were little short of amazed at the dramatically changed atmosphere in the classrooms. Needless to say, this was exciting to my graduate students and me. But, as scientists, we were not totally satisfied with these testimonials; we were seeking firmer, more objective evidence—and we got it. Because we had randomly introduced the jigsaw intervention into some classrooms and not others, we were able to compare the progress of the jigsaw students with that of the students in traditional classrooms in a precise, scientific manner. After only 8 weeks there were clear differences, even though students spent only a small portion of their class time in jigsaw groups. When tested objectively, jigsaw students expressed signifi-cantly less prejudice and negative stereotyping, were more self-confident, and reported that they liked school better then children in traditional classrooms. Moreover, this self-report was bolstered by hard behavioral data: For example, the children in jigsaw classes were absent less often than students in traditional classrooms. Finally, as mentioned earlier, on objective exams, the students in jigsaw classrooms performed significantly better than students learning the same material in traditional classrooms. Close inspection of the data revealed that the differences in objective exam performance were due primarily to improvements in the scores of minority students; the Anglo students per-formed equally well in jigsaw as in traditional classrooms (Lucker et al., 1977).

## COOPERATION: JIGSAW AND BASKETBALL

You might have noticed a rough similarity between the kind of cooperation that goes on in a jigsaw group and the kind of cooperation that is necessary for the smooth functioning of an athletic team. Take a basketball team, for example. If the team is to be successful, each player must play his or her role in a cooperative manner. If each player is hell bent on being the highest scorer on the team, then each would shoot whenever the opportunity arose. In contrast, on a cooperative team, the idea is to pass the ball crisply until one player manages to break clear for a relatively easy shot. If I pass the ball to Sam, and Sam whips a pass to Harry, and Harry passes to Tony who breaks free for an easy lay-up, I am elated even though I did not receive credit for either a field goal or an assist. This is true cooperation.

As a result of this cooperation, athletic teams frequently build a cohesiveness that extends to their relationship off the court. They become friends because they have learned to count on one another. There is one difference between the outcome of a typical jigsaw group and that of a typical high school basketball team, however, and it is a crucial difference. In high school, athletes tend to hang out with each other and frequently exclude nonathletes from their circle of close friends. In short, the internal cohesiveness of an athletic team often goes along with the exclusion of everyone else.

In the jigsaw classroom, we circumvented this problem by the simple device of shuffling groups every 8 weeks. Once a group of students was functioning well together, once the barriers had been broken down and the students showed a great deal of liking and empathy for one another, we would re-form the groupings. At first, the students would resist this re-forming of groups. Picture the scene: Debbie, Carlos, Tim, Patty and Jacob have just gotten to know and appreciate one another and they are doing incredibly good work as a team. Why should they want to leave this warm, efficient and cozy group to join a group of relative strangers?

Why, indeed? After spending a few weeks in the new group, the students invariably discover that the new people are just about as interesting, friendly, and wonderful as their former group. The new group is working well together and new friendships form. Then the students move on to their third group, and the same thing begins to happen. As they near the end of their time in the third group, it begins to dawn on most students that it is not the case that they happened to luck out and land in groups with four or five terrific people. Rather, they realize that just about *everyone* they work with is a worthy human being; all they need to do is pay attention to each person, to try to understand him or her and good things will emerge. That is a lesson well worth learning.

## LONG-TERM EFFECTS?

Jigsaw works. Moreover, jigsaw is compatible with other teaching methods. If jigsaw is used for as little as one hour per day, it has been shown to have positive effects. How permanent are the effects? If students participated in the jigsaw classroom in the fifth or sixth grade, would the positive impact remain even if they never experienced jigsaw again? Unfortunately, we do not have a definitive answer to this question. We do have some tangential evidence that the effects of jigsaw may become a permanent part of the individual's way of looking at the world. In a clever experiment, Diane Bridgeman showed that the empathy required by jigsaw takes on the form of a more or less permanent ability that generalizes and is used outside the confines of the classroom.

In Bridgeman's experiment, she worked with fifth graders, half whom had spent 2 months participating in jigsaw classes; the others had spent that time in traditional classrooms. Bridgeman showed them a series of stick-figure cartoons about a young boy their own age. In the first panel, the boy is looking sad as he waves good-bye to his father at the airport. In the next panel, a letter carrier delivers a package to the boy. In the final panel, the boy opens the package and finds a toy airplane inside and bursts into tears. Bridgeman asked the children why they thought the boy had burst into tears at the sight of the airplane. Nearly all of the children could answer correctly, because the toy airplane reminded him of how much he missed his father and that made him sad. Then Bridgeman asked the crucial question: "What did the letter carrier think when he saw the boy open the package and start to cry?"

Most children of this age make a consistent error; they assume that everyone knows what they know. Thus, the youngsters in the control group thought that the letter carrier would know the boy was sad because the gift reminded him of his father leaving. But the children who had participated in the jigsaw classroom responded differently. Because they were better able to take the perspective of the letter carrier—to put themselves in his shoes; they realized that he would be confused at seeing the boy cry over receiving a nice present because the letter carrier had not witnessed the farewell scene at the airport.

Offhand, this might not seem very important. After all, who cares whether kids have the ability to figure out what is in the letter carrier's mind? In point of fact, we should all care—a great deal. The extent to which children can develop the ability to see the world from the perspective of another human being has profound implications for empathy, prejudice, aggression, and interpersonal relations in general. When you can feel another person's pain, when you can develop the ability to understand what that person is going through, it increases the probability that your heart will open to that person, and it becomes difficult to harm him or taunt him. Moreover, because Bridgeman's data suggest that empathy, is a skill—not unlike riding a bike—that can be used in a variety of situations, the implication is that the major impact of the jigsaw classroom might have long-lasting effects.

I do have some additional evidence but I am afraid that it is merely anecdotal. Nevertheless, I will mention it for what it may be worth. Over the past 20 years, I have received unsolicited letters from young men and young women who, many years earlier, had undergone such a transformation. To give you some of the flavor of this experience, I would like to share one such letter with you.

Dear Professor Aronson:

I am a senior at——University. Today I got a letter admitting me to the Harvard Law School. This may not seem odd to you but, let me tell you something. I am the 6th of 7 children my parents had—and I am the only one who ever went to college, let alone graduate, or go to law school.

By now, you are probably wondering why this stranger is writing to you and bragging to you about his achievements. Actually, I'm not a stranger although we never met. You see, last year I was taking a course in social psychology and we were using a book you wrote called The Social Animal, and when I read about prejudice and jigsaw it all sounded very familiar—and then, I realized that I was in that very first class you ever did jigsaw in—when I was in the 5th grade in Austin. And as I read on, it dawned on me that I was the boy that you called Carlos. And then I remembered you when you first came to our classroom and how I was scared and how I hated school and how I was so stupid and didn't know anything. And you came in—it all came back to me when I read your book—you were very tall—about 6½ feet—and you had a big black beard and you were funny and made us all laugh.

And, most important, when we started to do work in jigsaw groups, I began to realize that I wasn't really that stupid. And the kids I thought were cruel and hostile became my friends and the teacher acted friendly and nice to me and I actually began to love school, and I began to love to learn things and now I'm about to go to Harvard Law School.

You must get a lot of letters like this but I decided to write anyway because let me tell you something. My mother tells me that when I was born I almost died. I was born at home and the cord was wrapped around my neck and the midwife gave me mouth to mouth and saved my life. If she was still alive, I would write to her too, to tell her that I grew up smart and good and I'm going to law school. But she died a few years ago. I'm writing to you because, no less than her, you saved my life too.

Sincerely,
XXXX XXX

As you might imagine, I was deeply touched by this letter. It is just about the most moving letter I have ever received. But when I read the signature I was startled to discover that it did not belong to the boy that I had in mind—the boy who in my previous writings I had referred to as "Carlos." The young man who wrote me that lovely letter was mistaken.

I have a clear memory of sitting there with the letter in my hand thinking about that young man and how wrong he was. After a few minutes, I fell into a reverie in which I began to realize that perhaps that young man was not mistaken after all. That is, although I had a specific fifth grader in mind when I wrote about Carlos, there are a great many children who come pretty close to fitting that description. In my reverie I began to grasp the implications of the possibility that, all over America, there are thousands of youngsters who think they are Carlos. And, in the deepest possible way, they *are* all Carlos. Carlos is any child who has been the unhappy recipient of put-downs, taunting, and rejection at the hands of his or her peers, leading to a diminution of his or her self-esteem, and who has managed to turn that around because the structure of the classroom changed, paving the way for a different set of responses. To the child involved, it feels like a miracle. To the social psychologist it is still another vivid example of the power of the situation: how what looks like a small, simple change in the structure of a social environment can have an enormous impact on the experience of the people in that environment. This is an experience that can last a lifetime.[1]

## A POSTSCRIPT

Following the Columbine massacre, there was a lot of negative publicity about the atmosphere at Columbine High School and how that atmosphere might have contributed to the tragedy. Some of it mentioned how athletes dominated the school and how unpopular students were taunted and excluded. The criticism, although not inaccurate, was unfair in the sense that the atmosphere at Columbine was no different than in almost every high school in the country. In response to the criticism, some of the Columbine students attempted to justify their exclusion of Harris and Klebold. Typical of these remarks was comment by a member of the Columbine football team:

> Columbine is a good clean place except for those rejects. Most kids didn't want them there. They were into witchcraft. They were into voodoo. Sure we teased them. But what do you expect with kids who come to school with weird hairdos and horns on their hats? If you want to get rid of someone, usually you tease 'em. (Quoted by Gibbs & Roche, December, 1999)

It is my belief that if the jigsaw technique had been widely used in the Littleton school system a few years earlier, the young man and his friends might have developed some additional compassion and empathy as well as a greater tolerance for diversity. If so, they would undoubtedly have been delighted rather than angered by the diversity represented by the kids "who come to school with weird hairdos." I may be wrong, but I am fairly certain that, if this had been the case, the Columbine massacre would never have occurred. Again, I may be wrong; but it certainly is worth thinking about.

## Teachers' Questions and Answers

**Q:**   As a teacher, I often use the jigsaw method with my students and it works extremely well. But, often there are some students, usually mainstreamed special education students, who have tremendous difficulty relaying the content specifics to their groups even after prepping in their their mastery group. How can the jigsaw be adapted to accommodate these stu-

---

[1] I should mention in passing that during the past two decades, educational researchers have developed and tested several alternative cooperative classroom methods. Although these alternative methods differ from jigsaw in several minor respects, they have in common a basic cooperative structure and produce similar positive effects. For a summary of these techniques, see Slavin, Aharan, Kagan, Hertz-Lazarowitz, Webb, and Schmuck (1985).

dents so that they can fully participate without their group missing essential information?

**A:**   I have found that, in situations like this, it is helpful to assign another student in the jigsaw group to the special-ed student, someone to serve as a coach. This would need to be a very bright, mature student. In addition to learning her own paragraph, she would learn enough about the special-ed student's paragraph to ask probing questions or to fill in where the special-ed student might have left something out. This is a special role that most bright, mature students take to like a duck to water. (If no such student exists in a particular jigsaw group, this is a role that the teacher might want to take on.)

**Q:**   I have found that we do not always have enough time to complete all of the parts of the jigsaw within one period. What are some ways you would recommend to divide up the process over 2 days? Or is there a way to shorten the process so as to fit it into one period?

**A:**   Needless to say, it works best if it can all be squeezed into one period. If not, I would do the learning of the material and the expert group in one period and save the final jigsaw group for the next period.

**Q:**   It's very clear to me that the jigsaw can be used effectively if the curriculum covers, say, the life of Eleanor Roosevelt. But I'm having trouble seeing how one could use the jigsaw method for teaching math. Is there a way to do so? Does it work as well as it does for more humanities-style curricula?

**A:**   You are absolutely right. It is easier to work with social studies than with a progressive subject like math, where it is difficult for students to grasp step 3 without having gone through steps 1 and 2. At the same time, I am happy to report that some math teachers have had very good success using jigsaw to teach arithmetic, mathematics, and statistics. Just to take one stunning, recent example, David Perkins and Renee Saris at Ball State University have used jigsaw, to great effect, in an undergraduate statistics course (see *Journal of Teaching of Psychology*, 2001, Vol. 28, pp.111–113).

## References

Aronson, E. (1978). *The jigsaw classroom*. Beverly Hills, CA: Sage.

Aronson, E. (1999). *The social animal* (Chap. 4). New York: Worth/Freeman.

Aronson, E. (2000). *Nobody left to hate: Teaching compassion after Columbine*. New York: Worth/Freeman.

Aronson, E., & Bridgeman, D. (1979). Jigsaw groups and the desegregated classroom: In pursuit of common goals. *Personality and Social Psychology Bulletin, 5,* 438–446.

Aronson , E., & Patnoe, S., (1997). *Cooperation in the classroom: The jigsaw method*. New York: Longman.

Bridgeman, D. (1981). Enhanced role-taking through cooperative interdependence: A field study. *Child Development 52*, 1231–1238.

Gibbs, N. (1999, October 25). A week in the life of a high school, Webster Groves. *Time Magazine.*

Gibbs, N., & Roche, C. (1999, October 25). Columbine. *Time Magazine.*

Gibbs, N., & Roche, T. (1999, December 20). The Columbine tapes. *Time Magazine.*

Goldberg, W., & Connelly, M. (1999, October 20). *New York Times.*

Lewin, T. (1999, May 2). Terror in Littleton: The teenage culture; Arizona high school provides glimpse into cliques. *New York Times.*

Lucker, W., Rosenfield, D., Sikes, J., & Aronson, E. (1977). Performance in the interdependent classroom: A field study. *American Educational Research Journal, 13*, 115–123.

Sizer, T., & Sizer, N. (1999). *The students are watching.* Boston: Beacon Press.

Slavin, R., Aharan, S. Kagan, S., Hertz-Lazarowitz, R., Webb, C., & Schmuck, R. (Eds.) (1985). *Learning to cooperate, cooperating to learn:* New York: Plenum.

Townsend, P. (1999, May 23). High school cliques. *Santa Cruz Sentinel*, p. A9.

# CHAPTER 11

# Intelligence Is Not Just Inside the Head: The Theory of Successful Intelligence

ROBERT J. STERNBERG

*Yale University, New Haven, Connecticut*

Many people believe that intelligence is just inside the head. According to this view intelligence can be defined in terms of a fairly narrow set of cognitive skills of the kinds measured by conventional intelligence tests—answering vocabulary questions, solving mathematical reasoning problems, manipulating images of geometric objects in the head, and so forth. In this chapter I argue that the notion of intelligence as inside the head and as operationalized in narrowly based intelligence tests is incomplete. I argue for a concept of successful intelligence, according to which intelligence is the ability to achieve success in life, given one's personal standards, within one's sociocultural context. One's ability to achieve success depends on one's capitalizing on one's strengths and correcting or compensating for one's weaknesses through a balance of analytical, creative, and practical abilities in order to adapt to, shape, and select

Preparation of this article was supported under the Javits Act Program (Grant No. R206R00001) as administered by the Office of Educational Research and Improvement, U.S. Department of Education. Grantees undertaking such projects are encouraged to express freely their professional judgment. This article, therefore, does not necessarily represent the position or policies of the Office of Educational Research and Improvement or the U.S. Department of Education, and no official endorsement should be inferred.

Requests for reprints should be sent to Robert J. Sternberg, Department of Psychology, Yale University, P.O. Box 208205, New Haven, CT 06520–8205.

environments (Sternberg, 1997, 1999). If we adopt this notion of intelligence, I argue, we immediately will have tools available to improve children's perform- ance in school and to enhance their achievements in life. This view requires us to view intelligence not just from a psychometric perspective or even a cognitive perspective, but from a social perspective as well.

I divide my argument into three main parts. First I argue that conventional notions of intelligence are incomplete. Second I suggest an alternative notion of successful intelligence that expands on conventional notions of intelligence. Finally I draw some conclusions about the nature of intelligence and its implications for schooling.

## INADEQUACY OF CONVENTIONAL NOTIONS OF INTELLIGENCE

Conventional notions of intelligence are incomplete. To the extent that one wishes to define intelligence very narrowly, perhaps they work. But in the modern world, where so many skills are needed to thrive and even to survive, perhaps narrow notions of intelligence are no longer adequate. Moreover, they are based on a doubtful premise. This premise is of intelligence as a unitary construct, a view that dates back to a proposal by British psychologist Charles Spearman (1904) and a view that is most likely not entirely correct. So contem- porary theories of intelligence based on this notion, such as those proposed by psychologists Arthur Jensen (1998) and John B. Carroll (1993), cannot be entirely correct either.

There now has accumulated a substantial body of evidence suggesting that, contrary to conventional notions, intelligence is *not* a unitary construct. This evidence is of a variety of different kinds. One of the main kinds of evidence traditionally adduced to support the unitary notion is the pattern of all positive correlations that is frequently observed among ability tests. The assumption has been that this pattern of all positive correlations among tests reflects an underlying common ability being measured by all the tests. This ability is often referred to as *g*, or general ability. But I believe there is good evidence to suggest that the general factor is not a function of some inherent structure of intellect. Rather, it reflects limitations in the kinds of individuals tested, the kinds of tests used in the testing, and the situations in which the individuals are tested.

One kind of evidence suggests the power of situational contexts in testing. For example, David Carraher, Terezinha Nuñes, and their colleagues have studied a group of children that is especially relevant for assessing intelligence as adaptation to the environment (see Nuñes, 1994). The group comprised Brazilian street children. Brazilian street children are under great contextual pressure to form a successful street business. If they do not, they risk death at the hands of so-called "death squads," which may murder children who, unable to earn money, resort to robbing stores (or who are suspected of resorting to robbing stores). The researchers found that the same children who are able to do the mathematics needed to run their street business areoften little able or unable to do school mathematics. In fact, the more abstract and removed from real-world contexts the problems are in their form of presentation, the worse the children do on the problems. These results suggest that differences in social context can have a powerful effect on performance.

Such differences are not limited to Brazilian street children. Jean Lave (1997) showed that Berkeley housewives who successfully could do the mathematics needed for comparison shopping in the supermarket were unable to do the same mathematics when they were placed in a classroom and given comparable problems presented in an abstract form. In other words, their problem was not at the level of mental processes but at the level of applying the processes in specific environmental contexts.

Steve Ceci and Steve Liker (1986) showed that, given tasks relevant to their lives, men would show the patterns of effects similar to those shown by women in the Lave studies. These investigators studied men who successfully handicapped horse races. The complexity of their implicit mathematical formulas was unrelated to their IQ. Moreover, despite the complexity of these formulas, the mean IQ among these men was only at roughly the population average or slightly below. Ceci and Liker also subsequently found that the skills were really quite specific: The same men did not successfully apply their skills to computations involving securities in the stock market. Again, context matters.

In our own research, we have found results consistent with those described above. These results have emanated from studies we have done around the world.

For example, in a study in Usenge, Kenya, near the town of Kisumu, we were interested in school-aged children's ability to adapt to their indigenous environment. In collaboration with others (Sternberg et al., 2001), I was involved in studies of practical intelligence for adaptation to the environment. We devised a test that measured children's informal tacit knowledge for natural herbal medicines that the villagers believe can be used to fight various types of illnesses. We do not know if all or any of these medicines are actually effective. But from the standpoint of our study, the important thing is that the villagers think they are and therefore that knowledge about them is worth possessing.

We measured the children's ability to identify the medicines and what they are used for. Based on work we had done elsewhere, we expected that scores on this test would not correlate with scores on conventional tests of intelligence. To test this hypothesis, we also administered to the children the Raven Coloured Progressive Matrices Test, which is a measure of fluid or abstract-reasoning-based abilities, as well as the Mill Hill Vocabulary Scale, which is a measure of crystallized or formal-knowledge-based abilities. In addition, we gave the children a comparable test of vocabulary in their own Dholuo language. The Dholuo language is spoken in the home, English in the schools.

We did indeed find no correlation between the test of indigenous tacit knowledge and scores on the fluid-ability tests. But to our surprise, we found statistically significant correlations of the tacit-knowledge tests with the tests of crystallized abilities. The correlations, however, were *negative*. In other words, the higher the children scored on the test of tacit knowledge, the lower they scored, on average, on the tests of crystallized abilities. This surprising result can be interpreted in various ways. But based on the ethnographic observations of the cultural anthropologists on our team, Geissler and Prince, we concluded that a plausible scenario takes into account the expectations of families for their children and the resultant ways in which the children are socialized.

Most families in the village do not particularly value formal Western schooling. There is no reason they should, as their children will for the most part spend their lives farming or engaged in other occupations that make little or no use of Western schooling. These families emphasize teaching their children the indigenous informal knowledge that will lead to successful adaptation in the environments in which they will live. At the same time, there are some families in the village that have different expectations for their children. They hope that their children eventually may be able to leave the village and to go to a university, perhaps the University of Nairobi. These families tend to emphasize the value of Western education and to devalue indigenous informal knowledge. Thus the families typically value and emphasize one or the other kind of knowledge but not both.

The Kenya study suggests that the identification of a general factor of human intelligence may tell us more about patterns of schooling and especially Western patterns of schooling than it does about the structure of human abilities. In Western schooling, children typically study a variety of subject matters from an early age and thus develop skills in a variety of skill areas. This kind of schooling prepares the children to take a test of intelligence, which typically measures skills in a variety of areas. Often intelligence tests measure skills that children were expected to acquire a few years before taking the intelligence test. But as Barbara Rogoff (1990) and others have noted, this pattern of schooling is not universal and has not even been common for much of the history of humankind. Throughout history and in many places still, schooling, especially for boys, takes the form of apprenticeships in which children learn a craft from an early age. They learn what they will need to know to succeed in a trade, but not a lot more. They are not simultaneously engaged in tasks that require the development of the particular blend of skills measured by conventional intelligence tests. Hence it is less likely that one would observe a general factor in their scores, much as we discovered in Kenya. The developing world provides a particularly interesting laboratory for testing theories of intelligence because many of the assumptions that are held as dear in the developed world simply do not apply. In particular, children receive very different socialization from the socialization they receive in the United States.

Even in the United States, however, children can receive very diverse kinds of socialization. Lynn Okagaki and I did a study in San Jose, California, of parents' and teachers' conceptions of what it means to have an intelligent child (Okagaki & Sternberg, 1991, 1993). We found that parents of children of different ethnic groups have somewhat different conceptions (sometimes called *implicit theories*) of what it means to have a smart child. In particular, Latino parents more emphasized the importance of social-competence skills, whereas Anglo and Asian parents more emphasized the importance of cognitive-competence skills. Teachers, however, had conceptions of smart children that were more similar to the conceptions of the Anglo and Asian parents than they were to the conceptions of the Latino parents. We found that the more the parents' conceptions of intelligence matched the conceptions of the teachers, the better the children performed in school. In other words, teachers are not evaluating children just on some "true" basis of what it means to be intelligent, but rather on their own conception of what it means to be intelligent. And of course, the teachers' conceptions of intelligence are likely to reflect the way *they* were socialized.

Another kind of socialization effect stems from familiarity with testing in the first place, a point that Patricia Greenfield (1997) has very much emphasized in her writings. We agree with Greenfield. A study done in Tanzania in which I collaborated with Elena Grigorenko points out the risks of giving tests, scoring them, and interpreting the results as measures of some fixed underlying intellectual ability or abilities (Sternberg, Grigorenko, Ngorosho, Tuntufye, Mbise, Nokes, Jukes, & Bundy, in press). We administered to young school children in Bagamoyo, Tanzania, tests such as a form-board test and a Twenty Questions Test, which measure the kinds of skills required on conventional tests of intelligence. Of course, we obtained scores that we could analyze and evaluate, ranking the children in terms of their supposed general or other abilities. However, we administered the tests dynamically rather than statically, loosely following a procedure first set out by Russian psychologist Lev Vygotsky (1978) and later carried out as well by Israeli psychologist Reuven Feuerstein (1979). Dynamic testing is like conventional static testing in that individuals are tested and inferences about their abilities are then made. But dynamic tests differ from conventional static tests in that children are given some kind of feedback to help them improve their scores. Vygotsky suggested that the children's ability to profit from the guided instruction the children received during the testing session could serve as a measure of children's zone of proximal development (ZPD), or the difference between their developed abilities and their latent or underlying capacities. In other words, testing and instruction are treated as being of one piece rather than as being distinct processes.

In our assessments, children were first given the ability tests. Then they were given a brief period of instruction in which they were able to learn skills that would potentially enable them to improve their scores. Then they were tested again. Because the instruction for each test lasted only about 15 minutes, one would not expect dramatic gains. Yet, on average, the gains were statistically significant. More importantly, scores on the pretest showed only weak although significant correlations with scores on the posttest. These correlations, at about the .3 level, suggested that when tests are administered statically to children in developing countries, they may be rather unstable and easily subject to influences of training. The reason, of course, is that the children are not accustomed to taking Western-style tests and so profit quickly even from small amounts of instruction as to what is expected from them. Of course, the more important question is not whether the scores changed or even correlated with each other, but rather how they correlated with other cognitive measures. In other words, which test was a better predictor of transfer to other cognitive performance, the pretest score or the gain from the pretest score to the posttest score? We found the gain score to be the better predictor, by a factor of 4. In other words, any general-factor score or, really, any other factor score obtained from the pretest, which was equivalent to a typical statically administered test, would be of substantially lower validity than would be a gain score measuring learning at the time of test as obtained from a dynamically administered test.

If intelligence is not just a single thing that can be measured by a conventional static test of intelligence, what is it? I argue that it comprises three things, each of which is a different aspect of intelligence.

## THREE ASPECTS OF SUCCESSFUL INTELLIGENCE

The intelligence one needs to attain success in life comprises analytical, creative, and practical aspects (Sternberg, 1985). According to my theory of successful intelligence, a common set of processes underlies these three aspects of intelligence. *Metacomponents*, or executive processes, plan what to do, monitor things as they are being done, and evaluate things after they are done. Examples of metacomponents are recognizing the existence of a problem, defining the nature of the problem, deciding on a strategy for solving the problem, monitoring the solution of the problem, and evaluating the solution after the problem is solved. In writing a term paper on patterns of child rearing, for example, a student has to recognize the need to write the paper, define a topic on which to write the paper, decide on a strategy for getting the paper done, monitor how the paper is going while he or she is writing it, and then evaluate it to make sure it is ready to be handed in. Performance components execute the instructions of the metacomponents. For example, inference is used to compare and contrast different approaches, say, to child rearing. Knowledge-acquisition components are used to learn how to solve problems or simply to acquire knowledge in the first place. For example, selective encoding is used to decide what information one is reading is relevant in the context of one's writing the term paper on which one is working

Although the same processes are used for all three aspects of intelligence, these processes are applied to different kinds of tasks and situations depending on whether a given problem requires analytical thinking, creative thinking, practical thinking, or a combination of these kinds of thinking.

## Analytical Intelligence

Analytical intelligence is involved when the components of intelligence are applied to analyze, evaluate, judge, or compare and contrast. It typically is involved when components are applied to relatively familiar kinds of problems where the judgments to be made are of an abstract nature.

In some of my early work, I showed how analytical kinds of problems, such as analogies and syllogisms, can be analyzed in terms of the core component processes underlying performance on these problems. In this research, I gave people problems such as testlike analogies or series problems, and collected their response times or error rates so that I could determine the underlying information-processing components people used when they solved these problems. The goal of this research was to understand the information-processing origins of individual differences in (the analytical aspect of) human intelligence.

Research on the components of human intelligence yielded some interesting results. For example, in a study of the development of figural analogical reasoning in second, fourth, and sixth graders, Bathsheva Rifkin and I found that although children generally became quicker in information processing with age, not all components were executed more rapidly with age (Sternberg & Rifkin, 1979). The encoding component, representing the time it takes to figure out what is in a stimulus, first showed a decrease in component time with age and then an increase. Apparently, older children realized that their best strategy was to spend more time in encoding the terms of a problem so that they would later be able to spend less time in operating on these encodings. A related finding was that better reasoners tend to spend relatively more time than do poorer reasoners in global, up-front metacomponential planning, when they solve difficult reasoning problems. Poorer reasoners, on the other hand, tend to spend relatively more time in local planning. Presumably, the better reasoners recognize that it is better to invest more time up front so as to be able to process a problem more efficiently later on.

The study with Rifkin also yielded another strange and totally unexpected finding. A substantial number of second graders received scores of zero on the analogical reasoning test. In other words, they got absolutely no problems correct. This was a puzzling finding indeed. Because it was hard to believe that the children could be so lacking in analogical reasoning skills, we decided to look closely at their data. We discovered that the children who got no problems correct, instead of circling one of the two answer options printed at the right of each page, had circled one of the two givens of the problem, printed at the left of each page. What were they doing?

It turned out that the children, who were students in a Hebrew day school, were accustomed to reading English in the morning and Hebrew in the afternoon. English is read left to right, but Hebrew is read right to left. Unfortunately for us, we had tested in the afternoon. So the children did what they were accustomed to doing in the afternoon, that is, they read from right to left. Note how even in what appears to be a wholly cognitive test, socialization matters. The children were responding in a way that made sense in terms of their socialization in the school.

Some of our studies concentrated on knowledge-acquisition components rather than performance components or metacomponents. For example, in one set of studies, Janet Powell and I (Sternberg, 1987b; Sternberg & Powell, 1983) were interested in sources of individual differences in vocabulary. We were not content just to write these off as individual differences in knowledge, because we wanted to understand why it was that some people acquired this knowledge and others did not. What we found is that there were multiple sources of individual and developmental differences. The three main sources were in knowledge-acquisition components, use of context clues, and use of mediating variables. For example, in the sentence, "The blen rises in the east and sets in the west," the knowledge-acquisition component of selective comparison is used to relate prior knowledge about a known concept, the sun, to the unknown word (neologism) in the sentence, "blen." Several context cues appear in the sentence, such as the fact that a blen rises, the fact that it sets, and the information about where it rises and sets. A mediating variable is that the information can occur after the presentation of the unknown word.

We did research such as that described above because we believed that conventional psychometric research sometimes incorrectly attributed individual and developmental differences. For example, a verbal analogies test that might appear on its surface to measure verbal reasoning might in fact measure primarily vocabulary and general information. The analogy MITIGATE: EXACERBATE :: AMELIORATE : (a. worsen, b. improve, c. extend, d. contract), for example, is more likely to measure individual differences in vocabulary than individual differences in reasoning, at least for most populations. In fact, in some populations, reasoning might hardly be a source of individual or developmental differences at all. And if we then look at the sources of the individual differences in vocabulary, we would need to understand that the differences in knowledge did not come from nowhere: Some children had much more frequent and better opportunities to learn word meanings than did others. For example, they may have grown up in a house with more books or more opportunities to be exposed to print in the English language. Note, therefore, how socialization matters even when one tests something as cognitive as vocabulary.

The kinds of analytical skills we studied in this research can be taught. For example, in one study, we tested whether it is possible to teach people better to figure out meanings of unknown words presented in context (Sternberg, 1987a). In one study, we gave participants in five conditions a pretest on their ability to figure out word meanings. Then the participants were divided into five conditions, two of which were control conditions that lacked formal instruction. In one condition, participants were not given any instructional treatment. They were merely asked later to take a posttest. In a second condition, they were given practice as an instructional condition, but there was no formal instruction, per se. In a third condition, they were taught knowledge-acquisition component processes that could be used to figure out word meanings. In a fourth condition, they were taught to use context cues. In a fifth condition, they were taught to use mediating variables. Participants in all three of the theory-based formal-instructional conditions outperformed participants in the two control conditions, whose performance did not differ. In other words, theory-based instruction was better than no instruction and better than practice without formal instruction.

Research on the componential bases of intelligence was useful in understanding individual differences in performance on conventional tests of intelligence. But it became increasingly clear to me that this research basically served to partition the variation on conventional tests in a different way, rather than serving to uncover previously untapped sources of variation. Children develop intellectually in ways beyond just what conventional psychometric intelligence tests or even Piagetian tests based on the theory of Jean Piaget (1972) measure. So what might be some of these other sources of variation? Creative intelligence seemed to be one such source of variation, a source that is almost wholly untapped by conventional tests.

## Creative Intelligence

Intelligence tests contain a range of problems, some of them more novel than others. In some of our work we have shown that when one goes beyond the range of unconventionality of the tests, one starts to tap sources of individual differences measured little or not at all by the tests. According to the theory of successful intelligence, (creative) intelligence is particularly well measured by problems assessing how well an individual can cope with relative novelty. Thus it is important to include in a battery of tests problems that are relatively novel. These problems can be either convergent or divergent in nature.

In work with convergent problems, some of it done in collaboration with Sheldon Tetewsky (Sternberg, 1982; Tetewsky & Sternberg, 1986), we presented individuals with novel kinds of reasoning problems that had a single best answer. For example, they might be told that some objects are green and others blue; but still other objects might be *grue*, meaning green until the year 2000 and blue thereafter, or *bleen*, meaning blue until the year 2000 and green thereafter. Or they might be told of four kinds of people on the planet Kyron: *blens*, who are born young and die young; *kwefs*, who are born old and die old; *balts*, who are born young and die old; and *prosses*, who are born old and die young. Their task was to predict future states from past states, given incomplete information. In another set of studies with Joyce Gastel (Sternberg & Gastel, 1989a, 1989b), people were given more conventional kinds of inductive reasoning problems, such as analogies, series completions, and classifications, but were told to solve them. But the problems had premises preceding them that were either conventional (dancers wear shoes) or novel (dancers eat shoes). The participants had to solve the problems as though the counterfactuals were true.

In these studies, we found that correlations with conventional kinds of tests depended on how novel or nonentrenched the conventional tests were. The more novel the items, the higher the correlations of our tests with scores on the conventional tests. We also found that when response times on the relatively novel problems were componentially analyzed, some components better measured the creative aspect of intelligence than did others. For example, in the "grue–bleen" task mentioned above, the information-processing component requiring people to switch from conventional green–blue thinking to grue–bleen thinking and then back to green–blue thinking again was a particularly good measure of the ability to cope with novelty.

In collaborative work with Todd Lubart (Sternberg & Lubart, 1995) using divergent reasoning problems having no one best answer, we asked people to create various kinds of products where an infinite variety of responses were possible. Individuals were asked to create products in the realms of writing, art, advertising, and science. In writing, they would be asked to write very short stories for which we would give them a choice of titles, such as "Beyond the Edge" and "The Octopus' Sneakers." In art, they were asked to produce art compositions with titles such as "The Beginning of Time" and "Earth from an Insect's Point of View." In advertising, they were asked to produce advertisements for products such as a brand of bow tie and a brand of doorknob. In science, they were asked to solve problems such as one asking them how people might detect extraterrestrial aliens among us who are seeking to escape detection. Participants created two products in each domain.

We found that creativity is relatively although not wholly domain-specific. Correlations of ratings of the creative quality of the products across domains were lower than correlations of ratings and generally were at about the .4 level. Thus, there was some degree of relation across domains, at the same time that there was plenty of room for someone to be strong in one or more domains but not in others. More importantly, perhaps, we found, as we had for the convergent problems, a range of correlations with conventional tests of abilities. As was the case for the correlations obtained with convergent problems, correlations were higher to the extent that problems on the conventional tests were nonentrenched. For example, correlations were higher with fluid than with crystallized ability tests, and correlations were higher, the more novel the fluid test was. Even the highest correlations, however, were only at the .5 level, suggesting that tests of creative intelligence tap skills beyond those measured even by relatively novel kinds of items on conventional tests of intelligence.

Creative-thinking skills can be taught, and in a collaborative endeavor with Wendy Williams, we have devised a program for teaching them. Insight skills, a form of creative-thinking skill, can also be taught. In collaborative work with Janet Davidson, we divided gifted and nongifted fourth grade children into experimental and control groups. All children took pretests on insightful thinking. Then some of the children received their regular school instruction whereas others received instruction on insight skills. After the instruction of whichever kind, all children took a posttest on insight skills. We found that children taught how to solve the insight problems using knowledge-acquisition components gained more from pretest to posttest than did students who were not so taught.

Tests of creative intelligence go beyond tests of analytical intelligence in measuring performance on tasks that require individuals to deal with relatively novel situations. But how about situations that are relatively familiar, but in a practical rather than an academic domain? Can we measure intelligence in the practical domain, and if so, what is the relation of practical intelligence to intelligence in more academic kinds of domains?

## Practical Intelligence

Practical intelligence involves individuals' applying their abilities to the kinds of problems that confront them in daily life, such as on the job or in the home (Sternberg, Forsythe, Hedlund, Horvath, Snook, Williams, Wagner, & Grigorenko, 2000). Practical intelligence involves applying the components of intelligence to experience so as to (a) adapt to, (b) shape, and (c) select environments. Adaptation is involved when one changes oneself to suit the environment. Shaping is involved when one changes the environment to suit oneself. And selection is involved when one decides to seek out another environment that is a better match to one's needs, abilities, and desires. People differ in their balance of adaptation, shaping, and selection, and in the competence with which they balance among the three possible courses of action.

Much of our work on practical intelligence has centered on the concept of tacit knowledge. We define this construct, for our purposes, as what one needs to know to work effectively in an environment that one is not explicitly taught and that often is not even verbalized. We represent tacit knowledge in the form of production systems or sequences of ''if–then'' statements that describe procedures one follows in various kinds of everyday situations.

We typically have measured tacit knowledge using work-related problems that present problems one might encounter on the job. We have measured tacit knowledge for both children and adults and, among adults, for people in various occupations such as management, sales, academia, and the military. In a typical tacit-knowledge problem, people are asked to read a story about a problem someone faces and to rate, for each statement in a set of statements, how adequate a solution the statement represents. For example, in a paper-and-pencil measure of tacit knowledge for sales, one of the problems deals with sales of photocopy machines. A relatively inexpensive machine is not moving out of the showroom and has become overstocked. The examinee is asked to rate the quality of various solutions for moving the particular model out of the showroom. In a performance-based measure for sales people, the test taker makes a phone call to a supposed customer, who is actually the examiner. The test taker tries to sell advertising space over the phone. The examiner raises various objections to buying the advertising space. The test taker is evaluated for the quality, rapidity, and fluency of the responses on the telephone.

In collaborative studies with Richard Wagner, we found that practical intelligence as embodied in tacit knowledge increases with experience, but it is profiting from experience, rather than experience per se, that results in increases in scores (Wagner & Sternberg, 1986). Some people can have been in a job for years and still have acquired relatively little tacit knowledge. We also have found that subscores on tests of tacit knowledge—such as for managing oneself, managing others, and managing tasks—correlate significantly with each other. Moreover, scores on various tests of tacit knowledge, such as for academics and managers, are also correlated fairly substantially (at about the .5 level). However, scores on tacit-knowledge tests do not correlate with scores on conventional tests of intelligence, whether the measures used are single-score measures or multiple-ability batteries. Despite their lack of correlation with conventional measures, the scores on tacit-knowledge tests predict performance on the job as well as or better than do conventional psychometric intelligence tests. In one study done at a management training center, the Center for Creative Leadership, we further found that scores on our tests of tacit knowledge for management were the best single predictor of performance on a managerial simulation. In a complex statistical procedure, scores on conventional tests of intelligence, personality, styles, and interpersonal orientation were considered first and scores on the test of tacit knowledge were considered last in predicting success on two simulations of managerial performance. Scores on the test of tacit knowledge were the single best predictor of managerial simulation score. Moreover, they also contributed significantly to the prediction even after everything else was entered first into the equation. In recent work on military leadership with Jennifer Hedlund, Joseph Horvath, Colonel George Forsythe, Wendy Williams, and others, we found that scores on a test of tacit knowledge for military leadership predicted ratings of leadership effectiveness, whereas scores on a conventional test of intelligence and on our tacit-knowledge test for managers did not significantly predict the ratings of effectiveness (Sternberg et al., 2000).

Craig Smith, Michael Barnes, and I also have done studies of social intelligence, which is viewed in the theory of successful intelligence as a part of practical intelligence (Sternberg & Smith, 1988; Sternberg & Barnes, 1988). In these studies, individuals were presented with photos and were asked to make judgments about the photos. In one kind of photo, they were asked to evaluate whether a male–female couple was a genuine couple (i.e., really involved in a romantic relationship) or a phony couple posed by the experimenters. In another kind of photo, they were asked to indicate which of two individuals was the other's supervisor. We found females to be superior to males on these tasks. Scores on the two tasks did not correlate with scores on conventional ability tests, nor did they correlate with each other, suggesting a substantial degree of domain specificity in the task.

Practical-intelligence skills can be taught. Williams, Blythe, White, Li, Gardner, and I have developed a program for teaching practical intellectual skills, aimed at middle-school students, that explicitly teaches students "practical intelligence for school" in the contexts of doing homework, taking tests, reading, and writing (Williams et al., 1996). We have evaluated the program in a variety of settings and have found that students taught via the program outperform students in control groups who did not receive the instruction.

## Combining Analytical, Creative, and Practical Intelligence

The studies described above looked at analytical, creative, and practical intelligence separately. But a full validation of the theory of successful intelligence would require research that looks at all three aspects of intelligence in conjunction. To date, we have done two such sets of studies.

In one set of studies in collaboration with Michel Ferrari, Pam Clinkenbeard, and Elena Grigorenko, we explored the question of whether conventional education in school systematically discriminates against children with creative and practical strengths. Motivating this work was the belief that the systems in schools strongly tend to favor children with strengths in memory and analytical abilities (Sternberg, Ferrari, Clinkenbeard, & Grigorenko, 1996; Sternberg, Grigorenko, Ferrari, & Clinkenbeard, 1999).

We devised a test for high school students of analytical, creative, and practical abilities that consisted of both multiple-choice and essay items. The multiple-choice items required the three kinds of thinking in three content domains: verbal, quantitative, and figural. Thus there were nine multiple-choice and three essay subtests. The test was administered to 324 children around the United States and in some other countries who were identified by their schools as gifted by any standard whatsoever. Children were selected for a summer program in (college-level) psychology if they fell into one of five ability groupings: high analytical, high creative, high practical, high balanced (high in all three abilities), or low balanced (low in all three abilities). Students who came to Yale were then divided into four instructional groups. Students in all four instructional groups used the same introductory psychology textbook [a preliminary version of Sternberg (1995)] and listened to the same psychology lectures. What differed among them was the type of afternoon discussion section to which they were assigned. They were assigned to an instructional condition that emphasized either memory, analytical, creative, or practical instruction. For example, in the memory condition, they might be asked to describe the main tenets of a major theory of depression. In the analytical condition, they might be asked to compare and contrast two theories of depression. In the creative condition, they might be asked to formulate their own theory of depression. In the practical condition, they might be asked how they could use what they had learned about depression to help a friend who was depressed.

Students in all four instructional conditions were evaluated in terms of their performance on homework, a midterm exam, a final exam, and an independent project. Each type of work was evaluated for memory, analytical, creative, and practical quality. Thus, all students were evaluated in exactly the same way.

Our results suggested the utility of the theory of successful intelligence. First, we observed when the students arrived at Yale that the students in the high creative and high practical groups were much more diverse in terms of racial, ethnic, socioeconomic, and educational backgrounds than were the students in the high-analytical group. In other words, just by expanding the range of abilities we measured, we discovered more intellectual strengths than would have been apparent through a conventional test. Moreover, the kinds of students identified as strong differed in terms of populations from which they were drawn in comparison with students identified as strong solely by analytical measures.

We found the general factor of intelligence to be very weak, suggesting that the general factor is probably relevant only when a fairly narrow range of abilities is measured, as is typically the case with conventional tests. We found that testing format had a large effect on results: Multiple-choice tests tend to correlate with other multiple-choice tests, almost without regard to what they measure. Essay tests show only weak correlations with multiple choice, however. We further found that after we controlled for modality of testing (multiple-choice versus essay), the correlations between the analytical, creative, and practical sections were very weak and generally nonsignificant, supporting the relative independence of the various abilities. We found that all three ability tests—analytical, creative, and practical—significantly predicted course performance. When multiple-regression analysis was used, at least two of these ability measures contributed significantly to the prediction of each of the measures of achievement. Perhaps as a reflection of the difficulty of deemphasizing the analytical way of teaching, one of the significant predictors was always the analytical score. (However, in a replication of our study with low-income African-American students from New York, Deborah Coates of the City University of New York found a different pattern of results. Her data indicated that the practical tests were better predictors of course performance than were the analytical measures, suggesting that what ability test predicts what criterion depends on population as well as mode of teaching.) Most importantly, there was an aptitude–treatment interaction whereby students who were placed in instructional conditions that better matched their pattern of abilities outperformed students who were mismatched. In other words, when students are taught in a way that fits how they think, they do better in school. Children with creative and practical abilities, who are almost never taught or assessed in a way that matches their pattern of abilities, may be at a disadvantage in course after course, year after year.

In a follow-up study with Bruce Torff and Elena Grigorenko, we looked at learning of social studies and science by third graders and eighth graders (Sternberg, Torff, & Grigorenko, 1998a, 1998b). The third graders were students in a very low income neighborhood in Raleigh, North Carolina. The eighth graders were students who were largely middle to upper-middle class studying in Baltimore, Maryland, and Fresno, California. In this study, students were assigned to one of three instructional conditions. In the first condition, they were taught the course that basically they would have learned had we not intervened. The emphasis in the course was on memory. In a second condition, they were taught in a way that emphasized critical (analytical) thinking. In the third condition, they were taught in a way that emphasized analytical, creative, and practical thinking. All students' performance was assessed for memory learning (through multiple-choice assessments) as well as for analytical, creative, and practical learning (through performance assessments).

As expected, we found that students in the successful-intelligence (analytical, creative, practical) condition outperformed the other students in terms of the performance assessments. One could argue that this result merely reflected the way they were taught. Nevertheless, the result suggested that teaching for these kinds of thinking succeeded. More important, however, was the result that children in the successful-intelligence condition outperformed the other children even on the multiple-choice memory tests. In other words, to the extent that one's goal is just to maximize children's memory for information, teaching for successful intelligence is still superior. It enables children to capitalize on their strengths and to correct or to compensate for their weaknesses, and it allows children to encode material in a variety of interesting ways.

Thus the results of two sets of studies suggest that the theory of successful intelligence is valid not just in its parts but also as a whole. Moreover, the results suggest that the theory can make a difference not only in laboratory tests, but in school classrooms as well.

## CONCLUSION

The time has come to move beyond conventional theories of intelligence and its development. In this chapter I have provided data suggesting that conventional theories and tests of intelligence are incomplete. The general factor of intelligence may be an artifact of limitations in populations of individuals tested, types of materials with which they are tested, and types of methods used in testing. Indeed, our studies show that even when one wants to predict school performance, the conventional tests are fairly limited in their predictive validity. I have proposed a theory of successful intelligence that fares well in construct validations, whether one tests in the laboratory, in schools, or in the workplace. The greatest obstacle to our moving on is in vested interests in a way of thinking that is no longer working, if it ever worked at all. If we want to maximize individuals' achievement in school and in the workplace, new notions are needed. We now have ways to move beyond conventional notions of intelligence; we need only the will.

## Teachers' Questions and Answers

**Q:** As an elementary school teacher, how could I enhance my students' analytical, practical, and creative skills? What kinds of interventions and exercises would you recommend?

**A:** Fortunately, we have written a book that addresses this question. The book is Teaching for Successful Intelligence (Sternberg & Grigorenko, 2000). In the book, we show the kinds of strategies that can be used. To develop analytical skills, children are encouraged to analyze, compare and contrast, judge, critique, and evaluate. To develop creative skills, children are encouraged to create, invent, explore, discover, and imagine. To develop practical skills, children are encouraged to use, apply, implement, and put into practice.

**Q:** Often, especially in highly competitive colleges and universities, the importance given to SAT scores far outweighs any other parameter used in the admissions process. In my experience, high scores on these standardized tests do not necessarily translate to outstanding performance in college. Can you comment on the validity of this observation? In the light of your findings do you think that universities ought to expand their selection criteria to include dimensions of successful intelligence? Do you see any evidence that colleges and universities may be moving in this direction?

**A:** Yes to everything! We are currently working with the College Board to experiment with new tests that we have developed that measure creative and practical in addition to analytical abilities. We hope that someday these tests will supplement measures such as the SAT. Ultimately, we hope to see a test battery that measures the complete set of skills proposed in the theory of successful intelligence.

# References

Carroll, J. B. (1993). *Human cognitive abilities: A survey of factor-analytic studies*. New York: Cambridge University Press.

Ceci, S. J., & Liker, J. (1986). Academic and nonacademic intelligence: An experimental separation. In R. J. Sternberg & R. K. Wagner, (Eds.), *Practical intelligence: Nature and origins of competence in the everyday world* (pp. 119–142). New York: Cambridge University Press.

Feuerstein, R. (1979). *The dynamic assessment of retarded performers: The learning potential assessment device theory, instruments, and techniques*. Baltimore, MD: University Park Press.

Greenfield, P. M. (1997). You can't take it with you: Why abilities assessments don't cross cultures. *American Psychologist, 52*, 1115–1124.

Jensen, A. R. (1998). *The g factor: The science of mental ability*. Westport, CT: Praeger/Greenwoood.

Lave, J. (1997). The culture of acquisition and the practice of understanding. In D. I. Kirshner & J. A. Whitson (Eds.), *Situated cognition: Social, semiotic, and psychological perspectives* (pp. 17–35). Mahwah, NJ: Erlbaum.

Nuñes, T. (1994). Street intelligence. In R. J. Sternberg (Ed.), *Encyclopedia of human intelligence* (Vol. 2, pp. 1045–1049). New York: Macmillan.

Okagaki, L., & Sternberg, R. J. (1991). Cultural and parental influences on cognitive development. In L. Okagaki & R. J. Sternberg (Eds.), *Directors of development: Influences on the development of children's thinking* (pp. 101–120). Hillsdale, NJ: Erlbaum.

Okagaki, L., & Sternberg, R. J. (1993). Parental beliefs and children's school performance. *Child Development, 64*, 36–56.

Piaget, J. (1972). *The psychology of intelligence*. Totowa, NJ: Littlefield Adams.

Rogoff, B. (1990). *Apprenticeship in thinking: Cognitive development in social context*. New York: Oxford University Press.

Spearman, C. (1904). 'General intelligence,' objectively determined and measured. *American Journal of Psychology, 15*, 201–293.

Sternberg, R. J. (1982). Nonentrenchment in the assessment of intellectual giftedness. *Gifted Child Quarterly, 26*, 63–67.

Sternberg, R. J. (1985). *Beyond IQ: A triarchic theory of human intelligence*. New York: Cambridge University Press.

Sternberg, R. J. (1987a). Most vocabulary is learned from context. In M. G. McKeown & M. E. Curtis (Eds.), *The nature of vocabulary acquisition* (pp. 89–105). Hillsdale, NJ: Erlbaum.

Sternberg, R. J. (1987b). The psychology of verbal comprehension. In R. Glaser (Ed.), *Advances in instructional psychology* (Vol. 3, pp. 97–151). Hillsdale, NJ: Erlbaum.

Sternberg, R. J. (1997). *Successful intelligence*. New York: Plume.

Sternberg, R. J. (1999). Successful intelligence: Finding a balance. *Trends in Cognitive Sciences, 3*, 436–442.

Sternberg, R. J., & Barnes, M. (Eds.) (1988). *The psychology of love*. New Haven, CT: Yale University Press.

Sternberg, R. J., Ferrari, M., Clinkenbeard, P. R., & Grigorenko, E. L. (1996). Identification, instruction, and assessment of gifted children: A construct validation of a triarchic model. *Gifted Child Quarterly, 40*, 129–137.

Sternberg, R. J., Forsythe, G. B., Hedlund, J., Horvath, J., Snook, S., Williams, W. M., Wagner, R. K., & Grigorenko, E. L. (2000). *Practical intelligence in everyday life*. New York: Cambridge University Press.

Sternberg, R. J., & Gastel, J. (1989a). Coping with novelty in human intelligence: An empirical investigation. *Intelligence, 13*, 187–197.

Sternberg, R. J., & Gastel, J. (1989b). If dancers ate their shoes: Inductive reasoning with factual and counterfactual premises. *Memory and Cognition, 17*, 1–10.

Sternberg, R. J., Grigorenko, E. L., Ferrari, M., & Clinkenbeard, P. (1999). A triarchic analysis of an aptitude–treatment interaction. *European Journal of Psychological Assessment, 15*, 1–11.

Sternberg, R. J., Grigorenko, E. L., Ngorosho, D., Tuntufye, E., Mbise, A., Nokes, C., Jukes, M., & Bundy, D. A. (in press). Assessing intellectual potential in rural Tanzania school children. *Intelligence*.

Sternberg, R. J., & Lubart, T. I. (1995). *Defying the crowd: Cultivating creativity in a culture of conformity*. New York: Free Press.

Sternberg, R. J., Nokes, K., Geissler, P. W., Prince, R., Okatcha, F., Bundy, D. A., & Grigorenko, E. L. (2001). The relationship between academic and practical intelligence: A case study in Kenya. *Intelligence, 29*, 401–418.

Sternberg, R. J., & Powell, J. S. (1983). Comprehending verbal comprehension. *American Psychologist, 38*, 878–893.

Sternberg, R. J., & Rifkin, B. (1979). The development of analogical reasoning processes. *Journal of Experimental Child Psychology, 27*, 195–232.

Sternberg, R. J., & Smith, E. E. (Eds.) (1988). *The psychology of human thought*. New York: Cambridge University Press.

Sternberg, R. J., Torff, B., & Grigorenko, E. L. (1998a). Teaching for successful intelligence raises school achievement. *Phi Delta Kappan, 79*, 667–669.

Sternberg, R. J., Torff, B., & Grigorenko, E. L. (1998b). Teaching triarchically improves school achievement. *Journal of Educational Psychology, 90*, 374–384.

Tetewsky, S. J., & Sternberg, R. J. (1986). Conceptual and lexical determinants of nonentrenched thinking. *Journal of Memory and Language, 25*, 202–225.

Vygotsky, L. S. (1978). *Mind in society: The development of higher psychological processes*. Cambridge, MA: Harvard University Press.

Wagner, R. K., & Sternberg, R. J. (1986). Tacit knowledge and intelligence in the everyday world. In R. J. Sternberg & R. K. Wagner (Eds.), *Practical intelligence: Nature and origins of competence in the everyday world* (pp. 51–83). New York: Cambridge University Press.

Williams, W. M., Blythe, T., White, N., Li, J., Sternberg, R. J., & Gardner, H. I. (1996). *Practical intelligence for school: A handbook for teachers of grades 5–8*. New York: HarperCollins.

## Suggested Reading

Ceci, S. J. (1996). *On intelligence...more or less* (expanded edition). Cambridge, MA: Harvard University Press.

Gardner, H. (1983). *Frames of mind: The theory of multiple intelligences*. New York: Basic.

Sternberg, R. J. (1997). *Successful intelligence*. New York: Plume.

# Current Lessons

# Being and Becoming a Good Person: The Role of Emotional Intelligence in Moral Development and Behavior

DAVID A. PIZARRO AND PETER SALOVEY

*Department of Psychology, Yale University, New Haven, Connecticut*

There can be little doubt that one of the primary concerns of parents and educators is that children under their care grow to develop a strong sense of moral responsibility. Within the past few years especially, a fear that something can go wrong—that the process by which children acquire this sense could fail—has led to increased attention to the formation of moral character. Nationwide, programs have been instituted that implement a standardized curriculum of moral and values education in classrooms. This has been due in part to the media exposure of shocking incidents involving children (in many cases very young children) acting violently in schools across the nation, but can also be understood as an attempt to apply what researchers have learned about moral development over the past decades to the home and the classroom. The topic itself has fascinated students of psychology for more than a century, and has inspired a great deal of research within the field. Indeed, it can be argued that moral development is one of the most important processes for psychologists to study, as one of the most critical conditions for the survival of society is that its members learn the differences between right and wrong.

Please address correspondence to Peter Salovey, Department of Psychology, P.O. Box 208205, New Haven, CT 06520–8205. E-mail: peter.salovey@yale.edu.

The study of emotion in psychology, on the other hand, has ebbed and flowed, enjoying periods of flourishing theory and research, yet also spending time on the "backburner" of psychological thinking. Despite its cyclical nature, the study of emotion has yielded valuable information to our understanding of human thinking and behavior. In recent years, psychology has experienced a surge of interest concerning the role of emotions in various psychological processes, including their role in judgment and decision making, and motivation. Part of this rebirth in interest about emotions has been due to a public fascination with popular theories of emotional intelligence and emotional competency—theories that describe a set of emotional skills that are important for social functioning. The surge of public interest in emotional intelligence has been accompanied by a plethora of books and articles on the topic (reviewed by Mayer, Salovey, & Caruso, 2000). Emotional intelligence has been implicated by many as an important skill or set of skills necessary for social adjustment and happiness, yet until present times relatively ignored. Some have gone as far as to equate emotional intelligence with moral character, making the terms "emotionally intelligent" and "moral" nearly synonymous (e.g., Goleman, 1995; Saarni, 1999). This interest has raised intriguing questions concerning the role emotions and emotion-related skills play in our moral lives. This chapter seeks to shed light on some of these important issues. Among the questions we address are, What role do various emotions play in the moral development and education of children, as well as in the moral decision-making of adults? And, is it necessary to be emotionally intelligent to be a moral person? Before we do so, however, let us first take a look at what we mean by "emotional intelligence."

## WHAT IS EMOTIONAL INTELLIGENCE?

Although emotions play a large role in the daily life of all people, it is clear that there are large individual differences in the way people deal with emotions; some people seem to be more adept emotional managers than others, for example. For instance, receiving a bad grade on a project might incite one child to intense anger, causing the child to act out in class, while another child, although angered at first, might use his or her feelings to motivate working harder on the next project. The various emotion-related skills that are employed by individuals have been grouped together and labeled *emotional intelligence* (Mayer & Salovey, 1997; Salovey & Mayer, 1990). The emotional intelligence framework was proposed as an attempt to organize the growing body of research on emotions and their influence on cognition and behavior into a single theory that highlighted the way individuals use these skills in their everyday lives. Emotional intelligence has been divided into four main branches, each focusing on a different set of emotional skills: (a) the ability to perceive, appraise, and express emotion; (b) the ability to use feelings in cognitive activities; (c) the ability to understand emotion and emotional knowledge; and (d) the ability to regulate or manage emotions to promote emotional and intellectual growth (Mayer & Salovey, 1997).

Many theorists, researchers, and journalists eagerly picked up on emotional intelligence, and framed it as a skill that was of critical importance to be a caring, moral, and otherwise well-adjusted person (e.g., Goleman, 1995). This characterization is not at all surprising. After all, perceiving, generating, and regulating emotions are generally things we do to maintain and improve relationships with others. Very often we enlist our abilities at managing emotions when we become angry with a best friend or have an argument with our spouse, for instance. In these situations, the ability to understand how the other person is feeling and to regulate our emotional reactions comes in very handy, and serves to fulfill the goals we have of remaining friends or of staying married for longer than a few months. It seems natural, then, that understanding how emotion-related skills affect social relations should be of primary importance to those interested in studying emotional intelligence.

The relationship between emotional intelligence and moral character is, however, not as clear-cut as might first appear. The same emotional skills that make some individuals good, caring people can also be used to achieve more nefarious goals. Criminals who are masters at deception or con artists who are trained to manipulate others may in some ways be among those highest in at least some of these emotional skills (Salovey & Mayer, 1990). Any discussion of how emotions and emotional skills relate to moral development and behavior must take this into account.

## A (VERY) BRIEF HISTORY OF MORAL PSYCHOLOGY AND EMOTION

Although research on moral development has grown enormously within the last 50 or so years, most of the interest has come from researchers within the tradition known as *cognitive-developmental*. Building on the work of Piaget (1932), Kohlberg (1969), and others, researchers from this tradition have had the strongest influence in the field of moral psychology. Unfortunately for those of us interested in emotions, this tradition has largely ignored the role of feelings in the way children grow to become moral individuals. Rather, it has focused on the development of the child's cognitive abilities and the way these developmental changes affect the child's moral world view. Kohlberg, for instance, viewed the child as progressing from an early morality based on parental authority to a fully autonomous morality, based on an understanding of universal moral principles. Although Kohlberg sometimes touched on the topic of emotions, his theory never adequately sought to describe the role of emotions in the development of a mature morality.

Within the last 20 years, however, social and developmental psychologists have turned their attention to emotional processes in the social development of children and in the judgments and behaviors of adults. Developmental researchers specifically have sought a description of how emotions work in fostering a child's moral sensibilities. There are at least two reasons why theorists consider emotions important for the study of moral development and behavior. First, emotions are powerful sources of motivation. In other words, most emotions are associated with what has been labeled an *action tendency*, or a propensity to engage in certain actions when experiencing a specific emotion. For instance, anger is associated with the tendency to attack and fright with the tendency to escape (Lazarus, 1991). Emotions such as empathy and guilt motivate prosocial behaviors [constructive behaviors that are also generally understood as moral (Eisenberg, 1986)]. Helping a person in need and apologizing for hurting someone are examples of these kinds of behaviors. Knowing in what circumstances emotions motivate us to do good is therefore an important component of understanding moral behavior in general. Even cognitive theories recognize this role of emotions as an energy source for moral functioning.

Because emotions are powerful motivators of action, they are also important mechanisms that aid in the process of socialization (the process by which children come to internalize the values, norms, and morals of their parents and society at large). Emotions, as naturally occurring events in children, are resources that can help in the transmission of norms and values. By inducing emotions such as guilt, empathy, shame, and even disgust (see Rozin, Haidt, & McCauley, 1993), parents can mold children's responses to behaviors, events, and people. In time, these emotional reactions come to occur naturally in the child in appropriate situations, and act as internal sources of motivation and constraint. It is these two features of emotion, their motivational arousal and their role in socialization, that have made the study of emotion an important area of inquiry to researchers interested in moral development and prosocial behavior.

When discussing the emotional intelligence of morality, we focus on those emotions that seem to have a distinctly moral nature, such as empathy and guilt. This is not to say that emotions such as happiness and sadness do not affect our moral lives. Certainly, we become happy when we do good things for others and sad when we ponder the misfortune of others. However, for the purposes of our discussion, we focus on the emotions investigators have generally lumped together as morally relevant. In our discussion, we organize the functions of these various emotions using the four branches of the emotional intelligence framework (Mayer & Salovey, 1997; Salovey, Woolery, & Mayer, 2000).

## PERCEIVING AND APPRAISING EMOTIONS

When discussing moral rights and wrongs, there seems to be room for a lot of disagreement. Issues such as abortion, the death penalty, and same-sex unions, for example, seem to draw a moral dividing line across our nation. Fortunately, however, there exists much more agreement about issues concerning right and wrong than it might seem. For instance, causing innocent individuals to suffer is rarely seen as anything but a morally reprehensible action. Because moral events usually center around the presence of victimization, encountering the suffering of innocent others in our daily lives is a strong indication that a moral event is taking place. It is generally not the case, however, that people wear signs around their neck that announce their pain, such as "I just got dumped by my girlfriend" and "My favorite aunt just passed away." Rather, there are subtle signals sent by those individuals that clue us in to their distress. These signals act as efficient forms of communication. However, as may seem obvious, a signal must be perceived and understood for it to be effective. The ability to perceive emotions accurately in others is thus a very important emotional skill, arguably the most fundamental skill of all when it comes to human relationships. This ability to know how others are feeling has been labeled *empathy* by many researchers (Eisenberg & Miller, 1991; Feshbach & Roe, 1968; Hoffman, 1987), and has been the most well-researched of all the so-called moral emotions.

What is empathy? Some researchers have defined empathy strictly in terms of the ability to take the perspective of others, a distinctly cognitive ability. However, empathy can be seen as having both a cognitive component and an emotional component, that of actually feeling an emotion that is more appropriate to the other person's situation (this is the definition offered by Hoffman, 1998). In fact, the word "empathy" literally means, "to feel oneself into" (Wispé, 1987). For our purposes, we restrict our definition of empathy to the emotional arousal one feels when presented with the emotional experience of another, particularly the distress of another. It is this empathic arousal that allows us to feel suffering when others are suffering and, thus, motivates us to help the individual in distress.

Most people are able to experience empathy, but some are better than others. For instance, there is evidence that some antisocial youth suffer from an inability to feel empathy, an "empathic dysfunction." As Gibbs (1987) states, "Empathy is available in most [juvenile] offenders but is not readily elicited and tends to be either an isolated impulse or a mawkish sentiment. In either case, the empathy is superficial and erratic; when it lingers, it is readily suppressed by self-centered motives or aggressive impulses. (p. 303)." It has also been argued that psychopathic individuals suffer from a lack of the capacity for empathic affect (Blair, 1995). This serves as further reason to consider empathy a truly moral emotion: if you cannot feel empathy, chances are you are not a very moral person.

What influences the ability to experience empathy? It is clear that a capacity for empathy is not all-or-nothing; individuals vary as to their degree of empathic responsiveness. Various factors have been pointed to as important for the development of empathy (for a review see Barnett, 1987; Davis, 1996, pp. 62–81). These include genetics (e.g., Matthews, Batson, Horn, & Rosenman, 1981), childhood temperament (e.g., Mehrabin, 1980), a stable and positive relationship with a caregiver (e.g., Mussen & Eisenberg-Berg, 1977), and disciplining techniques that focus on inducing empathy in children (e.g., Hoffman & Saltzstein, 1967). Summarizing the research on the development of empathy, Barnett (1987, p. 156) concluded:

> The development of empathy and related responses would appear to thrive in an environment that (1) satisfies the child's own emotional needs, (2) encourages the child to identify, experience, and express a broad range of emotions, and (3) provides numerous opportunities for the child to observe and interact with others who, through their words and actions, encourage emotional sensitivity and responsiveness to others.

Parents and educators should therefore strive to create an environment in which children are encouraged to take the perspective of others, to imagine what the other person is feeling, and to be active in speaking to their children about emotions.

Before we conclude that the capacity for empathy is sufficient to be a moral individual, we must discuss its limitations. As was mentioned above, empathic arousal motivates us to alleviate the suffering of others. It seems as if the distress we feel when in the presence of distressed others can be alleviated only by helping the individual in need. In fact, individuals tend to help even if there is an easier escape from the empathic distress, for instance, by leaving the situation (e.g., Batson, Dyck, Brandt, Batson, Powell, McMaster, & Griffitt, 1991). People high in dispositional empathy (people with an "empathic personality") are also more likely to engage in helping behavior (Davis, Mitchell, Hall, Lothert, Snapp, & Meyer, 1999). However, being "high" in empathy is not a surefire qualification for being a moral individual, nor is it a guarantee that a person will always do the right thing. One of the interesting features of empathy is that it is more easily elicited for people that we perceive as similar to us (e.g., Feshbach & Roe, 1968) and that we view as innocent (Betancourt, 1990). Conversely, the more different we perceive others to be, and the more at fault we think they are, the less likely we are to experience empathy for them and, thus, the less likely we are to help them if they are in need. This "empathic bias," as Hoffman (1987) has labeled it, is one reason we cannot always rely on our emotional reactions as a reliable guide to moral truth. Sometimes, we have to try very hard to feel empathy for others, by imagining ourselves in their position and by focusing on similarities rather than differences. Indeed, one of the primary tasks of parents and educators should be to make the empathic response available in children regardless of perceived differences between themselves and the victim.

Another problem with empathy is that sometimes we feel empathy for individuals who we know do not deserve it. For instance, we may feel sorry for a criminal who had a rough childhood, only to find out that he committed numerous brutal murders. In this situation, felt empathy must be "squashed" so that the motivational consequences (helping the murderer) dissipate.

When speaking of empathy as a moral emotion, then, one must be careful not to assume that the capability to feel what others are feeling is the same as making mature moral decisions. Indeed, the ability to perceive and appraise emotions in others is an ability that may even be used to manipulate others.

## EMOTIONS THAT HELP US THINK

The idea that emotions are forces that act contrary to reason has plagued Western thinking since the days of the earliest Greek philosophers. Plato (1988) characterized emotions as being akin to wild horses that need to be controlled by the "rational" rider. Freud (1977) also viewed most emotions as strong instinctual forces that must be conquered by the Superego, that portion of the mind that was in charge of matters of conscience. The notion that emotions disrupt cognitive activities persists even today in conceptions of emotional processes (Mandler, 1975; Simon, 1981). For example, labeling someone as being "too emotional" is synonymous with calling him or her irrational. Similarly, crimes of passion are punished less severely than cold, calculated acts because emotions are seen as temporarily seizing the will of the individual, rendering him or her unable to make informed decisions in the planning of actions.

Although there are some investigators who continue to maintain a strong position concerning the divide between reason and passion (e.g., Metcalfe & Mischel, 1999), most researchers agree that emotions often serve to facilitate reasoning, rather than hinder it (e.g., Damasio, 1994; Salovey & Mayer, 1990). Emotions prioritize events, pointing the individual toward problems in the environment that are of immediate importance (Easterbrook, 1959; Leeper, 1948). In this sense emotions serve to aid judgment, by steering thoughts in the right direction. For instance, negative moods encourage careful, deliberate ways of thinking, causing people to elaborate more on problems than they would in a more positive mood. The presence of happy moods, on the other hand, encourages a more creative style of thinking, leading some to listen to happy, upbeat music to facilitate creative thoughts (Isen, 1993; Palfai & Salovey, 1993; Schwarz, 1990).

Stated simply, emotional reactions focus our cognitive resources on the problem at hand. It is no different with moral emotions. Moral emotions prioritize thinking about our moral principles and beliefs, motivate appropriate moral judgments, and prepare us to take moral action. When we become distressed at the sight of another individual suffering, the negative arousal mobilizes our mental resources and facilitates thinking concerning moral questions such as why the individual is suffering, whose fault is it that she is suffering, and what course of action should be taken to help her. For example, when, on a winter day, we come across a man who is obviously cold and hungry, and who appears to be homeless, the empathy we feel turns our thoughts toward the plight of the homeless and the inequalities of society. Or, it may cause us to pronounce harsh moral judgments on the individual, attributing his or her position to some flaw of character. In either case, the immediate felt empathy is what served to stimulate thinking about the moral implications of the situation.

If empathy generally motivates us to help, guilt is what motivates us to make amends, either by seeking to repair the damage to a valued relationship, as when we ask forgiveness for offending a friend, or by correcting our behavior to be consistent with our principles concerning how one should act. Guilt is a negative evaluation of a specific behavior, and usually occurs when we feel as if we have violated one of our moral principles, for example, by hurting someone else or by otherwise acting in a manner unbecoming of how we think we should act. In contrast to shame, which usually causes us to focus on ourselves, guilt shifts the focus to the transgression and is associated with a desire to undo what has been done (Tangney, 1999). For instance, a young child who feels guilty for hitting his best friend will most likely find it hard to spend too much time organizing his baseball cards. The guilt he is experiencing will turn his thoughts toward how he hurt his friend and to what he should do to make things better. Similarly, if we have hurt the feelings of a good friend, we are easily distracted if we try to work, because our thoughts are constantly turning to the damage we have done. Although one can have maladaptive levels of guilt, in normal individuals guilt is an incredibly adaptive emotion, because it maintains relationship health by motivating individuals to repair any damage done to the relationship.

Once an emotion such as empathy is aroused in an individual, and thoughts turn to matters of a moral nature, one will naturally draw conclusions regarding the situation (Hoffman, 1998). Moral judgments, the conclusions drawn by individuals concerning the moral rightness or wrongness of actions or events, often influence the presence of subsequent emotions. If we feel empathy in the presence of a distressed other and realize that her or his distress is due to the unjust actions of some third party, our empathy is likely to turn into "empathic anger." For example, when viewing footage of police brutality directed toward an innocent African American man, the empathic distress we feel may turn into anger at such a violation of basic rights. If, on the other hand, we feel empathy for the distress of another, but realize that *we* are the cause of the others' distress, empathy transforms into guilt. For example, the distress aroused when seeing our younger siblings crying uncontrollably quickly turns into guilt when we realize that they are crying because of something we said. Empathy combines with attributions of blame and other moral judgments, and it is the motivational power of the emotion in combination with our judgments that informs our subsequent actions.

The knowledge that moral emotions will mobilize our thinking concerning moral issues (such as the plight of the homeless or the importance of not hurting those we love) is knowledge that can be used to serve our individual moral goals. By taking the perspective of other people, for instance, we can make ourselves feel empathy for someone with whom we may not have otherwise concerned ourselves. A pragmatic use of these emotional skills is therefore an advantage, in that the emotions encourage the critical thinking necessary to work through moral situations and moral dilemmas, and they harness the full motivational force of the emotion.

## EMPLOYING EMOTIONAL KNOWLEDGE

Human interactions are full of complex emotional information. The ability to understand and discern this emotional information adds quality and depth to our own lives, and allows us to understand better the lives of others. Knowledge such as what emotion an artist is trying to convey through her work or of the complex combination of emotions that are making us feel a certain way is considered a sign of a healthy emotional life. Knowledge concerning how emotions work and are communicated and the way that people employ this knowledge is organized under this third branch of emotional intelligence. Among the skills are the ability to define emotions, the ability to understand complex blends of emotions, and an accurate understanding of the likely transitions between emotions (Mayer & Salovey, 1997).

How is this emotional knowledge used in moral life? Thus far we have discussed how emotions work as motivation through their immediate action, as in the empathy we feel when we see someone in distress or the guilt we feel immediately after we hurt someone. But emotions also motivate us from a distance. In other words, merely anticipating that we might feel an emotion is sometimes enough to affect our present behavior. A child who is thinking about cheating on an exam might be motivated not to do so because she knows that she would feel guilty immediately following the act. In this case, knowledge of the emotional consequences of an act becomes an important determinant for whether or not a person will be motivated to avoid performing an "immoral" action.

This type of emotional knowledge, although crucial when it comes to behaving morally, takes time to develop. One of the most interesting findings concerning children's knowledge of moral emotions is the so-called "happy victimizer" effect (Arsenio & Kramer, 1992). Very young children expect that a wrongdoer will feel good after having committed a moral transgression. There is a clear age trend in this phenomenon; as children develop (usually between the ages of 6 and 10) they come to believe that a wrongdoer will feel badly after having committed a transgression. The development of this ability is critical; if a child is unaware of the emotional consequences of his or her act, there will be little motivation to avoid it (or to perform it). Pointing to the emotional consequences of an act can serve to strengthen the connections between transgressions and the feelings of guilt. In fact, there is evidence that disciplining children by pointing out how they feel after an act (what is called inductive discipline) is the most efficient form of discipline, because it pairs emotional consequences with certain acts.

A second type of emotional knowledge, which takes time to develop as well, is the knowledge of complex combinations of emotional states. This knowledge is one of the most important feats of mature emotional and cognitive development. When, for instance, we see an Olympic athlete in a track race fall, we are aware not only of the physical pain he is experiencing, but also of the disappointment he must feel at achieving so much and failing at such a critical moment, and also of the possible wound to his pride caused by falling in front of an audience of millions. Such an understanding of the complex emotions experienced by the individual is important in informing our subsequent actions. Should we help ease his physical pain? What types of things should we say to him to ease his emotional pain? Should we remain quiet rather than speak to him? An inability to answer these complex questions concerning the individual involved renders our helping abilities rather useless. If we were unable to figure out some answers to these questions, our helping behaviors would be similar to those of young children, who often offer a safety blanket or a favorite toy (decidedly not the kind of help that most adults would want). Adequately helping others means knowing how they may be feeling in the larger context of their life experiences.

## EFFECTIVELY REGULATING EMOTIONS IN OURSELVES AND IN OTHERS

### Regulating Emotions in Ourselves

Emotional regulation is perhaps one of the most important features of emotional intelligence when it comes to moral judgments and behaviors. Emotional reactions sometimes need to be guided in the right direction, lest they steer us into the wrong one. This is obvious for negative emotions such as anger; if anger is not regulated, it can motivate us to act inappropriately. It is less obvious why we would need to regulate emotions such as empathy. After all, empathy is a good thing, is it not?

This discussion should be prefaced with a point concerning emotions that is especially useful when discussing moral emotions. Sometimes emotions are elicited almost automatically (see Hodges & Wegner, 1997). When survival is threatened, we react immediately with fear. In the same manner, when the desire for social approval is threatened (e.g., by someone who made us look foolish in public), we immediately feel angry. We also have immediate and automatic reactions of empathy, disgust, jealousy, and nearly every other emotion. The bright side is that human beings are not mindless animals condemned to act on our every impulse, so we are constantly able to choose the emotions that are appropriate and those that are not by stepping outside the emotion and deciding whether or not it is appropriate, then regulating it accordingly (see Gross, 1999). If we have an emotion that we believe we should not be having, or at least that we think would be wrong to act on, we can enlist a higher-order desire to regulate that emotion. If we have an immediate emotional reaction, such as anger, and with it comes the desire to act on that emotion (attack our offender), we can step outside the emotion and act as judges of it. We can have desires about desires or emotions about emotions (Gottman, Katz, & Hooven, 1997). In the case of the anger, it is the greater desire to do the right thing that motivates us to regulate our emotional reaction.

Sometimes, it is the case that the immediate emotional reaction and the greater desires match up with each other nicely. For instance, the motivation brought on by empathy (the desire to help the person in need) goes along very well with our greater desire to "do good," and the end result is that we perform the action. In the cases where they do not match up, however, our skills in regulating our emotions are called into play, and we take on the role of emotional managers. When we become angry with a boss, for instance, we know that we cannot slap him in the face. Thinking about our anger and turning our thoughts toward constructive ways of dealing with the problem are strategies that are often effective in the regulation of the emotion.

Not all people have mastered this skill, as one might guess. Oftentimes, individuals allow inappropriate emotions to exert their full motivational force, with the end result sometimes being disastrous. The recently coined "road rage" phenomenon, where drivers become so angry that they stop at nothing until they satisfy their revenge on other drivers, certainly attests to the unfortunate consequences of poor emotional regulation.

This discussion of emotional regulation should not be taken as evidence that emotions are bad and that by regulating them we necessarily mean eliminating their effects. On the contrary, emotional reactions that are channeled constructively can act as excellent sources of motivation. Anger at the presence of societal injustices, when effectively regulated (which may mean letting ourselves experience the anger fully rather than suppressing it), can motivate individuals to great moral achievements, for instance. In fact, there are some instances in which regulating an emotion, by not allowing ourselves to fully experience it, may have drastic consequences for ourselves and others. For instance, suppressing anger is thought to affect various physiological mechanisms that are vital to our health (Petrie, Booth, Pennebaker, & Davison, 1995). Similarly, suppressing an emotion such as empathy might have disastrous moral consequences, allowing people to do things they would never otherwise do (such as harm innocent people).

## Regulating Emotions in Others

So far we have talked about the importance of regulating emotions in ourselves, but what about regulating emotions in other people? At first thought, this might seem rather manipulative. However, in everyday life we know individuals who are skilled at manipulating emotions in other people in ways that are considered constructive. For instance, the friend that everyone turns to when they are feeling down is often sought out because of his or her ability to "raise spirits" and make people feel better. Motivational speakers and preachers are also good regulators of emotion in others, and are applauded for these skills. So, while one can certainly see the manipulation that might occur by regulating the emotions of others, by and large people use these skills for the achievement of noble goals.

The ability to regulate the emotions of others is a critical skill when it comes to the socialization of children. As we have mentioned, effective disciplining is often achieved by using children's natural emotional reactions as sources of motivation. Parents can capitalize on these emotional reactions by generating them in children when appropriate. The induction of emotions or moods is something that psychologists interested in emotions often do in an experimental setting. For instance, in our emotions laboratory we often induce moods by asking people to watch sad movie clips or listen to happy music (e.g., Palfai & Salovey, 1993; Salovey, 1992; Salovey & Birnbaum, 1989). Similarly, when disciplining a child, caretakers can take advantage of the ease with which children are likely to experience emotions such as empathy and guilt, and use it to motivate appropriate moral behaviors.

The children of parents that tend to induce emotions such as empathy and guilt when a moral situation arises are more likely to internalize moral norms efficiently (Hoffman & Saltzein, 1967). For instance, pointing out the consequences of stealing, thus inducing empathy for the victim of the theft, is an effective way of teaching children not to steal. By repeatedly inducing empathy in similar situations, children come to associate the act of stealing with empathy for the victim, and this emotional energy provides an internal source of motivation in the children. This type of discipline stands in sharp contrast to disciplinary tactics in which caretakers merely exert their authority over children, threatening them with punishment if they do not act in a moral manner. In any future moral situations, children who were disciplined through the use of inductive methods will continue to act morally even in the absence of external authority or threat, as compared with children who were disciplined merely through an exertion of parental authority. Recent research on children's development of "conscience" has supported these ideas (Kochanska, 1995, 1997).

Empathy and guilt are not the only emotions recruited in the transmission of moral norms. Emotions such as shame and disgust are also implicated. Some authors have pointed to the power of feelings of disgust when it comes to certain moral practices. For instance, vegetarians (who are vegetarian for moral reasons) are more likely to find meat disgusting than vegetarians who become vegetarian for health reasons (Rozin, Markwith, & Stoess, 1997). Inducing disgust over certain practices may be one of the most powerful ways to get children (and adults, as some religious leaders can attest) to stop performing certain behaviors.

Inductive discipline works not merely as simple conditioning, i.e., the pairing of emotions with situations. Through time, caretakers elaborate on the moral principles involved in situations that arouse emotions, focusing on the similarities across situations such as hitting others, stealing, or lying, and teaching the child the appropriate principles involved. By linking moral principles to emotions like this, thinking about moral principles becomes an emotion-laden task, lending the principles greater motivational power. Every time there is a co-occurrence of moral principles with empathic affect, the association causes a bond between the two. Moral principles thus acquire a motivating power that they would not have acquired without the effective pairing of the empathic response. Moral principles come to elicit empathy and guilt, and conversely, empathy and guilt elicit thinking about moral principles, leading Hoffman (1987) to refer to them as "hot cognitions." This may help to explain why emotions become so intense when individuals disagree about their moral beliefs.

## A WORD ABOUT MORAL PRINCIPLES

In our discussion of emotions, we have briefly mentioned the importance of moral principles in guiding the regulation of emotions and in elaborating on them when disciplining children. As mentioned before, many psychologists studying morality have largely ignored moral emotions, choosing to focus on the development of cognitive abilities instead. They have focused on how maturing cognitive abilities affect children's thinking about moral principles, and how understanding these principles affects their judgments concerning right and wrong. However, moral theorists who do focus on emotions have been criticized for ignoring the role that an understanding of moral principles plays in the moral development of children, choosing rather to focus on how emotions act as rewards for doing good or punishments for doing wrong (e.g., Blasi, 1999).

It is our belief that any discussion of morality should ignore neither the role of moral principles nor the role of emotions. In the moral lives of individuals, it makes little sense to separate the two. We feel guilt when we violate what we believe to be a moral principle. Guilt does not exist without previous judgments that certain acts are wrong. In the same manner, were it not for the emotions of guilt and empathy we would have little motivation to act on our moral principles. Because the two cannot be separated in real life, we do not think they should be separated in our theoretical frameworks either.

# MORAL EDUCATION

Having covered a few key points concerning moral emotions and emotional intelligence, we are now in the position to take a closer look at the implications for moral and emotional education. There is a large push for the implementation of programs in schools across the nation that focus on the education of character, values, and morals. Although this is not intended to be a review of socio-moral-emotional education programs, there are a few points to be made concerning the broad approaches that are currently in favor. In his article "How Not to Teach Values," Kohn (1997) takes a critical look at many character education programs, guiding his criticism by asking five questions he considers vital. Among these are "What is the view of human nature [espoused by the program]?" and "What is the theory of learning [espoused by the program]?" Many character education programs adhere to an underlying assumption that children are intrinsically evil and that their natural impulses must be curbed. This bleak view of human nature, according to Kohn, leads to efforts at controlling behavior by "breaking the will" of the child, and by offering the child rewards for their good behavior. As Kohn correctly points out, this approach is directly contrary to psychological research on motivation; one way to extinguish behavior is to encourage it with extrinsic rewards (Lepper, Green, & Nisbett, 1973) . The rewarding of behavior (e.g., by giving tokens to children when they are "caught" performing a good behavior) may undermine intrinsic motivation.

Attempts to stop misbehavior by external punishments are just as ineffective. If character education is to work, it must foster internal motivation to do good, and not depend on the presence of external rewards and punishment. As discussed above, moral emotions are, by their very nature, internal sources of motivation and constraint. The easy solution seems to be just to "teach" emotional skills, focusing especially on moral emotions. In fact, it is strange that more moral education programs do not pay special attention to emotional education. But the goal sounds easier than it may actually be to accomplish it. Berkowitz (1995) lists some reasons why this may be the case. First, developmental evidence points to an early emergence (within the first 2 years of life) of empathy, making its presence dependent on factors that occur before children even reach school. Second, there is a general lack of research on how to educate moral emotions. As Berkowitz states, "[T]he role of the school is to direct the child to care for the good and abhor the bad; e.g., empathize with victims and despise injustice. *Unfortunately it is quite unclear how this is done.* The literature on moral education pays little attention to this issue" (p.25, emphasis added).

A more general approach to moral learning has also been popular in schools across the nation—programs that focus specifically on issues such as conflict resolution, emotional learning, and social development in children. Although in most cases more broadly focused than character education programs, these programs were also initiated because of the desire to minimize behaviors such as interpersonal violence, drug abuse, suicide, and lack of civility among students. There is only limited evidence at this point regarding the effectiveness of many of these programs (see Lopes & Salovey, in press, for a review). However, this is most likely due to a lack of controlled research (i.e., adequate comparisons between programs) rather than an inability of these programs to foster change in students.

Lest the state of affairs seem beyond remedy, it must be made clear that there are strategies that can promote moral emotions in children. We have already mentioned some strategies for effectively inducing emotions in others. For instance, pointing to the consequences of a child's actions is an effective method of promoting an empathic response in the child, and capitalizes on the child's natural tendency to feel for others. Below we present further strategies that may promote the education of moral character through the use of emotions:

1. Build an environment that encourages the expression and discussion of emotions. There is no substitute for having good models of emotional skills. The way in which parents and educators treat and talk about emotions has been shown to be an important part of the child's ability to adjust (Gottman et al., 1997).

2. Be an effective regulator of emotions in children, especially when confronted with moral situations. For instance, induce empathy for innocent victims of crime, or guilt when the child has hurt someone. The built-in motivation provided by these emotions will continue to exert an influence even in the absence of caretakers.

3. One strategy for inducing empathy in children is to point to the similarities between them and the victim, framing victims in ways that allow children to fully experience empathy. In contrast, framing victims as different preempts feelings of empathy. By fostering a universal respect for humanity, as opposed to drawing boundary lines across races, religions, and nationalities, parents and educators can ensure that children will not fail to experience emotions when presented with the victimization of others.

4. Although there may be a heritable component to the tendency to experience empathy, it is most certainly the case that we can improve this ability in ourselves and in children. Encourage children to be constant "perspective takers," to learn to see the world through the eyes of others. Encourage conversation about how others must be thinking or feeling. This is especially important in situations where there is a conflict between two parties. Encouraging both sides to take the perspective of others will help children not only to feel what the others may be feeling, but is also an important exercise in respecting the opinions of others. Make it a habit to verbalize your empathic feelings when presented with the suffering or victimization of others.

5. Discuss important moral principles, and link them to moral emotions. Discussions about justice and fairness will come naturally to the developing child (e.g., when having to share toys with other children, or when having to take the blame for mishaps). Seize these opportunities to engage children in a discussion of justice and fairness. Say, for instance, why feeling anger at the sight of unfair practices is okay (i.e., because the principle of justice has been violated). If a child is effective at reasoning about moral issues, it is usually the case that appropriate moral emotions will follow.

There is little reason to think that we are helpless when it comes to the emotional and moral education of children. The truth of the matter is that we can be systematic and effective in fostering the moral and emotional development of children.

## CONCLUSION

Emotions play an enormous role in the moral development, moral judgment, and moral behavior of individuals, and have often been ignored by researchers in moral psychology. For a full psychological understanding of morality, one must take emotional processes into account. The emotional intelligence framework provides a useful background by which to organize the various ways emotions work in moral processes. The ability to be effective in dealing with emotions—accurately perceiving them, using them to guide thinking, being knowledgeable about complex emotional states, and being effective regulators of emotions—comprises skills that come into play in being a moral individual. In fact, these skills can be used to teach children right from wrong more effectively. There is no doubt that people who are poor at dealing with emotions and emotional events would find it hard to maintain their moral character over time. As it is, moral judgments are nearly always affected by our emotions, and being bad at dealing with emotions would seem to imply being bad at dealing with moral situations.

In discussing emotions and emotional skills, however, we must be wary not to transform emotional intelligence into something it is not. Emotional skills are merely one subset of all human skills. Cognitive abilities, emotional abilities, and various other skills and talents are important in making us complete individuals. And, as we know, any human skill can be used to achieve destructive goals. Just as an individual who has the IQ of a genius could use her or his intelligence to hurt others (the notorious Hannibal Lecter of *The Silence of the Lambs* comes to mind), so can a person who is high in emotional intelligence use his or her skills to manipulate and hurt others. Being good at knowing how others feel, regulating the emotions of others, and controlling one's display of emotions are all skills that are prerequisites for any great leader, whether she or he chooses to lead people to do good things or evil things. Emotional intelligence is therefore not a cure-all for the ills of society. If tomorrow everyone in the world became emotionally intelligent, the world still might not be a paradise. However, by understanding the role of various emotional processes in the development of morality and in our everyday moral behavior, we are that much closer to being effective moral agents and effective moral educators.

## Teachers' Questions and Answers

**Q:** In the wake of the Columbine tragedy, what kinds of interventions can schools implement to help violent or withdrawn students deal more effectively with their emotions? How early should these interventions take place? Is there a point where it is simply too late to effect change?

**A:** Recent violent incidents reported in the news media have made the mental health of our youth very salient. Partly in response to these incidents, schools across the nation have implemented programs in an attempt to preempt any future tragedies [according to one count, more than 300 such programs are in place in the United States alone (Cohen, 1999)]. Although they often go by different names (character education, positive youth development, emotional intelligence, emotional literacy, social-emotional learning), they usually have as their main goal the teaching of skills surrounding the effective management of emotions, the building of healthy social relationships, and the achievement of positive social and personal goals.

It is too early to offer a critical evaluation of the success of these programs. However, there have been some optimistic reports. For instance, one of the first of such programs (instituted in the public schools of New Haven, CT), has contributed to the reduction of school violence and feelings of hopelessness among students (Shriver, Schwab-Stone, & DeFalco, 1999). A conflict-resolution program in New York City (Resolving Conflict Creatively) has also contributed to a reduction in aggressive behavior; children who received more conflict-resolution lessons were less aggressive overall (Aber, Brown, & Henrich, 1999). These early findings provide some assurance that we are headed in the right direction.

As far as the ideal age of implementation, the easiest answer is the earlier the better. This is not to say that older children and adults cannot benefit from such training. It seems as if old dogs can learn new tricks when it comes to emotional skills. It is never too late to teach a child to take the perspective of others, for instance, or to teach children to reappraise situations so as not to feel overwhelmed with violent emotions.

If there is a take-home message, however, it is that there is still much to learn about the motives of children such as those involved in the Columbine and Jonesboro incidents. It would be a mistake to say that emotional intelligence training could have prevented such a tragedy—we just do not know at this point. However, the hope remains that by paying closer attention to the social and emotional well-being of children at high risk for such behaviors, we may be able to prevent such tragedies in the future.

# References

Aber, J. L., Brown, J. L., & Henrich, C. C. (1999). *Teaching conflict resolution: An effective school-based approach to violence prevention.* New York: National Center for Children in Poverty, The Josephine L. Mailman School of Public Health, Columbia University.

Arsenio, W. F., & Kramer, R. (1992). Victimizers and their victims: Children's conceptions of the mixed emotional consequences of moral transgressions. *Child Development, 63,* 915–927.

Barnett, M. A. (1987). Empathy and related responses in children. In N. Eisenberg & J. Strayer (Eds.), *Empathy and its development: Cambridge studies in social and emotional development* (pp. 146–162). New York: Cambridge University Press.

Batson, C. D. (1991). *The altruism question: Toward a social-psychological answer.* Hillsdale, NJ: Erlbaum.

Batson, C. D., Dyck, J. L, Brandt, J. R., Batson, J. G., Powell, A. L., McMaster, M. R., & Griffitt, C. (1991). Five studies testing two new egoistic alternatives to the empathy–altruism hypothesis. In B. Puka (Ed.), *Reaching out: Caring, altruism, and prosocial behavior. Moral development: A compendium* (Vol. 7, pp. 76–101). New York: Garland.

Berkowitz, M. W. (1995). *The education of the complete moral person.* Aberdeen: Gordon Cook Foundation.

Betancourt, H. (1990). An attribution-empathy model of helping behavior: Behavioral intentions and judgments of help-giving. *Personality and Social Psychology Bulletin, 16,* 573–591.

Blair, R. J. R. (1995). A cognitive developmental approach to morality: Investigating the psychopath. *Cognition, 57,* 1–29.

Blasi, A. (1999). Emotions and moral motivation. *Journal for the Theory of Social Behaviour, 29,* 1–19.

Cohen, J. (1999). Social and emotional learning past and present: A psychoeducational dialogue. In J. Cohen (Ed.), *Educating minds and hearts: Social emotional learning and the passage into adolescence* (pp. 2–23). New York: Teachers College Press.

Damasio, A. R. (1994). *Descartes' error: Emotion, reason, and the human brain.* New York: Avon Books.

Davis, (1996) *Empathy: A social psychological approach.* Boulder, CO: Westview Press.

Davis, M. H., Mitchell, K. V., Hall, J. A., Lothert, J., Snapp, T., & Meyer, M. (1999). Empathy, expectations, and situational preferences: Personality influences on the decision to participate in volunteer helping behaviors. *Journal of Personality, 67,* 469–503.

Easterbrook, J. A. (1959). The effect of emotion on cue ultization and the organization of behavior. *Psychological Review, 66,* 183–201.

Eisenberg, N. (1986). *Altruistic emotion, cognition, and behavior.* Hillsdale, NJ: Erlbaum.

Eisenberg, N., & Miller, P. (1987). Empathy and prosocial behavior. *Psychological Bulletin, 17,* 273–282.

Feshbach, N., & Roe, K. (1968). Empathy in six- and seven-year olds. *Child Development, 39,* 133–145.

Freud, S. (1977). *Introductory lectures on psychoanalysis* (J. Strachey, Trans.). New York: Norton. (Original work published 1920).

Gibbs, J. C. (1987). Social processes in delinquency: The need to facilitate empathy as well as sociomoral reasoning. In W. M. Kurtines & J. L.Gewirtz (Eds.), *Moral development through social interaction* (pp. 301–321). New York: Wiley.

Goleman, D. (1995). *Emotional intelligence: Why it can matter more than IQ.* New York: Bantam.

Gottman, J. M., Katz, L. F., & Hooven, C. (1997). *Meta-emotion: How families communicate emotionally.* Mahwah, NJ: Erlbaum.

Gross, J. J. (1999). The emerging field of emotion regulation: An integrative review. *Review of General Psychology, 2,* 271–299.

Hodges, S. D., & Wegner, D. M. (1997). Automatic and controlled empathy. In W. Ickes (Ed.), *Empathic accuracy* (pp. 311–339). New York: Guilford Press.

Hoffman, M. L. (1987). The contribution of empathy to justice and moral judgment. In N. Eisenberg & J. Strayer (Eds.), *Empathy and its development.* New York: Cambridge University Press.

Hoffman, M. L. (1998). Varieties of empathy-based guilt. In J. Bybee (Ed.), *Guilt and children.* Boston: Academic Press.

Hoffman M. L., & Saltszein, H. D. (1967). Parental discipline and the child's moral development. *Journal of Personality and Social Psychology, 5,* 45–57.

Isen, A. M. (1993). Positive affect and decision making. In M. Lewis & J. M Haviland (Eds.), *The handbook of emotions* (pp. 261–277). New York: Guilford.

Kochanska, G. (1995). Children's temperament, mother's discipline, and security of attachment: Multiple pathways to emerging internalization. *Child Development, 66*, 597–615.

Kochanska, G. (1997). Multiple pathways to conscience for children with different temperaments: From toddlerhood to age 5. *Developmental Psychology, 33*, 228–240.

Kohlberg, L. (1969). Stage and sequence: The cognitive-developmental approach to socialization. In D. A. Goslin, (Ed.), *Handbook of socialization theory and research* (pp. 347–480). Chicago: Rand McNally.

Kohn, A. (1997). The trouble with character education. In A. Molnar (Ed.), *The construction of children's character* (pp. 154–162). Chicago: National Society for the Study of Education.

Lazarus, R. S. (1991). *Emotion and adaptation*. New York: Oxford University Press.

Leeper, R. W. (1948). A motivational theory of emotion to replace "emotion as diorganized response." *Psychological Review, 55*, 5–21.

Lepper, M. R., Greene, D., & Nisbett, R. E. (1973). Undermining children's intrinsic interest with extrinsic reward: A test of the "overjustification" hypothesis. *Journal of Personality and Social Psychology, 28*, 129–137.

Lopes, P., & Salovey, P. (in press). Emotional intelligence and social-emotional learning. In H.J. Walberg, M.C. Wang, R.P. Weissberg, & J.E. Zins (Eds.), *Building school success on social and emotional learning*. New York: Teachers College Press.

Mandler, G. (1975). *Mind and emotion*. New York: Wiley.

Matthews, K. A., Batson, C. D., Horn, J. & Rosenman, R. H. (1981). "Principles in his nature which interest him in the fortune of others": The heritability of empathic concern for others. *Journal of Personality, 49*, 237–247.

Mayer, J. D., & Salovey, P. (1997). What is emotional intelligence? In P. Salovey & D. Sluyter (Eds.), *Emotional development and emotional intelligence: Implications for educators* (pp. 3–31). New York: Basic Books.

Mayer, J. D., Salovey, P., & Caruso, D. (2000). Models of emotional intelligence. In R. J. Sternberg (Ed.), *Handbook of intelligence* (pp. 396–420). New York: Cambridge University Press.

Mehrabin, A. (1980). *Basic dimensions for a general psychological theory: Implications for personality, social, environmental, and developmental studies*. Cambridge: Oelgeschlager, Gunn, & Hain.

Metcalfe, J., & Mischel, W. (1999). A hot/cool system analysis of delay of gratification: Dynamics of willpower. *Psychological Review, 106*, 3–19.

Mussen, P., & Eisenberg-Berg, N. (1977). *Roots of caring, sharing, and helping: The development of prosocial behavior in children*. San Francisco: Freeman.

Palfai, T. P., & Salovey, P. (1993). The influence of depressed and elated mood on deductive and inductive reasoning. *Imagination, Cognition, and Personality, 13*, 57–71.

Petrie, K. J., Booth, R. J., Pennebaker, J. W., & Davison, K. P. (1995). Disclosure of trauma and immune response to a hepatitis B vaccination program. *Journal of Consulting and Clinical Psychology, 63*, 787–792.

Piaget, J. (1932). *The moral judgment of the child*. New York: Harcourt, Brace.

Plato (1988). *Phaedrus*. (Trans C.J. Rowe.) Warminster, England: Aris & Phillips.

Rozin, P., Haidt, J., & McCauley, C. R. (1993). Disgust. In M. Lewis & J. Haviland (Eds.), *Handbook of emotions* (pp. 575–594). New York: Guilford Press.

Rozin, P., Markwith, M., & Stoess, C. (1997). Moralization and becoming a vegetarian: The transformation of preferences into values and the recruitment of disgust. *Psychological Science, 8*, 67–73.

Saarni, C. (1999). *The development of emotional competence*. New York: Guilford Press.

Salovey, P. (1992). Mood induced self-focused attention. *Journal of Personality and Social Psychology, 62*, 699–707.

Salovey, P., & Birnbaum, D. (1989). Influence of mood on health-relevant cognitions. *Journal of Personality and Social Psychology, 57*, 539–551.

Salovey, P., & Mayer, J. D. (1990). Emotional intelligence. *Imagination, Cognition, and Personality, 9*, 185–211.

Salovey, P., Woolery, A., & Mayer, J.D. (2000). Emotional intelligence: Conceptualization and measurement. In G. Fletcher & M. Clark (Eds.), *The Blackwell handbook of social psychology: Interpersonal processes* (pp. 279–307). London: Blackwell.

Schwarz, N. (1990). Feelings as information: Informational and motivational functions of affective states. In E. T. Higgins & R. Sorrentino (Eds.), *Handbook of motivation and cognition: Foundations of social behavior* (Vol. 2, pp. 527–561). Elmsford, NY: Pergamon Press.

Shriver, T.P., Schwab-Stone, M., & DeFalco, K. (1999). Why SEL is the better way: The New Haven Social Development Program. In J. Cohen (Ed.), *Educating minds and hearts: Social emotional learning and the passage into adolescence* (pp. 43–60). New York: Teachers College Press.

Simon, H. (1981). Comments. In M. S. Clark & S. T. Fiske (Eds.), *Affect and cognition* (pp. 333–342). Hillsdale, NJ: Erlbaum.

Tangney, J. P. (1999). The self-conscious emotions: Shame, guilt, embarrassment and pride. In T. Dalgleish & M. J Power (Eds.), *Handbook of cognition and emotion* (pp. 541–568). Chichester: Wiley.

Wispé, L. (1987). History of the concept of empathy. In N. Eisenberg & J. Strayer (Eds.), *Empathy and its development: Cambridge studies in social and emotional development*. New York: Cambridge University Press.

# CHAPTER

# 13

# Mozart and the Mind: Factual and Fictional Effects of Musical Enrichment

FRANCES H. RAUSCHER

*Department of Psychology*
*University of Wisconsin, Oshkosh*
*Oshkosh, Wisconsin*

The "Mozart effect," a term coined by the *Los Angeles Times*, refers to the finding that college students who listened to the first 10 minutes of a Mozart sonata (K.448) scored higher on a spatial-temporal reasoning task immediately afterward—an effect that lasted approximately 10 minutes. The original research report, first published by my colleagues and me in the journal *Nature* (Rauscher, Shaw, & Ky, 1993), received a disproportionate amount of attention from the popular press. To our horror, the finding has spawned a Mozart effect industry which includes books, CDs, web sites, and all manner of hyperbole. Articles with titles such as "Mozart Makes You Smarter" and "Mozart Makes the Brain Hum" have led readers to believe that classical music in general, and Mozart in particular, can improve babies' math scores later in life, improve scores on the Scholastic Aptitude Test (SAT), and turn average healthy children into Einsteins. Unfortunately, press reports of scientific findings are powerfully seductive to parents, educators, and policymakers. In fact, Georgia Governor Zell Miller, based on his understanding of these results, asked legislators to purchase classical music CDs for every newborn baby in the state. "No one doubts that listening to music, especially at an early age, affects spatial-temporal reasoning that underlies math, engineering, and chess." Far from no one doubting it, there is no evidence at all for the claim that listening to classical music CDs improves children's spatial-temporal reasoning or any other aspect of intelligence, for that matter. The scientific reports made no claims about general intelligence, SAT scores, or babies.

Although the term *Mozart effect* initially referred to the transitory increase in certain visuospatial task scores following listening to a particular Mozart sonata, the phrase has generalized to include, for example, the effects of music instruction on spatial-temporal task performance. In numerous studies preschoolers, kindergartners, and second graders who received piano instruction scored higher on spatial-temporal tasks than control groups who received other instruction or no training (see, for example, Rauscher, 1999). My goal in this chapter is to share with you the most recent research in this area. Because this is an area where there is considerable temptation to overstate the scientific findings in the interest of a particular advocacy position, I caution the reader to employ a conservative interpretation of the data presented here. Although the research has strong implications for policy and practice, it is important to keep in mind that these studies were designed with an eye toward determining the parameters of a scientific effect rather than with an eye toward application. Questions to be addressed include: (1) What have researchers discovered about instrumental instruction and spatial-temporal reasoning? (2) What is the best age to begin instrumental instruction for spatial-temporal enhancement? (3) How long do the effects of instrumental instruction on spatial-temporal reasoning persist? (4) How might musical experiences affect cognitive development? (5) Does enhancing spatial-temporal reasoning improve mathematics scores? (6) What are the implications of this research for educators and public policy?

To understand the effects of instrumental instruction on children's spatial-temporal reasoning, it is necessary to understand what is meant by "spatial-temporal." Virtually every healthy human has some degree of spatial-temporal intelligence. To maneuver an armchair through a doorway and around a corner, for example, one needs to picture its shape and which way to turn it before one lifts it. Even animals can reason spatially. One researcher in the field of spatial cognition, for example, reports an event he noticed while watching a German shepherd play fetch with its owner (Cooper & Shepard, 1990). The owner threw a long stick over the backyard fence, and the dog pranced over and immediately placed his head through an opening where a board in the fence had fallen off. The dog grabbed the stick horizontally, jerked backward and, one moment before the stick would have rammed the fence, rotated his head 90° to pull the stick neatly through the hole in the vertical direction. One can never know whether the dog's foresight was conscious but, writes the researcher, "Might [there] not have been a preparatory mental rotation of the stick," a rotation, I might add, similar to the one that lets you picture this whole episode in your head as you read? Children show this form of intelligence as soon as they start building block towers or putting together puzzles, and later as they reason about ratios and fractions. Individuals with highly developed spatial skills often become architects, sculptors, engineers, graphic designers, painters, mathematicians, physicists—and musicians.

Lois Hetland, a researcher from Harvard University, recently published a statistical review (i.e., meta-analysis) of all the causal studies she could find that explored the effects of instrumental instruction on spatial abilities (Hetland, 2000). Although not all studies showed positive effects, overall the data were convincing. Hetland concluded, "Active instruction in music does appear to enhance spatial-temporal performance for preschool and elementary-aged children, at least while instruction is occurring and at least up through two years of instruction. The effect is…remarkably consistent across this population of studies. …It is a solid finding."

The typical study included in Hetland's analysis compared spatial-temporal scores of two to four groups of children. One group received music instruction and the other(s) received either no instruction or instruction in an alternative activity to control for the Hawthorne effect.[1] Instruction was provided either individually or in groups of approximately 10 children, and lasted 10 to 60 minutes for periods ranging from 6 weeks to 2 years. In most studies children were taught the piano or xylophone, generally in conjunction with Orff or Kodàly techniques that included listening, singing, movement, and learning to read music. Spatial-temporal reasoning was typically tested before and after instruction began.

The primary outcome of Hetland's analysis was that active music instruction led to dramatic improvement of children's spatial-temporal task scores. In addition to this finding, Hetland made several other interesting discoveries. To determine if the effect was stronger for younger than older children, Hetland compared the posttest scores of children aged 3 to 5 years with those of children aged 6 to 12. Her results suggest that the spatial abilities of younger children are more enhanced by active music instruction than are those of older children. This finding is consistent with the notion that the age at which music instruction begins is related to structural changes in the brain. The 4-year study reported below illustrates the importance of Hetland's finding.

## SCHOOL DISTRICT OF KETTLE-MORAINE STUDY

### Kindergarten

Children from four kindergarten classrooms at two Wisconsin public elementary schools in the school district of Kettle-Moraine participated. Some children received piano keyboard instruction (keyboard group) and others received

---

[1]The Hawthorne effect is the phenomenon that whenever one introduces something new into a curriculum or program, it has an enhancing effect on a variety of behaviors.

no special training (no music group). We began by pretesting all the children using two spatial-temporal tasks, a puzzle-solving task and a block-building task, and one pictorial memory task. Based on previous research, we predicted improvement for the spatial-temporal tasks only.

Immediately following the pretesting, a music specialist visited each classroom to provide the keyboard group with 20-minute piano lessons two times per week for the remainder of the school year (8 months). Children were taught in groups of 8 to 10. The instruction involved singing and moving to the compositions of the current and subsequent weeks, rhythmic clapping and solfège, ear training, music notation, improvisation, interval and dynamic exercises, and keyboard performance. The children in the no music group engaged in journaling activities with their kindergarten teacher during music lessons. These children were not permitted access to the keyboards.

Children were posttested twice, once following 4 months of lessons and a second time following 8 months. For both spatial-temporal tasks the children who had received the keyboard lessons scored significantly better than the children who had not. Although no differences in pretest scores were found between the two groups of children, after only 4 months of instruction the keyboard group's puzzle-solving scores were 38% higher than those of the no music group. The keyboard group's scores had improved by 52%. These enhancements were similar in magnitude to those found in similar studies using preschoolers as participants, despite the chaotic setting of the kindergarten classroom and the participation of older (5- to 6-year-old) children. Furthermore, after 8 months of lessons the difference between the two groups' scores had increased in magnitude. The keyboard group scored 46% higher than the no music group, representing a 65% improvement. Similar results were found for the other spatial-temporal task, block building. As predicted, scores on the memory task did not differ significantly for the two groups following lessons. Thus, in contrast to what the Mozart zealots would claim, music training effects were limited to spatial-temporal skills; they did not generalize to other skills.

## First Grade

We returned to the schools the following year, at the end of the first grade, to retest the children. The school district had partially expanded its kindergarten keyboard program into the first grade. Therefore, some first grade children received keyboard lessons and others did not, depending on the logistics of classroom assignment. We thus had three groups of children to retest. Some children received keyboard instruction for 1 year (in kindergarten) and did not receive instruction the second year (in first grade). These children therefore had a 1-year gap in their instruction, after which they were retested. A second group of children received music instruction for 2 years (in kindergarten and first grade) and were retested after each year of instruction. Finally, a third group received no music instruction at all. All children were tested using the same three tasks used earlier.

Results indicated that the children who received keyboard instruction only in kindergarten scored 15% lower on the puzzle-solving task 1 year after their lessons had ended. In fact, these children's scores were not significantly different from the scores of the children who had never received lessons. However, the scores of the children who continued lessons through the first grade had increased by approximately 17% since kindergarten. Finally, the children who received no lessons showed only the improvement one would expect from age. The block-building task followed a similar trend. Again, no effects were found for the memory task. *These data suggest that 1 year only of keyboard music instruction will not induce long-term effects on spatial-temporal task performance.* Either the instruction must continue indefinitely for the effects to persist (use it or lose it), or some critical amount of training is required to produce lasting effects on spatial cognition. Unfortunately, it is too early in the research to determine which of these two explanations is correct.

## Second Grade

The following year we returned to the schools to retest the children yet again. After viewing the data, the district superintendent had decided to provide keyboard lessons to all her elementary school children. All children were to receive instruction every year. This decision provided us with three groups of children to retest, all of whom had participated in our study in previous years. One group had received keyboard instruction in kindergarten and second grade only (not in first grade), a second group had received the instruction in all three grades (kindergarten, first grade, and second grade), and a third group had received instruction in the second grade only. We administered the same three tasks as before, after the children had completed the second grade.

The data show that the children who received lessons in kindergarten and second grade, but not in first grade, improved by approximately 37% after their lessons were reinitiated in the second grade. The children who received lessons for all 3 years continued to improve, although the improvement from first to second grade was not significant (14%). This may be due to the presence of a ceiling effect.[2] Finally, children who received the lessons in the second grade only did not improve significantly. Consistent with Hetland's (2000) analysis, these data suggest that the effects of keyboard instruction on spatial-temporal task performance are found primarily for those children who begin training at the earliest ages.

---

[2]"Ceiling effect" refers to the failure to observe any improvement in performance owing to the fact that the participant is already performing at maximum capacity.

## Third Grade

We collected additional data from these children the following year, after they had completed the third grade. This time we used a more difficult version of the puzzle-solving task. The block-building and memory tasks were not administered.

As before, three groups of children were retested, some of whom received lessons in kindergarten, second grade, and third grade, some of whom received lessons from kindergarten through third grade, and some of whom received lessons in second and third grades only. Because of the difference in task difficulty between the test items we administered in third grade and those administered earlier, we did not compare the data collected following the third grade with those collected in previous years. However, we were able to compare the scores of the three groups of third grade children.

The data are compelling. The children who received keyboard instruction for 4 consecutive years (through the third grade) scored 30% higher on the task than children who received instruction in kindergarten, second grade, and third grade, and 52% higher than the children who began instruction in second grade. This lends further support to the importance of beginning the instruction early.

## Summary

Consistent with previous studies this longitudinal study found that young children who were provided with music instruction scored higher on spatial-temporal tasks compared with children who did not receive the instruction. The effect was significant after 4 months of instruction. No enhancement was found for a nonspatial task: pictorial memory. However, when the music instruction was terminated the children's scores began to decrease. The children who received instruction over the entire 4 years of the study continued to score higher on the spatial-temporal tasks. Finally, scores of the children who began instruction in the second grade did not improve significantly, and these children continued to score lower than all other groups in the third grade.

Lois Hetland's meta-analysis provides further information regarding several variables of interest to researchers and educators. In addition to age-of-onset differences, she found that one-on-one instruction may lead to stronger spatial skills than group lessons, although group lessons, as demonstrated above, do appear to be effective. Furthermore, Hetland's analysis revealed that instruction on the keyboard, rather than another musical instrument, may not be necessary for spatial enhancement, although she recommends caution in interpreting this finding: Only five of the studies included in her analysis did not include keyboard instruction. Also, the inclusion of movement in the music instruction did not affect spatial skills. Programs that included movement produced similar effect sizes as those that did not include movement. Finally, learning to read music may play a role. Although learning standard musical notation does not appear to be necessary for spatial enhancement, programs of music instruction that included literacy resulted in greater spatial-temporal enhancements than programs of instruction that did not.

## THEORETICAL INTERPRETATIONS

The effects of music instruction on spatial-temporal abilities have been explained by two types of theories. Neuroscientific theories assert that music instruction induces physiological changes in brain structure that consequently affect spatial-temporal processing (Leng & Shaw, 1991). Indeed, recent research suggests that the brains of musicians are different from those of nonmusicians. For example, two structural magnetic resonance imaging (MRI) studies have found that musicians who began piano instruction prior to age 6 or 7 had larger corpus callosi and greater asymmetry of the planum temporale (the brain's sound signal processor) relative to nonmusicians (Schlaug, Jancke, Huang, & Steinmetz, 1995; Schlaug, Jancke, Huang, Staiger, & Steinmetz, 1995). Furthermore, violinists who began training prior to age 12 displayed greater cortical representation of the digits of the left hand than nonmusicians (Elbert, Pantev, Wienbruch, Rockstroh, & Taub, 1995). Finally, one study found that musicians who started playing before age 9 showed greater auditory cortical representation than those who began instruction after age 9 or nonmusicians (Pantev, Oostenveld, Engelien, Ross, Roberts, & Mannfried, 1998). Again, there was a significant positive correlation between effect size and the age at which subjects initiated instruction: musicians who began instruction before age 9 displayed the largest effects. These differences in the brains of musicians and nonmusicians may be related to findings of improved spatial-temporal abilities in children who began music instruction at an early age.

Transfer theories, on the other hand, suggest that playing a musical instrument and performing a spatial-temporal task require similar cognitive skills, and thus the skills involved in making music may transfer to spatial-temporal task performance (Rauscher, 1999). One approach to examining the nature of the relationship between music and spatial-temporal reasoning is to analyze the cognitive requirements shared by these two domains. For example, several of the musical elements described by Serafine (1988), including temporal succession, nontemporal closure, transformation, and abstraction, may have parallel elements in the visuospatial domain. Perhaps the cognitive skills required to process this type of information are used in performing both musical and spatial-temporal tasks.

## THE LINK BETWEEN MUSIC AND MATH

An important practical question remains: Will children who score higher on spatial-temporal tasks as a function of music instruction also score higher on mathematical tasks? Although significant correlations have been found between spatial-temporal task performance and mathematical ability, only two studies have addressed the hypothesis that music instruction affects mathematical reasoning. The first study (Gardiner, Fox, Knowles, & Jeffrey, 1996) found that first and second grade children who received 7 months of supplementary music and visual arts classes achieved higher standardized mathematics scores than children who received the schools' typical music and arts training. However, because the two treatments were initiated together it is difficult to determine which intervention, music or art training, may have been responsible for the improvement.

The second study (Graziano, Peterson, & Shaw, 1999) compared the mathematical reasoning (in particular reasoning about ratios and fractions) of second grade children assigned to four groups: (1) keyboard instruction coupled with exposure to a computer game designed to develop spatial-temporal reasoning; (2) English instruction coupled with the same spatial-temporal training; (3) spatial-temporal training only; (4) no treatment. Results indicated that the mathematical reasoning scores of the children whose treatment included the music instruction were significantly higher than those of the children in the other groups. It is unfortunate that the researchers did not include a fifth group of students who received keyboard instruction only. However, this study does suggest that music instruction may enhance reasoning related to certain mathematical abilities, and confirms the role of spatial-temporal reasoning in some mathematical operations.

## IMPLICATIONS FOR PUBLIC POLICY

The research reported in this paper has public policy implications. It seems clear that children derive measurable educational benefits from music training beyond those directly related to music. I believe that the results of these studies must be included in music education advocacy efforts. Arguments that emphasize the extra-musical benefits of music instruction are effective and have saved school music programs. Disadvantaged children, whose caregivers can afford neither the time nor the money to provide music lessons, stand to lose the most if school music programs are cut back or eliminated. I suggest that music advocates use all available evidence to convince policymakers of the importance of a music education for all our children.

Nevertheless, I feel it is important to acknowledge the possible dangers associated with an argument of music for math's sake. Care must be taken to ensure that scientific goals do not displace developmentally appropriate instruction. Decisions regarding music education curricula should be based on musical goals only. Consistent with recent recommendations of the National Association for the Education of Young Children (Bredekamp & Copple, 1997), a position statement containing guidelines for the establishment of age-appropriate music curriculum has been published by the Music Educator's National Conference (*The School Music Program*, 1994). MENC recommends a focus on singing, listening, movement, instrumental instruction, creativity, and music literacy as well as the development of musical knowledge of melody, rhythm, timbre, and form. Musical play is also highly recommended, as is the encouragement of individual creativity. Kenney (1997) outlines specific teaching strategies relevant to these instructional goals for newborns to children aged 8. I encourage scientists and educators to attend carefully to these guidelines when considering the application of these research findings.

John Bruer, president of the James S. McDonnell Foundation and a leader in the funding of educational research, cautions us that "neither neuroscientists nor behavioral scientists have the vaguest notion of how differences in brains translate into differences in IQ or how a brain that can pass third grade differs from one that cannot" (Bruer, 1994). He further comments that "I don't want to discount [brain research] because eventually we will know much more. In twenty years, it's conceivable we will understand the brain circuitry involved in reading, for example, and how learning to read changes neural circuitry as the skills mature." However, today's students and teachers cannot wait 20 years for neuroscience to unequivocally demonstrate the nature of the link between brain function and cognition. The current research suggests that music instruction improves children's spatial abilities, whether due to neurophysiological mechanisms or not. I believe that to exclude this research from discussions arguing for music in the schools is to do a disservice to the children whose lives will be affected when music programs are eliminated. Yes, much more research is needed to provide converging evidence, and no, music is not a panacea for poor academic achievement. However, it seems clear that music has benefits to intellectual development that transcend music itself.

## Teachers' Questions and Answers

**Q:** You say that the original effect of listening to Mozart on test performance lasted only 10 minutes. What does this mean, exactly? Does it mean that 10 minutes into the test, there was no difference between a group that listened to Mozart and a group that did something else? What if there was music playing constantly say before, during, and after a test, or piped into classrooms constantly, could this limited effect be stretched out? If not, why would such an effect be so ephemeral?

**A:** Our claim that the cognitive effects of listening to Mozart are short-term came from the fact that a 10-minute delay between music exposure and spatial-temporal testing eradicated the enhancement. In delay circumstances, participants' scores were essentially the same as when they had been exposed to relaxation instructions or silence. The answer to your question regarding why the effect is so ephemeral ultimately rests in determining the cause of the Mozart effect. There are some data suggesting that the effect is due to arousal, which would suggest that when the music-induced arousal ends, so does the cognitive enhancement. I find this argument plausible, but it does not account for all of the data. For example, my own research finds that other arousing music, such as Mendelssohn, does not improve performance on spatial-temporal tasks. Why would a Mozart sonata improve task performance while a Mendelssohn symphony, which subjects reported as equally arousing, not affect performance? What we need is an experiment in which actual physiological measurements (e.g., heart rate and galvanic skin response) are made of participants before, during, and after exposure to Mozart and other music and also during a subsequent spatial-temporal test. Only then can we determine if arousal is a viable explanation.

**Q:** You argue very passionately for the importance of music programs. Is your assumption that because music can improve spatial-temporal reasoning, we should use it? Is there actually an advantage to developing these skills indirectly through music, as opposed to teaching children spatial-temporal skills directly, for example, by giving them lots of puzzles to solve?

**A:** I strongly believe that music should be included in the core curriculum for the beauty and joy it brings into our lives. The fact that music instruction has also been shown to enhance children's spatial abilities is an added benefit. I am often asked by my own music specialists if there is anything "special" they should be doing to enhance the children's spatial abilities. I tell them that they should teach the children using their best musical judgment, and the effects will follow.

A study by Gordon Shaw and his colleagues at the University of California, Irvine, directly pertains to the second portion of your question. Shaw compared the spatial-temporal reasoning scores of several groups of children, including one group who received spatial-temporal training alone and another group who received the same spatial-temporal training coupled with piano keyboard instruction. The spatial-temporal training consisted of several months of playing a computer game designed to train spatial skills. The children were then tested using items similar to those used in the computer training. Although both groups scored higher than a group of children who received language or no special training, results indicated that the group who studied the piano along with the spatial-temporal training scored significantly higher than the group who received the spatial-temporal training alone. This is particularly interesting because the children who received the spatial-temporal training alone had twice as much direct spatial-temporal training (via the computer) than the children in the keyboard group. (For example, if the spatial-temporal alone group was given 40 minutes of spatial-temporal computer training, then the spatial-temporal/piano group would be given 20 minutes of computer training and 20 minutes of piano training.) It seems that adding the music instruction to the training provided the children with an advantage that the computer training did not. Perhaps it is the multisensory nature of the piano instruction, which requires kinesthetic, auditory, and visual skills, that contributes to its effects on spatial learning. Only further research will tell.

**Q:** Does the Mozart effect work both ways? That is, is there any evidence to suggest that practicing with puzzles or other spatial-temporal activities improves one's ability to learn music?

**A:** No one has explored the possibility that spatial-temporal training can improve music learning, although I think it is a feasible hypothesis. I have thought about conducting such an experiment for quite some time, but have encountered major difficulties in the design of the study. For example, what would be a suitable measure of "music learning"? Those of us who study music cognition recognize that learning to play a musical instrument requires an integration of several types of knowledge, physical coordination, listening skills (including aural discrimination for pitch, duration, and intensity), planning skills, and so forth.

I am currently conducting a study with Head Start children to try to separate some of the musical skills that may be affecting cognitive performance. We are providing the children with different types of music instruction (e.g., rhythmic training, singing instruction, and piano instruction) and are then testing a broad range of spatial abilities. I am hoping that the information gained from this study will lead to a better understanding of the components of musical learning that may be contributing to the enhancement. If we can eventually determine precisely which aspect(s) of music learning is affecting spatial-temporal skills, perhaps then we can determine if the effect works both ways.

## References

Bredekamp, S., & Copple, C. (Eds.) (1997). *Developmentally appropriate practice in early childhood programs: Revised edition.* Washington, DC: National Association for the Education of Young Children.

Bruer, J. (1994). *Schools for thought: A science of learning in the classroom.* Bradford, UK: Bradford Books.

Cooper, L. A., & Shepard, R. N. (1990). Turning something over in the mind. In R. R. Llinás (Ed.), *The workings of the brain: Development, memory, and perception.* New York: Freeman.

Elbert, T., Pantev, C., Wienbruch, C., Rockstroh, B., & Taub, E. (1995). Increased cortical representation of the fingers of the left hand in string players. *Science, 270,* 305–307.

Gardiner, M. F., Fox, A., Knowles, F., & Jeffrey, D. (1996). Learning improved by arts training. *Nature, 381,* 254.

Graziano, A., Peterson, M., & Shaw, G. L. (1999). Enhanced learning of proportional math through music training and spatial-temporal training. *Neurological Research, 21,* 139–152.

Hetland, L. (2000). Learning to make music enhances spatial reasoning. *Journal of Aesthetic Education, 34,* 179–238.

Kenney, S. H. (1997). Music in the developmentally appropriate integrated curriculum. In C. H. Hart, D. C. Burts, & R. Charlesworth (Eds.), *Integrated curriculum and developmentally appropriate practice*. Albany, NY: SUNY Press.

Leng, X., & Shaw, G. L. (1991). Toward a neural theory of higher brain function using music as a window. *Concepts in Neuroscience, 2*, 229–258.

Pantev, C., Ooostenveld, R., Engelien, A., Ross, B., Roberts, L. E., & Manfried, H. (1998). Increased auditory cortical representation in musicians. *Nature, 392*, 811–813.

Rauscher, F. H. (1999). Music exposure and the development of spatial intelligence in children. *Bulletin of the Council for Research in Music Education, 142*, 35–47.

Rauscher, F. H., Shaw, G. L., & Ky, K. N. (1993). Music and spatial talk performance. *Nature, 365*, 611.

Schlaug, G., Jancke, L., Huang, Y., & Steinmetz, H. (1995a). In vivo evidence of structural brain asymmetry in musicians. *Science, 267*, 699–701.

Schlaug, G., Jancke, L., Huang, Y., Staiger, J. F., & Steinmetz, H. (1995b). Increased corpus callosum size in musicians. *Neuropsychologia, 33*, 1047–1055.

*The school music program: A new vision*. (1994). MENC: Reston, VA: Music Educators National Conference.

Serafine, M. L. (1988). *Music as cognition: The development of thought in sound*. New York: Columbia University Press.

## Suggested Reading

Hetland, L. (2000). Learning to make music enhances spatial reasoning. *Journal of Aesthetic Education, 34*, 179–238.

Rauscher, F. H., & Zupan, M. (2000). Classroom keyboard instruction improves kindergarten children's spatial-temporal performance: A field experiment. *Early Childhood Research Quarterly, 15*, 215–228.

Shaw, G. L. (2000). *Keeping Mozart in mind*. San Diego, CA: Academic Press.

# Stereotype Threat: Contending and Coping with Unnerving Expectations

JOSHUA ARONSON

*Department of Applied Psychology, New York University, New York*

When my friends and I entered junior high school in the mid-1970s, we quickly noticed something that our teachers seemed to miss: the black and Latino kids bused into our district were a lot smarter than the adults at the school seemed to think. It was not necessarily that our teachers held the prejudiced view that minorities were dumb. Rather, as students, we had the advantage of seeing these kids in a variety of classes and situations. And their behavior from one situation to the next was often remarkably different. For example, there were many kids like Ricky, the star pupil in my electronics class. Always the first to finish his project, Ricky would go from table to table, patiently helping the electronically challenged kids like me make sense of the complex diagrams for assembling the strobe light, radio, or whatever we happened to be struggling with. There were also kids like my friend Darryl, a black eighth grader, whom I hung around with at lunch and after school. Darryl was one of the most thoughtful, intelligent, and articulate kids I knew, and no one who knew him well thought otherwise. But in some of the classes I had with Ricky and Darryl, you would never get an inkling of how bright they were. In these more "academic" classes like English, Math, and History, they simply ceased to be the same kids we knew. Like most of the minority students in the school, they fell into one of two camps. Either they were rowdy and disruptive, or they were meek and withdrawn, quietly sitting in their seats as though they were trying to become invisible to the teacher. In either case, they were not themselves in these classes, and they performed terribly, no doubt considered losers by the teachers and the administration. My friends were not extraordinary cases. I think they were typical of a trend of underachievement that has perplexed educators and policy makers for several decades. It is a depressing trend: on whatever measure of academic success one looks at—test scores, grades, engagement, dropout rates, and so on—black and Latino students from grade school through college tend to perform worse than white students (National Center for Education Statistics, 1998). But why? What happens to students like my junior high classmates to suppress their performance, learning, and engagement in school? And what can educators do to help them perform up to their potential?

For the past decade I have been trying to find answers to these questions. My colleagues and I started by considering the standard explanations for minority underachievement. Some of these explanations have been widely discussed and hotly debated in the scientific literature and in the popular press. Most notorious is the view that some groups are by nature intellectually inferior. This is the argument put forth in the highly controversial book, *The Bell Curve* by Hernnstein and Murray (1994), who assembled a massive amount of information on test performance and school achievement, casting it as evidence for genetically determined differences in general intelligence. Most scientists who study intelligence reject this argument in favor of the view that some combination of environmental factors (e.g., poverty, poor schooling) hinders black and Latino students from developing the skills necessary to do well on tests and in school (see Jencks & Phillips, 1998). Certainly these structural factors make a difference, but can they explain why kids like Ricky or Darryl, so undeniably competent and engaged in certain circumstances, could be so incompetent and "out of it" in others? Our hunch was that the standard explanations fell short. Something was missing.

National statistics supported this hunch. For example, every year the College Board releases statistics on how students across the country score on the Scholastic Achievement Test (SAT). And every year the same pattern: blacks and Latinos score substantially lower than the Asians and whites, regardless of income level. To be sure, the gaps are *widest* between poor black and Latino students and their more well-to-do white counterparts. Income level clearly matters. But even at the same level of family income, the gap is substantial. Thus, by itself, socioeconomic status does not explain the problem, though it is a factor (Steele, 1997; Jencks & Phillips, 1998). Indeed, group-level differences in ability or preparation seem inadequate to fully explain the low performance of minority students. For example, when we look at how students perform in college as a function of their SAT scores (which are associated with ability, preparation, and motivation), we find a sizable discrepancy between the grades of blacks and whites. Specifically, blacks with a given SAT score earn significantly worse grades than whites with the same score, even when the score they share is extremely high, say at the 98th percentile. Thus, something else appears to be depressing the test performance and the school achievement of these students at every level of income, ability, and preparation —something beyond skill, preparation, or any of the other things to which we customarily attribute achievement.

Claude Steele, Steven Spencer, and I (e.g., Steele, Spencer, & Aronson, in press) have been studying these issues for the past decade, and we believe that this "something else" is psychological in nature, a social psychological predicament rooted in stereotypical images of certain groups as intellectually inferior. It has long been known that stereotypes—the "pictures in the head" that simplify our thinking about other people—produce expectations about what people are like and how they are likely to behave (e.g., Allport, 1954). We also know such expectations on the part of a teacher can influence the performance of his or her students. The process (described by Rosenthal in Chapter 2 in this volume) proceeds like this: a teacher develops expectations about a student's ability based on some prior information about the student (e.g., a test score) or based on the student's race, ethnicity, gender, or social class. Then the teacher inadvertently acts on these expectations and in so doing, treats the student in a way that makes those expectations come true. Thus, let us suppose that because of the widespread images of blacks as intellectually inferior, a teacher unconsciously assumes a black boy in her class does not have much potential. During the teacher's interactions with him she sends subtle signals that reflect her expectations: perhaps she's less warm or attentive, perhaps she fears embarrassing him, so she sets the bar lower, asking easy, unchallenging questions, or perhaps she does not call on him at all. And so on. The student in turn, responds to this differential treatment as anyone would—with less learning. Such a process undoubtedly plays a role in the relatively low achievement of black students (e.g., Ferguson, 1998). Thus, stereotypes have been thought to undermine minority children in large part, because the stereotype influences the way they are treated by others.

## STEREOTYPE THREAT

But this is just part of the equation. What my colleagues and I have found is that a "self-fulfilling prophecy" of this sort can occur without a teacher's help. That is, even in the absence of differential treatment, stereotypes can spoil a person's experience—in school or in many social situations—just by suggesting to the target of a stereotype that a negative label might apply to one's self or one's group. Consider the image elicited by the term *absentminded professor*, a label that could conceivably be applied to me, because I am a professor and because, like anyone, I am capable of absentmindedness. My familiarity with this image can make me wonder if this description fits me and perhaps make me worry that my behavior could be viewed with this rather unflattering stereotype in mind. When the stereotype is relevant to a particular situation—say, when I am trying to locate my lecture notes or trying to remember if I have an appointment after lunch—the question may cross my mind: *Am I behaving like an absentminded professor?* If I'm in the company of my students, I may become apprehensive, wondering if *they* think I am an absentminded professor, and I may start to worry that they do. And perhaps as a result of this, I may become less effective in finding my notes or remembering my schedule. This predicament, this apprehensiveness about confirming a stereotype, both in my own eyes and other people's eyes, is what we have called "stereotype threat" (Aronson, Quinn, & Spencer, 1998; Steele, 1997; Steele & Aronson, 1995). In form, it is a predicament that can beset anyone, given that all of us belong to one group or another that has some sort of reputation, and given that each of us can develop our own individual reputation. When the stereotype or individual reputation alleges an importantly negative quality—like the low intelligence stereotypes allege for blacks and Latinos—the expectations that come with it can be quite unnerving, and stereotype threat can have critically disruptive effects.

Consider, for example, an African-American or Latino student trying to solve difficult items on a test, or called on in class to answer a complex question. As for anyone, low performance in such situations can bring discouragement and shame. But the stereotype alleging African-American or Latino intellectual inferiority poses the additional risk of confirming a deeply negative, racial inferiority, a suspicion of being unalterably limited and of not belonging in the academic arena. Negative stereotypes alleging low intelligence among blacks and Latinos are particularly problematic, both because intelligence is universally valued and because these stereotypes are so widely known. By the age of about 5, virtually everyone in our culture is aware of the content of a variety of ethnic and racial stereotypes. Whether or not people agree with stereotypes, the mere awareness of their content is enough to bias people's perceptions and treatment of individuals from stereotyped groups (Devine, 1989). Moreover, opinion polls suggest that the stereotypes *are* widely believed. About half of white Americans endorse common stereotypes about blacks and Latinos, which, among other things, portray them as being unintelligent (e.g., Smith, 1990). And this fact is not lost on blacks and Latinos; research indicates that they are well aware how the are viewed by the mainstream. Indeed, some research suggests a tendency for targets to be *hyperaware* of people's negative expectations about their group, considerably overestimating the extent to which they are viewed as less intelligent, more likely to commit crime, live off welfare, and so on (Sigelman & Tuch, 1997). Given this climate of stereotype awareness, there are ample grounds for black and Latino students to feel a burden of suspicion, to feel at risk of confirming stereotypes through their behavior, and to wonder if they belong in environments where academic ability is prized. Such feelings, our research suggests, can play a significant role in undermining the achievement of students who belong to groups stereotyped as lacking some academic ability—blacks, Latinos, and women in math and science domains. This would appear to be bad news given the ubiquity of social stereotypes and the fact that they are notoriously resistant to change. But as the research I will now discuss demonstrates, stereotype threat is partly situational; it is induced by features of the situation that can be changed, and it can be minimized by teaching students adaptive ways of coping with it.

## CONTENDING WITH STEREOTYPE THREAT

Stereotype threat arises in situations where a negative stereotype is relevant to evaluating performance. The classic example is a black student taking a standardized test of intelligence. If, in such cases, performance is depressed by the extra cognitive and emotional burden of worrying that low performance will confirm the stereotype, then somehow removing that extra burden should improve performance. This was the initial hypothesis in our research, and we have tested it with a number of very simple experiments (Steele & Aronson, 1995). In our first experiment, we had African-American and white college students take a very challenging standardized test (the verbal portion of the Graduate Record Examination). In the control condition of the experiment, we presented the test as these tests are always presented—as a measure of intellectual ability and preparation. In the experimental condition, we sought to reduce stereotype threat by removing the relevance of the stereotype. To do so, we simply told our test takers that we were not interested in measuring their ability with the test; we just wanted to use the test to examine the psychology of verbal problem solving. This was the only difference between the two conditions of the experiment: the test was the same, the students were equally talented, they were given the same amount of time, and so on. But this little difference in the way we presented the test made a big difference for the African-Americans. When the test was presented in this nonevaluative manner, they solved about twice as many problems on the test as when it was presented in the standard way! Moreover, there was no difference between the performance of the black test takers under no stereotype threat and that of the white test takers. For the white students, incidentally, the way the test was presented had no effect whatsoever on their performance.

What caused this dramatic rise in performance among black students? Further analyses and additional studies suggested a number of things. First, by reducing the evaluative scrutiny in the situation, we reduced our black students' anxiety—the sort of debilitating test anxiety that we have all experienced at times, and which appears to be aroused in black and Latino students under traditional testing situations where their intelligence is being evaluated. One thing was also very clear from our studies: stereotype threat did not impair performance simply by prompting our test takers to give up or to try less hard.

On every measure of effort available to us, we have found the same thing: if anything stereotype threat makes people try *harder* on tests. We think this increase in effort and anxiety reflects a kind of "I'll show *you*" response, aimed at invalidating the stereotype. Such a reflex can be an advantage in situations where brute effort or a rush of adrenaline is desirable, and indeed, stereotype threat can actually *boost* performance on easy or well-learned tasks where more effort pays off (O'Brien & Crandall, under review). But on difficult standardized tests, as with brain surgery, free-throw shooting, or chess, a sort of relaxed concentration is critical, and anything that compounds performance pressure is likely to be a handicap. The data from our studies suggest strongly that this extra motivation reflected the desire to disprove the negative stereotype or, at least, to deflect it from being self-characteristic. In one study (in Steele & Aronson, 1995) with a setup similar to that described above, just after describing the test as either ability evaluative or nonevaluative, we gave our test takers a questionnaire to fill out. Part of the questionnaire asked about the kinds of activities they enjoyed—the kinds of sports they played, the kind of music they enjoyed, and so on. Some of these preferences were clearly stereotypic of African-Americans (e.g., liking rap music, playing basketball, being lazy, and so on). There was a very telling difference in the way that black students filled out these measures depending on whether or not they were told the upcoming test was a measure of intelligence. Stereotype threat led them to distance themselves from the stereotypic portrayals of themselves. That is, when they thought the upcoming examination was going to be used to measure their intelligence, they reported liking basketball, enjoying rap music, being lazy, and so on, significantly *less* than their counterparts who thought the upcoming examination was not going to diagnose their abilities. Feeling at risk of being viewed stereotypically, they did what they could not to portray themselves in a stereotype-consistent manner.

Thus, people in stereotype threatening situations appear to be thinking about the stereotype and its implications. In addition to whatever thoughts they bring to bear on their test, they are also contending with the stereotype and the extra burden of the possibility of confirming it. Evaluative scrutiny, our studies make clear, activates thoughts about race in the minds of black students. Stereotype threat thus appears to involve the salience of race. The converse seems to be true as well; we have found that just making race salient in some way spoils performance, even in a nonevaluative situation. For example, in one of our experiments (Steele & Aronson, 1995) we replicated the conditions of the no-stereotype threat test described earlier. That is, all of our black and white test takers were assured that their intelligence would not be evaluated. For half of these students, we added one detail designed to inject thoughts about race into the situation: we merely included an item on the cover of the test booklet that asked them to indicate their race. As in the prior study, when the test was presented as a nonevaluative exercise, blacks performed just as well as the whites. But in the race-salient condition, in which students were asked to indicate their race, black students' anxiety went up and their test performance plummeted. They solved about half as many items as their counterparts who were not asked to indicate their race. Such is the power of a stereotype; the mere mention of race can turn an otherwise nonevaluative situation into an unpleasant defense of one's competence and worth.

The studies I have just described have been replicated in one way or another numerous times, not only by my colleagues and my students, but by researchers working around the country. Thus we are convinced not only that the effects are real, but also that they are not dependent on a particular population of students or limited to a particular set of procedures or settings. Some of this work has greatly extended our understanding of the stereotype threat phenomenon: the groups that regularly experience stereotype threat, the situations that can either exacerbate or reduce stereotype threat, and some important individual differences in people's vulnerability to stereotype threat. Rather than exhaustively go through all of these studies, I will instead focus on findings that shed light on some of the more pressing issues that educators may face, such as trying to identify students likely to experience stereotype threat, creating conditions that can reduce stereotype threat, and helping students overcome its more pernicious effects.

## Who Contends with Stereotype Threat?

An obvious question is who is likely to be affected by stereotype threat? Researchers have found that virtually any group can experience it to a meaningful degree in certain circumstances. The basic effect of impaired test performance has been replicated in studies of Latino students taking tests of verbal ability and with women taking math tests, at a variety of levels of schooling from grade school (Ambady et al., 2001; Good & Aronson, in press) through college (Aronson & Salinas, 1997; Spencer et al., 1999), in elite private colleges like Stanford (Steele & Aronson, 1995) and large state universities such as the University of Texas (Aronson, 1997, 1999). Stereotype threat can affect students who are highly confident in their abilities and those who are less confident; highly able and prepared students and the not so able and prepared. It is clear as well that to feel stereotype threat, the stereotype need not pertain to race, ethnicity, or gender. For example, Jean-Claude Croizet has found that French students of low socioeconomic status performed worse on a test when reminded of their social status, which in France, as in the United States, is stereotypically associated with low academic achievement (e.g., Croizet & Claire, 1998). Similarly, elderly individuals can be disrupted by the stereotype suggesting that their mental abilities are on the decline. When the elderly participants in one experiment were subtly reminded of the stereotype regarding old age and senility, they performed worse on a test of short-term memory than when they were reminded of the more positive old-people-are-wise stereotype instead (Levy, 1996). Indeed, it is clear that in certain circumstances, one need not even be a member of a stigmatized minority group suspected of inability to feel the pressure associated with stereotype threat. In a simple experiment I performed with my colleagues (Aronson, Lustina, Good, Keough, Steele, & Brown, 1999), we asked highly competent white males, (both at Stanford University and at the University of Texas) to take a difficult math test. Two groups were told that the test was aimed at determining their math abilities. For one group we added a stereotype threat: we told them that one of our reasons for doing the research was to understand why Asians seemed to perform better on these tests. In this condition, these test-takers stumbled on the test. Pressured by the stereotype of Asian mathematical superiority, they solved significantly fewer of the problems on the test and felt less confident about their performance. These students were highly competent and confident males: most of them were mathematics majors and most of them of them had earned near-perfect scores on the math portion of the SAT. It is safe to say that they were not minorities and, thus, not conditioned by stereotypes to doubt the intellectual abilities of their group. Thus, if they can experience stereotype threat, anyone who can be plausibly targeted by a stereotype can feel it. The rather exotic situation that we imposed on them—a direct comparison with a supposedly superior group—is not exotic for blacks and Latinos; they contend daily with this sort of implied comparison in most integrated academic settings. That such undeniably smart and accomplished students like our high-scoring math whizzes underperform on a test when faced with a stereotype should make us think twice about casually assuming that the low performance of blacks and Latinos reflects a lack of ability. Instead, we need to appreciate the power of the circumstances they face.

Importantly, stereotype threat can arise without any special attempt to raise the issue of the stereotype, either explicitly as with in study with the Asian stereotype, or implicitly as with the study with the elderly or the study with poor students in France. In a study with particular relevance for educators, Michael Inzlicht and Talia Ben-Zeev (2000) showed how just the way students are grouped can matter. In their study, they had highly competent female under-graduates take a difficult math examination in small groups. Depending on the condition of the experiment, the researchers added one or more men to this testing session. The effects were dramatic. The mere presence of only one male test taker was enough to significantly lower the performance of the female test takers in the group. Moreover, each male introduced into the testing session produced an increase in stereotype threat and a corresponding drop in the women's performance, a perfectly linear effect of gender integration on under-performance. To my knowledge, no similar study has been conducted with race or ethnicity integration systematically varied in this way, but there is no theoretical reason to doubt that these effects would not occur with black or Latino students in the company of whites. The implications of this finding for race and gender composition of classrooms would appear to be self-evident. If classes are simply integrated, without any attention paid to attenuating the intimidating intellectual environment that can ensue, many students will perform at levels beneath their potential. This study raises critical questions not only about testing, but more generally about how classroom learning may be impeded in environments where stereotype threat arises by mixing students alleged to differ in ability.

## Stereotype Vulnerability: Individual Risk Factors for Underperformance

Stereotype-based expectations are not equally unnerving to all individuals. Important individual differences make some individuals more vulnerable than others to the kind of underperformance I have been talking about. I refer to the sum of these risk factors as "stereotype vulnerability." The following factors, which I describe only briefly, appear to contribute to an individual's level of stereotype vulnerability.

### Domain Identification

One of the sad ironies uncovered by our research is that stereotype threat is most keenly felt by the individuals who care most about doing well. In a number of studies, we have measured the degree to which people care about a particular domain: how much they value doing well in math, science, or any particular domain of academic achievement, and how much doing poorly in the domain threatens their self-esteem. What we find is that underperformance under stereotype threat is more pronounced for those who really want to do well (Aronson et al., 1999; Aronson & Good, 2001a). This is quite logical, of course. We would not expect to be critically unnerved by a stereotype alleging a lack of ability if that ability was trivial. The irony is this: to the extent that we increasingly see high-stakes testing used to evaluate our students' progress or suitability for admissions to institutions of higher learning, it is unfortunate that we, in a sense, punish those minority students who care the most about high achievement.

### Group Identification

It appears also to be the case that people who feel a deep sense of attachment to their ethnic or gender group are also more at risk for feeling stereotype threat. Some individuals are less invested than others in their gender or racial identity, and initial research into this area of research, although not yet definitive, suggests that the less investment in one's own group, the less one will be bothered by stereotypes impugning that group's abilities (e.g., Schmader, Johns, Keiffer, Healy, & Fairchild-Olivierre, 2001). Thus in an intriguing set of studies, Rosenkrantz (1994) found that all other things being equal (e.g., ability and preparation), Latinos who are "bicultural," that is, who feel just as firmly grounded in mainstream culture as in their culture of origin, are less stereotype vulnerable than Latinos who are more heavily identified with Latino culture. Specifically, in one situation biculturals were less defensive about receiving negative feedback on an academic task from a white evaluator and, in a subsequent study, less likely to underperform on a standardized test under stereotype threat. Apparently, in some cases, there can be an unfortunate trade-off for feelings of group pride and solidarity; deep identification with one's own group can create difficulty navigating integrated situations where stereotypes may be relevant.

## Stigma Consciousness

One reason that group pride may exact a toll in terms of discomfort in integrated intellectual environments is that it often comes along with higher expectations for discrimination. Studies of "racial socialization" find that African–Americans who have experienced discrimination in their lives often attempt to prepare and shield their children from such discrimination by teaching them to expect it and to counter it with pride in their group (e.g., Hughes & Chen, 1999). Thus along with a sense of group pride, some children also develop a heightened sense of what Elizabeth Pinel (1999) calls "stigma consciousness." Pinel and her colleagues have found that students perform worse on standardized tests the more stigma conscious they are—the more they have experienced discrimination and the more they expect to experience it in the future (e.g., Brown, Pinel, Rentfrow, & Lee, 2001).

## Acceptance of the Stereotype

A person need not believe a stereotype to feel threatened by its unflattering allegations. After all, even if one rejects the premise of a stereotype, one must still contend with the perceptions of other people. A person can still feel uneasy or alienated in academic settings if he or she feels devalued or suspected of inferiority by others, and these feelings, we have shown, are sufficient to undermine performance (Aronson et al., 1999; Good & Aronson, 2001). But it seems reasonable to assume that some people may suspect that a stereotype may have some validity, a "kernel of truth," and such individuals would presumably be more threatened by the stereotype. Interestingly, survey research suggests that this should not be a big problem, because most black and Latino students reject negative stereotypes as untrue. Yet questionnaires can be very misleading; they often fail to detect people's underlying attitudes. But other methods can, and they tell a very different story. Thus, in a remarkable study by developmental psychologist Niobe Way (1998), in-depth interviews with minority adolescents revealed the degree to which they wrestle with stereotypes, wanting to reject them, but unable to do so with confidence. A large percentage of the teens she interviewed admitted, with shame, that they lived up to stereotypes portraying them as lazy and incompetent. They did not like the stereotypes, but they could not deny that they lived up to them. Because it is easy to reject a proposition on a survey, questionnaires fail to capture this ambivalence, and thus they paint a distorted picture of what minority students may be thinking about the stereotypes applied to their group. But using more subtle measures of people's implicit acceptance of stereotypes, recent research shows that the more people accept the stereotypes as true, the more vulnerable they are to stereotype threat (Spicer & Monteith, 2001; Schmader et al., 2001).

## Beliefs about Intelligence

An important individual difference for achievement-related behavior is the way people think about intelligence. People differ in how fixed they think it is: some think it can be expanded with hard work and mental challenge, whereas others think you are either smart or not smart, and your intelligence cannot really develop. Dweck (1999; Chapter 3 in this volume) discusses the various advantages conferred on students who believe in malleable intelligence. Such students tend to maximize their academic potential—they respond better to challenges and difficulties because they are less threatened by them. In my own research, I have found that black students performed better under stereotype threat to the extent that they saw intelligence as something they could expand. This makes good sense. If one believes that intelligence is fixed, a stereotype alleging low intelligence is a condemnation of one's ability and future prospects for success. Thus the risk of low performance is very keenly felt. If, on the other hand, one believes that intelligence is malleable, the stereotype should have less impact. As I will discuss shortly, these findings hold considerable promise for helping students cope with stereotype threat. As for the other individual differences, no research to my knowledge has addressed whether understanding these risk factors can help us remediate stereotype threat, but they can certainly help us identify students who may be particularly vulnerable.

## COPING WITH STEREOTYPE THREAT

Test performance is but one manifestation of stereotype threat. There are a number of ways that this apprehension can hinder students; some are more troubling than low performance on a test. Some of the most troubling manifestations arise as attempts to cope with the unpleasant threat to self that stereotype threat poses. People need ways of shielding themselves from threatening intellectual environments, such as the stereotype-dense environment of most integrated schools. Social psychology is replete with examples of how people adapt to psychological threats to self-esteem (e.g., Steele, 1988;

Tesser, 1988). The social psychologist Daniel Gilbert, in noting the variety of ways that people unconsciously cope with threats to the self, speaks of the "psychological immune system" we all posses (e.g., Gilbert et al., 1998). In much the same way that our physiological immune system wards off threats from microbes, that is, without our awareness that it is working, this psychological system rationalizes, minimizes, and otherwise attempts to neutralize threats to the self. Research has examined a number of such unconscious defenses that arise as way of coping with stereotype threat as well. And just as sometimes happens physiologically (e.g., with allergies), our psychological immune systems can turn traitor on us, offering a defense that is harmful both in the short run and in the long run.

## Self-Defeating Defenses

### Self-handicapping

For example, a common defense for people who feel at risk of low performance is what psychologists refer to as "self-handicapping" (see Rhodewalt & Tragakis, Chapter 6 in this volume). In an attempt to minimize the negative implications of low performance, a person may make claims that some external factor impeded performance ("the sun was in my eyes"; "I didn't get any sleep last night"; "the test was biased against minorities"). Or, alternatively, they may create actual performance impediments that allow them or others to attribute low performance to some external cause. They may, for example, not try as hard, get drunk the night before an examination, or create some other kind of excuse that defeats their own performance. While self-esteem may be protected in this way, learning, performance, and enjoyment of academics can suffer. Thus, the protection of self-esteem can become a liability for learning and growth.

Moises Salinas and I (Aronson & Salinas, 1997) have documented this trade-off in a series of studies examining the consequences of a very common excuse among minorities: the claim of test bias. First we noted that in many stereotype threat studies, when students are led to believe that a test was going to be used to diagnose their abilities, they claimed that standardized tests were far more biased than if they were led to believe the same test was nonevaluative. Like a warrior going into battle, they raised the self-protective notion of bias like a shield. In our own studies, we wanted to see how their heightened sense that the test was biased would affect their performance. We tested this by having Latino students take a long standardized test, which we divided into two parts. During a "rest period" between the two parts, half the test takers were asked if they thought standardized tests were biased. Those who were asked this question solved significantly fewer of the items on the second half of the test than those who were not asked. It was also the case that those who were asked about bias were less upset about their overall performance than those who were not. Thus, the shield effectively protected their self-esteem, but it undermined their performance. The disruptive power of suspicions of bias is underscored by a study conducted by Steven Spencer and his colleagues (1999), which showed how preventing students from making an attribution to bias can reduce anxiety and lift performance. In this experiment, women's performance on a math test improved dramatically when they were assured that the test had never shown gender differences.

Suspicions of bias extend well beyond testing. There is a clear tendency among African–Americans and Latinos to reject critical yet instructive feedback from white evaluators as a means of protecting self-esteem (e.g., Cohen, Steele, & Ross, 1999; Crocker & Major, 1989; Rosenkrantz, 1994), a rejection based on the presumption of bias. But such presumptions are a double-edged sword here, too, as motivation and learning from the feedback are traded away for self-esteem protection. Cohen and Steele (Chapter 15 in this volume) discuss ways that teachers can deliver critical feedback in a way that maximizes trust and, thus, minimizes this trade-off.

## Avoidance of Challenge

A recent study I performed with Catherine Good (see Good & Aronson, 2001) illustrates another, perhaps more pernicious self-protective tendency among stereotype targets. We had sixth grade girls and boys (both Latino and white) take tests under evaluative (stereotype threat) or nonevaluative (no stereotype threat) conditions. Before they took the test, we told them that they would be taking a second test of both math and reading, but that on this second test, they would get to select the difficulty of the problems. We then offered them a choice of solving problems that were easy, right at their level, or very challenging. The results showed a clear effect of the stereotype threat manipulation: the girls selected easy problems in math (where they are stereotyped to lack ability), whereas the Latinos selected easier problems in reading (where they are stereotyped to lack ability). The implications of this are very clear. One way to cope with stereotype threat is to arrange things so that you are at the least risk of confirming the stereotype. Thus when there is a choice between challenge and high performance, stereotype threat leads people to play it safe by avoiding the challenge. It is a truism in educational psychology that challenge is required for intellectual growth and for developing the kind of skills and confidence needed to do well. Thus settings that are highly evaluative may actually impede the *learning*, not just the performance, of stereotype targets. Every year the Princeton Review offers free standardized test preparation to minority and low-income students. Jay Rosner, who runs this program, reports that despite the fact that African-Americans could raise their scores by hundreds of points by taking this course, they seldom avail themselves of the opportunity, even when the price of the course is reduced or waived. Rosner's explanation, based on years of working with minority students, is that for these students, even the prospect of practice is threatening.

## Self-Suppression

Stereotypes, by creating expectancies for performance, also send messages about who is valued by the norms of the setting and who is not, who is "in" and who is "out." In an eloquent essay introducing the notion of stereotype threat, Claude Steele (1992) described this aspect of the predicament as a significant part of the barrier that keeps African-Americans from fully embracing academic achievement: "Black students quickly learn that acceptance, if it is to be won at all, will be hard won." Looked at through this lens, the withdrawn behavior of my junior high classmates 25 years ago is less surprising. In some settings they belonged, they were not suspected of inferiority so they were free to be themselves; in other settings, they were afraid to make a wrong move. One black woman I interviewed told me this about her experience in college: "When I talk in class, I feel as though I'm totally on stage, like everyone's thinking, 'oh what's the black girl going to say?' I pretty much never speak up in class though, so I guess it's not a big problem." The effects of this feeling of not fitting in and attempts to cope with it have been compellingly documented for women in the male-dominated domains of math and science. Seymour and Hewitt (1996), for example, report that female math majors feel less free to be their true selves when interacting with their peers in the major. They show an interesting trend of "dressing down," that is, dressing less femininely in their math classes than in their humanities classes. This suggests that in situations where people feel at risk of confirming a negative stereotype, they cope both by suppressing themselves and by adjusting or concealing themselves, or certain aspects of themselves, to better fit the image of those who do seem to belong (see also Pronin, Steele, & Ross, 2001). Although one could argue about how "self-defeating" such defenses are, it seems clear that one price students pay to cope with stereotype threatening environments is the free expression of their genuine selves. As I discuss below, self-supression can make persevering in a threatening domain especially difficult.

## Disidentification

After a failure or a mistake of some kind most people have a tendency to rationalize it in some way. When a person claims to not care about math after a failure on a math test, we refer to this response as *devaluing*, and everyone does it to some degree (e.g., Aronson, Blanton, & Cooper, 1995). It is a natural reflex. But when the response becomes so chronic that the person adjusts her or his self-concept, divesting self-esteem from the threatened domain, this response can have disastrous effects on achievement. We call this chronic adaptation *disidentification*. I noted earlier that stereotype threat is strongest among students who are most invested in doing well, those who are highly identified with an intellectual domain. Disidentification solves the problem for students because it removes sensitivity to failure. Although failure in and of itself is enough to prompt disidentification, stereotype threat appears to make it a far more common response among blacks and Latinos because the stereotype suggests not only a general lack of ability, but also, as discussed above, limited belongingness in the domain (Osborne, 1997; Steele, 1997). The problem with disidentification is the same as with a number of other modes of self-esteem protection—one trades away motivation and engagement for protection from self-threat. Commenting on the basic human need for psychic insulation, the critic Louis Menand recently observed that "if we didn't learn how not to care, our failures would destroy us." Disidentification with particular domains of academics is to be expected as children mature and their interests and specialties narrow. We all must choose what to major in and what domains of competence to build our self-esteem on. Disidentification with areas of weakness is natural and adaptive. But for blacks and Latinos, whose performance and belongingness are broadly threatened in the academic arena, disidentification with academics can be maladaptive. Thus, if we cannot succeed in reducing stereotype threat, perhaps what we need to do for these students is help them learn alternate ways "not to care." Biographical portraits of successful black Americans often make reference to the critical insight offered by a parent or mentor, which helped them persevere in the face of adversity: learning not to care about *what others think* (e.g., Jordan, 2001). Perhaps we can teach this kind of disidentification to our students, and thereby prevent wholesale divestment from academics.

## REDUCING STEREOTYPE THREAT: WHAT TEACHERS CAN DO

### Presenting Tests Differently

#### Reducing Diagnosticity

The initial studies we performed offer some practical clues as to how to reduce stereotype threat. Recall that we improved performance among black students by presenting a test, not as a measure of ability, but rather as a nonevaluative task. This might be hard to pull off in a school setting, particularly with the recent drive toward "standards and accountability" that is turning the modern elementary school into a standardized testing center. It is unlikely that one could convince a child that you do not care about his or her performance when so much of the curriculum gets dictated by what is on the statewide standardized test. Yet there are some possible variations in presentation that can reduce the onus on the child. Consider the clever idea of a teacher, who, after hearing about this research, tried the following with her students: she introduced the test as a measure of how well we (the school administration) are doing our job of teaching. According to the teacher, the students were more relaxed and performed better. The Spencer et al. studies further suggest that presenting a test as not showing gender or race differences can accomplish similar results. What teachers should try to avoid is anything that unduly raises the stakes in an effort to motivate the students.

## Learning Curve Protection

Earlier I noted that stereotype threat seems especially disruptive to individuals who believe that intelligence is fixed. In a number of studies, researchers have improved performance by reminding people of the malleability of human ability and skill. These studies suggest practical ways of reducing stereotype threat in educational contexts.

In one study, Josephs and Schroeder (1997) successfully reduced the under-performance of women taking a math test by manipulating these women's performance on a prior unrelated task. Women in this condition were given problems and feedback on their performance that emphasized that they had made substantial gains in skill improvement throughout the course of this first task. Awareness of this "learning curve" appears to have inoculated these participants from the deleterious effects of stereotype threat. Women given this prior experience completed a later math test with performance equal to that of a male control group, and better than that of women who completed the same set of problems and solved the same number correct, but who were not given the impression that their performance was improving. Thus in this study the attribution that participants could improve their performance seemed to reduce stereotype threat.

## Malleable Skill versus Fixed Ability

In a similar study performed with African-American college students (Aronson, 1999), I presented a difficult verbal test as a test of an ability that was either malleable or fixed, reasoning that one would experience more anxiety if the test measured an ability of which a person had little hopes of improving. As pre-dicted, the African-Americans, as well as the whites, performed much better and reported lower performance anxiety when the test was said to diagnose an ability that could be expanded with practice. Many teachers have told me that they have had good success with students by presenting tests to their students in this way—as a marker of their current level of skill rather than a measure of their permanent ability. This experiment backs up their perceptions.

The usefulness of thinking of ability as malleable is further underscored in a similar study (Aronson, 1997). In this study, undergraduates were led to believe they had either performed well or poorly on a test measuring their speed-reading ability. Prior to receiving the feedback, the test takers had been led to believe either that speed reading was a highly improvable skill or that it was an endowed ability that could not be improved much with practice. At issue was how the feedback and the conception of the ability would interact to influence how much students ultimately valued the importance of speed reading. The results were quite clear. When speed reading was presented as a trait that could not be improved, test takers who received positive feedback gave it high ratings ("speed reading is an extremely valuable skill"). In contrast, test takers who received negative feedback did not believe that speed reading was an important skill. This devaluing did not occur when the test takers were led to believe that they could get better at speed reading. In this condition, both those who received positive feedback and those who received negative feedback said that speed reading was an important skill. Thus thinking of a skill as malleable can reduce the tendency to disidentify in the face of failure.

## Reconceptualizing Intelligence

Two larger-scale interventions (Aronson, Fried, & Good, in press; Aronson & Good, 2001b) built on these two findings. One program involving African-American and European-American college students employed numerous tactics of attitude change to get them to adopt—and make highly accessible—the belief that intelligence expandable. Attitudes toward academic achievement and actual performance were assessed 4 months later at the end of the school year. The results were highly encouraging. Not only did the African-American students who took part in the intervention report enjoying and feeling more identified with academics, their GPAs at year's end reflected these positive attitudes. On average these African-American students improved their grades (overall GPA) by four-tenths of a grade point. In a second program college students mentored Latino and European-American junior high students. The mentors conveyed to their students different attitudes that we hypothesized would help the students navigate the difficult transition year from elementary school to junior high school. For one group of students, the mentors focused on the idea that intelligence is expandable; for another group of students, the mentors discussed the perils of drug use. At year's end, students mentored in the malleability of intelligence received higher scores on the statewide standardized test of reading ability than students who received the antidrug message. Similar results were found for girls' math performance on the statewide test. When the malleability message was not incorporated into the mentoring, girls underperformed relative to boys. When they were taught about the expandability of intelligence, their performance increased substantially.

## Reducing Stereotype Threat Through Contact

The research by Inzlicht and Ben-Zeev (2000) suggests that just mixing students together can spoil minority student performance and their enjoyment of classroom activities. But if structured properly, diversity can be used to reduce stereotype threat. Steele, Spencer, Hummel, Carter, Harber, Schoem, and Nisbett (1997) designed a comprehensive program for first-year students at the University of Michigan. This program sought to reduce stereotype threat through three means: (1) Students were "honorifically" recruited by emphasizing that they had already met the tough admission standards at the University of Michigan. (2) Students participated in weekly seminars through the first semester that allowed students to get to know one another and to learn some of the common problems they shared. (3) Students participated in subject master workshops in one of their courses that exposed the students to advanced material that went beyond material in the class. The elements sought to convey the message that instructors and peers thought they could excel academically, would not stereotype them, and believed they belonged at the University. Several years of the program demonstrate that such practices can lead to a substantial increase in African-Americans' performance in school. On average African-Americans randomly assigned to the program do four-tenths of a grade point better than African-Americans randomly assigned to a control group. In addition, this increase in performance, although it diminishes, is evident throughout the college years and leads to higher retention rates. Why is the program effective? Analysis of survey data collected from the program participants and the control group suggests that the program decreases stereotype threat, which in turn promotes identification with school, which leads to better grades.

## Cooperation

Stereotypes and intergroup tensions flourish in competitive settings. There have been numerous interventions that have yielded impressive gains in the academic achievement of minority youth by structuring classroom or study environments in a way that minimizes the performance-undermining processes akin to those I have discussed here. E. Aronson and colleagues' "Jigsaw classroom" (e.g., Aronson & Patnoe, 1997; E. Aronson, Chapter 10 in this volume) and Uri Treisman's work (e.g., Treisman, 1992) with African–American math students are outstanding examples in this regard. Studies on the Jigsaw classroom show that the technique typically raises the minority students' grades (by about a letter grade), raises their self-esteem, increases friendships between ethnic group members, and leads to greater enjoyment among students of all backgrounds. In Treisman's work, group study in a calculus workshop that stressed challenge lifted the African–Americans' achievement to surprising levels; they earned grades as high as those of the Asian students in Treisman's classes. Importantly, part of the success of Treisman's work depends on presenting difficult work, which stresses challenge—as opposed to remediation. Getting children or adult students to work cooperatively on highly challenging work not only reduces prejudice (and thus stereotype threat), it also ensures that all students feel a sense of belongingness. These studies are touchstones; they prove that the group differences are tractable, that they can disappear under the proper social conditions. If I could make only one change in classrooms, I would adopt cooperative learning techniques because they elegantly address so many of the causes and consequences of stereotype threat.

## CONCLUSION

Decades of psychological research shows us that stereotypes are more than just benign "pictures in the head." Rather, they are expectations that can undermine performance, either through prompting differential treatment of the stereotyped or by inducing stereotype threat in the stereotyped. Most likely, both processes occur at the same time in a self-confirming spiral of low expectations, hindered performance, and threatened belongingness. Our research suggests that how people contend and cope with these unnerving expectations can have a dramatic effect on their academic achievement. The good news that I hope has come through in this chapter is that because stereotype threat is partly induced by situations, such as the situations that turned bright kids like Ricky and Darryl into low-performing students, there is much that concerned educators can do to reduce stereotype threat in classrooms and other academic settings.

### Teachers' Questions and Answers

**Q:**   Your research makes me wonder if students at schools or in classrooms where they are not in the minority might fare better than when they are outnumbered by majority group members. Is there any research on this?

**A:**   There has been some research that bears on these issues. Recall the research by Inzlicht and Ben-Zeev (2000), showing that it takes only one male to undermine the performance of women taking a math test. This would seem to suggest that any level of integration is disruptive. But it is not that simple. Bryant Marks (e.g., Marks & Jackson, 2001) conducted an interesting study comparing the test performances of African–Americans at primarily black colleges versus primarily white colleges, essentially a replication of the Steele –Aronson studies I described earlier, but examining the role of school environment. The other twist that Marks added was to look at the difference between freshmen and seniors. With freshmen, he found the same pattern of results: the students underperformed on a standardized test under stereotype threat conditions. But the seniors were not affected by stereotype threat. Marks interprets these results as indicating that the seniors learned to cope effectively with stereotype threat—to develop their abilities as well as some useful attitudes that unseated their vulnerability. Thus, under certain conditions at least, integration can be detrimental, but people can learn to be less vulnerable. What remains to be seen, however, is how students like Marks' seniors fare at higher levels of schooling, like graduate or medical school, where they may find themselves in the minority, in an extremely challenging and competitive environment.

**Q:** Not all stereotypes are negative. For example, Asians are widely perceived to be smarter and harder working than other students. Do these positive stereotypes have any effects comparable to the negative stereotypes you have discussed?

**A:** Indeed they do, and it's a very interesting story. When stereotypes are subtly activated, it appears that people tend to behave or perform in line with the stereotype. But when the stereotype is so salient that it is brought to conscious awareness, people can get caught up in trying to prove or disprove the stereotype. Thus, in a remarkable study conducted by Margaret Shih and her associates (Shih, Pittinsky, & Ambady, 1999), Asian women were subtly reminded (with a questionnaire) of either their Asian identity or their female identity prior to taking a difficult math test. The results were clear: the women reminded of their Asianness performed better than the control group, whereas those reminded of their female identity performed worse than the control group. Sapna Cheryan and Galen Bodenhausen (2000) found that when Asian women were made conscious that their Asian identity was relevant to a math test they were taking, they choked. Thus, model minority status can be a burden or a boon, depending on whether one consciously thinks about it. The implications of negative stereotypes for blacks and Latinos are also clear: whether or not the stereotype is so salient that one thinks about it is, to some degree, irrelevant; with or without conscious awareness, the stereotype undermines performance.

**Q:** You have described a number of laboratory studies that are very compelling. But I wonder how applicable these studies are to real-world testing. Does stereotype threat have as big an effect on the real tests that students take?

**A:** This is an important question. Our studies were designed to test a theory, and as such, we constructed a very controlled—some would say *sterile*—environment in which to test it. So you are right to wonder if stereotype threat has effects on performance in the real world, where so much else is going on that cannot be controlled for. A number of researchers, including us, have conducted studies in schools with children, outside the sterile confines of our university psychology laboratories. The results have generally paralleled the laboratory studies. But there is even more compelling research that bears on your question. Not long ago researchers at the Educational Testing Service, which develops many of the college entrance examinations like the SAT, conducted a series of studies to see if stereotype threat depressed the performances of women and minorities on real tests, with real-life consequences.

These studies are notable in that it was clear from the reporting that the researchers wanted dearly to show that stereotype threat has no effects on actual test performances outside the laboratory. After all, our research had raised the possibility that their tests were unfair to women and minorities, a claim they have been disputing for decades.

In one notable study (Stricker, 1998), the test administrators had students indicate their ethnicity and gender either before or after a difficult test, the Advanced Placement (AP) test of calculus. This is an important test, one that determines whether students get college credit for their high school studies; it can also play a big role in college admissions. Although stereotype threat should have been high for women and minorities taking either version of the test, it should have been even higher for those who indicated their gender and ethnicity before the test (which, incidentally, is the way the test is actually administered by the College Board). And to the apparent chagrin of the researchers, this is exactly what was found. Above and beyond the stereotype threat already depressing performance, there was a clear effect on the female and minority students asked about ethnicity and gender before the test—their test scores were lower. The author of this study was clearly unhappy with these results, and therefore argued that the performance differences, although *statistically* significant, were nonetheless trivial—that the small number of items missed as a result of indicating gender or ethnicity could hardly add up to much in the real world. I disagree, and so do most of the scientists who have read this report. A commentary by social psychologist Christian Crandall, who carefully analyzed the report, makes clear precisely why. Crandall notes that if the College Board made the simple change of asking for the ethnicity and gender information *after* the test, in a typical year approximately 2837 additional young women (out of about 17,000) would start college with calculus credit—and stand a better chance of getting into the college of their choice. I think that most of us would agree that this is not trivial, especially if you happen to be one of the thousands of students who take these tests every year. In sum, all the available data suggest that stereotype threat is a real phenomenon with real consequences for students.

## References

Allport, G. (1954). *The nature of prejudice*. New York: Doubleday.

Ambady, N., Shih, M., Kim, A., & Pittinsky, T. (2001). Stereotype susceptibility in children: Effects of identity activation on quantitative performance. *Psychological Science, 12*, 385–390.

Aronson, E., & Patnoe, S. (1997). *The jigsaw classroom*. New York: Longman.

Aronson, J. (1997). *The effects of conceptions of ability on task valuation*. Unpublished manuscript, New York University.

Aronson, J. (1999). *The effects of conceiving ability as fixed or improvable on responses to stereotype threat*. Unpublished manuscript, New York University.

Aronson, J., Blanton, H., & Cooper, J. (1995). From dissonance to disidentification: Selectivity in the self-affirmation process. *Journal of Personality and Social Psychology, 58*, 1062–1072.

Aronson, J., Fried, C., & Good, C. (in press). Reducing the effects of stereotype threat on African-American college students by shaping theories of intelligence. *Journal of Experimental Social Psychology*.

Aronson, J., & Good, C. (2001a). *Personal versus situational stakes and stereotype threat: A test of the vanguard hypothesis*. Manuscript in preparation, New York University.

Aronson, J., & Good, C. (2001b). *Theories of intelligence, stereotype threat, and the transition to middle school*. Unpublished data, New York University.

Aronson, J., Lustina, M. J., Good, C., Keough, K., Steele, C. M., & Brown, J. (1999). When white men can't do math: Necessary and sufficient factors in stereotype threat. *Journal of Experimental Social Psychology, 35*, 29–46.

Aronson J., Quinn, D., & Spencer, S. J. (1998). Stereotype threat and the academic performance of minorities and women. In J. Swim & C. Stangor (Eds.), *Prejudice: The target's perspective*. San Diego: Academic Press.

Aronson, J., & Salinas, M. F. (1997). *Stereotype threat, attributional ambiguity, and Latino underperformance*. Unpublished manuscript, New York University.

Brown, R. P., Pinel, E. C., Rentfrow, P., & Lee, M. (2001). *Stigma on my mind: Individual differences in the experience of stereotype threat*. Unpublished manuscript, University of Oklahoma.

Cheryan, S., & Bodenhausen, G. V. (2000). When positive stereotypes threaten intellectual performance: The psychological hazards of ''model minority'' status. *Psychological Science, 11*, 399–402.

Cohen, G., & Steele, C. M. (2002). A barrier of mistrust: How negative stereotypes affect cross-race mentoring. In J. Aronson (Ed.), *Improving academic achievement: Impact of psychological factors on education*. San Diego: Academic Press.

Cohen, G. L., Steele, C. M., & Ross, L. D. (1999). The mentor's dilemma: Providing critical feedback across the racial divide. *Personality and Social Psychology Bulletin, 25*, 1302–1318.

Crocker, J., & Major, B. (1989). Social stigma and self-esteem: The self-protective properties of stigma. *Psychological Review, 96*, 608–630.

Croizet, J., & Claire, T. (1998). Extending the concept of stereotype threat to social class: The intellectual underperformance of students from low socioeconomic backgrounds. *Personality and Social Psychology Bulletin, 24*, 588–594.

Devine, P. (1989). Stereotypes and prejudice: Their automatic and controlled components. *Journal of Personality and Social Psychology, 56*, 5–18.

Dweck, C. S. (1999). *Self-theories: Their role in motivation, personality, and development*. Philadelphia: Taylor & Francis.

Dweck, C. S. (2002). Messages that motivate: How praise molds students' beliefs, motivation, and performance (in surprising ways). In J. Aronson (Ed.), *Improving academic achievement: Impact of psychological factors on education*. San Diego: Academic Press.

Ferguson, R. F. (1998). Teacher's perceptions and expectations and the black–white test score gap. In C. Jencks & M. Phillips (Eds.), *The black–white test score gap*. Washington, DC: Brookings Institution Press.

Gilbert, D. T., Pinel, E. C., Wilson, T. D., Blumberg, S. J., & Wheatley, T. (1998). Immune neglect: A source of durability bias in affective forecasting. *Journal of Personality and Social Psychology, 75*, 617–638.

Good, C., & Aronson, J. (in press). The development and consequences of stereotype vulnerability in adolescents. In F., Pajares & T. Urdan (Eds.), *Adolescence and education, Vol. 2: Academic motivation of adolescents*. Greenwich, CT: Information Age.

Good, C., & Aronson, J. (2001). *Stereotype threat in the absence of a kernel of truth: Unfounded stereotypes can depress women's calculus performance*. Unpublished manuscript, Columbia University.

Herrnstein, R. J., & Murray, C. (1994). *The bell curve. Intelligence and class structure in American life*. New York: Free Press.

Inzlicht, M., & Ben-Zeev, T. (2000). A threatening intellectual environment: Why females are susceptible to experiencing problem-solving deficits in the presence of males. *Psychological Science, 11*, 365–371.

Jordan, V. (2001). *Vernon can read!* New York: Public Affairs.

Levy, B. (1996). Improving memory in old age through implicit self-stereotyping. *Journal of Personality and Social Psychology, 71*, 1092–1107.

Marks, B. T., & Jackson, J. S. (2001). *Stereotype threat and African-American college students: The role of experience, racial identity, and racial context.* Unpublished manuscript, University of Illinois, Chicago.

National Center for Education Statistics (1998). *Trends in academic progress* (NCES 97–985).

O'Brien, L., & Crandall, C. (under review). *Stereotype threat and arousal: Effects on women's math performance.*

Osborne, J. W. (1997). Race and academic disidentification. *Journal of Educational Psychology, 89*, 728–735.

Pinel, E. C. (1999). Stigma consciousness: The psychological legacy of social stereotypes. *Journal of Personality and Social Psychology, 76*, 114–128.

Pronin, E., Steele, C. M., & Ross, L. (2001). *Stereotype threat and the feminine identities of women in math.* Manuscript under review.

Rhodewalt, F., & Tragakis, M. W. (2002). Self-handicapping and school: On academic self-concept and self-protective behavior. In J. Aronson (Ed.), *Improving academic achievement: Impact of psychological factors on education.* San Diego: Academic Press.

Rosenkrantz, S. L. (1994). *Attributional ambiguity among Mexican-Americans: The role of acculturation and ethnic identity.* Doctoral dissertation, Stanford University.

Rosenthal, R. (2002). The pygmalion effect and its mediating mechanisms. In J. Aronson (Ed.), *Improving academic achievement: Impact of psychological factors on education.* San Diego: Academic Press.

Schmader, T., Johns, M., Keiffer, V., Healy, E., & Fairchild-Ollivierre, S. (2001) *"Double devaluation": The role of personal and social identity in stereotype threat effects.* Manuscript submitted for publication.

Seymour, E., & Hewitt, N. (1996). *Talking about leaving. Why undergraduates leave the sciences.* Boulder, CO: Westview Press.

Shih, M., Pittinsky, T. L., & Ambady, N. (1999). Stereotype susceptibility: Identity salience and shifts in quantitative performance. *Psychological Science, 10*(1), 80–83.

Sigelman & Tuch (1997). Meta-stereotypes: Blacks' perceptions of whites' stereotypes of blacks. *Public Opinion Quarterly, 61*, 87–101.

Smith, T. W. (1990). *Ethnic images.* GSS Topical Report No. 19. National Opinion Research Center.

Spicer, C. V., & Monteith, M. J. (2001). *Implicit outgroup favoritism among African-Americans and vulnerability to stereotype threat.* Unpublished manuscript, College of Charleston.

Steele, C. M. (1988). The psychology of self-affirmation: Sustaining the integrity of the self. In L. Berkowitz (Ed.), *Advances in experimental social psychology* (Vol. 21, pp. 261–302). Hillsdale, NJ: Erlbaum.

Steele, C. M. (1992, April). Race and the schooling of black Americans. *The Atlantic Monthly.*

Steele, C. M. (1997). A threat in the air: How stereotypes shape intellectual identity and performance. *American Psychologist, 52*, 613–629.

Steele, C. M., & Aronson, J. (1995). Stereotype threat and the intellectual test performance of African-Americans. *Journal of Personality and Social Psychology, 69*, 797–811.

Steele, C. M., Spencer, S. J., Hummel, M., Carter, K., Harber, K., Schoem, D., & Nisbett, R. (1997). *African-American college achievement: A "wise" intervention.* Unpublished manuscript, Stanford University.

Steele, C. M., Spencer, S. J., & Aronson, J. (in press). Contending with images of one's group: The psychology of stereotype and social identity threat. *Advances in Experimental Social Psychology.*

Stricker, L. J. (1998). *Inquiring about examinee's ethnicity and sex: Effects on AP Calculus AB Examination performance* (College Board Rep. 98–1; ETS Research Rep. No. 98–5). New York: College Entrance Examination Board.

Tesser, A. (1988). Toward a self-evaluation maintenance model of social behavior. In L. Berkowitz (Ed.), *Advances in experimental social psychology* (Vol. 21, pp. 181–228). Hillsdale, NJ: Erlbaum.

Treisman, U. (1992). Studying students studying calculus: A look at the lives of minority mathematics students in college. *College Mathematics Journal, 23*, 362–372.

Way, N. (1998). *Everyday courage: The lives and stories of urban teenagers.* New York: New York University Press.

CHAPTER

15

# A Barrier of Mistrust: How Negative Stereotypes Affect Cross-Race Mentoring

GEOFFREY L. COHEN

*Department of Psychology, Yale University,*
*New Haven, Connecticut*

CLAUDE M. STEELE

*Department of Psychology, Stanford University*
*Stanford, California*

A short time ago, a friend of ours began a job as a teacher in an inner-city school. He had studied education for several years, and now he had a chance to practice what he loved. For the first weeks, however, he found the work far more demanding than he had anticipated. The academic theory he had learned concerning the classroom had failed, it seemed, to prepare him for what actually occurred there. What surprised him most was the significance of race. Even among his young students, most of whom were ethnic minorities, racial stereotypes had shaped their expectations about him as a white teacher and about their prospects in school more generally. His students talked about the images that the media, and society at large, painted of their groups—and how these images presented, at worst, an insulting portrayal of their ethnic groups, and at best a pessimistic one. They worried that such images might bias the treatment they received not only from teachers but from other

Correspondence concerning this article should be addressed to Geoffrey Cohen, Department of Psychology, Yale University, 2 Hillhouse Avenue, P.O. Box 208205, New Haven, CT 06520-8205. E-mail: geoffrey.cohen@yale.edu.

gatekeepers of educational opportunity. In a system tarnished by racism, they wondered, what assurance did they have that their efforts in school today would lead to advancement tomorrow?

While this anecdote raises several issues, we use it here to illustrate an often underappreciated concept in the psychology of motivation—trust. To excel at almost any endeavor, people need to trust that relevant authority figures have their best interests at heart (see also Tyler, Smith, & Huo, 1996). Of course, a given teacher, school, or institution may not deserve trust. But when trust is warranted, students are best served if they can feel certain that educators believe in their potential and care about their welfare.

Given the key role that trust plays in academic settings, members of historically oppressed groups may suffer a disadvantage, insofar as the past treatment of their groups in society gives them grounds to mistrust authority figures. In fact, personal experience alone may provide African-Americans, Latino-Americans, and Native Americans with ample reason to fear being judged or treated prejudicially. Without trust in the integrity of educators and academic institutions, their motivation in school may falter, particularly in situations that trigger concerns about their group's acceptance. Indeed, much of the well-documented scholastic achievement gap between ethnic minority students and their white peers reflects, we argue, the devastating consequences of racial mistrust (see Steele, 1997). A crucial challenge faced by educators working across racial lines, the present chapter thus suggests, is to forge trusting relationships (Marx, Brown, & Steele, 1999; Steele, 1999; see also Bryk & Schneider, 1996).

The analysis presented in this chapter rests on three claims. The first claim asserts that stigmatization impedes trust. Being a member of a socially devalued group can cause a student to question whether teachers, schools, or societal institutions more generally will provide reliably fair and kind treatment. The second claim asserts that the mistrust elicited by stigmatization can, in turn, cause motivation and performance to suffer. Students will feel reluctant to invest themselves in a domain where they could be subjected to biased judgment or treatment. The final claim asserts that allaying the threat of stigmatization will help to create trust and to improve motivation. Students who feel assured that they will not be viewed through the lens of a negative stereotype, that is, will be more likely to trust their educators. They will thus feel safe to invest their effort, and even their identity, in scholastic pursuits.

Below we present a selective review of research to buttress each of these three theoretical claims. Next, we describe work conducted in our own laboratory, where we applied this theory to a key educational dilemma—the challenge to provide critical but constructive feedback across lines of difference, specifically across the racial and gender divides. In a later section of the chapter, we use the same conceptual framework to understand how a "stigma of racism" may hamper the performance of *teachers* who work in demographically diverse classrooms. Then, in a final section, we review several additional intervention strategies. Each one boosts the achievement of minority students, we argue, by allaying the threat of stigmatization and thus creating a basis for trust.

## STIGMATIZATION IMPEDES THE ESTABLISHMENT OF TRUST

Because minority students know that members of their ethnic group have long faced prejudice, and because they may have experienced such prejudice personally, they may rightfully feel wary of people who do not belong to their ethnic group, especially in evaluative situations where negative racial stereotypes could be used against them. Theorists have long noted the potentially large costs incurred by trusting someone who could ultimately prove untrustworthy (Gambetta, 1990; see also Fukuyama, 1995; Lewis & Weigert, 1985). For that reason, minority students may reasonably view white teachers with suspicion until they have evidence that they are worthy of trust.

The default assumption may thus be that people outside one's ethnic group are biased, even when these outsiders do not explicitly harbor prejudicial beliefs. In one study, both black undergraduates and their white classmates vastly overestimated the degree to which peers of the other racial group stereotyped their own race (Krueger, 1996). In fact, members of both ethnic groups reported similarly positive feelings toward blacks and whites. Nevertheless, they predicted that members of the *other* race would express far more negative evaluations of their *own* race than they actually did. Because they are aware of our country's history of racial prejudice and conflict, people may reasonably suspect—sometimes accurately, sometimes inaccurately—that the hearts and minds of those beyond the boundary of their ethnic group are biased.

In any specific interaction, racial mistrust is apt to prove particularly acute when the possibility of being discredited on the basis of one's race is plausible rather than implausible. Features of the situation that alter the salience or relevance of one's race—and thus affect its potential to bias another person's response—can dramatically influence trust. In one study, black college students and their white peers received negative interpersonal feedback from a white student who, they were led to believe, sat on the other side of a one-way mirror (Crocker, Voelkl, & Major, 1991). Black students proved more likely than white students to believe that the feedback was motivated by the evaluator's prejudice. However, this race difference in trust was most pronounced when the curtains of the one-way mirror were open rather than closed and, students thus could presume that the evaluator was aware of their race. Stigmatization leads to mistrust primarily when group members recognize that a stereotype could plausibly be used against them, in situations, that is, where their race is known, and where the stereotype impugns their general worth or their specific abilities at the task at hand (Crocker, Major, & Steele, 1998).

Not only may members of ethnic minority groups show decrements in trust as a result of stigmatization. Rather, anyone who fears being rejected on the basis of a personal characteristic might anticipate being judged with prejudice rather than viewed with respect (Goffman, 1963). Even ordinarily nonstigmatized individuals may thus respond mistrustfully when the situation causes them to feel suspect in the eyes of others. In one classic experiment, for example, subjects were temporarily given a stigma by having a simulated scar cosmetically applied to their face (Kleck & Strenta, 1980). While ostensibly touching it up, however, the experimenter wiped off the scar without the subject's knowledge. Feeling physically disfigured gives people grounds to wonder if others will accept them (Davis, 1961; Goffman, 1963; Hastorf, Wildfogel, & Cassman, 1979). Subjects in the present study, believing that a scar was visible on their face, thus had reason to question whether others would treat them with fairness and kindness.

In fact, the results of the study yielded dramatic support for this reasoning (Kleck & Strenta, 1980). After the scar had been removed, subjects participated in a discussion with a fellow student, and then later commented on their partner's demeanor. Subjects reported that the scar had caused their partner to treat them in an awkward and patronizing manner—the person, they felt, had been unable to get past their physical disfigurement. However, the scar's removal prior to this interaction ensured that subjects were *not* treated differently on the basis of a facial deformity, and in fact independent observers found no evidence of systematic differences in the partner's behavior as a function of whether subjects believed they possessed a scar or not. Rather, subjects who thought that they appeared facially disfigured engaged in a fine-grained analysis of their partner's behavior, finding evidence of bias in non-verbal cues that they would otherwise overlook (Strenta & Kleck, 1984; see also Vorauer & Ross, 1993).

Clearly, it is an oversimplification to equate the stigmatization felt by subjects in the present study with that faced by ethnic minorities. In many cases, the prejudice minority students sense is real rather than merely perceived. Their mistrust, moreover, derives not from an illusory scar, but from the lessons of history and personal experience. Because racism can be subtle in its manifestations, and because its effects can prove costly, it is adaptive to be vigilant for prejudice (see Frable, Blackstone, & Scherbaum, 1990). Nevertheless, the results described in this experiment offer at least one important lesson: The relationship between stigmatization and trust is general rather than specific to any one group. Even a *transitory* stigma, conferred to persons from a historically *nonstigmatized* group, can create mistrust, wherein the good will of other people comes to be questioned rather than assumed (see also Aronson, Lustina, Keough, Brown, & Steele, 1999; Leyens, Désert, Croizet, & Darcis, 2000).

## MISTRUST UNDERMINES MOTIVATION
## AND PERFORMANCE

Persistence in an endeavor is sustained by a faith that one will both be viewed as an individual and be included in important relationships. Negative stereotypes erode this trust, and thus reduce the likelihood of scholastic success. Students who suspect racial bias, for example, may prove less motivated to comply with teachers' specific instructions for improvement. Black students in one study thus discounted the objectivity of performance feedback more from a white evaluator than from a black one; and they also chose to perseverate in their own strategies rather than adopt those recommendations made by the white evaluator (Banks, Stitt, Curtis, & McQuarter, 1977). Moreover, people who fear being stereotyped are apt to suffer dramatic decrements in self-confidence (Stangor, Carr, & Kiang, 1998).

At each level of achievement, one's race may raise doubts about the quality of treatment that one can expect from relevant authorities. Students may thus be discouraged from fully investing themselves in school. As much research attests, the quality of relationships with school authorities conveys important information about one's standing and general prospects within relevant academic domains (see Tyler et al., 1996). Unfair, inattentive, or disrespectful treatment suggests that the student (and perhaps the student's race) has a low standing and unfavorable prospects. By contrast, fair, attentive, or respectful treatment communicates good standing and favorable prospects. As social psychologists have long noted, people who evaluate their position and prospects favorably within a group are apt to internalize relevant group norms and values, and they seek to fulfill group-based standards of behavior and performance (Tyler et al., 1996; Huo, Smith, Tyler, & Lind, 1996). To the extent that minority students believe that they might be excluded or rejected on the basis of race, they may thus view school as irrelevant to their self-interests and identity.

In an impressive line of research, Tom Tyler, Allan Lind, and their colleagues underscore the role of trust in motivation. In a variety of settings, including school, family, and work, they find that judgments about the quality of one's relationships with authorities prove to be among the strongest predictors not only of whether individuals comply with the decisions of authorities, but also of whether they adopt the values of their organization (Huo et al., 1996; Tyler et al., 1996). Employees are more likely to embrace the ideals of their company, and they even will go beyond the formal requirements of their position, when they feel that management is "on their side" and generally responsive to their needs. In fact, trust appears more important in determining identification with an organization (and subsequent motivation) than the objective rewards and punishments provided by the authority (Smith, Tyler, Huo, Ortiz, & Lind, 1998; Tyler et al.,1996; Huo et al., 1996).

People decide whether to trust individuals or organizations by assessing the consistency with which they apply rules and the fairness with which they make decisions (Tyler et al., 1996; Huo et al., 1996). The objective grades and feedback students receive thus seem to matter less than the perceived fairness of the system that provides them. If students believe that the academic system is fair—if they trust the legitimacy of the *procedures* it uses—they will maintain motivation in the face of most decisions or outcomes. Only when students think that the system could be biased against them or their ethnic group will they focus on a given outcome and the potential bias that motivated it.

The reasoning outlined here dovetails with the body of research on "stereotype threat" (Aronson, Quinn, & Spencer, 1998; Spencer, Steele, & Quinn, 1999; Steele & Aronson, 1995; Steele, 1997; see also Aronson, Chapter 14 in this volume). As that work demonstrates, minority students working on a standardized GRE test, or for that matter on any demanding intellectual task, may worry about confirming a negative stereotype about their ethnic group. They must contend with the threatening possibility that, should their performance falter, it could substantiate the racial stereotype's allegation of limited ability. In the short term, stereotype threat can cause anxiety and distraction debilitating enough to undermine academic performance. In the long term, it can lead students to disidentify from scholastic pursuits, prompting them to invest their efforts and identity in areas where they are less subject to doubt. Stereotype threat, it could be argued, sprouts from a crack in social trust. Students cannot trust that their performance will be judged fairly, inasmuch as they worry that a specific failure on their part could be viewed as evidence of racial inferiority.

A recent study conducted by Joseph Brown and Claude Steele specifically highlighted the role of trust in stereotype threat. They began by documenting a familiar pattern: black college students performed worse than did their white peers on a difficult GRE test (see Marx, Brown, & Steele, 1999). The researchers wondered, however, if black students would do better if they could trust that the test would not be used to substantiate racial stereotypes—if they were assured, in Tyler's language, that it was procedurally fair. Students in one experimental condition were presented with the same GRE test, but they were first informed that the designers of the test, many of whom were said to be black, had ensured that it was *racially fair*. Students thus knew that their poor performance would not be taken as evidence of a racial inferiority, because any biased test content that would produce a racial difference had allegedly been removed. In fact, the performance of black students in this condition improved so dramatically that it equaled that of their white peers. Notably, more commonplace strategies to enhance performance, such as boosting self-efficacy, proved ineffective. It was not low self-confidence that hurt black students on the test; it was a lack of trust.

## ALLAYING STIGMATIZATION ENHANCES
## MOTIVATION AND PERFORMANCE

Both teacher and student thus face a challenge. The teacher must communicate that he or she is trustworthy, despite the potential for racism that exists both in the academic system in particular and in society more generally. The student, in turn, has to make a risky leap of faith, going beyond at times inconclusive evidence to assume that a given teacher or academic institution is worthy of trust. The first step, we believe, lies with teachers and the schools they represent. They must educate in a "wise" manner, that is, in a way that communicates to students that they will neither be viewed nor be treated in light of a negative stereotype. The term *wise* is borrowed from the sociologist Erving Goffman (1963), who had borrowed it from the gay subculture of the 1950s. In its original usage, the term referred to straight individuals who were recognized for their ability to see the full humanity of gay men and women. The present use of the term *wise* evokes a similar connotation. Wise strategies are those that assure stigmatized students that they will not be judged or treated stereotypically—that their abilities and belonging are assumed rather than doubted. Such strategies lift the threat of stigmatization, allowing minority students both to trust their educators and to safely invest themselves in school.

Assuring students of the racially fair nature of the testing and decision procedures, as in the study conducted by Brown and Steele noted above, can constitute one wise intervention. But even strategies that do not *explicitly* refer to race can be wise. The effectiveness of such strategies is suggested by the many educators and intervention programs who, in defiance of troubling statistics on minority achievement, have raised the grades, test scores, and college prospects of at-risk and minority youth (see Cohen, Steele, & Ross, 1999, for a review). The educators in these programs all refute negative stereotypes by conveying a faith in each student's intellectual potential. But they do not impart this message by assigning easier work to ensure student success, or by offering heavy doses of unstinting praise—all-too-common tactics of well-meaning but unwise teachers. In fact, several researchers offer detailed discussions of the dangers of "overpraising" and "underchallenging" students (Barker & Graham, 1987; Massey, Scott, & Dornbusch, 1975; Brophy, 1981; Mueller & Dweck, 1998). Rather, minority students in all of these otherwise diverse success stories are challenged with high performance standards, standards that *presume* their motivation and ability to succeed. The educators in these programs often go an important step further by explicitly assuring students of their capacity to meet those standards through greater effort.

Jaime Escalante (whose work was portrayed in the movie *Stand and Deliver* and documented in a book by Mathews, 1988) challenged his East Los Angeles Latino students to take and pass the advanced placement (AP) exam in calculus (see Cohen et al., 1999). Escalante's students met this standard. In fact, for a time, they accounted for 27% of all Mexican Americans receiving college credit on their AP exam, and the rate of advanced placement compared favorably with that obtained in many privileged suburban schools. Xavier University, which despite its small size and scant endowment, sends more black students to medical schools than any other university, and Georgia Tech, which enjoys exceptional success in graduating minority students from its engineering curriculum, similarly set highly demanding standards (see also Rosenthal, Chapter 2 in this volume; Rosenthal & Jacobson, 1968).

The benefits conferred by the invocation of high standards are apt to be limited unless the student is also assured, implicitly or explicitly, that he or she is capable of reaching the higher standards (Cohen et al., 1999). Effective interventions thus continually convey the message that students can succeed through effort and persistence. In a sense, the message is that academic ability, or even so-called intelligence, is not fixed or immutable (Dweck, Chiu, & Hong, 1995; see also Chapter 3 by Dweck and Chapter 14 by Aronson in this volume). Rather, it can be enhanced through effortful practice and the cultivation of specific skills. Norman Francis, the president of Xavier University, explains his institution's educational philosophy eloquently: "From the very beginning, we always believed that every youngster could learn, that the mind was an unlimited facility, that if you gave the support, provided the environment and the teachers, young people would exceed even their own potential" (quoted in Cose, 1997). To drive home that message, Xavier's prospective premedical students are bombarded with information on careers, especially those in the areas of science and health, from the outset. The lesson conveyed is clear: "success is attainable  becoming a physician is not an impossible dream" (Cose, 1997).

## THE MENTOR'S DILEMMA: A SPECIFIC APPLICATION

In a series of experiments conducted with our colleague Lee Ross, we focused on what we call the "mentor's dilemma"—the challenge to provide critical but constructive feedback without undermining the student's motivation to succeed (Cohen et al., 1999). Along with tutorial instruction, the quality of feedback that students receive constitutes one of the strongest predictors of scholastic accomplishment (Bloom, 1984; Walberg, 1984). The mentor's dilemma, we reasoned, should prove particularly acute when critical feedback must be conveyed across racial lines. Because they know that their abilities are negatively stereotyped, minority students may mistrust the person providing the feedback. Following the receipt of critical feedback, they may consequently feel less motivated to undertake further efforts to improve their work.

The real-world success stories noted above highlighted the effectiveness of combining an invocation of high standards with an assurance of students' capacity to reach those standards. Such a strategy should prove particularly helpful to the mentor who is obliged to provide critical feedback across racial lines. The invocation of high standards would encourage students to view the critical nature of the feedback as a reflection of rigorous performance standards rather than racial bias. Moreover, the assurance would allay students' fear of confirming the stereotype by failing to meet the critic's demanding standards. The *explicitness* of these two messages, we reasoned, would prove disproportionately important for minority students. White students receiving rigorous criticism, that is, should be more inclined than minority students to automatically *infer* that high standards are being applied and to further *assume* that they are seen as capable of meeting those standards.

In our first study, African American undergraduates and their white peers wrote a letter of commendation for their favorite teacher. They were informed that the best letters would be published in an education journal. The following week, students returned and received a "revise and resubmit" verdict on their letter, ostensibly from a member of the journal's editorial board, along with critical feedback pointing out areas of weakness and suggesting strategies for improvement. Our experiments pitted the effect of "unbuffered" criticism, that is, criticism unaccompanied by any additional information, against that of "wise" criticism, that is, criticism accompanied by the stigmatization-dispelling combination of high standards and personal assurance.

Two experimental details were added to lead black participants to view the feedback as potentially biased. At the first session, prior to receiving the criticism, students had their photograph taken with an instant camera, and this photograph was then appended to their letter. Students were thus alerted that anyone who evaluated their letter would be aware of their race. In addition, at the second session, students learned the name of the reviewer who ostensibly evaluated their letter, and this name was recognizably Caucasian: "Dr. Gardiner Lindsay."

When provided with unbuffered feedback in this manner, black students proved more inclined than white students to suspect bias on the part of the evaluator. This mistrust, in turn, undermined motivation: black students felt less interested than their white classmates in undertaking a revision of their letter. However, when the same critical feedback was accompanied by the combination of an invocation of high standards and a personal assurance of the student's capacity to reach those standards, black students suspected little if any bias on the part of the evaluator, and their motivation improved so dramatically that it surpassed, slightly, that of their white peers. In addition, *all* students in this treatment condition reported greater interest in pursuing career possibilities that demand writing skills. The wise, two-faceted intervention proved more effective than the commonplace tactic of preceding critical feedback with a buffer of performance praise. Indeed, one striking result was that although the criticism suggested that a major revision of their work was necessary, black students receiving "wise criticism" felt as efficacious and motivated as students in an additional condition who received *only* positive feedback.

A later study disentangled the effect of invoking high standards from that of assuring students of their capacity to reach those standards. Accompanying critical feedback with only a warning that high standards would be imposed deflected attributions of racial bias, but by itself failed to raise motivation on the part of black students. Indeed, in the absence of the personal assurance, such a forewarning of heightened standards seemed to exacerbate threat. Black students still had to wonder if their capacity to reach such daunting standards was in doubt, and they thus benefited from the additional personal assurance featured in fully wise feedback.

## GENERALIZING THE FRAMEWORK: WOMEN WORKING IN THE NATURAL SCIENCES

The theory outlined here asserts that stigmatization impedes trust, which in turn undermines motivation. Dispelling stigmatization, for example, with the wise intervention used in our research, establishes a basis for trust, and thus improves motivation. The theory should generalize to other populations who face group-based doubts about their abilities. In fact, women working in math, science, and engineering have long confronted negative stereotypes about their potential and belonging in these fields (Spencer, Steele, & Quinn, 1999). As early as elementary school, girls receive less encouragement than boys in math and science; and as late as college, women abandon the study of math and science at a rate nearly three times that of men, even though they earn grades in relevant coursework that equal and even slightly exceed those of their male peers (see Steele, 1997).

We began with the observation that women working in scientific disciplines are apt to receive much of their instruction from male superiors. It seemed plausible that the male–female achievement gap in the sciences may be due, at least in part, to gender mistrust and its detrimental effects on motivation and performance. In fact, one study found that doctoral graduates who had worked with a mentor of the *opposite* sex later achieved an average publication rate only a fourth that of graduates who had worked with mentors of the *same* sex (Goldstein, 1979; see also Crosby, 1999). Because they know that their scientific abilities are negatively stereotyped, women may wonder if they are granted as much respect as men in pursuits that demand such skills, and this mistrust could diminish their prospects for success.

In one of our studies, science and engineering majors of both sexes received either "wise" or "unwise" critical feedback on a task relevant to their skills and long-term prospects in scientific pursuits—preparing and delivering a research presentation. One week later, they received a critical review of their performance ostensibly from a male science professor. Our study went beyond self-report measures of motivation to examine the effect of feedback on *performance*. Specifically, upon receiving feedback about their initial performance, students had an opportunity to give their presentation again, after being provided with sufficient time to incorporate the suggestions for improvement offered in the context of the feedback.

Compared with men, women receiving *unbuffered* critical feedback responded mistrustfully. They felt that the reviewer had been unfair and biased in his assessment of their presentation. Women receiving this unbuffered feedback also proved less likely, in their revisions, to comply with the reviewer's recommendations for improvement. Finally, women in this condition also produced worse overall presentation revisions, and they communicated less technically difficult subject matter, than did subjects in any other condition of the experiment. Interestingly, the performance of female students showed only slight improvement when the same critical feedback was accompanied only by a personal assurance of their capacity to "do better." Without the additional invocation of high standards used in fully wise feedback, it seems, such an assurance can send the discouraging message that hard work on the student's part can only raise the level of their performance from utter deficiency to mere adequacy.

When, however, the same critical feedback featured the wise combination of high standards and assurance, women felt greater trust, and they showed stunning gains in *performance*. In fact, the percentage of women who complied with a central suggestion made by the critic—to incorporate an outline at the beginning of their presentation—was far greater in the wise criticism condition (72%) than it did in the condition featuring unbuffered criticism (11%). Indeed, in the wise criticism condition, women's *overall* performance improved so dramatically that the average overall quality of their presentations proved superior to that of subjects—male or female—in any other condition of the experiment.

The explicit invocation of high standards and assurance of personal capacity will prove particularly beneficial, we believe, at junctures where students receive feedback more critical than what they believe their performance merits. In such cases, they may be particularly liable to mistrust the evaluator's motives. Teachers, managers, and coaches may recall analogous situations, where the feedback they provided or the decisions they made conflicted with what their subordinates expected or simply wanted to be told. Beyond the confines of the lab, such situations often arise in academic settings when students go from one scholastic environment to a more rigorous one—moving from high school to college, or from college to graduate school—and the standards for what constitutes an adequate performance rise sharply (Dweck et al., 1995). At these transitions, students may be surprised to find that the amount of effort that they had previously invested in their work no longer suffices to earn them the praise or favorable grades that they had once received. How they make sense of the abrupt increase in critical feedback and scholastic frustration will affect their motivation and sense of belonging in school.

Nonstereotyped students may readily view the increased difficulty they experience as a reflection of elevated performance standards. Stereotyped students, by contrast, could potentially view it as a sign that they do not belong, as evidence that they have reached, in the eyes of others and perhaps in their own eyes as well, the limitation in ability alleged by the stereotyped. It may be no coincidence that, in at least one large longitudinal study, black students saw their GPA fall more than three times that of their white peers during the first major academic transition—as students left elementary school to enter junior high school (Simmons, Black, & Zhou, 1991). No doubt, this result reflects the institutional racism, school tracking policies, and inadequate academic preparation that put many black students at a disadvantage relative to white students. But the abrupt nature of the decline in achievement also raises the possibility that racial mistrust grows particularly acute when high standards are abruptly imposed without explanation or forewarning.

The wise intervention used in our studies is beneficial, it seems, because it makes explicit to negatively stereotyped students precisely the message that is apt to be implicit at least for the more privileged of nonminority students. Minority students and female science majors, that is, have grounds to wonder if the critical feedback they receive or the newly encountered academic hurdles they face imply that their race or gender puts them at risk. Our findings, we believe, offer an optimistic message about the potential to remedy such mistrust. Both minority students and female science majors seem *eager* to believe that they belong. In fact, they responded to the critical feedback provided in our studies as favorably as their nonstereotyped peers (indeed, somewhat *more* favorably), as long as that feedback was delivered in a manner that assured them that the stereotype would not be used against them.

## THE OTHER SIDE: SOME EFFECTS OF STIGMATIZATION ON TEACHER FEEDBACK

The present chapter has focused on the role of stigmatization in undermining the achievement of students who face negative stereotypes. However, stigmatization may also undermine the performance of teachers who work across ethnic lines. Because they know that their group is stereotyped as being racially biased, white teachers working with minority students may worry that they will be viewed as insensitive or even prejudiced. In numerous studies, in fact, whites and other ordinarily nonstereotyped individuals seem to feel stigmatized when interacting with members of socially devalued groups. Their body language thus stiffens, their speech becomes fragmented, and they seek to end the interaction sooner rather than later (Word, Zanna, & Cooper, 1974; see also Kleck, Ono, & Hastorf, 1966). Majority group members may also hold "meta-stereotypes"—beliefs about what members of a minority group think about members of a majority group (Vorauer, Main, & O'Connell, 1998). Specifically, whites and members of other majority groups tend to believe that minority group members stereotype their group as prejudiced, unfair, or complacent about existing power imbalances; and they may fear being personally assimilated to that stereotype (Vorauer et al., 1998). In fact, in at least one study, meta-stereotypic beliefs on the part of whites proved superior to conventional measures of prejudice at predicting aversion to cross-race interaction (Vorauer et al., 1998). Both white educators and their minority students may thus face a similar dilemma. They both want to break free of an identity to which they fear the other has consigned them.

Inasmuch as white educators cannot trust that minority students will interpret their behavior charitably, their performance may suffer accordingly. They may focus less on teaching effectively, and more on projecting an egalitarian self-image, than they otherwise would. When working with minority students, white teachers may thus use critical feedback only sparingly for fear of appearing prejudiced and, instead, offer generous dollops of performance praise. Empirical research, in fact, buttresses this reasoning. Several studies find that, in the classroom, minority students are praised more and criticized less than their nonminority peers (for notable exceptions, see the review by Ferguson, 1998). In a schoolwide survey, black students reported receiving the *most* praise of any ethnic group, even though they spent the fewest number of hours on homework and received the worst grades (Massey et al., 1975). Moreover, white evaluators in a series of experiments responded to a poorly written essay with more positive feedback when they were led to believe that its author was *black* rather than *white* (Harber, 1996, 1998).

A stigma of racism appears to motivate the provision of the favorable commentary provided to minority students. In one study, the positive feedback bias proved most acute when evaluators' egalitarian self-image had been threatened (Harber, 1996). Subjects who were told that they had scored poorly on a test of racial tolerance thus offered the most positive assessments of a black student's essay. The number of favorable comments made also rose sharply if the subject provided the feedback publicly, and the black student responded with a sullen demeanor, neither smiling nor making eye contact, and thereby insinuated a suspicion that the evaluator was racist (Harber, 1996). The results suggest that instructors use positive feedback to fend off a stigma of racism, and that their minority students may thus be provided with *more* positive feedback and *less* negative feedback than their white peers.

At first consideration, such a practice might seem beneficial. Both conventional wisdom and empirical research attest to the pedagogical value of praise. Students receiving positive feedback in laboratory studies tend to like their evaluator more, feel more intrinsically motivated, and perform better at relevant tasks than do students receiving negative feedback or even no feedback (see Koestner, Zuckerman, & Koestner, 1987; Miller, Brickman, & Bolen, 1975).

On further consideration, however, it becomes clear that although praise can confer benefits, it can also exact costs (see Dweck, Chapter 3 in this volume; also Graham, 1990). In an illustrative study outside the classroom, for example, high school athletes who received the lion's share of praise from their coaches were, by the end of the season, the *least* confident in their athletic skills, even after individual differences in preseason ability were statistically controlled (Horn, 1985).

At least in certain circumstances, it seems, positive feedback can thus prove counterproductive. To the extent that teachers substitute praise for criticism, and easily achieved success for hard-won accomplishment, students are apt to learn less than they otherwise would. In addition, recent research underscores the negative *motivational* consequences of superfluous praise. As Carol Dweck and her colleagues have found, teachers who praise students' intelligence can send the harmful message that current performance provides evidence of innate ability rather than of the application of effort or the use of appropriate strategy (Mueller & Dweck, 1998; see also Dweck, Chapter 3 in this volume). Students who are praised for their ability may thus respond to later failure not by trying harder, or by implementing a new problem-solving strategy, but by concluding that they lack the requisite skills to continue. Ability praise communicates that scholastic performance provides a gauge of intelligence and even of self-worth, and it can thus lead students to view the inevitable scholastic setback as reason to withdraw effort.

Positive feedback can cause further harm to the extent that it communicates low expectations for future achievement. Praise for substandard performance, or for easy work, can send the message that little more is expected from the student (see Anderson, Evertson, & Brophy, 1979). Inasmuch as students recognize that the positive feedback provided was motivated by low expectations rather than by the merit of their work, they may suffer a drop in self-confidence. In one study, students who had been praised for their performance on an easy task felt *less* confident that they would do well on a new, more difficult set of problems (Meyer, Plöger, & Bachman, 1978, cited in Meyer, Bachmann, Biermann, Hempelmann, Plöger, & Spiller, 1979). By contrast, students who had received criticism felt *more* confident in the likelihood of future success. Critical feedback sent the galvanizing message that their initial performance, though perhaps adequate for another student, was not worthy of their potential.

Beyond communicating low expectations, the superfluous praise provided to minority students may exact at least two additional costs. First, it may lull students into accepting low performance standards, or otherwise deter them from trying to attain a higher level of achievement. The study by Massey and colleagues (1975) noted above found that although black high school students spent the least time on homework and earned the lowest grades, they rated their effort and performance in school as high as their white and Asian peers did. Positive feedback may have led them to believe that they were doing better in school than they actually were (Massey et al., 1975).

Teachers who overpraise minority students may also exacerbate racial mistrust rather than assuage it. Inasmuch as minority students recognize that the evaluation they receive is more positive than what their performance merits, they may view it as patronizing and even insulting. In one study, black students and their white peers were praised for their interpersonal qualities by a white stranger (Crocker et al., 1991). White students saw the feedback as a reflection of their own social graces, and subsequently their self-esteem *increased*. By contrast, black students who thought that the evaluator was aware of their race could reasonably wonder if the feedback was motivated by racial sympathy, and their self-esteem *decreased*. Minority students presumably recognized that the evaluator, having had no previous contact with them, had little if any basis for providing such a positive assessment. The feedback thus signaled that they had been viewed not as an individual, but as a token of their race (see Harber, 1996). Over time, moreover, minority students may rightfully come to doubt the genuineness behind whites' displays of approval, and they may thus ultimately discount even well-earned positive feedback.

The same theoretical framework used to understand the role of stigmatization in *student* performance can thus be used to understand its role in *teacher* performance. Educators may mistrust the way that their feedback in particular and their actions more generally could be interpreted in the minds of minority students. Their ability to teach in racially diverse classrooms may thus suffer because their attention is drawn from teaching effectively to deflecting charges of racial bias. Ironically, however, the feedback that teachers offer to entrust and encourage minority students may sow the seeds of further mistrust and discouragement.

## ADDITIONAL STRATEGIES FOR CREATING TRUST

The need to combat the effects of stigmatization does not oblige the educator to withhold critical feedback, to lavish praise, or to otherwise lower performance standards in the hope of sustaining student motivation. Indeed, as noted above, doing so may cause the student more harm than good. Rather than alter the *content* of instruction, the educator (and student) might be better served by modifying the *context* in which such instruction occurs (Cohen et al., 1999). In the case of the highly selected black students and female science majors featured in our own research on feedback, motivation and performance were raised not by diluting the critical feedback offered or by softening its tone. What proved effective was providing that criticism in a context where its critical nature could be readily attributed to the existence of high and consistent standards and to the instructor's belief in the student's capacity to reach them. The challenge to the wise mentor, accordingly, is to establish a learning *context* that assures students that they will neither be judged nor be treated stereotypically. Beyond invoking high standards, and assuring students of their capacity to reach those standards, other strategies may prove effective in the classroom, business, or playing field contexts outside the narrow confines of the psychology laboratory. The effectiveness of each strategy derives, at least in part, from its ability to lift the situational threat of stigmatization. Students are thus free to trust their teachers and to safely invest their effort, and their identity, in school.

## Providing Sufficient Support

Wise educators and interventions succeed not simply by imposing high standards and assuring students of their capacity to reach them. They also provide the resources and guidance—in the form of teacher feedback, student services, and tutoring opportunities—that students need to attain the level of performance demanded. Selective colleges, for example, offer more generous financial aid programs, generally provide smaller classes with more personal attention, and supply more counseling and support services than do less well-endowed institutions. Such colleges yield graduation rates nearly twice the national average, and produce students who go on to earn salaries almost 70% greater than those of their peers who attend less selective schools; in fact, 10 to 50% of the advantage of attending a well-endowed, selective college remains even after student socioeconomic status, SAT scores, high school grades, and gender are statistically controlled (Bowen & Bok, 1998). Furthermore, attendance at elite schools appears to confer greater benefit to black students than to white students (Bowen & Bok, 1998). Even students who enter such schools with fewer academic credentials than their peers, for example, those admitted under affirmative action or through athletic scholarships, on average achieve superior graduation rates, earn higher salaries, and even become more civically involved than do similarly qualified peers who attend less competitive schools (Bowen & Bok, 1998).

## Cultivating Relationships

Criticism delivered in the context of a trusting relationship, where recipients can effortlessly attribute such feedback to benevolent intentions, may not require explicit assurances or evocations of standards to prove beneficial. Outside such a relationship, it seems, minority students may reasonably view academic authorities with mistrust. But as they develop a close relationship with a teacher or mentor, they may come to view racial bias as an increasingly implausible explanation for the treatment they receive, at least in the context of that specific relationship (see also Slavin & Cooper, 1999). Indeed, stereotype-based suspicions exert far less influence on judgment once people have gathered even minimally diagnostic information about another person (e.g., Locksley, Borgida, Brekke, & Hepburn, 1980). The messages of respect and regard that at first must be made explicit may thus become implicit in the context of a trusting relationship. The mentor's continuing support and demonstrated concern, that is, can communicate that the student is accepted and viewed as capable.

## Conveying a Message of Personal Concern

It is likely that the rigor of the feedback featured in our own studies communicated the critic's *interest* in helping the student to reach the higher standard (Cohen et al., 1999). Many students in our own studies remarked in the postexperimental debriefing session that they had felt impressed by the attentiveness of the criticism, and that seldom in their undergraduate careers had a teacher or professor taken their efforts so seriously. In fact, students who face negative stereotypes may feel particularly uncertain about whether their mentors, teachers, and even academic institutions support and care about the welfare of students from their gender or racial group. Detailed critical feedback, at least when accompanied by personal assurance and evidence of high standards, may help to resolve this uncertainty.

Beyond communicating high standards and a belief in the student's capacity for success, the mentor may thus be obliged to convey, implicitly or perhaps even explicitly, a personal concern for the student. While this notion is consistent with our theoretical analysis, it also resonates with research examining the factors that distinguish effective intervention programs from ineffective ones (Comer, 1988, 1997; Schorr, 1997). According to one recent review, it is an ethos of care and commitment that is essential. In fact, "[I]n their responsiveness and willingness to hang in there, effective programs are more like families than bureaucracies" (Schorr, 1997). Effective teachers are likely to take similar steps to communicate a personal interest in their students, often an interest that goes beyond scholastic concerns. For example, the ability of teachers to connect with the lives of students *outside* of school appears critical to the success of several academic intervention programs (see Schorr, 1997). Indeed, strategies as simple as providing opportunities for high-risk youth to develop caring relationships with peers, teachers, and role models in the context of extracurricular activities dramatically reduce rates both of high school dropout and of criminal arrest (Mahoney, 2000).

Cross-cultural research on Japanese preschool and elementary education offers a similar lesson. According to one comprehensive ethnography, the Japanese place importance on the development and maintenance of caring relationships between teachers and children, an emphasis that arguably accounts for their superior achievement on international tests of science and mathematics (Lewis, 1995). Through the cultivation of close relationships, Japanese students come to view school "as a place that has their best interests at heart," and they thus feel motivated to persist even when faced with challenging work (Lewis, 1995).

## Managing Attributions

Small features of the situation can override the effects of race or gender on students' expectations and attributions. In our research, the invocation of high standards led black students to attribute the criticism to the reviewer's demands for excellence rather than to personal or group animus. Even simpler attributional strategies may also prove effective. Presenting the evaluator as motivated by self-interest can, surprisingly, help to deflect attributions of bias. In one study, for example, black students' reluctance to trust a white evaluator's feedback was eliminated when they were told that the evaluator would win money if participants excelled at the task (Banks et al., 1977). Because they knew that their evaluator had a stake in their performance, participants could feel certain that the feedback was fair and objective. Of course, we do not suggest that mentors let self-interest motivate their actions. Our point is merely that simple interventions can ward off counterproductive attributions.

Other attributional strategies are suggested by observations of expert tutors. Rather than cater to the presumed deficiencies of at-risk children with an abundance of positive feedback, such tutors present the work in a manner that forestalls destructive attributions on the part of the student (Lepper, Aspinwall, & Mumme, 1990, see also Lepper & Woolverton, Chapter 7 in this volume). They might, for example, describe a problem as particularly difficult so that the student can readily attribute frustration to the demands of the work rather than to a personal limitation (Lepper et al., 1990). Expert tutors wisely use attributional techniques to keep the child optimistic in the face of challenge (Lepper et al., 1990). They are thus able to produce gains in student achievement of up to two standard deviations, more than twice the effect size of any other conventional educational intervention (Bloom, 1984; Walberg, 1984).

## Framing Ability as Malleable Rather Than Fixed

Much of the effectiveness of the wise intervention used in our own feedback studies may lie in the message that it conveys about the malleable nature of ability—the message that abilities are enhanced through practice and effort, and that more practice and greater effort will yield performance that surpasses the capacities demonstrated to date (Dweck et al., 1995; see also Dweck, Chapter 3 in this volume). The malleability message should prove particularly important for students who are targets of ability-stigmatizing stereotypes, because these stereotypes are accompanied by the implicit assumption or even explicit claim that ability (or lack of ability) is a fixed group limitation rather than a malleable aspect of the self (Aronson, Chapter 14 in this volume; Cohen et al., 1999).

At least one intervention specifically illustrated the possibility of raising black students' GPA by leading them to view intelligence as expandable (Aronson, Chapter 14 in this volume). More generally, the guiding philosophy of many of the most successful programs aimed at minority youth is an emphasis on the malleable nature of academic ability—the message that "Intelligence can be taught" (Whimbey, 1975). Effective educators and academic programs convey an unflagging faith in their students' *potential*. But, like our wise criticism, they do not hesitate to call attention to the gap between students' current performance and the level they could achieve with unstinting effort.

## Increasing Diversity

Increasing the representation of historically excluded racial or gender groups, it seems obvious, should also help to counteract the effects of stigmatization. Students are apt to trust that same-race educators will not use the stereotype against them. Indeed, one ethnographic study found that graduate students of color derive great benefit by working with African American mentors who can help them to negotiate the trials and challenges of being a minority in academia (Antony & Taylor, in press). The benefits of diversity are further underscored by experimental evidence that being a token minority, or simply a solitary group member, can activate concerns about being judged stereotypically and thereby cause motivation and performance to suffer (Inzlicht & Ben-Zeev, 2000; see also Stangor et al., 1998).

But increasing diversity alone may not automatically help minority students. For example, research suggests that inner-city black students do not necessarily achieve higher test scores when working with same-race teachers (Alexander, Entwisle, & Thompson, 1987; Ferguson, 1998). Rather, they perform better with black teachers of *low* socioeconomic status and worse with black teachers of *high* socioeconomic status (see Ferguson, 1998). It is possible that even minority teachers may be perceived as potentially biased beneficiaries of a white system, inasmuch as high socioeconomic status serves as cue that a given minority teacher is more "white" than "black." Poignantly, minority teachers may thus face a double barrier of mistrust. Minority students may wonder if they have sold out to a white system. Moreover, nonminority students may doubt their expertise and thus question the validity of the criticism they provide (Sinclair & Kunda, 1999). Nevertheless, many minority teachers surmount such barriers, and examining the strategies they use constitutes a fruitful topic for future research (see Antony & Taylor, in press).

We also think that mentors and students alike can derive great benefit not only by working *within* racial and gender lines, but also by working *across* them. Clearly, individuals are apt to learn new perspectives by establishing working relationships with members of different ethnic and gender groups. Furthermore, cross-race and cross-gender mentoring can offer unique *motivational* benefits to students. The power of the wise intervention used in our research, for example, might rest in its affirmation of respect despite racial difference. The white reviewer may have been perceived as reaching out across the racial divide—as a person willing to provide honest and validating treatment despite his group's reputation for prejudice. Such a gesture may allay doubts on the part of minority students about whether academic authorities in a predominantly white institution care about the welfare of their ethnic group. In addition, receiving respectful help from someone who is different or dissimilar can confer benefits to self-esteem, inasmuch as the recipient attributes the assistance to the uniquely kind motives of the person who provides it or to the uniquely special merit of his or her own performance (see Fisher & Nadler, 1974).

### Promulgating a Positive Ideology

The potential for mistrust may also be attenuated when feedback is interpreted in light of a shared ideology or value system. For example, the usual effect of race and socioeconomic status on student achievement may vanish in certain liberal Catholic schools (Bryk, 1993; Bryk & Schneider, 1996). These religious institutions succeed, it seems, by creating a shared and inspirational ideology (Bryk, 1993). Practitioners in such schools stress the fundamental worth of every individual, and emphasize the importance of ethical treatment in even the most mundane interactions. These values are woven into the school curriculum, and their effect is to establish "organic trust" (Gambetta, 1990). Students come to trust their educators because of shared assumptions about mutual benevolence and regard.

## CONCLUSION

Educators who work across racial or gender lines must communicate that they are not biased, despite the potential for prejudice that exists in the larger system. The strategies reviewed here may help teachers, managers, and tutors to accomplish just this. But even if students feel convinced that they personally are accorded respect, they may still face the threat that *other* members of their ethnic or gender group could be judged or treated stereotypically. With our colleague Julio Garcia, we have documented a phenomenon called "collective threat," and it refers to the shame, embarrassment, and doubt an individual feels in situations where the reputation of his or her group might be damaged. As such, collective threat can be elicited not only by one's own actions, but by those of fellow group members who could also confirm a negative stereotype about one's group.

African-American students in one study simply observed a black student who appeared likely to flunk an intelligence test and thereby substantiate a racial stereotype. Compared with their black peers who did not witness this event, subjects showed many of the symptoms of stigmatization, including a large drop in self-esteem. The situation caused distress not because it posed a specific threat to subjects' sense of personal worth based on their own performance. Rather, the situation imperiled their self-worth due to its implications for the larger representation of their racial group. Intervention programs may thus need to assure students that respect is granted not only to them personally but to members of their *group* more generally.

The present chapter focused on minority students, but we believe that the theoretical framework offered here applies to any individuals who fear that their abilities or worth is doubted rather than assumed. The threat of stigmatization may be felt by whites in the arena of competitive sports, where their group is stereotyped as lacking ability (Stone, Lynch, Sjomeling, & Darley, 1999), by students plagued with low self-esteem (Brockner, 1979; Brockner & Hulton, 1978), by children from low socioeconomic backgrounds (Croizet & Clair, 1998), by people making the transition to a more rigorous school or job (Simmons et al., 1991), and so on. In each case, people may question whether others view them with respect, and their motivation and performance may thus falter.

Perhaps it would have been equally useful to have focused much of our analysis not on stereotyped students performing in the classroom, but on *nonstereotyped* students (cf. Miller, Taylor, & Buck, 1991). In our own work, for example, we were surprised to find that nonstereotyped students responded to the criticism in an equally favorable manner regardless of whether it was accompanied by a personal assurance or not. For them, it seems, such assurances are *implicit*. At least among the highly select populations used in our own research, nonstereotyped students may thus enjoy a social-psychological advantage. They navigate the demands of the classroom equipped with trust. They can feel assured that neither their personal worth nor the worth of their group is automatically subject to doubt. Our attention is thus turned from stigma to privilege. Exploring both concepts, and their implications for mentoring and other teacher–student relationships, constitutes a central challenge for educators and researchers alike, as is using such relationships to cultivate the fertile ground of trust.

## Teachers' Questions and Answers

**Q:** I find your research on trust very compelling. At the same time, I wonder if you have any research or ideas on how I could facilitate this kind of trust-building dynamic in a classroom full of 30 or so kids, rather than the one-on-one situation you used to test your theory.

**A:** While we have not investigated this issue empirically, it is a very interesting question worthy of further research. We suggest, however, that many of the intervention strategies we describe in this chapter could be applied in a classroom context. For example, teachers could emphasize, at the beginning of the year, that they hold their entire class to high standards, and that they will help each student to reach those standards. In fact, it seems possible that some of the interventions we describe could prove more effective in a classroom context rather than less effective. For example, anecdotal evidence suggests that many successful teachers instill in their students a sense of shared fate and common identity. Jaime Escalante, while holding his students to a high standard, also communicated to students that they would work *together* to reach that standard—indeed, that they would be unable to succeed without one another's help. [Several intervention programs, such as E. Aronson's jigsaw classroom (see Chapter 10 in this volume), also promote a spirit of cooperation.] Students in Escalante's class thus came to view one another as members of a team striving for a shared goal. Rather than merely mentioning his high standards and belief in students' potential, Escalante made his personal belief in the importance of scholastic success a publicly shared group norm. And, as much research in social psychology attests, group norms can be powerful determinants of behavior.

**Q:** Is there not also an identity problem for the teacher when kids misbehave? For example, urban teachers face twice the problems—academic *and* disciplinary. Since the inception of the zero tolerance policies in schools, I hear teachers ask ''How am I supposed to handle discipline problems with minority children when their peers think I'm unfair to that minority group?'' Doesn't this exacerbate the problem of a teacher then bending over backward not to look unfair, and the students mistrusting the classroom authority?

**A:** This is an important question, and only further research could do this issue the justice it deserves. We can only suggest that teachers can preserve trust, especially when they must make decisions unpopular among their students, by making the justification for their actions explicit rather than leaving it implicit. If the rules of good conduct are laid down in a clear manner, at the beginning of the school year, and if students can be encouraged to see the merit of those rules—indeed, perhaps they can even help to generate those rules—then they may be less likely to view disciplinary action on the part of their teachers with mistrust. Teachers could frame any punitive steps they must take as the necessary response to the rules of good conduct that the students themselves helped to establish.

## Acknowledgments

We are grateful to Julio Garcia, Sarah Wert, Eric Uhlmann, Gregory Walton, and Joshua Aronson for their valuable comments and suggestions.

## References

Alexander, K. L., Entwisle, D. R., & Thompson, M. S. (1987). School performance, status relations, and the structure of sentiment: Bringing the teacher back in. *American Sociology Review, 52,* 665–682.

Anderson, L., Evertson, C., & Brophy, J. (1979). An experimental study of effective teaching in first grade reading groups. *Elementary School Journal, 79,* 193–223.

Antony, J. S., & Taylor, E. (2001). Graduate student socialization and its implications for the recruitment of African American Education Faculty. In W. G. Tierney (Ed.), *Faculty work in schools of education: Rethinking roles and rewards for the twenty-first century*. New York: SUNY Press.

Aronson, J., Lustina, M., Keough, K., Brown, J. L., & Steele, C. M. (1999). When white men can't do math: Necessary and sufficient factors in stereotype threat. *Journal of Experimental Social Psychology, 35*, 29–46.

Aronson, J., Quinn, D. M., & Spencer, S. J. (1998). Stereotype threat and the academic underperformance of minorities and women. In J. K. Swim & C. Stangor (Eds.), *Prejudice: The target's perspective* (pp. 83–103). San Diego: Academic Press.

Banks, W. C., Stitt, K. R., Curtis, H. A., & McQuarter, G. (1977). Perceived objectivity and the effects of evaluative reinforcement upon compliance and self-evaluation in blacks. *Journal of Experimental Social Psychology, 13*, 452–463.

Barker, G. P., & Graham, S. (1987). Developmental study of praise and blame as attributional cues. *Journal of Educational Psychology, 79*, 62–66.

Bloom, B. S. (1984). The 2 sigma problem: The search for methods of group instruction as effective as one-to-one tutoring. *Educational Researcher, 13*, 4–16.

Bowen, W. G., & Bok, D. (1998). *The shape of the river: Long-term consequences of considering race in college and university admissions*. Princeton, NJ: Princeton University Press.

Brockner, J. (1979). Self-esteem, self-consciousness, and task performance: Replications, extensions, and possible explanations. *Journal of Personality and Social Psychology, 37*, 447–461.

Brockner, J., & Hulton, A. B. (1978). How to reverse the vicious cycle of low self-esteem: The importance of attentional focus. *Journal of Experimental Social Psychology, 14*, 564–578.

Brophy, J. (1981). Teacher praise: A functional analysis. *Review of Educational Research, 51*, 5–32.

Bryk, A. S. (1993). *Catholic schools and the common good*. Cambridge: Harvard University Press.

Bryk, A. S., & Schneider, B. (1996). *Social trust: A moral resource for school improvement*. Madison, WI: Center on Organization and Restructuring of Schools, *Office of Educational Research and Improvement*.

Cohen, G. L., Steele, C. M., & Ross, L. D. (1999). The mentor's dilemma: Providing critical feedback across the racial divide. *Personality and Social Psychology Bulletin, 25*, 1302–1318.

Comer, J. P. (1988). Educating poor minority children. *Scientific American, 259*, 42–48.

Comer, J. P. (1997). *Waiting for a miracle*. New York: Penguin Putnam.

Cose, E. (1997). *Color-blind: Seeing beyond race in a race-obsessed world*. New York: HarperCollins.

Crocker, J., Major, B., & Steele, C. (1998). Social stigma. In D. T. Gilbert, S. T. Fiske, & G. Lindzey (Eds.), *The handbook of social psychology* (Vol. 2, pp. 504–553). New York: McGraw–Hill.

Crocker, J., Voelkl, K., & Major, B. (1991). Social stigma: The affective consequences of attributional ambiguity. *Journal of Personality and Social Psychology, 60*, 218–228.

Croizet, J., & Clair, T. (1998). Extending the concept of stereotype threat to social class: The intellectual underperformance of students from low socioeconomic backgrounds. *Personality and Social Psychology Bulletin, 24*, 588–594.

Crosby, F. J. (1999). The developing literature on developmental relationships. In A. J. Murrell, F. J. Crosby, & R. J. Ely (Eds.), *Mentoring dilemmas: Developmental relationships within multicultural organizations*. Mahwah, NJ: Erlbaum.

Davis, F. (1961). Deviance disavowal: The management of strained interaction by the visibly handicapped. *Social Problems, 9*, 120–132.

Dweck, C. S., Chiu, C., & Hong, Y. (1995). Implicit theories and their role in judgments and reactions: A world from two perspectives. *Psychological Inquiry, 6*, 267–285.

Ferguson, R. F. (1998). Teachers' perceptions and expectations and the black–white test score gap. In C. Jencks & M. Phillips (Eds.), *The black–white test score gap* (pp. 273–317). Washington, DC: Brookings Institution.

Fisher, J. D., & Nadler, A. (1974). The effect of similarity between donor and recipient on recipient's reaction to aid. *Journal of Applied Social Psychology, 4*, 230–243.

Frable, D. E. S., Blackstone, T., & Scherbaum, C. (1990). Marginal and mindful: Deviants in social interactions. *Journal of Personality and Social Psychology, 59*, 140–149.

Fukuyama, F. (1995). *Trust: The social virtues and the creation of prosperity*. New York: Free Press.

Gambetta, D. (1990). *Trust: The making and breaking of cooperative relations*. Cambridge.

Goffman, E. (1963). *Stigma: Notes on the management of a spoiled identity*. Englewood Cliffs, NJ: Prentice–Hall.

Goldstein, E. (1979). Effect of same-sex and cross-sex role models on the subsequent academic productivity of scholars. *American Psychologist, 34*, 407–410.

Graham, S. (1990). Communicating low ability in the classroom: Bad things good teachers sometimes do. In S. Graham & V. S. Folkes (Eds.), *Attribution theory: Applications to achievement, mental health, and interpersonal conflict* (pp. 17–36). Hillsdale, NJ: Erlbaum.

Harber, K. (1996). *Feedback to minorities: Egalitarian motives, biased consequences*. Unpublished doctoral dissertation.

Harber, K. (1998). Feedback to minorities: Evidence of a positive bias. *Journal of Personality and Social Psychology, 74*, 622–628.

Hastorf, A. H., Wildfogel, J., & Cassman, T. (1979). Acknowledgement of handicap as a tactic in social interaction. *Journal of Personality and Social Psychology, 37*, 1790–1797.

Horn, T. S. (1985). Coaches' feedback and changes in children's perceptions of their physical competence. *Journal of Educational Psychology, 77*, 174–186.

Huo, Y. J., Smith, H. J., Tyler, T. R., & Lind, E. A. (1996). Superordinate identification, subgroup identification, and justice concerns: Is separatism the problem; is assimilation the answer? *Psychological Science, 7*, 40–45.

Inzlicht, M., & Ben-Zeev, T. (2000). A threatening intellectual environment: Why females are susceptible to experiencing problem-solving deficits in the presence of males. *Psychological Science, 11*, 365–371.

Kleck, R., Ono, H., & Hastorf, A. H. (1966). The effects of physical deviance upon face-to-face interaction. *Human Relations, 19*, 425–436.

Kleck, R. E., & Strenta, A. (1980). Perceptions of the impact of negatively valued characteristics on social interaction. *Journal of Personality and Social Psychology, 39*, 861–873.

Koestner, R., Zuckerman, M., & Koestner, J. (1987). Praise, involvement, and intrinsic motivation. *Journal of Personality and Social Psychology, 53*, 383–390.

Krueger, J. (1996). Personal beliefs and cultural stereotypes about racial characteristics. *Journal of Personality and Social Psychology, 71*, 536–548.

Lepper, M. R., Aspinwall, L. G., & Mumme, D. L. (1990). Self-perception and social-perception processes in tutoring: Subtle social control strategies of expert tutors. In J. M. Olson & M. P. Zanna (Eds.), *Self-inference processes: The Ontario symposium* (Vol. 6, pp. 217–237). Hillsdale, NJ: Erlbaum.

Lewis, C. C. (1995). *Educating hearts and minds: Reflections on Japanese preschool and elementary education*. New York: Cambridge University Press.

Lewis, J. D., & Weigert, A. (1985). Trust as a social reality. *Social Forces, 63*, 967–985.

Leyens, J., Désert, M., Croizet, J., & Darcis, C. (2000). Stereotype threat: Are lower status and history of stigmatization preconditions of stereotype threat? *Personality and Social Psychology Bulletin, 26*, 1189–1199.

Locksley, A., Borgida, E., Brekke, N., & Hepburn, C. (1980). Sex stereotypes and social judgment. *Journal of Personality and Social Psychology, 39*, 821–831.

Mahoney, J. L. (2000). School extracurricular activity participation as a moderator in the development of antisocial patterns. *Child Development, 71*, 502–516.

Marx, D. M., Brown, J. L., & Steele, C. M. (1999). Allport's legacy and the situational press of stereotypes. *Journal of Social Issues, 55*, 491–502.

Massey, G. C., Scott, M. V., & Dornbusch, S. M. (1975, November). Racism without racists: Institutional racism in urban school. *Black Scholar*, pp. 10–19.

Mathews, J. (1988). *Escalante: The best teacher in America*. New York: Henry Hold.

Meyer, W. U., Bachmann, M., Biermann, U., Hempelmann, M., Plöger, F. O., & Spiller, H. (1979). The informational value of evaluative behavior: Influences of praise and blame on perceptions of ability. *Journal of Educational Psychology, 71*, 259–268.

Miller, R. L., Brickman, P., & Bolen, D. (1975). Attribution versus persuasion as a means for modifying behavior. *Journal of Personality and Social Psychology, 31*, 430–441.

Miller, D. T., Taylor, B., & Buck, M. L. (1991). Gender gaps: Who needs to be explained. *Journal of Personality and Social Psychology, 61*, 5–12.

Mueller, C. M., & Dweck, C. S. (1998). Praise for intelligence can undermine children's motivation and performance. *Journal of Personality and Social Psychology, 75*, 33–52.

Rosenthal, R., & Jacobson, L. (1968). *Pygmalion in the classroom: Teacher expectation and pupils' intellectual development.* New York: Holt.

Schorr, L. B. (1997). *Common purpose: Strengthening families and neighborhoods to rebuild America.* New York: Anchor Books.

Simmons, R. G., Black, A., & Zhou, Y. (1991). African-Americans versus white children and the transition into junior high school. *American Journal of Education, 99*, 481–520.

Sinclair, L., & Kunda, Z. (1999). Reactions to a black professional: Motivated inhibition and activation of conflicting stereotypes. *Journal of Personality and Social Psychology, 77*, 885–904.

Slavin, R. E., & Cooper, R. (1999). Improving intergroup relations: Lessons learned from cooperative learning programs. *Journal of Social Issues, 55*, 647–663.

Smith, H. J., Tyler, T. R., Huo, Y. J., Ortiz, D. J., & Lind, E. A. (1998). The self-relevant implications of the group-value model: Group membership, self-worth, and treatment quality. *Journal of Experimental Social Psychology, 34*, 470–493.

Spencer, S. J., Steele, C. M., & Quinn, D. M. (1999). Stereotype threat and women's math performance. *Journal of Experimental Social Psychology, 35*, 4–28.

Stangor, C., Carr, C., & Kiang, L. (1998). Activating stereotypes undermines task performance expectations. *Journal of Personality and Social Psychology, 75*, 1191–1197.

Steele, C. M. (1997). A threat in the air: How stereotypes shape the intellectual identities and performance of women and African-Americans. *American Psychologist, 52*, 613–629.

Steele, C. M. (1999). Thin ice: "Stereotype threat" and black college students. *The Atlantic Monthly, 284*, 44–54.

Steele, C. M., & Aronson, J. (1995). Stereotype threat and the intellectual test performance of African Americans. *Journal of Personality and Social Psychology, 69*, 797–811.

Stone, J., Lynch, C. I., Sjomeling, M., & Darley, J. M. (1999). Stereotype threat effects on black and white athletic performance. *Journal of Personality and Social Psychology, 77*, 1213–1227.

Strenta, A. C., & Kleck, R. E. (1984). Physical disability and the perception of social interaction: It's not what you look at but how you look at it. *Personality and Social Psychology Bulletin, 10*, 279–288.

Tyler, T. R., Smith, H. J., & Huo, Y. (1996). Member diversity and leadership effectiveness: Procedural justice, social identity, and group dynamics. *Advances in Group Processes, 13*, 33–66.

Vorauer, J. D., Main, K. J., & O'Connell, G. B. (1998). How do individuals expect to be viewed by members of lower status groups: Content and implications of meta-stereotypes. *Journal of Personality and Social Psychology, 75*, 917–937.

Vorauer, J. D., & Ross, M. (1993). Making mountains out of molehills: An informational goals analysis of self- and social perception. *Personality and Social Psychology Bulletin, 19*, 620–632.

Walberg, H. J. (1984). Improving the productivity of America's schools. *Educational Leadership, 41*, 19–27.

Whimbey, A. (1975). *Intelligence can be taught.* New York: Dutton.

Word, C. O., Zanna, M. P, & Cooper, J. (1974). The nonverbal mediation of self-fulfilling prophecies in interracial interaction. *Journal of Experimental Social Psychology, 20*, 109–120.

# Toward a Resolution of an American Tension: Some Applications of the Helping Model of Affirmative Action to Schooling

ANTHONY R. PRATKANIS

*Department of Psychology, University of California, Santa Cruz*
*Santa Cruz, California*

MARLENE E. TURNER AND STANLEY B. MALOS

*Department of Organization and Management, San Jose State University*
*San Jose, California*

There is a fundamental tension in the American schooling system—an unresolved dilemma between the ideals of what a school should be in a democracy and what American schools actually offer its citizens. At the heart of this tension is what Gunnar Myrdal (1944) referred to as the American dilemma —the demand of democracy that all human beings are endowed with certain unalienable rights is in direct conflict with the belief that one race is superior to another.

Educational institutions are seen as the engine of democracy. The ideal of American schools is to educate the masses to become informed citizens;

Correspondence concerning this article can be sent to Anthony R. Pratkanis at the Department of Psychology, University of California, Santa Cruz, CA 95064, and Marlene E. Turner and Stanley B. Malos at the Department of Organization and Management, San Jose State University, San Jose, CA 95192.

*Improving Academic Achievement*

schools should provide access to skills and knowledge so that all citizens can rise to the heights of their talents and should teach the tolerance and respect of others needed in a democracy. Such ideals go back to the founding of the nation and are represented in the thought of Thomas Jefferson. He believed that a strong public education system was essential for a democracy because it would allow a strong middle class to prosper and thus thwart attempts to reestablish a monarchy or other forms of autocratic government. Indeed, Jefferson considers one of his greatest achievements his founding of the University of Virginia because, in his vision, it would allow any capable citizen to pursue a course of knowledge and enlightenment.

Critics of schooling in America, however, have claimed that it does little more than maintain and promote the status quo. Visit most of the classrooms in this nation and you will find a pattern of winners and losers. The winners sit in the front of the class; they raise their hands when the teacher asks a question; they score well on the tests; they will have the opportunity for more and more schooling should they so desire. The losers, on the other hand, sit in the back of the class; they have a tacit agreement with the teacher not to call on them; they feel that school is not the place for them. Sadly, for the Jeffersonian ideal of democracy, the losers in this American system of education are often minority group members—an African-American, a child of Hispanic descent, or a girl in a math or science class. Thus, instead of fostering the skills needed for democracy and challenging the status quo, the American school comes to mirror the social relationship and inequalities found in American society as a whole.

One of the educational facts of life is that in-group members often outperform members of America's out-groups while they are in school. For example, African-Americans are less likely to graduate from high school and 50% less likely to graduate from college than white Americans (Jones, 1988; 1997). Black and Hispanic students typically score 30 points lower than their white counterparts on the reading component of the National Assessment of Educational Progress exam and perform significantly poorer on the SAT (Miller, 1999). Although there is no difference in the scores of girls and boys on standardized math tests during the elementary and middle school years, males start to out score females in math in high school, with gender differences in performance increasing during college (Hyde, Fennema, & Lamon, 1990). In college, women drop out of the physical sciences, math, and engineering at a rate two and a half times that of men (quoted in Steele, 1997).

These group differences can be accounted for by the many barriers—both in school and in society—that the out-group member must face. For example, until the 1950s African-Americans in many parts of the country were not permitted to attend the same schools as their white counterparts. To justify such exclusion, an ideology developed claiming that African-Americans and other out-groups were innately inferior and/or came from a culture of poverty that precluded them from achieving. Jones (1997) calls this a culture of racism—the wholesale emphasis through individual prejudice and societal institutions of the superiority of one race over another. The culture of racism can be seen in a survey of white New Englanders showing that the majority of respondents endorsed at least one stereotypic belief that blacks are born inferior [such as they experience less pain, have an extra muscle (Plous & Williams, 1995)]. Other studies have shown more "subtle" manifestations of racism, finding that whites are less likely to help blacks in casual social settings, less likely to follow the directions of a black leader, and more likely to use inadmissible testimony in court cases to convict black (as opposed to white) defendants (Gaertner & Dovidio, 1986).

The culture of racism can impact school performance for targeted minorities (Miller, 1999). As Booker T. Washington (1901/1993) put it: "The Negro boy has obstacles, discouragements, and temptations to battle that are little known to those not situated as he is. When a white boy undertakes a task, it is taken for granted that he will succeed. On the other hand, people are usually surprised if the Negro boy does not fail. In a word, the Negro youth starts out with the presumption against him" (p. 28). In other words, expectations of failure create for the target of racism the potential of a self-fulfilling prophecy (Rosenthal & Jacobson, 1968, see Chapter 2 in this volume). This "presumption against" places what Steele and J. Aronson (1995; Steele, 1997, see Chapter 14 in this volume) call "a threat in the air" or stereotype threat where members of a targeted group fear being reduced to the stereotype; this fear directly interferes with performance, and the targeted student may come to disidentify with the domain of schooling (Ogbu, 1986). The culture of racism carries with it a legacy of segregation. America's housing is still highly segregated by race (Yinger, 1995) and thus children of out-group parents may live in residential areas marked by health risks and poorer educational facilities. Chances are their parents did not attend institutions of higher education and thus cannot provide the mentoring needed to navigate the complexities of a university.

A similar although not as extreme story can be told about the schooling of American females. Historically, the schooling of girls consisted of the basics —reading, writing, and arithmetic. "Advanced" study was often limited to those things that would make the woman a better homemaker and socialite; she was not expect to engage in the affairs of state and commerce and thus did not need courses in higher math, sciences, and more technical domains. Spencer, Steele, and Quinn (1997) document the legacy of this exclusion, showing that women experience the threats of a stereotype by performing poorer on standardized tests of math abilities but not on similar tests in the domain of literature.

There have been times when Americans have attempted to enact their ideals and dismantle discriminatory barriers. In this chapter, we look at two such attempts: school desegregation and affirmative action. Our goal is to review the attempts made in these two areas to find out what works and what does not. In the process, we develop further a model for effectively changing America's schools, which we call the helping model of affirmative action. At the core of this model is the proposition that effective affirmative action focuses on the proactive removal of discriminatory barriers and not on remedial efforts to somehow change the target of prejudice to fit into a prejudicial society. We use this model to suggest principles of change that we believe will help promote democracy in the classroom and relieve America's schoolroom tension. To provide a historical context for our efforts, we begin by reviewing the history of legal efforts to remove discrimination in the classroom.

## LEGAL MANIFESTATIONS OF AN AMERICAN TENSION

The battle over the nature and purpose of American schools has been fought in the nation's courtrooms, legislative bodies, and the White House. Table 1 is a chronological listing of major legal actions taken with respect to school desegregation and affirmative action.

**TABLE 1**

Legal Milestones Related to School Desegregation and Affirmative Action

| Year | Case or Statutory Provision | Summary of case holding or statutory provision |
|------|------------------------------|-------------------------------------------------|
| 1849 | *Roberts v. City of Boston* | Ruled that Boston could provide different schools for black and white children. |
| 1866 | Freedman's Bureau Act | Established education and other programs for black soldiers and freedmen. |
| 1896 | *Plessy v. Ferguson* | With Justice John Harlan, a former slaveholder, dissenting, Supreme Court allows state imposed segregation via a "separate but equal" facilities rule. |
| 1899 | *Cumming v. Richmond County Board of Education* | Supreme Court rules that a Georgia school's failure to provide a high school education for African-Americans is constitutional; thus, the doctrine of separate but equal becomes in practice separate but not equal. |
| 1954 | *Brown v. Board of Education I* | Supreme Court unanimously outlaws school segregation by race and overturns *Plessy v. Ferguson;* Court finds racially segregated schools inherently unequal. |
| 1955 | *Brown v. Board of Education II* | Supreme Court furthers dismantling of "separate but equal" doctrine, ordering school districts to "desegregate with all due deliberate speed." |
| 1964 | *Griffin v. The County School Board of Prince Edward County* | Supreme Court rules that schemes to fund private schools to circumvent *Brown* decision are unconstitutional; ruled that there was too much deliberation and not enough speed. |

*continues*

*continued*

| Year | Case or Statutory Provision | Summary of case holding or statutory provision |
| --- | --- | --- |
| 1964 | Civil Rights Act of 1964 | Title VII of the Act forbade discrimination on the basis of race, sex, color, religion, or national origin and established the Equal Employment Opportunity Commission. |
| 1965 | Executive Order 11246 | Signed by Lyndon Johnson, it required federal contractors to take affirmative action in business practices. |
| 1968 | *Green v. County School Board of New Kent Co.* | Supreme Court strikes down "freedom of choice" school attendance, finding segregated schools have an affirmative duty to eliminate discrimination "root and branch." |
| 1971 | *Swann v. Charlotte-Mecklenburg Board of Education* | Supreme Court confirms power of courts to fashion remedies ensuring desegregation. |
| 1972 | *Title IX, Education Amendments 20 U.S.C. §1681(a)* | Congress enacts statute prohibiting gender discrimination in educational activities that receive federal funding. |
| 1974 | *Milliken v. Bradley I* | Supreme Court invalidates metropolitan-wide desegregation plan involving both city and suburban schools, effectively limiting court-ordered plans to single school districts. |
| 1977 | *Milliken v. Bradley II* | Supreme Court reaffirms broad powers of courts to order specific elements of desegregation plans if needed to remedy proven past instances of discrimination. |
| 1978 | *University of California Regents v. Bakke* | In plurality opinion, Supreme Court finds reservation of admission slots at University of California Medical School for minorities unconstitutional; however, Court allows consideration of race in admissions as factor promoting the "compelling interest" of diversity in educational environment. |
| 1982 | *Mississippi University for Women v. Hogan* | Supreme Court finds policy of state-supported university limiting enrollment in nursing program to women and denying admission to otherwise qualified males unconstitutional. |
| 1984 | *Grove City College v. Bell* | Supreme Court issues interpretation of Title IX, holding that the statute applies only to specified programs receiving federal funding, not to all programs or activities at schools receiving federal funds. |
| 1987 | *Civil Rights Restoration Act* | Congress enacts statute applying Title IX to all operations of a university receiving federal financial aid, overturning *Grove City College v. Bell.* |

*continues*

*continued*

| Year | Case or Statutory Provision | Summary of case holding or statutory provision |
| --- | --- | --- |
| 1991 | *Board of Education of Oklahoma City v. Dowell* | Supreme Court rules that judicial supervision of schools will end on showing good faith compliance with court orders and elimination of desegregation "to the extent practicable." |
| 1992 | *Freeman v. Pitts* | Supreme Court reaffirms *Dowell* holding that judicial supervision of formerly segregated schools should be temporary and limited to the effects of officially caused segregation; Court also notes that "where resegregation is a product not of state action but of private choices, it does not have constitutional implications." |
| 1994 | *Podberesky v. Kirwan* | 4th Circuit Court of Appeals invalidates race-based scholarship at University of Maryland as unconstitutional. |
| 1995 | *Hopwood v. Texas* | 5th Circuit Court of Appeals invalidates affirmative action plan at University of Texas Law School as unconstitutional; although affirmative action remains an appropriate remedy for past discrimination, the court ruled such programs are no longer needed because the effects of past discrimination had been eliminated. |
| 1995 | *Missouri v. Jenkins* | In case where "vestiges of discrimination have been eliminated to the extent practicable," Supreme Court overturns measures to implement desegregation; Court reaffirms interdistrict limitations of *Milliken* and limits remedial court orders to "restoring the victims of discriminatory conduct to the position they would have occupied absent that conduct" and no more. |
| 1999 | *Tuttle v. Arlington County School Board* | 4th Circuit Court of Appeals invalidates weighted lottery admissions system designed to promote racial diversity at public kindergarten. |
| 2000 | *Gratz et al. v. Bollinger et al.* | District court judge rules in favor of University of Michigan undergraduate affirmative action program, finding that diversity of student body is a compelling state interest. |
| 2001 | *Grutter et al. v. Bollinger et al.* | A different district court judge rules against University of Michigan law school affirmative action program, finding that diversity of student body is not a compelling state interest. |

During the antebellum period, African-Americans and other minorities were mostly excluded from participation in America's schools. The case of Frederick Douglass, a slave who later escaped to the North, is a case in point (see

Douglass 1881/1993). As a young slave, Douglass' master, Mrs. Lucertia Auld, began to teach him to read. Mrs. Auld was criticized by other slaveholders for her attempts to educate a black child and soon forbade Douglass to read. However, the fire of knowledge had been lit. Douglass recounts how he took every opportunity to sneak a chance to learn to read, working through lessons from a discarded copy of *Webster's Spelling-Book* whenever he could. The life of Frederick Douglass personifies the American tension, simultaneously demonstrating the power of an education to change lives and the power of institutions to regulate who has the opportunity to learn.

America's first formal attempt to open access to education came with the passage of the Freedman's Bureau Act of 1866. As part of Reconstruction efforts, the Bureau was charged with, among other things, providing educational opportunities for black soldiers and freed slaves. The effort was short-lived. Beginning around 1877, reconstruction was dismantled and in its place "Jim Crow" laws appeared. In 1896, the U.S. Supreme Court ruled in *Plessy v. Ferguson* that segregation via separate but equal educational facilities rule was constitutional. Of course, while the "separate" part of the equation was put into practice, the "equal" part remained little more than a theory.

Segregation in American schools was legal until 1954 when the Supreme Court rendered its historic judgment in *Brown v. Board of Education.* In this case, the Court ruled that segregated schools are inherently unequal and ordered desegregation with all due deliberate speed. Significantly, the research of social psychologists on the effects of segregation appeared as Footnote 11 in the decision and was instrumental in the court's ruling (see Clark, 1963, for the text of this statement). The *Brown* decision set off a legal debate over the direction of America's schools. At first, the courts were sympathetic to the goal of desegregation, but over time increasingly narrowed the scope of this effort until it was effectively abandoned in the 1980s.

A similar history can be told for America's other most recent attempt to remove discriminatory barriers in education—affirmative action. The policy of affirmative action began with the passage of the *Civil Rights Act of 1964* (which forbade discrimination on the basis of race, sex, color, religion, or national origin) and Lyndon Johnson's Executive Order 11246 (which required federal contractors to take affirmative action in selection decisions). In 1978, the U.S. Supreme Court in *University of California Regents v. Bakke* limited the use of set aside programs for university admissions. In 1995, the courts placed further limitations on affirmative action by ruling in *Hopwood v. Texas* that, although affirmative action remains an appropriate remedy for discrimination, such policies are improper today because the effects of past discrimination have been eliminated. More recently, two court rulings involving the University of Michigan have added confusion to the legal standing of affirmative action. In *Gratz et al. v. Bollinger et al.*, a U.S. District Court judge ruled in favor of the University of Michigan's affirmative action program for undergraduate admissions, arguing that racial diversity is a compelling issue of the state. Three months later, another U.S. District Court judge ruled the complete opposite in *Grutter et al. v. Bollinger et al.*—that the University of Michigan's affirmative action program for law school admissions was unconstitutional and the state has no compelling interest in diversity. Needless to day, these issues will be revisited as these cases are appealed.

School desegregation and affirmative action represent two of America's most concerted efforts to proactively remove discriminatory barriers in education. What did they accomplish? We now turn our attention to social psychological research that has looked at these two efforts in an attempt to learn what these efforts have to teach us about resolving America's tension.

## WHAT HAVE WE LEARNED FROM ATTEMPTS AT SCHOOL DESEGREGATION?

In response to the 1954 U.S. Supreme Court mandate to end segregated schooling, most school desegregation efforts took place during the period 1964 to 1974. These efforts involved a number of tactics for reducing segregation including magnet schools, redrawing of district lines, placement of new schools in strategic locations, and school busing. What have been the fruits of these efforts? We investigate these efforts by answering three questions about school desegregation (see also Gerard & Miller, 1975; Rossell & Hawley, 1983; Stephan & Feagin, 1980).

### Are American Schools Desegregated?

A look at the demographics of school populations suggests that the objective of dismantling separate schools has been only partially obtained. In the early 1960s, less than 2% of black children in the South attended public school with white children. In the early 1970s, that figure climbed to 46.3%. Outside of the South, however, only 28.3% of black children attended public schools with white children (Pettigrew, 1975). By 1980 nationwide, 70% of black students attended school with a white, whereas only 61% of whites attended a school that had few or no blacks (Stephan, 1991). However, since the late 1980s, the level of desegregation has been slowly decreasing to levels that existed before 1971 (Orfield & Eaton, 1996).

### What Are the Effects of Desegregation on Students?

Desegregation was expected to affect three outcomes: (a) an improvement in the academic performance of minority students, (b) an increase in self-esteem in black students, and (c) a reduction in racial prejudice.

## Academic Performance of Minorities in Desegregated Schools

In a review of 34 studies of school desegregation, Stephan (1978, 1986) finds that most show that desegregation had no or mixed effects on minority academic performance, 29% showed improvements, and only 3% show a decrement in minority achievement. Mahard and Crain (1983) also find that desegregation does have some positive effects on black achievement and that these gains are stronger when students are desegregated in earlier grades and when there is a critical mass of at least between 15 and 20% minorities in the school.

## Self-Esteem of Minorities in Desegregated Schools

In contrast to academic achievement, desegregation has not had its hoped for effects with respect to the promotion of self-esteem. In a review of 27 studies, Stephan (1986) finds that, although in the majority of desegregation cases black self-esteem is unaffected, in 25% of the studies black self-esteem was actually higher in segregated schools. One explanation for this finding is that minorities in desegregated schools may more often come into contact with negative stereotypes about their groups.

## Racial Prejudice in Desegregated Schools

In Stephan's (1978, 1986, 1991) reviews, he finds that, for blacks, school desegregation is more likely to result in less prejudice towards whites. However, for whites, school desegregation is more likely to increase prejudice towards blacks. In other studies an unexpected result is obtained: after their children attend a desegregated school, white parents evaluate school desegregation efforts to be successful, are more positive in their support of desegregation, and rate their child's experience in school as more successful (than parents of children in segregated schools; see Rossell, 1983).

## When Is Desegregation Most Likely to Achieve Its Goals?

In hindsight, it was naïve to think that merely bringing people together from different social groups would have dramatic consequences for academic performance, self-esteem, and intergroup attitudes. Schools can be competitive places, with winners and losers declared on such important dimensions as athletic and academic abilities and interpersonal attraction. In such a mix, there is little reason to expect that well-learned racial and gender stereotypes will not be used as one ingredient in sorting the winners from the losers, which, in turn, reinforces the well-learned racial and gender stereotypes.

It does not have to be that way. Considerable research has consistently shown that a restructuring of the classroom along democratic lines using

Allport's (1954) equal status contact principle will reduce prejudice, improve academic performance, and increase student self-esteem (Schofield & Sagar, 1983). According to Allport (1954), positive intergroup relations are most likely to occur when members from two groups (a) possess equal status, (b) seek common goals, (c) are cooperatively dependent on each other, and (d) interact with the support of authorities, customs, and laws.

Desegregation was most effective in schools that either had elements of the equal status contact principle or engaged in activities to create equal status contact. For example, Pettigrew (1961) found that peaceful integration occurred where authorities made it clear that integration was inevitable but that violence occurred where authorities did not support desegregation and hinted that it might be reversed. A series of studies show that children at schools with principals who were committed to the goals of desegregation were more likely to interact with other children from a different race (Schofield & Sagar, 1983). E. Aronson and his colleagues (E. Aronson, Chapter 11 in this volume; Aronson, Blaney, Stephan, Sikes, & Snapp, 1978) have developed what they call the jigsaw classroom in which students from diverse backgrounds are each given a part of a topic to be studied and then must work together to learn the material; jigsaw classrooms have been shown to produce dramatic reductions in prejudice and improvement in the academic performance of minority students. Cohen and Roper (1972) reversed the typical statuses in a classroom by having black students teach white students how to build a radio; subsequent interactions between the students were marked by more equality and less white dominance. Even something as simple as mixing races in classroom seating assignments can have a positive effect on interracial interactions outside the classroom (Schofield & Sagar, 1983).

## WHAT HAVE WE LEARNED FROM RECENT ATTEMPTS AT AFFIRMATIVE ACTION?

The second attempt to resolve America's schoolroom tension took the form of affirmative action. In attempting to implement affirmative action, schools have adopted a number of policies and programs. At primary and secondary schools, affirmative action has resulted mostly in attempts to secure a diverse work force. In this case, the school, in accordance with federal guidelines, sets employment targets based on the proportion of qualified female or minority applicants and then engages in various recruitment, retention, and promotion activities to meet this goal (see Pratkanis & Turner, 1996, for a list of common affirmative action procedures). Welch and Gruhl (1998) surveyed university affirmative action efforts and found that most universities have affirmative action offices with the responsibility of diversifying their faculty and student bodies. These offices typically engage in such activities as personally interviewing and meeting with minority candidates, preparing recruitment publications targeted at minorities, helping to secure funding and scholarships, serving on university admission committees, and offering summer workshops and short courses to encourage minority students to pursue advanced degrees. What is the effect of these practices on American schools and what do they tell us about successful affirmative action programs? We look at these issues by answering five specific questions about the effects of affirmative action on schools.

## Has Affirmative Action Been Successful in Meeting Its Goals?

Two of the primary goals of affirmative action are to increase access to educational institutions for those who were previously excluded and to provide for a more diverse work force in schools. Has affirmative action met its mission? In a nutshell, the glass is half-empty or half-full, depending on your perspective. In other words, affirmative action has resulted in a more diverse student body and educational work force, but it has not removed completely the barriers that many social groups still face (Turner & Pratkanis, 1994; Pratkanis & Turner, 1996).

Some illustrative research should make the point. Eberts and Stone (1985) found that Equal Employment Opportunity programs implemented in elementary and secondary schools in Oregon and New York reduced discriminatory hiring practices by about half. In an analysis of admissions to law and medical schools, Welch and Gruhl (1998) found that minority enrollment rates increased from the early 1970s, coinciding with the adoption of affirmative action, until the *Bakke* decision in 1978. After *Bakke*, minority enrollment rates rose and fell in an erratic manner until they leveled off in the mid-1980s. After examining admission practices at elite undergraduate universities, Bowen and Bok (1998) concluded that the elimination of affirmative action at these schools would result in a substantial drop in minority enrollment, with bigger losses at the most prestigious universities.

## Has Affirmative Action Produced Other Benefits?

In addition to increasing minority access to higher education, affirmative action has also been shown to produce some unexpected, but positive benefits for the organization and society (see Turner & Pratkanis, 1994; Pratkanis & Turner, 1996, for additional examples). For example, in an evaluation of minority physicians who graduated from medical schools in 1975 (many admitted via affirmative action programs), Keith, Bell, and Williams (1987) found that minority physicians are more likely to enter primary care specialties (in accord with the federal health work force policy of the 1970s) and are more likely to serve poorer patients in areas that normally experience physician shortages. Bowen and Bok (1998) found that white students who attended elite institutions that employed affirmative action reported that their contact with minority group members in college later allowed them to function more effectively in a multicultural society. A recent Gallup Poll survey of law students at Harvard and the University of Michigan showed that two-thirds reported that having students of different racial and ethnic backgrounds improves class discussions and, by a ratio of 10 to 1, those who had been in both single-race and multiracial classes said racially diverse classes were superior (Mollison, 1999).

## Does Affirmative Action Stigmatize the Recipient as Less Qualified?

One reason given by opponents for dismantling affirmative action is that it leads to the perception that recipients are unqualified for their positions and thus places an additional burden on women and minorities. Four sets of studies have found some support for this proposition, although there are some important conditions under which this stigmatization does not occur.

First, many people misunderstand the meaning of affirmative action and view it as just preferential selection or quota. For example, Kravitz and Platania (1993) found that college students could not identify the components of a typical affirmation action plan and instead believed that it consists of quotas, which are, of course, illegal. Golden, Hinkle, and Crosby (2000) found that such confusion leads to the rejection of affirmative action, with those most opposed to the policy defining it in terms of quotas.

Second, more than half a dozen studies find that preferential selection and quota systems are seen as unfair (see Pratkanis & Turner, 1996, for a review). However, research has also identified factors that influence these judgments including: (a) selection based on gender alone is seen as less fair than selection on the basis of gender and ability combined (Austin, Friedman, Martz, Hooe, & Ball, 1977; Nacoste, 1987); (b) affirmative action is seen as fairer when the institution is shown to have a history of discrimination (Nacoste, 1985, 1987; Nacoste & Lehman, 1987); and (c) affirmative action in principle is seen as fairer than in practice (Ayers, 1992).

Third, when a woman or minority member enters a previously all male or all-white organization, she or he is often accorded the status of solo or, in Kanter's (1977a) terms, the only "X" in a field of "O's." This solo status brings with it special treatment. Research finds that solos (a) tend to receive more attention and scrutiny than in-group members, (b) are evaluated either negatively or more extremely as a result of exaggerated low and high expectations, and (c) are seen as playing a special, often stereotypic role in the group (Kanter, 1977a, 1977b; Pettigrew & Martin, 1987; Taylor, 1981).

Finally, research finds that those who are perceived as preferentially selected are *sometimes* seen as less qualified (Garcia, Erskine, Hawn, & Casmay, 1981; Jacobson & Koch, 1977; Turner, Pratkanis, & Hardaway, 1994).

## Why Does Affirmative Action Sometimes Result in Stigmatization?

One possibility is that affirmative action actually selects and promotes less qualified students and employees and thus the stigma is deserved. Although the research base is limited to a handful of studies, there is no evidence to date that the perception of affirmative action recipients as less qualified is true, and some evidence to show that productivity improves as a result of implementing affirmative action (Turner & Pratkanis, 1994; Pratkanis & Turner, 1996). For example, Bowen and Bok (1998) found that the standardized test scores of those minorities who would be excluded from elite universities if affirmative action were discontinued did not differ significantly from those of minority students who would still be eligible for enrollment. If differences in productivity are not the cause, what then is the root of negative attitudes toward affirmative action and the perception that affirmative action recipients are less qualified? Social psychological research finds support for four explanations.

First, considerable research reveals that racism is the leading cause of opposition to affirmative action (Bobo & Kluegel, 1993; Kluegel and Smith, 1986; Malos, 2000; Murrell, Dietz-Uhler, Dovidio, Gaertner & Drout, 1994). Racial attitudes can provide a context for how recipients of affirmative action are perceived. For example, a racist student or co-worker must resolve two discrepant cognitions: "I believe minorities are inferior, and this minority member is now enrolled at a prestigious university." One way to do this is to conclude that the minority group member was admitted through preferential treatment. Second, support for affirmative action diminishes when white Americans see the causes of poverty in terms of personal factors (lack of motivation or ability of the person who lives in poverty) as opposed to social factors (discriminatory barriers preventing equal opportunities) (Kluegel & Smith, 1986). Third, affirmative action programs based on universalistic procedures (applicant qualifications given the most weight with some weight given to group membership) are perceived as fairer than those relying on particularistic procedures [giving more weight to group membership than qualifications (Nacoste, 1985)]. Finally, attitudes are often held to enhance and defend the self (Pratkanis & Greenwald, 1989). Attitudes toward affirmative action recipients can serve a scapegoating or ego-defense function, especially when a person feels relatively deprived. In other words, the affirmative action recipient is used as an excuse for one's own shortcomings.

## Does the "Preferentially Selected" Stigma Affect Recipients of Affirmative Action?

Research shows that being perceived as preferentially selected for a position can impact affirmative action recipients in at least three ways (Turner & Pratkanis, 1994).

First, those who believe they were hired as a result of preferential selection often doubt their ability to do job-related tasks (Heilman, Lucas, & Kaplow, 1990; Heilman, Simon, & Repper, 1987; Turner, Pratkanis, & Hardaway, 1991). In these laboratory experiments, subjects are told they can perform a desired task either because of meritorious performance or because of their gender (i.e., we do not have enough females). The results consistently show that females in the preferentially selected conditions evaluated their specific abilities and performance as poorer in quality compared with females who perceived they merited the position. However, consistent with the work of Crocker and Major (1989; see also Branscome, Schmitt, & Harvey, 1999), self-evaluations of global abilities are not impaired. Finally, this tendency to devalue performance can be mitigated by providing the recipient with unambiguous, explicit, and focused information regarding qualifications for the task or job.

Second, women who believe they were selected for a position on the basis of their gender are more likely to choose less demanding tasks than women who perceived they were selected by merit (Heilman, Rivero, & Brett, 1991) and show less interest in the position (Chacko, 1982; Heilman & Herlihy, 1984; Nacoste, 1987). In other words, they disidentify with the task. As with self-evaluations of ability and performance, these effects are mitigated by providing information about personal qualifications.

Finally, Turner and Pratkanis (1993) found that performance is complexly affected by selection processes and conceptualization of task requirements. In their experiment, female subjects were told that they were assigned to a position on the basis of either merit or preferential selection (that is, because they were female) and that successful performance on an upcoming brain-storming task required either extra effort or inherent capabilities. The results showed that preferentially selected women performed poorer when the task required effort rather than ability. (Merit selected women showed the opposite pattern.) Interestingly, self-evaluation of task performance was affected only by the selection procedures with women who believed they were preferentially selected devaluing their performance. Replicating part of the Turner and Prat-kanis design, Brown, Charnsangavej, Keough, Newman, and Rentfrow (2000) found that females who believed they were preferentially selected for a leader-ship task of answering GRE questions showed less motivation for the task (attempted fewer problems) and lower overall performance. Turner and Pratka-nis (1993) interpret these results in terms of self-handicapping (see Rhodewalt & Tragakis, Chapter 6 in this volume). Preferentially selected individuals experience uncertainty regarding the likelihood of achieving successful performance (Crocker & Major, 1989; Pettigrew & Martin, 1987). Under these conditions, people self-handicap; that is, they seek to protect against the negative implications of failure by actively setting up possible excuses for poor performance (Higgins, 1990). One common self-handicapping tactic is the allocation of reduced effort—"I failed because I didn't try as opposed to I couldn't do it"—which in turn results in poorer performance. When no ready-made excuse is available (such as when a task requires inherent ability), preferentially selected individuals find it difficult to self-handicap and, as a result, their performance is not adversely affected.

## AN OVERVIEW OF THE HELPING MODEL OF AFFIRMATIVE ACTION

Our review of desegregation and affirmative action revealed some consistent findings. First, both desegregation and affirmative action were able to achieve their goals, although not completely. Second, desegregation and affirmative action worked better under certain conditions including when: (a) the intervention had the support of authorities, (b) the conditions of equal status contact were met, (c) the situation did not stigmatize and carry other self-threatening messages, (d) the intervention was seen as fair because it involved universalistic principles or was done to counter violations of American laws and tradition, and (e) recipients and others were provided with unambiguous, explicit, and focused information regarding qualifications. Third, and perhaps unexpectedly, both school desegregation and affirmative action often resulted in positive effects on the white majority, who found the experience to be useful for their lives.

To account for these results, Turner and Pratkanis (1994; Pratkanis & Turner, 1996; 1999) have developed a helping model of affirmative action. In this model, the key to understanding the effects of interventions such as school desegregation and affirmative action is the nature of the underlying helping relationship between the in-and out-group members. Both school desegregation and affirmative action represent an attempt by the in-group member to help the out-group member. How this assistance is rendered makes all the difference. Sometimes help can imply a superior–inferior relationship between the donor and recipient of aid—that the recipient lacks the ability to make it on her or his own and must depend on the good graces of the in-group member for success. In such cases, affirmative action and classroom interaction raise self-doubts in the minority group member and may serve to stigmatize that person further. The donor continues to believe (falsely) in her or his own superiority.

Sometimes, however, help can be rendered as cooperation between group members of equal status. In such cases, the aid is not focused on remedial measures to somehow "fix" the recipient, but instead is targeted toward removing discriminatory barriers for mutual benefit. When this occurs, the aid does not raise feelings of self-doubt in the recipient and can provide lasting benefits to both the donor and the recipient of affirmative action. In the helping model, the conditions that led to more effective school desegregation and affirmative action interventions are also more likely to lead to a form of help as mutual cooperation and not recipient-threatening aid. To understand the dynamics of this helping process, let us look at affirmative action from both the donor's and the recipient's perspectives.

## AFFIRMATIVE ACTION AS HELP: A DONOR'S PERSPECTIVE

To understand the donor's perspective, we need to answer two questions: What motivates anyone to help another (through affirmative action or other means)? What are the consequences of this help for the donor?

The literature on helping suggests that help will be given under a number of conditions such as when norms specify that help is appropriate, the situation is interpreted as requiring help, or the donor experiences personal conflicts (Schroeder, Penner, Dovidio, & Piliavin, 1995). In other words, a donor with needs, perceptions, and beliefs is placed in a social situation with certain norms, barriers, and social forces. Often in such cases, the individual experiences tensions and conflicts that must be resolved, resulting in attitudes and behavior. We explore these motivations below (see Pratkanis & Turner, 1999, for more details).

In terms of consequences, help can sometimes have a dark side, given out of egotistic motivations. Although this aid may bring about positive outcomes, it defines a power hierarchy with the donor cast in the role of a powerful figure whereas the recipient is relegated to the position of needy and low power (Batson, 1991; Pratkanis, 2000; Worchel, 1984). However, not all helping has a dark side. For example, cooperation, or the mutual working together for a common goal, does not necessarily create a power hierarchy. Cooperation requires mutual and equal exchange between parties and thus does not create a dependency relationship (Worchel, 1984; Worchel, Wong, & Scheltema, 1989).

Thus, a majority group member can take one of three routes of helping or delivering affirmative action. First, the potential helper can outright refuse the opportunity to lend assistance, that is, reject any attempt at taking affirmative action. Second, the help can be given begrudgingly; the result is ambivalent aid that maintains the current power relationships. (It is this form of aid that the recipients of affirmative action find most threatening.) Finally, help can be rendered as cooperation, that is, working together toward the goals of a democratic society. These three routes of helping correspond to three common forms of prejudice (see Allport, 1954; Kovel, 1970): (1) the bigot who openly acts out racist beliefs, (2) the aversive racist who tries to avoid and deny her or his racism, and (3) the tolerant personality who views affirmative action, not as a form of remedial care, but as a basic responsibility of a citizen in a democracy to protect the rights of minorities and thus one's own rights. Let us now look at the antecedents and consequences of each route of affirmative action as help.

## Race as Excuse: Rejecting the Helping Role

### The Antecedents of Bigotry and Scapegoating

What causes a person to reject a group of people and to argue violently against all efforts at affirmative action? According to the frustration–aggression model (Berkowitz, 1962; Dollard, Doob, Miller, Mowrer, & Sears, 1939), one cause of intergroup hostility is the frustration felt by a dominant group member who then takes out (displaces) this frustration on a minority group member. In other words, the individual faces a self-threat such as frustrations, goal blocking, or relative deprivation. This threat to one's self-esteem raises the question: Who am I and why have I failed? As Ezekiel (1995) noted, neo-Nazis and Klan members often find an answer to this question in racist ideology: The white race is superior to the mud races (people of color); any threat to self is met by blaming minorities and by promoting one's own special status as a member of a superior race.

Of course, not all self-threats lead to aggression and out-group hostility. Four factors that increase the likelihood of translating frustrations into hate include: (a) norms of prejudice that hold that the in-group is superior to the out-group (see Pettigrew 1958, 1959, 1991), (b) racist propaganda that derogates an out-group member, (c) a tendency to seek autocratic relationships (Altemeyer, 1988; Pratto, Sidanius, Stallworth, & Malle, 1994), and (d) a lack of coping skills or other ways of responding to a self-threat other than aggression and scapegoating.

### The Psychological Consequences of Using Race as an Excuse

What happens to individuals when they accept the myth of racial supremacy and use race as an excuse for their problems? The identity of dominant group members can become transformed so that all psychological energy must be directed at maintaining the excuse for one's shortcomings and for preserving the myth of racial superiority. If the excuse fails, all is lost. The myth of racial supremacy can result in some short-term positive feelings: a sense of power and strength along with immediate satisfaction that one is superior. However, maintaining the myth is not without its psychological costs including a unidimensional self, extremist identity, high susceptibility to propaganda supporting the identity, perpetuation of the problems that led to the failure and frustration in the first place, and establishment of a vicious cycle of self-justification whereby cruelty toward others is justified by a hardening of the soul, which in turn increases the likelihood of more aggression.

# Ambivalent Aid and the Maintenance of Power

## Antecedents of Aversive Racism

At the heart of aversive racism is Myrdal's (1944) American dilemma. On the one hand, democracy demands that the rights of all citizens to life, liberty, and happiness be protected. According to this creed, taking affirmative action to stop and prevent the negative effects of racism is the only morally defensible position. On the other hand, racism brings with it the fruits of social domination (Sidanius, 1993; Sidanius & Pratto, 1999). Taking affirmative action can result in a loss of this position of dominance for the in-group member.

As Festinger (1957, p. 7) noted, Myrdal's dilemma establishes the conditions of cognitive dissonance: the in-group member holds two conflicting beliefs (support for democracy and for racism), which create an unpleasant tension state. In an attempt to resolve this dissonance, the behavior of the in-group member can vary wildly. For example, Harvey and Oswald (2000) found that inducing white guilt about racism (by showing a civil rights video) led to less support of programs for African-Americans (dissonance over white guilt was resolved by rejecting claims of racism) but more support for such programs if the person first listed positive aspects of her- or himself (such self-affirmations reduce dissonance directly and allow the person to empathize with the out-group member).

In terms of attitudes toward affirmative action, the aversive racist can show an astonishing range of responses including: (a) believing that out-group members are genetically inferior or come from a culture of poverty and therefore affirmative action is useless, (b) denying that the government (or anyone else) has a responsibility for protecting the rights of citizens, (c) desiring social equality but disliking all means suggested for obtaining it, (d) rationalizing that affirmative action programs violate justice norms (Bobocel, Son Hing, Dravey, Stanley, & Zanna, 1998), (e) supporting affirmative action as remedial care, and (f) actively attempting to remove discriminatory barriers. However, with the exception of attempting to remove discriminatory barriers, all of these policies maintain the basic structure of group dominance and therefore do not resolve the American dilemma.

What determines how the American dilemma will be resolved by the aversive racist? We should note that attempts to resolve this conflict can result in highly variable behavior, with the same person exhibiting behavior that may oscillate between the blatantly racist and the truly integrative depending on some often subtle social factors. Some of these factors with respect to affirmative action include: (a) norms that specify the socially appropriate behavior and how to resolve the dilemma (Pettigrew, 1991), (b) the ambiguity of the situation [e.g., prejudice responses are more likely when the person can get away with it; (Gaertner & Dovidio, 1986)], (c) the existence of a clear standard to justify the prejudice behavior, and (d) political ideology [a conservative as opposed to a liberal ideology can be used to justify the rejection of affirmative (see Pettigrew et al., 1998; Sidanius, Pratto, & Bobo, 1996)].

## The Psychological Consequences of an Unresolved Dilemma

The unresolved American dilemma can result in four possible psychological responses. First, suppressing racist tendencies can provide a doubly false sense of self-worth, with aversive racists feeling superior to more blatant racists who practice an outdated form of prejudice and to the out-groups who they begrudgingly help. Second, this unresolved inconsistency can be played upon by politicians or demagogues who gain by offering a false solution to the conflict. Third, power tends to corrupt, becoming an end in itself and replacing other more moral values; the powerless are devalued and considered to be of little worth (see Kipnis, 1976). Finally, the aversive racist feels unappreciated because any aid (affirmative action) may be threatening and rejected by the recipient. This, in turn, reinforces perceptions that affirmative action is a poor tool for resolving social problems, thus perpetuating the tension.

## Democratic Altruism: Help as Cooperation

In this route, affirmative action is not viewed as remedial help, but as the promotion of democracy by protecting the rights of all citizens including minorities. Affirmative action is thus the proactive removal of discriminatory barriers to provide opportunity to all citizens living in a democracy. It is not one group begrudgingly helping another out of some misplaced emotion, but the cooperation of citizens from different backgrounds to ensure a democratic structure that all can enjoy.

### Antecedents of Cooperation Between Groups

What leads a person to cross social barriers to render democratic aid to an out-group member? Perhaps, the answer to this question can be seen most clearly in those who rendered the ultimate help—rescuers or those who saved Jewish persons from the Nazi death campaign. According to a survey conducted by Oliner and Oliner (1988) rescuers differed from nonrescuers in a number of ways [many of these factors have also been found to increase altruism in general (see Schroeder et al., 1995)]. The parents of rescuers buffered their children from negative stereotypes of the out-group and were less likely to express negative stereotypes of Jews. In addition, rescuers were more likely to have contact with Jews as either friends or neighbors or in an employer –employee relationships. An important principle held by rescuers, instilled through socialization, is that each person has a social responsibility for promoting the principles of democracy, that is, a strong commitment to core democratic principles of equality and the protection of minority rights. They defined their group in inclusive terms, reported feeling connected and close to diverse people, and could easily see how they were personally similar to other people. Building on this sense of inclusion, rescuers found it easy to empathize with others and especially to feel another person's pain. The parents of rescuers were more likely to use what has been termed an inductive style of discipline—the use of reason with their children and suggestions on ways to remedy the harm done by their misbehavior—as opposed to the use of physical punishment and punishment that was gratuitous and unrelated to misbehavior. Finally, rescuers showed more self-efficacy and feelings of personal control; that is, they felt that they could affect events and had a responsibility to do so.

### The Consequences of Intergroup Cooperation

As Bowen and Bok (1998) found, affirmative action can establish the conditions that lead to a more satisfying social interaction for the majority group member. No longer does the in-group member need to engage in torturous self-justifications and deceptions to maintain false power. Instead, he or she is free to learn from others and from life situations and to develop and grow as a person. Rendering cooperative help can yield seven benefits: (a) improved productivity and decision making (Johnson and Johnson, 1989); (b) ability to learn from others; (c) deprovincialization or a thoughtful reappraisal of the in-group's norms, customs, values, and lifestyles (Pettigrew, 1997); (d) a coherent, complex social self; (e) a sense of connectedness and belonging; (f) a purpose larger than one's self; and (g) happiness.

## AFFIRMATIVE ACTION AS HELP: A RECIPIENT'S PERSPECTIVE

What is the experience of affirmative action from the recipients' point of view? Nadler and Fisher (1986) have developed a model of reactions of recipients to aid. In this model, they specified the factors that lead aid to be self-threatening and the consequences of self-threatening as opposed to self-supporting help. We use this model to specify the conditions under which affirmative action is most effective (see Turner & Pratkanis, 1994; Pratkanis & Turner, 1996).

## Self-Threatening Affirmative Action

### Antecedents of Self-Threatening Help

The helping model identifies three conditions that foster self-threatening affirmative action. First, affirmative action is more likely to be perceived as self-threatening when the implementation strategy conveys negative self-relevant messages; that is, the recipient lacks the requisite qualifications, is inferior, and could not have obtained the position without assistance. This affirmative action stigma stems in part from long-held stereotypes that women and minorities do not have what it takes to compete in school coupled with the ego needs of others to use minorities and women as excuses for their own relative deprivation. Further, this stigma is supported by a fundamental attribution error, which downplays the role of social structure in determining employment and advancement (Kluegel & Smith, 1986; Ross, 1977). Second, affirmative action is more likely to be viewed as self-threatening when it seems to conflict with societal values and norms. For example, when not coupled with explicit, unambiguous, and focused information about qualifications, affirmative action can imply that the recipient is dependent and lacks self-reliance. Finally, affirmative action that does not convey instrumental benefits is more likely to be perceived as self-threatening. Specifically, affirmative action is likely to be viewed as self-threatening if it does not clearly confirm the possibility of the recipient's future success, implies a need for future assistance, and fails to remove discriminatory barriers.

## The Consequences of Self-Threatening Aid

The helping model predicts short- and long-term consequences. Three immediate responses are suggested. First, the self-threat translates into an immediate negative self-perception of ability and performance. Affirmative action unaccompanied by explicit, unambiguous, and focused evidence about a recipient's qualifications engenders self-doubt about one's task-related abilities. Second, self-threatening aid results in negative evaluation of the procedure (Nacoste, 1990) and of the provider. Finally, individuals attempt to deal with the self-threat by engaging in defensive behaviors designed to protect the self and to alter the threatening situation. For example, Turner and Pratkanis (1993) found that preferentially selected subjects took advantage of a self-handicapping strategy when it was available. Turner et al. (1991) found that preferentially selected subjects devalued specific abilities but not their overall self-evaluations, thus limiting the attack to a specific domain. Nadler and Fisher (1986) suggested that recipients of self-threatening help should be highly motivated to alter the dependency relationship. In other words, recipients may attempt to terminate the relationship (drop out of school), reduce contact with the provider (e.g., be absent), disidentify with the task (e.g., "education is not for me"), or engage or appear to engage in strategies for "self-improvement" so that the purported need for assistance is terminated.

The long-term consequences of self-threatening aid may be either learned helplessness or achievement. According to Nadler and Fisher (1986), the level of perceived control determines the ultimate result. Recipients who lack control exhibit learned helplessness or a feeling that nothing can be done to change the current negative state of affairs. On the other hand, recipients who perceive a high degree of control are likely to engage in behavior to reduce the dependency relationship. For example, Templeton (1994) found that successful black executives sought to achieve control of a situation and had developed a number of techniques for doing so.

# Self-Supportive Affirmative Action

## Antecedents of Self-Supporting Help

Not all aid is self-threatening nor do all affirmative action programs entail negative consequences. According to our model, three factors will increase the degree of self-support associated with affirmative action. First, affirmative action is more likely to be perceived as self-supportive if the process carries positive self-relevant messages highlighting the recipient's unique qualifications and not implying inferiority or that the recipient is in need of help. Second, the procedure is more likely to be viewed as self-supportive if it confirms societal norms and values such as procedural fairness, independence, self-reliance, and rewarding excellence. Finally, affirmative action is seen as self-supportive if it provides instrumental benefits such as removing discriminatory barriers.

## The Consequences of Self-Supporting Aid

The immediate consequences of self-supportive affirmative action are largely positive and nondefensive. We have seen that affirmative action that is supportive, in other words, that provides unambiguous, explicit, and focused evidence of recipient qualifications, is more likely to result in positive self-perceptions of ability, performance, and affect and perceptions that the procedure was fair. In contrast to self-threatening aid, self-supportive affirmative action does not result in defensive behavior (or, at least, no more defensive behavior than human beings typically engage in).

The long-term consequences of self-supportive affirmative action depend on the objective need for help. Self-supportive aid to an individual truly needing help results in low motivation and a low degree of subsequent self-help that could ultimately result in a harmful helplessness-like dependency. However, there is no reason to suspect that women and minorities are inferior to others (although some stereotypes suggest otherwise), and thus there is little objective need for help (other than to remove discriminatory barriers). Recipients of such aid should not experience helplessness assuming that the aid is successful in removing discriminatory barriers.

## TOWARDS COOPERATIVE AND DEMOCRATIC HELP

One of the major ironies of the American educational system is that it is a most undemocratic place charged with the maintenance and promotion of a democracy. In the typical classroom, the teacher stands autocratically at the head of the classroom, ready to spew forth knowledge to eager followers. The relationships among students are guided by the social inequalities of race, class, and gender. It does not need to be that way. Based on our helping model of affirmative action and on research in social psychology, we can identify 18 strategies for bringing about a more democratic classroom (for concrete illustrations of some of these strategies in action see Pratkanis & Turner, 1994a, 1994b).

## 18 Strategies for Helping to Resolve America's Schooling Tension

1. *Focus helping effort away from the recipient and toward removing discriminatory barriers.* As we have seen, this is the key ingredient for successful affirmative action interventions. It is the responsibility of everyone in the school to identify possible barriers that are preventing some from obtaining their educational goals and to help find effective means for removing those barriers. When this occurs, everyone is the beneficiary.

2. *Establish unambiguous, explicit, and focused qualifications criteria to be used in any selection decision.* Our review indicates that the negative consequences of the perception of preferential selection do *not* occur when qualifications are included as selection criteria.

3. *Clearly communicate the requisite criteria.* One of the problems many affirmative action programs face is that they have clear selection criteria, but these criteria are not clearly communicated to relevant audiences. For example, the voters of California rejected affirmative action plans used at the University of California because they thought that such plans admitted unqualified minorities to the university. (Almost all students admitted are UC qualified; the small percentage that are not typically have a special skill such as music and are mostly white.) A clearer communication plan could avoid some of this confusion.

4. *Be certain that selection procedures are perceived as fair by the relevant audiences.* The procedure for admission to any institution of higher education must take into consideration complex factors; this ambiguity coupled with traditional patterns of racism makes such procedures ripe for claims of bias. However, it is the responsibility of the educational institution to ensure that relevant audiences perceive a sense of fair play. For example, consider two "objective" measures used by the University of California for admission: the GPA and the SAT score. Both can be biased against minorities. Students who attend elite high schools have the opportunity to take advanced placement courses

(where in calculating a GPA an "A" counts as "5" points instead of "4", a B as "4" instead of "3", and so on). Thus, such a student has the opportunity to receive a higher GPA (often above the traditional maximum of 4.0). Similarly, the SAT test is standardized on middle-class students and can be taken under conditions of stereotype threat as outlined by Steele (2000) in his testimony in the recent University of Michigan affirmative action case. Communicating information about biases in selection procedures can help observers understand the fairness in differentially weighting criteria.

5. *Reinforce the fact that affirmative action is not just preferential selection.* Given the ubiquity of this misbelief about affirmative action, it is imperative that all those who are interested in promoting diversity within education take the responsibility to clearly communicate that quotas are illegal and are not part of affirmative action.

6. *Provide specific information testifying to the competencies of the recipient of affirmative action.* It is difficult and stressful being the "new kid" in the class and being relegated to the solo status. Thus it is important to provide unambiguous, specific feedback to overcome the adverse consequences that may be associated with perceptions of being preferentially selected. More global feedback (e.g., "you did well") does not appear to be as effective. Further, when providing negative feedback to minority students it is important to couple that feedback with a reminder of the high standards used in the evaluation and an assurance to the student that he or she has the capacity to reach those standards (Cohen, Steele, & Ross, 1999).

7. *Emphasize the recipient's contributions to the organization.* It is important that observers perceive the affirmative action recipient as a unique contributor and not just in terms of old stereotypes. Affirmative action can result in a diversity of skills and perspectives that can be useful for a school. By making clear such contributions, the qualifications of the recipient are tangibly demonstrated. Further, the recipient has reciprocated the purported help to the provider. Fellow students' belief that the person "got in by preference" is replaced with a belief that the student is an important contributor to the educational setting.

8. *Develop socialization strategies that deter attributions fostering helplessness-like behavior.* The goal of these strategies should be to preclude student recipients of affirmative action from making attributions that they do not belong and are likely to fail. One approach to executing this principle is what Steele (1997) terms *wise* programs—educational programs that do not offer self-threatening remedial programs for minorities, but challenging "honors" level work that carries the message, "since the work is difficult, success is to your credit; a setback is a reflection of the challenge." Similarly, Zweigenhaft and Domhoff (1991) found that the most successful preparatory schools for African-Americans were those that challenged the student with rigorous academics and numerous cultural activities.

9. *Practice the psychology of the inevitable in implementing affirmative action.* We have seen that the support of authorities for the inevitability of change is a key ingredient for successful school desegregation and affirmative action. The support of authorities legitimizes the helping effort, signaling that affirmative action does not run counter to social norms. In contrast, when authorities do not support affirmative action, it conveys a message that such efforts are not needed, thereby reinforcing old in-group/out-group patterns.

10. *Establish the conditions of equal status contact.* We also saw that Allport's (1954) equal status contact principle is one of the most effective means of reducing intergroup prejudice (Pettigrew, 1998). Sometimes the conditions of equal status contact are inherent in a situation and merely need to be emphasized. However, in many schools these conditions need to be created; this can be accomplished with the tactics we listed above. From the perspective of the helping model, equal status contact is a simple and effective means of establishing the conditions needed to produce intergroup cooperation and democracy.

11. *Create a common in-group identity.* A sense of inclusiveness can be created by giving members of different groups a superordinate common identity. For example, Gaertner, Dovidio, Anastasio, Bachman, and Rust (1993) induced laboratory groups either to think of themselves as two separate groups or to recategorize themselves as one group. The results showed less group bias when the two groups thought of themselves as one.

12. *Counter negative stereotypes and norms.* It is clear that racist stereotypes provide the fuel for constructing the myth of in-group supremacy. Citron, Chein, and Harding (1950) found that the best way to handle bigoted remarks is to point out, in a calm voice, that such behavior is inconsistent with the American creed. Aboud and Fenwick (1999) provide three additional strategies for counteracting prejudicial norms: instructing students how to explain behavior in terms other than race, exploring ways to respond to racial remarks, and engaging in discussions of race with a low-prejudice friend.

13. *Promote empathy.* Empathy or feeling someone else's emotions makes it difficult to treat that person with cruelty and increases the likelihood of democratic altruism. Batson (1991) describes a program for teaching empathy which includes: (a) making salient the needs of others, (b) encouraging the adoption of perspective taking, and (c) teaching how to respond to needs in an effective manner. In their training sessions for leaders, the Army requires role-playing: whites see situations from the standpoint of blacks and blacks see situations from the standpoint of whites (Moskos & Butler, 1996). Role-play provides participants with a range of new information and helps them empathize with others (Pratkanis, 2000). One dramatic example of the use of role-playing to reduce prejudice (and promote empathy) is Jane Elliott's classroom exercise that divides students on the basis of their eye color (see Peters, 1987).

14. *Recognize the worth of each person.* One factor that leads to racism is a threat to self that questions the worth of an individual. Recently, Fein and Spencer (1997) showed that merely giving a person the opportunity to affirm the essential aspects of his- or herself was enough to reduce the use of negative stereotypes. In a world were winning is everything, it is unrealistic to expect that there will not be losers who will need to somehow find an excuse for failure. This is especially true if their self-esteem is over inflated and not built on true competencies. However, that does not mean that steps cannot be taken to prevent this from happening such as (a) providing coping skills and positive ways to resolve attacks on the self and (b) valuing and developing the competencies of all persons so that they feel worthwhile and not excluded from society.

15. *Teach democratic relationships.* It is important that our schools teach the basic machinery of democracy (checks and balances, deliberative persuasion, respect for minority rights) and why each of these components is important. In addition, for democratic altruism to flourish, it is essential that citizens see relationships as egalitarian and equal as opposed to autocratic and hierarchical. As the work of Hoffman (1984) has shown, empathy and an appreciation for democratic relations can be fostered by inductive child rearing or explaining why a behavior is wrong and how it impacts others as opposed to the use of strong punishment as a power tactic (see also Shure, 1994, for additional ideas on how to accomplish this goal).

16. *Be aware that desegregation and affirmative action programs do not operate in isolation within the school setting.* Such programs are part of the larger schooling and societal context. As such, efforts are doomed to fail if they are not diffused throughout the school; efforts limited to a single subunit are likely to be regarded as a ghetto. Further it is also important to develop meaningful rewards for those educators who advance the goals of the program.

17. *Recognize that affirmative action is not a panacea.* In actuality, affirmative action programs are but one tool for overcoming discrimination in schools. These programs should *not* be expected to solve all problems faced by targeted groups but should work in conjunction with other programs such as Head Start to eliminate discriminatory barriers.

18. *Monitor the affirmative action program to see what works and what does not.* As affirmative action succeeds and previously excluded persons achieve in the school setting, new discriminatory barriers are likely to be identified that will require new solutions. A good assessment program can identify these new needs along with tracking the progress in general.

## A DEMOCRATIC VISION FOR SCHOOLS

By now it should be clear that it will take more than just showing a film strip about Martin Luther King during Black Awareness Week to resolve the tension in American schools. To accomplish this goal, classrooms need to be fundamentally restructured. To promote democracy, the classroom must be a democracy. That does not mean that the teacher gives up the role of educator and allows students to run the classroom; this is not democracy but merely laissez-faire rule. The teacher needs to be a democratic leader to teach democratic relationships.

A classic study by Kurt Lewin and his colleagues illustrates the role of teacher as democratic leader (Lewin, Lippitt, & White, 1939; White & Lippitt, 1960). In this research, boys were led by an adult who was trained to exhibit an authoritarian, laissez-faire, or democratic leadership style. The authoritarian leader determined policy and dictated the tasks the group would perform; communication was unidirectional from the leader to the followers; group members were rewarded for conforming to the leader's wishes. The boys led by an authoritarian showed high levels of productivity, but this productivity lacked creativity and was highly dependent on the leader's instructions. In addition, their social relationships were marked by hostility and distrust; scapegoating was common. The laissez-faire leader had limited participation in the group and allowed the boys to do whatever they wanted; ironically, this group had the lowest level of participation and productivity. The democratic leader structured activities by encouraging group discussion; rewards and power were used to advance the group's agenda, objectives, and tasks. Under this form of leadership, the boys produced highly original work; they enjoyed their relationships with the other group members. The moral of this research should be clear: a democratic classroom not only is more productive (increased learning) but also helps to establish the social relationships that are needed by democracies.

This vision of a democratic classroom was outlined more than 85 years ago by John Dewey (1916) who viewed education as a way of expanding the horizons of its participants, providing opportunity for people of different social groups to share common interests, and building character appropriate to democratic life including cooperation, flexibility, and concern for the welfare of others. As Dewey (1916) put it:

> [I]t is the office of the school environment to balance the various elements in the social environment, and to see to it that each individual gets an opportunity to escape the limitations of the social group in which he was born. …The intermingling in the school of youth of different races, differing religions, and unlike customs creates for all a new and broader environment. (pp. 20–21)

It is by affirming our fundamental principles that we can resolve a fundamental tension in the American classroom and rediscover our democracy anew.

## Teachers' Questions and Answers

**Q:** Does this mean that schools are to provide equality of knowledge, teaching, and education to all students, or more to those who are at a disadvantage due to the historical barriers of access so as to "level the playing field"?

**A:** We concur with John Dewey that humans do not begin as neutral blank slates and that unfairness, not fairness, results when equality is treated as an original given. In other words, each student is special and deserving of the resources required to reach her or his potential. The question is, "how to do this?" One method is tracking: putting students into classrooms that are grouped on ability level. This seems more to reinforce old stereotypes as opposed to changing them.

In our mind, the fundamental problem is with the autocratic structure of the typical classroom: a teacher with the answers talking at a mass of students whose job it is to guess those answers. A more democratic way to structure a classroom is based on Dewey's notion of occupations or what Howard Gardner calls projects: each student comes with a set of interests (a love of trains, dance, baseball, or whatever) and learns by pursuing his or her interests (e.g., by studying train routes a student learns geography, train history becomes a scaffold for history in general, and train operations become a vehicle for learning math). In this classroom, the teacher is a resource that guides the student as he or she pursues a project. Lectures become a way of opening horizons and motivating inquiry. Group work structured as in the jigsaw class-room can reinforce the student's project or occupation. And there is no reason not to use teaching machines that allow students to learn on their own.

This would be the ideal. Given that it is not likely to happen in the short run, it would be nice, at least, to see those students who face discriminatory barriers get at least as many resources as other students. Schools located in inner cities and poverty zones get far fewer resources than other schools.

**Q:** Given that the trend is to remove affirmative action, what types of programs need to be implemented to continue the goal of democratically, fairly educating all students?

**A:** Given the history of school desegregation and affirmative action, we should expect that there will be legal battles that may prevent or radically change some programs. Our view of affirmative action as the proactive removal of discriminatory barriers is in some sense independent of court challenges. It requires that each teacher look at her or his environment and ask: "What obstacles stand in the way of my students' learning?" And "What is the best way to remove those obstacles?" Sometimes this may be as simple as resched-uling the time of the PTA meeting or paying attention to social interactions on the playground. At other times it may mean explaining to others the inherent bias in many standardized tests. And at yet other times it may mean taking political action in support of programs that we feel are the best way to remove discriminatory barriers.

**Q:** In two separate cases involving the University of Michigan, different U.S. District Court judges rendered opposite rulings, with one claiming that a diverse classroom is a compelling issue of the state and the other claiming that it is not. What is your opinion about these rulings?

**A:**   The promotion of diversity in America's schools is a compelling issue of the state because the promotion of democracy is a compelling issue of the state. From its very beginning, America has been a nation of people from different races, religions, ethnicities, and backgrounds. To function as a democracy and as a nation, we must learn how to live and work with each other and to prosper with each other. When any group of people is systematically excluded from the opportunities that others take for granted, it sows the seeds for discontent and rebellion that will ultimately lead to intergroup hatred. The promotion of diversity in America's schools provide us with one means for learning how to live with each other and for ensuring that each person, no matter his or her social group, has the opportunity to develop to his or her fullest potential.

# References

Aboud, F., & Fenwick, V. (1999). Evaluating school-based interventions to reduce prejudice in preadolescents. *Journal of Social Issues, 55*, 767–785.

Allport, G. W. (1954). *The nature of prejudice*. Reading, MA: Addison–Wesley.

Altemeyer, B. (1988). *Enemies of freedom*. San Francisco: Jossey–Bass.

Aronson, E., Blaney, N., Stephan, C., Sikes, J., & Snapp, M. (1978). *The jigsaw classroom*. Beverly Hills, CA: Sage.

Austin, W., Friedman, J. S., Martz, R. A., Hooe, G. S., & Ball, K. P. (1977). Responses to favorable sex discrimination. *Law and Human Behavior, 1*, 283–298.

Ayers, L. R. (1992). Perceptions of affirmative action among its beneficiaries. *Social Justice Research, 5*, 223–238.

Batson, C. D. (1991). *The altruism question*. Hillsdale, NJ: Erlbaum.

Berkowitz, L. (1962). *Aggression: A social psychological analysis*. New York: McGraw–Hill.

Bobo, L., & Kluegel, J. R. (1993). Opposition to race-targeting: Self-interest, stratification ideology, or racial attitudes? *American Sociological Review, 58*, 443–464.

Bobocel, D. R., Son Hing, L. S., Davey, L. M., Stanley, D. J., & Zanna, M. P. (1998). Justice-based opposition to social policies: Is it genuine? *Journal of Personality and Social Psychology, 75*, 653–669.

Bowen, W. G., & Bok, D. (1998). *The shape of the river*. Princeton, NJ: Princeton University Press.

Branscome, N. R., Schmitt, M. T., & Harvey, R. D. (1999). Perceiving pervasive discrimination among African Americans: Implications for group identification and well-being. *Journal of Personality and Social Psychology, 77*, 135–149.

Brown, R. P., Charnsangavej, T., Keough, K. A., Newman, M. L., & Rentfrow, P. J. (2000). Putting the "affirm" into affirmative action: Preferential selection and academic performance. *Journal of Personality and Social Psychology, 79*, 736–747.

Chacko, T. I. (1982). Women and equal employment opportunity: Some unintended effects. *Journal of Applied Psychology, 67*, 119–123.

Citron, A. F., Chein, I., & Harding, J. (1950). Anti-minority remarks: A problem for action research. *Journal of Abnormal and Social Psychology, 45*, 99–126.

Clark, K. B. (1963). *Prejudice and your child*. Boston: Beacon Press.

Cohen, E., & Roper, S. (1972). Modification of interracial disability interaction: An application of status characteristics theory. *American Sociological Review, 36*, 643–657.

Cohen, G. L., Steele, C. M., & Ross, L. D. (1999). The mentor's dilemma: Providing critical feedback across the racial divide. *Personality and Social Psychology Bulletin, 25*, 1302–1318.

Crocker, J., & Major, B. (1989). Social stigma and self-esteem: The self-protective properties of stigma. *Psychological Review, 98*, 608–630.

Dewey, J. (1916). *Democracy and education*. New York: MacMillian.

Dollard, J., Doob, L. W., Miller, N. E., Mowrer, O. H., & Sears, R. R. (1939). *Frustration and aggression*. New Haven, CT: Yale University Press.

Douglass, F. (1881/1993). *Life and times of Frederick Douglass*. New York: Gramercy Books.

Eberts, R. W., & Stone, J. A. (1985). Male–female differences in promotions: EEO in public education. *Journal of Human Resources, 20*, 504–521.

Ezekiel, R. S. (1995). *The racist mind*. New York: Viking.

Fein, S., & Spencer, S. J. (1997). Prejudice as self-image maintenance: Affirming the self through derogating others. *Journal of Personality and Social Psychology, 73*, 31–44.

Festinger, L. (1957). *A theory of cognitive dissonance*. Stanford, CA: Stanford University Press.

Gaertner, S. L., & Dovidio, J. F. (1986). The aversive form of racism. In J. F. Dovidio & S. L. Gaertner (Eds.), *Prejudice, discrimination, and racism* (pp. 61–89). San Diego, CA: Academic Press.

Gaertner, S. L., Dovidio, J. F., Anastasio, P. A., Bachman, B. A., & Rust, M. C. (1993). The common ingroup identity model: Recategorization and the reduction of intergroup bias. In W. Stoebe & M. Hewstone (Eds.), *European Review of Social Psychology* (Vol. 4, pp. 1–26). Chichester: Wiley.

Garcia, L. T., Erskine, N., Hawn, K., & Casmay, S. R. (1981). The effect of affirmative action on attributions about minority group members. *Journal of Personality, 49*, 427–437.

Gerard, H. B., & Miller, N. (1975). *School desegregation*. New York: Plenum.

Golden, H., Hinkle, S., & Crosby, F. (2001). Reactions to affirmative action: Substance and semantics. *Journal of Applied Social Psychology, 31*, 73–88.

Harvey, R. D., & Oswald, D. L. (2000). Collective guilt and shame as motivation for white support of black programs. *Journal of Applied Social Psychology, 30*, 1790–1811.

Heilman, M. E., & Herlihy, J. M. (1984). Affirmative action, negative reaction? Some moderating conditions. *Organizational Behavior and Human Performance, 33*, 204–213.

Heilman, M. E., Lucas, J. A., & Kaplow, S. R. (1990). Self-derogating consequences of sex-based preferential selection: The moderating role of initial self-confidence. *Organizational Behavior and Human Decision Processes, 46*, 202–216.

Heilman, M. E., Rivero, J. C., & Brett, J. F. (1991). Striking the competence issue: The effects of sex-based preferential selection on task choices of women and men. *Journal of Applied Psychology, 76*, 99–105.

Heilman, M. E., Simon, M. C., & Repper, D. P. (1987). Intentionally favored, unintentionally harmed? Impact of sex-based preferential selection on self-perceptions and self-evaluations. *Journal of Applied Psychology, 72*, 62–68.

Higgins, R. L. (1990). Self-handicapping: Historical roots and contemporary approaches. In R. L. Higgins, C. R. Snyder, & S. Berglas (Eds.), *Self-handicapping: The paradox that isn't* (pp. 1–35). New York: Plenum.

Hoffman, M. L. (1984). Parental discipline, moral internalization, and development of prosocial motivation. In E. Staub, D. Bar-Tal, J. Karylowski, & J. Reykowski (Eds.), *Development and maintenance of prosocial behavior* (pp. 117–137). New York: Plenum.

Hyde, J. S., Fennema, E., & Lamon, S. J. (1990). Gender differences in mathematics performance: A meta-analysis. *Psychological Bulletin, 107*, 139–155.

Jacobson, M. B., & Koch, W. (1977). Women as leaders: Performance evaluation as a function of method of leader selection. *Organizational Behavior and Human Performance, 20*, 149–157.

Johnson, D. W., & Johnson, R. T. (1989). *Cooperation and competition: Theory and research*. Edina, MN: Interactive Book.

Jones, J. M. (1988). Racism in black and white: A bicultural model of reaction and evolution. In P. A. Katz & D. A. Taylor (Eds.), *Eliminating racism* (pp. 117–135). New York: Plenum.

Jones, J. M. (1997). *Prejudice and racism*. New York: McGraw-Hill.

Kanter, R. M. (1977a). Some effects of proportions in group life: Skewed sex ratios and responses to token women. *American Journal of Sociology, 82*, 965–990.

Kanter, R. M. (1977b). *Men and women of the corporation*. New York: Basic Books.

Keith, S. N., Bell, R. M., & Williams, A. P. (1987). *Assessing the outcome of affirmative action in medical schools: A study of the class of 1975*. Santa Monica, CA: Rand.

Kipnis, D. (1976). *The powerholders*. Chicago: University of Chicago Press.

Kluegel, J. R., & Smith, E. R. (1986). *Beliefs about inequality*. New York: Aldine de Gruyter.

Kovel, J. (1970). *White racism*. New York: Columbia University Press.

Kravitz, D. A., & Platania, J. (1993). Attitudes and beliefs about affirmative action: Effects of target and of respondent sex and ethnicity. *Journal of Applied Psychology, 78,* 928–938.

Lewin, K., Lippitt, R., & White, R. K. (1939). Patterns of aggressive behavior in experimentally created social climates. *Journal of Social Psychology, 10,* 271–299.

Mahard, R. E., & Crain, R. L. (1983). Research on minority achievement in desegregated schools. In C. H. Rossell & W. D. Hawley (Eds.), *The consequences of school desegregation* (pp. 103–125). Philadelphia: Temple University Press.

Malos, S. B. (2000). The new affirmative action: Socioeconomic preference criteria in college admissions. *Journal of Applied Behavioral Sciences, 36,* 5–22.

Miller, L. S. (1999). Promoting high academic achievement among Non-Asian minorities. In E. Y. Lowe (Eds.), *Promise and dilemma: Perspectives on racial diversity and higher education,* (pp. 47–91). Princeton, NJ: University of Princeton Press.

Mollison, A. (1999, August 4). Students back diversity. *San Jose Mercury News,* p. 6A.

Moskos, C. C., & Butler, J. S. (1996). *All that we can be*. New York: Basic Books.

Murrell, A. J., Dietz-Uhler, B. L., Dovidio, J. F., Gaertner, S. L., & Drout, C. (1994). Aversive racism and resistance to affirmative action: Perceptions of justice are not necessarily color blind. *Basic and Applied Social Psychology, 15,* 71–86.

Myrdal, G. (1944). *An American dilemma*. New York: McGraw–Hill.

Nacoste, R. W. (1985). Selection procedure and responses to affirmative action. *Law and Human Behavior, 9,* 225–241.

Nacoste, R. W. (1987). But do they care about fairness? The dynamics of preferential treatment and minority interest. *Basic and Applied Social Psychology, 8,* 177–191.

Nacoste, R. W. (1990). Sources of stigma: Analyzing the psychology of affirmative action. *Law and Policy, 12,* 175–195.

Nacoste, R. W., & Lehman, D. (1987). Procedural stigma. *Representative Research in Social Psychology, 17,* 25–38.

Nadler, A., & Fisher, J. D. (1986). The role of threat to self-esteem and perceived control in recipient reactions to help: Theory development and empirical validation. In L. Berkowitz (Ed.), *Advances in experimental social psychology* (Vol. 19, pp. 81–122). Orlando, FL: Academic Press.

Ogbu, J, (1986). The consequences of the American caste system. In U. Neisser (Ed.), *The school acheivement of minority students: New perspectives* (pp. 19–56). Hillsdale, NJ: Erlbaum.

Oliner, S. P., & Oliner, P. M. (1988). *The altruistic personality*. New York: Free Press.

Orfield, G., & Eaton, S. (1996). *Dismantling desgregation*. New York: New Press.

Peters, W. (1987). *A class divided: Then and now*. New Haven, CT: Yale University Press.

Pettigrew, T. F. (1958). Personality and sociocultural factors in intergroup attitudes: A cross-national comparison. *Journal of Conflict Resolution, 2,* 29–42.

Pettigrew, T. F. (1959). Region differences in anti-Negro prejudice. *Journal of Abnormal and Social Psychology, 59,* 28–36.

Pettigrew, T. F. (1961). Social psychology and desegregation research. *American Psychologist, 16,* 105–112.

Pettigrew, T. F. (1975). *Racial discrimination in the United States*. New York: Harper & Row.

Pettigrew, T. F. (1991). Normative theory of intergroup relations: Explaining both harmony and conflict. *Psychology and Developing Societies, 3,* 3–16.

Pettigrew, T. F. (1997). Generalized intergroup contact effects on prejudice. *Personality and Social Psychology Bulletin, 23,* 173–185.

Pettigrew, T. F. (1998). Intergroup contact theory. *Annual Review of Psychology, 49,* 65–85.

Pettigrew, T. F., Jackson, J. S., Brika, J. B., Lemaine, G., Meertens, R. W., Wagner, U., & Zick, A. (1998). Outgroup prejudice in Western Europe. In W. Stoebe & M. Hewstone (Eds.), *European review of social psychology* (Vol. 8, pp. 241–273). Chichester: John Wiley.

Pettigrew, T. F., & Martin, J. (1987). Shaping the organizational context for black American inclusion. *Journal of Social Issues, 43*, 41–78.

Plous, S., & Williams, T. (1995). Racial stereotypes from the days of American slavery: A continuing legacy. *Journal of Applied Social Psychology, 25*, 795–817.

Pratkanis, A. R. (2000). Altercasting as an influence tactic. In D. J. Terry & M. A. Hogg (Eds.), *Attitudes, behavior, and social context* (pp. 201–226). Mahwah, NJ: Erlbaum.

Pratkanis, A. R., & Greenwald, A. G. (1989). A socio-cognitive model of attitude structure and function. In L. Berkowitz (Ed.), *Advances in experimental social psychology* (Vol. 22, pp. 245–285). New York: Academic Press.

Pratkanis, A. R., & Turner, M. E. (1994a). The year Cool Papa Bell lost the batting title: Mr. Branch Rickey and Mr. Jackie Robinson's plea for affirmative action. *Nine: A Journal of Baseball History and Social Policy Perspectives, 2*, 260–276.

Pratkanis, A. R., & Turner, M. E. (1994b). Nine principles of successful affirmative action: Mr. Branch Rickey, Mr. Jackie Robinson, and the integration of baseball. *Nine: A Journal of Baseball History and Social Policy Perspectives, 3*, 36–65.

Pratkanis, A. R., & Turner, M. E. (1996). The proactive removal of discriminatory barriers: Affirmative action as effective help. *Journal of Social Issues, 52*, 111–132.

Pratkanis, A. R. & Turner, M. E. (1999). The significance of affirmative action for the souls of white folk: Further implications of a helping model. *Journal of Social Issues, 55*, 787–815.

Pratto, F., Sidanius, J., Stallworth, L. M., & Malle, B. F. (1994). Social dominance orientation: A personality variable predicting social and political attitudes. *Journal of Personality and Social Psychology, 67*, 741–763.

Rosenthal, R., & Jacobson, L. (1968). *Pygmalion in the classroom: Teacher expectation and pupils' intellectual development*. New York: Holt, Rinehart, & Winston.

Ross, L. (1977). The intuitive psychologist and his shortcomings: Distortions in the attribution process. In L. Berkowitz (Ed.), *Advances in experimental social psychology* (Vol. 10, pp. 173–220). New York: Academic Press.

Rossell, C. H. (1983). Desegregation plans, racial isolation, white flight, and community response. In C. H. Rossell & W. D. Hawley (Eds.), *The consequences of school desegregation* (pp. 13–57). Philadelphia: Temple University Press.

Rossell, C. H., & Hawley, W. D. (Eds.) (1983). *The consequences of school desegregation*. Philadelphia: Temple University Press.

Schofield, J. W., & Sagar, H. A. (1983). Desegregation, school practices, and student race relations. In C. H. Rossell & W. D. Hawley (Eds.), *The consequences of school desegregation* (pp. 58–102). Philadelphia: Temple University Press.

Schroeder, D. A., Penner, L. A., Dovidio, J. F., & Piliavin, J. A. (1995). *The psychology of helping and altruism*. New York: McGraw–Hill.

Shure, M. B. (1994). *Raising a thinking child*. New York: Henry Holt.

Sidanius, J. (1993). The psychology of group conflict and the dynamics of oppression: A social dominance perspective. In S. Iyengar & W. J. McGuire (Eds.), *Explorations in political psychology* (pp.183–219). Durham, NC: Duke University Press.

Sidanius, J., & Pratto, F. (1999). *Social dominance*. Cambridge: Cambridge University Press.

Sidanius, J., Pratto, F., & Bobo, L. (1996). Racism, conservatism, affirmative action, and intellectual sophistication: A matter of principled conservatism or group dominance? *Journal of Personality and Social Psychology, 70*, 476–490.

Spencer, S., Steele, C. M., & Quinn, D. (1999). Stereotype threat and women's math performance. *Journal of Experimental Social Psychology, 35*, 4–28.

Steele, C. M. (1997). A threat in the air: How stereotypes shape intellectual identity and performance. *American Psychologist, 52*, 613–629.

Steele, C. M. (2000). Expert testimony in defense of affirmative action. In F. J. Crosby & C. VanDeVeer (Eds.), *Sex, race, and merit: Debating affirmative action in education and employment* (pp. 124–133). Ann Arbor: University of Michigan Press.

Steele, C. M., & Aronson, J. (1995). Stereotype threat and the intellectual performance of African Americans. *Journal of Personality and Social Psychology, 69,* 797–811.

Stephan, W. G. (1978). School desegregation: An evaluation of predictions made in *Brown v. Board of Education. Psychological Bulletin, 85,* 217–238.

Stephan, W. G. (1986). The effects of school desegregation: An evaluation 30 years after *Brown.* In M. J. Saks & L. Saxe (Eds.), *Advances in applied social psychology* (Vol. 3, pp. 181–206). New York: Academic Press.

Stephan, W. G. (1991). School desegregation: Short-term and long-term effects. In H. J. Knopke, R. J. Norrell, & R. W. Rogers (Eds.), *Opening doors* (pp. 100–118). Tuscaloosa: University of Alabama Press.

Stephan, W. G., & Feagin, J. R. (1980). *School desegregation.* New York: Plenum.

Taylor, S. E. (1981). A categorization approach to stereotyping. In D. L. Hamilton (Ed.), *Cognitive processes in stereotyping and intergroup behavior* (pp. 83–114). Hillsdale, NJ: Erlbaum.

Templeton, J. W. (1994). *Success secrets of black executives.* San Francisco: Electron Access.

Turner, M. E., & Pratkanis, A. R. (1993). Effects of preferential and meritorious selection on performance: An examination of intuitive and self-handicapping perspectives. *Personality and Social Psychology Bulletin, 19,* 47–58.

Turner, M. E., & Pratkanis, A. R. (1994). Affirmative Action as help: A review of recipient reactions to preferential selection and affirmative action. *Basic and Applied Social Psychology, 15,* 43–69.

Turner, M. E., Pratkanis, A. R., & Hardaway, T. J. (1991). Sex differences in reactions to preferential selection: Towards a model of preferential selection as help. *Journal of Social Behavior and Personality, 6,* 797–814.

Turner, M. E., Pratkanis, A. R., & Hardaway, T. (1994, April). *Observer interpretation of affirmative action: The role of performance information.* Kailua–Kona, HI: Western Psychological Association.

Washington, B. T. (1901/1993). *Up from slavery.* New York: Gramercy Books.

Welch, S., & Gruhl, J. (1998). *Affirmative action and minority enrollment in medical and law schools.* Ann Arbor: University of Michigan Press.

White, R. K., & Lippitt, R. (1960). *Autocracy and democracy: An experimental inquiry.* New York: Harper & Brothers.

Worchel, S. (1984). The dark side of helping: The social dynamics of helping and cooperation. In E. Staub, D. Bar-Tal, J. Karylowski, & J. Reykowski (Eds.), *Development and maintenance of prosocial behavior* (pp. 379–395). New York: Plenum.

Worchel, S. W., Wong, F. Y., & Scheltema, K. E. (1989). Improving intergroup relations: Comparative effects of anticipated cooperation and helping on attraction for an aid-giver. *Social Psychology Quarterly, 52,* 213–219.

Yinger, J. (1995). *Closed doors, opportunities lost.* New York: Russell Sage Foundation.

Zweigenhaft, R. L., & Domhoff, G. W. (1991). *Blacks in the white establishment?* New Haven, CT: Yale University Press.

# Social Exclusion in the Classroom: Teachers and Students as Agents of Change

AMANDA W. HARRIST

*Oklahoma State University,
Stillwater, Oklahoma*

K. DENISE BRADLEY

*Department of Educational Psychology, University of Texas at Austin*

After the school shootings in Colorado, a Columbine classmate told a radio journalist about his life in elementary school: how other children taunted him, threw food at him, called him names, and constantly bullied him. In junior high, he said, he and other outcast boys realized they were not alone, and banded together to form the Trenchcoat Mafia, the group the two teenagers responsible for the shooting were part of. Stories like this, of rejection by peers, are common among many of the histories of the adolescents involved in the school violence of recent years. The media have brought these stories to our national attention, and they support what a decade and a half of empirical study suggests, that peer rejection is one of the more serious problems in the schools today. Teachers, principals, parents, counselors, and researchers hold this concern, but so do the children themselves. Even though only about 10 to 15% of children are consistently rejected by their peers (Coie & Dodge, 1988), schoolchildren report worrying about peer relations as much or more than any other issue in their lives (Ladd, 1990).

Being excluded by school peers is a truly painful social and emotional experience. Elementary school children who are sociometrically rejected (i.e., rated by peers as disliked) are often targets of aggression from peers, both overt aggression (Coie & Kupersmidt, 1983)—physical abuse or verbal threats —and what is called "relational aggression" (Crick & Grotpeter, 1995), where harm is deliberately inflicted through more subtle means, such as ignoring, declaring "I'm not your friend," and spreading rumors (e.g., a child one of us once interviewed said that if she were mad at her classmate, she would get even by telling everyone the classmate had peed in her pants). The pain of exclusion is evidenced by higher-than-average levels of loneliness and depression among rejected children, and by the fact that children in therapy are twice as likely to have peer relationship problems than other children (Achenbach & Edelbrock, 1981).

In addition to the day-to-day struggles excluded children face, there appear to be long-term consequences. Longitudinal studies have shown the link between early peer relationship problems and later adjustment problems in adolescence and adulthood manifest as mental health difficulties, or involvement in delinquent or other criminal activities. It is estimated that somewhere around half of "disordered adults" have a history of problems in their peer relationships, and in some cases these problems begin even before the child reached school age (Parker & Asher, 1987; Vitaro, Tremblay, Gagnon, & Pelletier, 1994).

## SOCIAL EXCLUSION AS A SCHOOL PROBLEM

Social exclusion is more than an emotional and social problem, though, it also is an academic problem. Children's sociometric status (their classification as rejected, neglected, or accepted) is often associated with their academic achievement (e.g., Green, Forehand, Beck, & Vosk, 1980). Peer rejection in kindergarten and first grade, for example, predicts poor second grade academic achievement (Pettit, Clauson, Dodge, & Bates, 1996), and if social status improves over the 2 years, so does academic performance. Academic problems associated with exclusion are reflected in multiple ways: In the early school years, sociometrically rejected children tend to have trouble meeting teachers' expectations for classroom behavior (Volling, MacKinnon-Lewis, Rabiner, & Baradaran, 1993), have poor work habits (O'Neil, Welsh, Parke, Wang, & Strand, 1997), develop unfavorable perceptions of school (Ladd, 1990), and eventually begin to avoid school (DeRosier, Kupersmidt, & Patterson, 1994). Given this picture of early school experience, it is not surprising that children who are frequently rejected are at risk for failing at least one grade (Kupersmidt, 1983; Ollendick, Weist, Borden, & Greene, 1992). In fact, one of the best predictors of leaving school in adolescence is the combination of aggressive behavior with low peer and teacher acceptance (see Parker & Asher, 1987; Williams & Gilmour, 1994).

There are several possible explanations for the link between lack of peer acceptance and academic problems. One explanation begins with the peer group and ends with achievement problems. It may be that children who are excluded are adversely affected by the exclusion, become lonely and depressed, and their school performance suffers (Cole, 1990; Leon, Kendall, & Garber, 1980). A second explanation begins with poor academic performance and ends with peer exclusion: Perhaps when children do not do well in school, their peers are not as likely to accept them, either because it marks them as being deviant or because classmates resent the disruption and attention that the child's academic problems cause in the classroom. Studies of children with learning disabilities, for example, find that they are less liked by classmates than are their higher-achieving peers (Haager & Vaughn, 1995). A final explanation is that academic and peer problems stem from a common source. This model posits that the kind of behavior contributing to a child's being excluded (e.g., antisocial or aggressive behavior) also lends itself to poor study habits (not staying on task, not doing homework, etc.), so the child's behavior contributes to both social exclusion and academic problems concurrently, but neither causes the other. None of these explanations have been tested explicitly over time, though, and so are only speculative at this point.

To better understand social exclusion as a classroom problem, it helps to explore the profile of the excluded child. There have been many studies examining commonalities among young poorly accepted children, and they have uncovered behavioral as well as nonbehavioral characteristics.

## WHY ARE CHILDREN EXCLUDED?

The clearest reason children are excluded is simple: They act in ways that other children do not like. And the behavior children seem to dislike most is aggression, by far the most common trait among sociometrically rejected children, characterizing up to half of them (Coie & Cillessen, 1993). Other children appear to be disliked due to their social withdrawal, and still other low-accepted children display both aggression and withdrawal. [In fact, it is these aggressive-withdrawn children who appear to have the most academic difficulty (Ledingham & Schwartzman, 1984)]. Behaviors other than aggression that are disliked by peers include being disruptive, uncooperative, hyperactive, anxious, immature, and lacking in prosocial skills such as sharing (Putallaz & Gottman, 1981). When thinking about intervention, this offers some hope: If we could alter the child's behavior, we might decrease the level of their exclusion by peers. But not all exclusion is caused by inappropriate or unlikable behavior.

Children also are excluded or disliked for being different, for having qualities—behavioral or physical—that make them stand out. As many as 40% of sociometrically rejected children are neither aggressive nor withdrawn, and differ little (behaviorally) from average status children (Cillessen, van IJzendoorn, van Lieshout, & Hartup, 1992). Being a racial minority within the classroom increases the chances of rejection, particularly among girls (Kistner,

Metzler, Gatlin, & Risi, 1993), as does being unattractive or disabled in some way (Bierman, Smoot, & Aumiller, 1987; Hartup, 1983). It is some comfort that if peers perceive a child's "differentness" to not be the child's fault (e.g., if the child is thought to be obese due to a medical condition rather than because of overeating), they react less negatively than if the child is blamed for his or her deviance (Juvonen, 1992). However, this is not often the case.

Children's exclusionary behavior is not solely due to their assessment of each other. They also take cues from teachers, and teachers do not treat all children equally. Teachers respond more positively to their attractive students than to their unattractive ones, for example (Algozzine, 1977). And, as it turns out, teacher preference is related to peer acceptance. One researcher found that teacher preference in kindergarten predicted sociometric rejection by peers 2 years later, even after statistically accounting for subsequent behavior problems (Taylor & Trickett, 1989). Some have speculated that teacher preference accounts for the link between low academic achievement and poor peer acceptance, that teachers convey negative perceptions of students with learning difficulties and peers follow suit (Haager & Vaughn, 1995).

There remains another reason children are excluded by their peers: They are excluded because they have been excluded in the past. This may be true for two reasons. First, disliked children develop reputations that are hard to shake, so even if their behavior changes, the rejection continues (Hymel, Wagner, & Butler, 1990) Second, the experience of being excluded, per se, appears to have negative consequences for children, and these consequences contribute to continued rejection in the future. One study of preschoolers (Olson, 1992), for example, showed that at the beginning of the year, children contributed to their own rejection by initiating "socially aversive exchanges" with peers, but by the end of the year, peers had begun to actively victimize those children, so the rejected children's aggression was mostly reactive (i.e., in reaction to the victimization); they were, nonetheless, aggressive, and peers do not like aggression. Several recent studies (e.g., Burks, Dodge, & Price, 1995; Parke, O'Neil, Spitzer, Isley, Welsh, Wang, Lee, Strand, & Cupp, 1997) have compared the effects of being sociometrically rejected for more than one school year, and have found that there seems to be a threshold, with rejection for 2 consecutive years being the threshold. In other words, that appears to be the point at which the experience of rejection itself takes over and causes a downward spiral for the child.

Given the serious negative short- and long-term consequences of early exclusion by the peer group, recent research attention has been directed at developing and assessing various interventions for children at risk for or currently experiencing peer problems. Following is an overview and critique of such interventions. Note that peer relations interventions may target sociometrically rejected children, sociometrically neglected children, children who are behaviorally withdrawn, or various combinations or subgroups of these categories. The following overview includes studies of each of these types, with the overriding theme being interventions whose target populations are children who are socially excluded, regardless of whether they are disliked by the peer group, ignored by the peer group, or choose to hang on the periphery of the group.

## CURRENT INTERVENTIONS

Intervention programs designed to decrease rejection or isolation among children are, as a rule, targeted at changing the unaccepted child, rather than dealing with the behavior of the peer group. Typically, this has been attempted through changing the target child's behavior either directly, by teaching the child more socially appropriate behaviors and skills, or indirectly, by focusing on the underlying social-cognitive processes that are thought to drive the child's problem behavior. As a result, current intervention programs vary widely. Some seek to change specific social skills, and others tend to focus more on global skills such as social problem solving, perspective taking, and/or negotiation of peer interaction. Though a number of approaches have been developed to address the problem of peer exclusion, there are currently three major types of intervention programs: social skills training, social-cognitive training, and peer-mediator approaches (Asher & Coie, 1990).

### Social Skills Training

A commonly used intervention for low-accepted children is social skills training. Social skills training is based on the underlying assumption that these children lack the knowledge and social skills necessary for positive peer relations. For example, some children may not be good at group entry, but others may lack conversational skills. Many of these programs select children based on sociometric ratings, so that all rejected (or all rejected and neglected) children are the target of the intervention. Other programs are more focused and choose children who have shown specific social skill deficits or children who are classified as a specific "subtype" (e.g., aggressive-rejected) based on peer nominations, teacher reports, or observations done by the researcher. Regardless of the content taught, procedures used, or group of children targeted, the objective of these interventions remains the same: to teach children social skills that will help them engage in more positive peer interactions and, ultimately, acceptance by peers.

The skills taught in social skills training programs vary from program to program. Some programs focus on specific interactional skills such as smiling and eye contact, whereas others emphasize more general concepts such as participation, cooperation, and communication. Other skills targeted may include initiating interaction, making and maintaining friends, avoiding the initiation and receipt of negative behaviors, laughing, greeting, extending invitations, sharing, verbal complimenting, physical appearance/grooming, offering suggestions and directions, asking questions, responding to criticism, listening, using self-control, and dealing with peer pressure (see Asher, Parker, & Walker, 1998). Typically, programs consist of a series of steps whereby the child is taught the deficient social skills, including direct instruction of the skill, modeling, role-playing, reinforcement, and feedback, and also provided with an explanation of why the skill is important to social interaction. The idea is for the child to practice and develop the skills necessary for positive social interactions within a safe social context (see Malik & Furman, 1993).

Results from social skills training programs vary widely. Though many programs have yielded significant improvements in social acceptance, not all studies have. Even the most successful social skills training programs benefit at most 50 to 60% of the target children (Zakriski, Jacobs, & Coie, 1997). Though this type of intervention is successful with some children, it has been ineffective with others. It is also unclear whether or not social skills programs are successful at the classroom level (Malik & Furman, 1993). Regardless of these limitations, the primary focus of most interventions for low-accepted children remains social skills training.

## Social-Cognitive Training

Another major type of intervention for low-accepted children is social-cognitive skills training. The child with peer-relations problems is again the target of this type of intervention program. Although some of these programs are aimed at low-accepted children in general, others have focused on sub-groups, particularly on aggressive-rejected children. However, in contrast to social skills training, the primary objective is not to teach the child specific social skills, but to attempt to change the cognitive processes underlying the child's behavior. Programs intended to increase self-control, for example, generally seek to teach children a series of questions to think about when faced with difficult social situations [e.g., Bash & Camp's (1985) "Think Aloud" program teaches children to ask "What is my problem?" "How can I solve it?" "Am I using the best plan?" and "How did I do?"], and assume that children will generalize from hypothetical scenarios to real-life situations.

As with social skills training programs, the content of social-cognitive training programs also varies significantly depending on the specific cognitive processes targeted for intervention (perceptions, self-statements, attributions, problem-solving skills, etc.), yet share as their goal the modification of cognitive processes that foster negative behavior so that a more positive behavioral outcome—and eventually peer acceptance—will occur.

## Peer-Mediator Approaches

The third type of intervention program aimed at reducing peer rejection or isolation is the peer-mediator approach. Research has shown that peers have the potential to positively influence the behavior of the rejected child (see review by Kalfus, 1984). Through positive social interaction with their peers, excluded children may acquire the cognitive and social skills necessary for effective peer relations. Based on this theory, the peer-mediator approach involves pairing the target child with a peer-trainer (or "peer-helper") who has been selected according to specific guidelines (e.g., same age as excluded child, compliant with rules and teacher requests, attends school regularly, demonstrates age-appropriate play and social skills, lacks a negative history with target child). The peer-trainer may then act as a model or reinforcer to the target child in an effort to change the rejected child's behavior. This approach has two distinguishing characteristics (Mathur & Rutherford, 1991): (a) rather than employing an adult as the behavior change agent, this type of intervention uses peers as models and reinforcers; and (b) rather than attempting to first change the child's behavior, the primary objective of this approach is to alter the child's social environment in a way that will facilitate the sociability of the target child. By increasing the amount of interaction with accepted peers, it is hypothesized that the nonaccepted child will learn the behaviors and skills necessary for successful peer relations.

Peer-mediator approaches attempt to influence the target child either indirectly or directly. In interventions that seek to affect the excluded child's behavior indirectly, the peer does not prompt or reinforce any behaviors of the target child; instead, the peer serves as a model. The underlying premise of this type of intervention is that by watching a socially competent child enact desirable interactional skills and behaviors, excluded children will be able to reproduce those behaviors and be more effective in their peer relations. Interventions that attempt to directly affect the excluded child's acquisition of social or social-cognitive skills generally take on the form of peer-tutoring. In this case, the peer-mediator is trained to teach the target child socially appropriate behaviors by providing instruction, prompting social interaction, and offering corrective feedback when necessary. Peer-tutoring can be accomplished one-on-one, or in some cases, several peer-tutors may be used to facilitate the social skills of the target child. Though some interventions involving peer-tutoring have provided evidence for its effectiveness, not all programs have been successful, showing increases in positive social behaviors for some children, but no difference in others.

## Summary and Critique

To summarize, a wide range of interventions have been implemented to reduce childhood rejection and isolation, all focusing to greater or lesser degrees on changing the behavior of the poorly accepted child. These interventions have generally yielded modest success. Though some have shown changes in both the target child's behavior and in the child's sociometric status, some have shown changes in only of these areas, and others have shown no change at all. Many are relatively costly and time-consuming to implement, and may require the use of a trained staff. Of more concern may be the recurring finding that changing the behavior of the target child does not guarantee acceptance by the peer group.

Reviews of interventions targeting rejected children (Malik, & Furman, 1993; Mathur & Rutherford, 1991) have suggested that factors contributing to the limited effectiveness of programs include: (a) lack of generalization and maintenance of treatment effects (i.e., program effects do not continue beyond the intervention itself, perhaps because training often is with adults, and the problems lie within the peer group; (b) use of heterogeneous groups (because excluded children are not all the same, generic, ''one size fits all'' interventions that do not consider why children are not accepted might be less effective than those targeted to the specific cognitive or behavioral problems of the excluded child); and (c) the intransigence of a negative reputation.

Recently, an intervention known as The FAST Track Program (Conduct Problems Prevention Research Group, 1992) has been implemented that takes into consideration many of the limitations of past programs. This program combines features of both social skills training and social-cognitive skills training, in a multifaceted intervention that includes the child, family, and school. To date, this intervention has proven to be highly effective. One possibility for its success may be the broader perspective from which these researchers are approaching the problem of social relations, by not limiting the intervention to the rejected child. Although its results are encouraging, FAST Track is really an efficacy study: It has demonstrated that the trajectory for children at risk for peer rejection *can* be altered. Yet its comprehensive approach and the amount of capital necessary to fund such a large-scale project do not make it a practical method for most researchers or teachers.

Clearly, the peer group plays a large role in preserving the poorly accepted child's social situation, yet, to date, most intervention programs choose to ignore this crucial part of the equation. Excluded children are part of a social context; the act of exclusion involves others. What would be the effect of aiming an intervention effort at the peer group itself, rather than just at the ''problem'' children?

## INTERVENING IN THE PROCESS OF EXCLUSION

### Punishing the Victims

It could be argued that, by trying to change the behavior of the poorly accepted child and doing nothing to address the exclusionary behavior of the peer group, current intervention programs are akin to teaching a child who is abused by a parent how to avoid abuse, rather than dealing with the parent's abusive behavior. Why not, instead of (or in addition to) dealing with the behavior of the excluded child, deal with the exclusionary behavior of peers? Vivian Paley, author and kindergarten teacher at the University of Chicago's Laboratory School, suggests just that in her book, *You Can't Say You Can't Play* (Paley, 1992).

## *You Can't Say You Can't Play*

Paley's book highlights a fact that seems to be overlooked by most attempts at intervention: that peer exclusion is a group phenomenon, that there is a whole group of children doing the excluding who are ignored by clinicians, counselors, and researchers. Paley (p. 3) questions why teachers allow children to reject each other, why, "long after hitting and name-calling have been outlawed by teachers, a more damaging phenomenon is allowed to take root"? She claims, with poignant anecdotes from her own experience and from the mouths of children in her school, that exclusion becomes a habit for the children doing the excluding, and that the academic and social learning of the excluded children is impeded. She toys with the idea of implementing a rule that disallows overt rejection, a "you can't say you can't play" rule, and eventually uses it in her own class. Before doing so, however, she explores the ramifications of the rule by talking to children and to other teachers.

Both teachers and children are ambivalent about the rule. On the one hand, they realize the seriousness of social exclusion and how unaccepted children become sad, which must affect their learning. On the other hand, they also believe that children have the right to choose their friends (When we told a colleague about this idea, he said, "sounds like Nazism to me"), that children are rejected because they do not play well with others (so it is, in essence, the rejected children's fault, and why should the others have their play spoiled?), that friendship comes before fairness. Paley counters with the notion that school is different from home: At home you can make your own choices but school is for everybody, and fairness should come before friendship. Two subgroups of children are less ambivalent about the rule, however: The excluded children are pretty much convinced it is a good thing, and the "bosses"—the children at the top of the dominance hierarchies, alpha males and females, if you will—are totally against it. This makes sense, of course. If they cannot choose who gets to play and who does not, they lose power. In one of the most poignant moments of Paley's narrative, one of the bosses, named Lisa, asks if everyone is allowed to play, "then what's the whole point of playing?" (p. 20).

After much class discussion and through the use of a beautifully written fairy tale about a bird named Magpie and the Kingdom of Tall Pines, Paley implements the rule in her kindergarten classroom. Children are somewhat resistant in the beginning, and several common practices (such as using "time out" as a disciplinary measure and choosing who you want to act out the characters in your story) have to be revised, but by the end of the year Paley feels it is making a difference in how her children treat each other.

## Potential Positive Consequences

Approaching social exclusion as a problem in peer behavior—as a classroom social problem—has several potential benefits. First, it could destabilize the phenomenon for children with behavior problems that develop into negative reputations that are, in turn, hard to break out of. About one-third of children rejected in kindergarten maintain their status over 1, 2, or 3 years, and stable rejection is much worse than temporary rejection (Vitaro, Gagnon, & Tremblay, 1990). Also, an intervention at the group level might affect the experience of children who are being excluded for nonbehavioral reasons; teaching social skills does not change the ethnic background or physical characteristics of a child. Finally, being accepted by peers, even just a few, seems to have its own benefits. Children who are accepted by peers have a stronger sense of belonging at school than other children (Legault, Caron, Montgomery, David, & Paquette, 1997), and if rejected children have a mutual friend, they are not any lonelier than nonrejected children (Sanderson & Siegal, 1995). Children with more classroom friends at the beginning of kindergarten develop more favorable school perceptions by the second month of school, and if their friends are maintained, children like school better over the course of the year (Ladd & Price, 1987). Furthermore, gains in school performance have been associated with making new friends during the school year. Why? Resiliency theorists suggest that successful peer interactions may serve a "prophylactic" function, offering social and instrumental support to help buffer the effects of stress, including academic stress (Cicchetti, Toth, & Bush, 1988; Ollendick et al., 1992). It may be that intervening at the group level could not only ameliorate some of the pain of exclusion, but also equip children with social/emotional resources to face other types of adversity.

## Why Kindergarten?

There are several reasons to believe that the place to aim a class-level intervention such as Paley's is in kindergarten. In U.S. culture, kindergarten teachers are expected to teach socialization. Also, the problem of reputation is not an issue for most children in early kindergarten. And there is evidence that what happens early is particularly important in the process of peer acceptance. In the preschool classroom, for example, high levels of cooperative play early in the year forecast gains in peer acceptance over the year (Ladd, Price, & Hart, 1988); if cooperative play could be facilitated in an intervention effort in early kindergarten, this naturally occurring phenomenon might take over and prevent or lessen exclusion during the year. Another argument for early intervention comes from Patterson and his colleagues, who describe a "limited shopping" hypothesis, where the behavior of antisocial children alters the contexts in which they engage (Patterson, Reid, & Dishion, 1992). Over time, these children have fewer and fewer chances to have positive social experiences that might steer them down a better path, so the later an intervention is implemented, the less likely it is to succeed. An intervention such as Paley's would try to alter the child's interactional context, enlarging it even though the natural reaction of the group might be to cut the child off.

Beginning early would not just be important for the children at risk for social exclusion; it would also be important for the peer group. If exclusion is a habit, as Paley argues, habits are best broken early or replaced with the habit of inclusion. A group of fourth and fifth graders interviewed by Paley say it is too late for them, but that starting the rule in kindergarten might work for two reasons. First they point out that children wear seatbelts without question because they have always worn seatbelts (in contrast, getting a parent who did not grow up wearing seatbelts to develop that habit is difficult), and second, they claim that kindergartners trust their teachers, and will not question it. "They'll believe you that it's a rule. You know, a law" (p. 63). The intervention we recently piloted was an attempt to introduce this kind of "law" to a group of kindergartners and gauge how it affected their social/emotional experiences in the classroom.

## AN ALTERNATIVE INTERVENTION APPROACH

### The Pilot Study

We conducted a pilot study to see if young school children and their teachers could adopt a nonexclusion policy in their classrooms, and whether adoption of that policy would affect the interactions among the children and their feelings about themselves and each other (see Harrist et al., 1999). Ten kindergarten classes representing diverse socioeconomic statuses at three schools in an urban area were selected for the study. Students, mostly Mexican- or Euro-American, were given 6 weeks to get to know each other before the study began. We then interviewed the children to determine who the socially excluded (rejected and neglected) children in each class were. These children were then observed interacting during freeplay so that we could estimate their typical level of time spent playing alone, as well as the average rate of acceptance by their classmates when they attempted to join ongoing play. (Observers were never told which classes were participating in the intervention and which were not.) All children were interviewed about their feelings of acceptance and social satisfaction, and their teachers filled out questionnaires assessing their perception of the excluded children's social isolation. After the winter break, we asked teachers in half the classes (the intervention classes) to read Paley's book, and helped them introduce "you can't say you can't play" as a classroom rule.

To introduce the rule, research assistants read aloud to the children Paley's fairy tale addressing the notions of inclusion and exclusion during play; the children were fascinated by this long story (it took 8–10 sessions to read), and seemed to fall in love with the Magpie character. Research assistants led group discussions (asking children if they ever remembered being left out or leaving someone out of play, how that made them feel, etc.) and role-play (having small groups enact in front of the other students group-entry scenarios with various inclusion/exclusion endings, and leading them in discussion about what they had just seen). Children were also led in discussion specifically about the rule, why it was being implemented, and how it should work. Children seemed to give the rule lots of thought, and challenged the research assistants with "borderline" inclusion scenarios, such as whether they had to let someone sit with them at lunch if they did not want to, or whether, if there were only three children allowed in the block area and a fourth child wanted to play, they would have to let the child play. Intervention classrooms were supplied with reminders of the rule, such as colorful banners, bookmarks, and coloring pages depicting Magpie, and the rule was officially instituted.

Once the rule was introduced, research assistants returned weekly to continue discussions with the children. They asked for instances when the rule had been used and when the rule had not been used, and encouraged children to share their feelings about how it was working. Teachers were invited to share in these discussions, but in most cases were somewhat reticent during these sessions.

Freeplay observations continued throughout the school year, and at the end of the year child interviews were conducted and teacher questionnaires again completed. Because research assistants reported incidents where teachers did not appear to be actively helping children enact the rule, we decided to have the assistants make ratings of teacher "fidelity" at the conclusion of the project. We then divided the teachers into two groups, a high-fidelity group, who endorsed the principles behind the intervention and were observed to implement the intervention at appropriate times (e.g., when a child was being excluded), and a low-fidelity group, who tended to express negative or ambivalent feelings about the intervention and/or were observed to be inconsistent in their implementation of the intervention.

## What We Found

When we compared data in intervention classrooms with data in the other classrooms, an interesting pattern emerged. Although in some cases, the rule did not seem to make a difference—we observed no differences in playground behavior nor in teachers' reports of the children's isolation—there were differences in two arenas. First, classmates' ratings of how much they liked to play with each other increased significantly in the intervention classes compared with the other classes. We found this particularly striking given that the "you can't say you can't play" rule was imposed on the children (and the teachers). Second, the children's self-reported level of social dissatisfaction showed a significant intervention effect, but in a surprising direction: As a group, children in the intervention classes became *more* dissatisfied by the end of the year, whereas children's social dissatisfaction decreased in the other classes; in other words, the nonexclusionary rule appeared to cause some discomfort among the children.

At first, these two findings might appear to be in conflict. Could it be that children in the intervention classes liked each other more at the end of the year, but were not happy about that change? Examination of the changes within subgroups offers some insight. The ratings of how well-liked classmates were increased for all groups of children, but increased the most among the excluded subgroup of children. This was the finding we had hoped for, that the children whom peers did not like to play with at the beginning of the year would become more well-liked play partners by the end. But, if this increase was due to increased inclusion—chidlren playing with classmates they had never played with before—then the social structure of the class must have been altered; the dominance hierarchy was destabilized. And who would be most disturbed by a destabilization of the hierarchy? The children who were doing fine before the intervention began, the nonexcluded children. When we further examined our data, this speculation was supported: There was a trend for nonexcluded children to be the ones who became socially dissatisfied over the course of the intervention, not the excluded children (whose social dissatis-faction score actually decreased during the year). It may be, then, that when nonexcluded children were asked about individual classmates, they admitted to liking them better, but they were somehow threatened by the changes—or at least the discussion of changes—in the classroom. If this is true, it could be a temporary phenomenon; nonexcluded children may just take a while to get used to the notion of inclusion. If the rule had been implemented from the beginning of the year, discontent may have dissipated by the end of the year. It is interesting to note that, in our study, the children who had the greatest increase in dissatisfaction were those in the low-fidelity classes, suggesting that teachers who were more committed to the project may have been able to mitigate some of the negative consequences for the nonexcluded children.

Why did we not see an increase in inclusion on the playground? One possibility is that behavior changed, but our methods were inadequate to detect it. We found that the likelihood of observing group-entry attempts was very low, and many more and/or longer periods of observation were needed. Regarding the lack of teacher-reported change in children's problem behavior, we know that teachers are, themselves, subject to forming reputational biases and, therefore, may not have tuned in to less-than-dramatic changes in children's interaction patterns. The other possibility is that no behavioral change occurred as a result of the intervention. If this is the case, what may have been happening is that our discussions about the ''you can't say you can't play'' rule changed children's thinking, but not their behavior. We may have heightened children's awareness of the pain of exclusion, and this may have affected their feelings about classmates (possibly by increasing empathy) as well as their level of social dissatisfaction. Whether or not a change in thinking would eventually have led to observable behavioral change, and ultimately to an increased feeling of acceptance among the originally excluded children, is not clear.

## SUGGESTIONS FOR FUTURE RESEARCH AND CLASSROOM PRACTICE

In evaluating this pilot project, we have identified several things that might have improved the project's effectiveness. If classroom teachers are considering using a nonexclusion rule, or if similar research/intervention projects are conducted in the future, the following issues might be helpful to consider.

1. *Begin as early as possible.* We suggest teachers introduce the nonexclusion rule during the first week of class, along with other classroom rules. In this way the ideas behind the rule could be part of the "emotional climate" of the classroom. Because we needed to collect pretest data (we had to let the children get to know each other before conducting sociometric interviews, we could not conduct observations until we had completed sociometrics, etc.), the rule was not introduced until late in the kindergarten year. It may be that children's patterns of interaction are immutable by the second half of the school year—Paley talks about "the habit of rejection"—or it may be that, in our pilot, the rule was simply not in effect long enough for us to observe more striking effects. Either way, the longer the rule is in place, the better the test of its efficacy.

2. *Focus on comprehensive training for all involved.* As with any intervention program, you need to train those who will be involved in the implementation. In retrospect, we did not focus enough attention on training, particularly with teachers.

    a. *Teachers need to understand the principle behind the intervention.* Simply reading Paley's book may not be enough; some teachers may disagree with the underlying assumptions of the book, and the researcher needs to be sure that this assumption is understood and agreed with (and if not, of course, the teacher should not be part of the intervention effort).

    b. *Teachers need to understand the mechanics of the intervention.* Teachers need to know how and when to implement the rule, how to lead group discussion and role-play, and how to respond to the children when they are not using the nonexclusion rule. (One of our teachers was so enthusiastic about the rule she implemented it before all of our pretest data were collected!)

    c. *Teachers need to think about classroom practices that might impede or facilitate internalization and generalization of the inclusion principle.* Teachers might think about the impact of curriculum content and implementation, as well as classroom management practices. Recent research has demonstrated, for example, that preschoolers' social cognitions can be enhanced by teachers' reading literature and developing activities with "peer relationship" themes (Bhavnagri & Samuels, 1996). Other studies have shown a link between kindergarten cooperative learning programs and children's prosocial behavior in the classroom (Nowak, 1996; Solomon, Watson, Battistich, Schaps, & Delucchi 1996). Teachers who integrate introduction of the nonexclusion rule with classroom practices such as these might be most successful. Teachers might also examine how they deal with children's misconduct in the room: Do they use social exclusion as a punishment? Is time-out social exclusion? If so, what might be an alternative way to deal with misconduct? In our pilot, we encouraged intervention teachers not to use time-out or other exclusion practices, but some of them could think of no other effective way to punish their students than by excluding them from recess. In one intervention classroom, in fact, directly beneath our "you can't say you can't play" poster, was a handwritten list the teacher had made of names of children who were not allowed to play during recess; the list began, "Can't play...". What were the children to make of that?

d. *Student preparation needs to be in-depth.* The children must first see the rule as necessary before they will use it. Class discussions including children's sharing their own experiences are probably most helpful in this regard. In the pilot project, children immediately began sharing stories of exclusion: a friend would not let a young girl play chase, or a classmate told a child he could not play blocks because he and a friend were already building a house. Let the children share these stories as a way to illustrate why the new rule would be so beneficial. Paley's book offers invaluable insight into the ability to facilitate students' sharing their thoughts and feelings. In our study, the fairy tale, group discussion, and role-playing seemed to the research assistants to hold the students' interest and involve them emotionally; however, we observed no significant change in playground behavior, suggesting that perhaps children needed more concrete experience in the use of the rule. Maybe working with children in vivo—interjecting in observed instances of freeplay exclusion—would be most effective. This type of training would require more time, but might be possible for teachers to implement if not researchers.

e. *Generalization needs to be facilitated during student training.* In retrospect, we suspect that some of our intervention children were interpreting the rule narrowly (i.e., they would allow a child to play when the child asked "Can I play?", but *only* if the child asked to play). In fact, there are many ways to exclude a child. A teacher in a private school in Dallas told one of us that his school endorses a "you can't say you can't play" rule, but the children will say things like, "Yes, you can play, but you have to be the maid" (or the dog, etc.). Paley acknowledges this in her narrative, and uses lots of group discussion and storytelling to address the issue of embracing only the "letter of the law." Researchers or teachers implementing an intervention should bear this in mind and, for example, broaden the scope of the role-play to include exclusion scenarios that involve more than just asking "Can I play?", such as the situation where a child approaches the group but hovers without asking to join.

f. *Children's social status needs to be considered during training.* Separate group discussion with children identified as excluded versus accepted might be helpful, followed up with full-group discussions. Excluded children might be hesitant at first to speak of their own experiences in the larger group, although it would be important for the accepted children to eventually hear these children's points of view. Given our findings, there might be a way to address the experiences of the accepted children so that they do not become more dissatisfied after the rule is implemented. In her book, Paley discusses the obstacles she faced in dealing with children who were resistant to the rule—the "bosses"—and describes ways she was able to overcome this particular challenge.

3. *Assess fidelity of project implementation.* Future attempts at a research-type intervention should carefully assess teacher attitude and commitment, and do more extensive monitoring of teachers' accurate implementation of the intervention. Our assessment of fidelity was nonsystematic and conducted in a post hoc fashion, but we were motivated to do it anyway because of anecdotal reports from various classrooms. Researchers need to know whether the teacher believes the rule is important and whether she or he is committed to modeling and "enforcing" the rule (including doing away with time-out, e.g., as discussed earlier). More careful assessment of teacher fidelity might include classroom observations including recording the number of times the teacher enforced the rule and the number of times the rule was observed being used by the children, as well as the use of a teacher log, where teachers record time spent discussing the rule with the students and illustrative issues of the rule's use.

4. *Consider involving parents.* Interventions might prove more successful if the child's broader social context was taken into consideration. It might be helpful to send home a brief summary of the program, explaining why social exclusion is such a problem, telling the parents about the intervention, and providing them with some guidelines on how they could talk to their children about the new rule and the issue of social exclusion. Many parents are searching for answers to the puzzle of school violence right now and, therefore, might be open to the implementation of a program that could offer them some sort of hope.

# POSTSCRIPT

The Society for Research in Child Development just released a Social Policy Report entitled "Youth Civic Development: Implications of Research for Social Policy and Programs" (Flanagan & Faison, 2001). The authors argue that to have a civil society, children need to be taught a civic ethic, a desire to "identify with the common good and become engaged members of their communities" (p. 1). One way to do this, they suggest, is to ensure that school environments are places of tolerance, where students treat each other equally and with respect, where each voice is heard. This would enable students to view America as a society where justice prevails, differences are embraced, and all citizens are treated equally. The implication of this for our discussion is that, by intervening in the social exclusion practices of young schoolchildren, not only would a small group of children be spared the pain of rejection, but all children might be learning lessons about what a true democracy is.

## Teachers' Questions and Answers

**Q:** Are parents giving kids mixed messages about inclusion and exclusion?

**A:** Yes! But this is not something that is talked about much by peer relations researchers. Judy Langlois, a researcher who studies physical attractiveness, has pointed out that parents give mixed messages about how children should treat each other. Parents teach children platitudes such as "Don't judge a book by it's cover" and "Pretty is as pretty does," yet when it comes right down to it, many discourage their children from playing with scruffy-looking children, or children who are different, or children whom they perceive as "losers," while encouraging their children to do whatever is necessary to fit in with the most popular children.

**Q:** How do you reinforce messages [of inclusion] as kids develop cognitively at later ages?

**A:** This raises a good point. As children develop cognitively, their perspective-taking abilities also develop. So an educator working to enlighten children about issues of exclusion and inclusion would want to tailor the discussion to the children's perspective-taking level: With young children, using stories that can be discussed in a rather concrete way and related to their own experiences and feelings ("Why was the princess sad?" Have you ever felt like that?" etc.) probably works best; with older children, more abstract notions such as justice can be discussed. In fact there is a time—around middle school—when children *love* to find fault in adult behavior and to identify hypocrisy in others; this might be a prime time to discuss and critique adult practices of exclusion and how they contradict what children are taught (see the first question, above).

**Q:**    Are there kids who will grow out of their cliquish behavior after high school, when they feel more confident of themselves?

**A:**    Peer relations researchers typically do not study peer-group relationships beyond adolescence (they tend to study close friendships or romantic relationships, instead). Here are some things we do know, however. Studies of peer pressure show that the height of susceptibility to peer pressure is early adolescence, and that older adolescents are more willing to think for themselves by the end of high school. Also, researchers have found that cliques tend to be less "tight" toward the end of high school. It may be, then, that you are right, and exclusionary behavior might decline as children get older (except, of course, it becomes institutionalized on the college campus in groups like sororities and fraternities!). Even if this is true, though, we would argue that the pain of peer rejection remains with the rejected child long after the actual rejection, that, for many children, the damage has been done.

# References

Achenbach, T. M., & Edelbrock, C. S. (1981). Behavioral problems and competencies reported by parents of normal and disturbed children aged four through sixteen. *Monographs of the Society for Research in Child Development, 46* (1, Serial No. 188).

Algozzine, O. (1977). Perceived attractiveness and classroom interaction. *Journal of Experimental Education, 46*, 63–66.

Asher, S. R., & Coie, J. D. (Eds.) (1990). *Peer rejection in childhood: Origins, consequences, and intervention.* New York: Cambridge University Press.

Asher, S. R., Parker, J. G., & Walker, D. L. (1998). Distinguishing friendship from acceptance: Implications for intervention and assessment. In W. M. Bukowski, A. F. Newcomb, & W. W. Hartup (Eds.), *The company they keep: Friendship in childhood and adolescence.* New York: Cambridge University Press.

Bash, M. A. S., & Camp, B. W. (1985). *Think aloud: Increasing social and cognitive skills: A problem-solving program for children.* Champaign, IL: Research Press.

Bhavnagri, N. P., & Samuels, B. G. (1996). Children's literature and activities promoting social cognition of peer relationships in preschoolers. *Early childhood Research Quarterly, 11*, 307–332.

Bierman, K. L., Smoot, D. L., & Aumiller, K. A. (1987). *Distinguishing characteristics of aggressive-rejected, aggressive (non-rejected) and rejected (non-aggressive) boys.* Paper presented at the biennial meeting of the Society for Research in Child Development, Baltimore, MD.

Burks, V. S., Dodge, K. A., & Price, J. M. (1995). Models of internalizing outcomes of early rejection. *Development and Psychopathology, 7*, 683–695.

Cicchetti, D., Toth, S., & Bush, M. (1988). Developmental psychopathology and incompetence in childhood. In B. B. Lahey & A. E. Kazdin (Eds.), *Advances in clinical child psychology (Vol. 11, pp. 1–71).* New York: Plenum.

Cillessen, A. H. N., van IJzendoorn, H. W., van Lieshout, C. F. M., & Hartup, W. W. (1992). Heterogeneity among peer-rejected boys: Subtypes and stabilities. *Child Development, 63*, 893–905.

Coie, J. D., & Cillessen, A. H. N. (1993). Peer rejection: Origins and effects on children's development. *Current Directions in Psychological Science, 2*, 89–92.

Coie, J. D., & Dodge, K. A. (1988). Multiple sources of data on social behavior and social status in the school: A cross-age comparison. *Child Development, 59*, 815–829.

Coie, J. D., & Kupersmidt, J. (1983). A behavioral analysis of emerging social status in boys' groups. *Child Development, 54*, 1400–1416.

Cole, D. A. (1990). Relation of social and academic competence to depressive symptoms in childhood. *Journal of Abnormal Psychology, 99*, 422–429.

Conduct Problems Prevention Research Group. (1992). A developmental and clinical model for the prevention of conduct disorder: The FAST Track Program. *Development and Psychopathology, 4*, 509–527.

Crick, N. R., & Grotpeter, J. K. (1995). Relational aggression, gender, and social-psychological adjustment. *Child Development, 66*, 710–722.

DeRosier, M. E., Kupersmidt, J. B., & Patterson, C. J. (1994). Children's academic and behavioral adjustment as a function of the chronicity and proximity of peer rejection. *Child Development, 65*, 1799–1813.

Flanagan, C. A., & Faison, N. (2001). Youth civic development: Implications of research for social policy and programs. *Social Policy Report, XV*(1). Ann Arbor, MI: Society for Research in Child Development.

Green, K. D., Forehand, R., Beck, S. J., & Vosk, B. (1980). An assessment of the relationship among measures of children's social competence and children's academic achievement. *Child Development, 51*, 1149–1156.

Haager, D., & Vaughn, S. (1995). Parent, teacher, peer, and self-reports of the social competence of students with learning disabilities. *Journal of Learning Disabilities, 28*, 207–231.

Harrist, A. W., Bradley, K. D., Powdrill, L. A., Terry, L. N., Barrett, D. C., Wood, T., Selvig, L., Locasio, A. L., Summers, J. J., Smith, M. A., Robillard, R., & Ota, M. (1999, April). *"You can't say you can't play": Using peers and teachers as agents of change in the process of rejection*. Paper presented at the biennial meeting of the Society for Research on Child Development, Albuquerque, NM.

Hartup, W. W. (1983). Peer relations. In E. M. Hetherington (Ed.), P. H. Mussen (Series Ed.), *Handbook of child psychology, Vol. 4: Socialization, personality, and social development* (pp. 103–198). New York: Wiley.

Hymel, S., Wagner, E., & Butler, L. J. (1990). Reputational bias: View from the peer group. In S. R. Asher & J. D. Coie (Eds.), *Peer rejection in childhood*. New York: Cambridge University Press.

Juvonen, J. (1992). Negative peer reactions from the perspective of the reactor. *Journal of Educational Psychology, 84*, 314–321.

Kalfus, G. R. (1984). Peer mediated intervention: A critical review. *Child & Family Behavior Therapy, 6*(1), 17–43.

Kistner, J., Metzler, A., Gatlin, D., & Risi, S. (1993). Classroom racial proportions and children's peer relations: Race and gender effects. *Journal of Educational Psychology, 85*, 446–451.

Kupersmidt, J. B. (1983). *Predicting delinquency and academic problems from childhood peer status*. Paper presented at the biennial meeting of the Society for Research in Child Development, Detroit, MI.

Ladd, G. W. (1990). Having friends, keeping friends, making friends, and being liked by peers in the classroom: Predictors of children's early school adjustment? *Child Development, 61*, 1081–1100.

Ladd, G. W., & Price, J. M. (1987). Predicting children's social and school adjustment following the transition from preschool to kindergarten. *Child Development, 58*, 1168–1189.

Ladd, G. W., Price, J. M., & Hart, C. H. (1988). Predicting preschoolers' peer status from their playground behavior. *Child Development, 59*, 986–992.

Ledingham, J. E., & Schwartzman, A. E. (1984). A 3-year follow-up of aggressive and withdrawn behavior in childhood: Preliminary findings. *Journal of Abnormal Child Psychology, 12*, 157–168.

Legault, F., Caron, D., Montgomery, C., David, M, & Paquette, M. (1997, April). *Peer acceptance and friendship: Their relation to self-esteem, peer attachment, school belonging and attitudes toward school* Paper presented at the biennial meeting of the Society for Research in Child Development, Washington, DC.

Leon, G. R., Kendall, P. C., & Garber, J. (1980). Depression in children: Parent, teacher, and child perspectives. *Journal of Abnormal Child Psychology, 8*, 221–235.

Malik, N. M., & Furman, W. (1993). Practitioner review: Problems in children's peer relations: What can the clinician do? *Journal of Child Psychology and Psychiatry and Allied Disciplines, 34*, 1303–1326.

Mathur, S. R., & Rutherford, R. B. (1991). Peer-mediated interventions promoting social skills of children and youth with behavioral disorders. *Education and Treatment of Children, 14*, 227–242.

Nowak, T. A. (1996). *Promoting academic and social behaviors of children in integrated kindergarten classes: The effects of cooperative learning* [CD-ROM]. Abstract from: PsychINFO_1887: Dissertation Abstract Item: 1996-95021-016.

Ollendick, T. H., Weist, M. D., Borden, M. C., & Greene, R. W. (1992). Sociometric status and academic, behavioral, and psychological adjustment: A five-year longitudinal study. *Journal of Consulting and Clinical Psychology, 60,* 80–87.

Olson, S. L. (1992). Development of conduct problems and peer rejection in preschool children: A social systems analysis. *Journal of Abnormal Child Psychology, 20,* 327–350.

O'Neil, R., Welsh, M., Parke, R. D., Wang, S., & Strand, C. (1997). A longitudinal assessment of the academic correlates of early peer acceptance and rejection. *Journal of Clinical Child Psychology, 26,* 290–303.

Paley, V. G. (1992). *You can't say you can't play.* Cambridge: Harvard University Press.

Parke, R. D., O'Neil, R., Spitzer, S., Isley, S., Welsh, M, Wang, S., Lee, J., Strand, C., & Cupp, R. (1997). A longitudinal assessment of sociometric stability and the behavioral correlates of children's social acceptance. *Merrill-Palmer Quarterly, 43,* 635–662.

Parker, J. G., & Asher, S. R. (1987). Peer relations and later adjustment: Are low-accepted children "at risk"? *Psychological Bulletin, 102,* 357–389.

Patterson, G. R., Reid, J. B., & Dishion, T. J. (1992). *Antisocial boys.* Eugene, OR: Castalia.

Pettit, G. S., Clauson, M. A., Dodge., K. A., & Bates, J. E. (1996). Stability and change in peer-rejected status: The role of child behavior, parenting, and family ecology. *Merrill-Palmer Quarterly, 42,* 267–294.

Putallaz, M., & Gottman, J. M. (1981). Social skills and group acceptance. In S. R. Asher & J. M. Gottman (Eds.), *The development of children's friendships* (pp. 116–149). Cambridge: Cambridge University Press.

Sanderson, J. A., & Siegal, M. (1995). Loneliness and stable friendship in rejected and nonrejected preschoolers. *Journal of Applied Developmental Psychology, 16,* 555–567.

Solomon, D., Watson, M., Battistich, V., Schaps, E., & Delucchi, K. (1996). *American Journal of Community Psychology, 24,* 719–748.

Strayer, F. F., & Trudel, M. (1984). Developmental changes in the nature and function of social dominance among young children. *Ethology and Sociobiology, 5,* 279–295.

Taylor, A. R., & Trickett, P. K. (1989). Teacher preference and children's sociometric status in the classroom. *Merrill-Palmer Quarterly, 35,* 343–361.

Vitaro, F., Gagnon, C., & Tremblay, R. E., (1990). Predicting stable peer rejection from kindergarten to grade one. *Journal of Clinical Child Psychology, 19,* 257–264.

Vitaro, F., Tremblay, R. E., Gagnon, C., & Pelletier, D. (1994). Predictive accuracy of behavioral and sociometric assessments of high-risk kindergarten children. *Journal of Clinical Child Psychology, 23,* 272–282.

Volling, B. L., MacKinnon-Lewis, C., Rabiner, D., & Baradaran, L. P. (1993). Children's social competence and sociometric status: Further exploration of aggression, social withdrawal, and peer rejection. *Development and Psychopathology, 5,* 459–483.

Williams, B. T. R., & Gilmour, J. D. (1994). Annotation: Sociometry and peer relationships. *Journal of Child Psychology and Psychiatry, 35,* 997–1013.

Zakriski, A., Jacobs, M., & Coie, J. (1997). Coping with childhood peer rejection. In S. A. Wolchik & I. N. Sandler (Eds.), *Handbook of children's coping: Linking theory and intervention.* New York: Plenum.

## Suggested Reading

Asher, S. R., & Coie, J. D. (Eds.) (1990). *Peer rejection in childhood: Origins, consequences, and intervention.* New York: Cambridge University Press.

Corsaro, W. (1985). *Friendship and peer culture in the early years.* Norwood, NJ: Ablex.

Malik, N. M., & Furman, W. (1993). Practitioner review: Problems in children's peer relations: What can the clinician do? *Journal of Child Psychology and Psychiatry and Allied Disciplines, 34,* 1303–1326.

Paley, V. G. (1992). *You can't say you can't play*. Cambridge: Harvard University Press.

Ramsey, P. G. (1991). *Making friends in school: Promoting peer relationships in early childhood*. New York: Teacher's College Press.

# Index